Teaching and Mainstreaming Autistic Children

Peter Knoblock
Syracuse University

LOVE PUBLISHING COMPANY
Denver · London

Photographs by David Tobin

Copyright © 1982 Love Publishing Company

Printed in the U.S.A.
ISBN 0-89108-111-9
Library of Congress Catalog Card Number 81-84572
10 9 8 7 6 5 4 3 2 1

Contents

I Designing Mainstreamed Therapeutic Environments   1

1 Introduction to Teaching Autistic Children   3
   Peter Knoblock

2 Models of Mainstreamed Programs   15
   Peter Knoblock

3 So You Want to Start a Mainstreamed Classroom or
   Program?   31
   Peter Knoblock

4 Case Study of a Stage One Classroom   49
   Sandra Mlinarcik

II Curriculum Approaches   69

5 Case Study of An Autistic Child   71
   Margaret Ninno and Susan Vermeulen

6 Teaching Autistic Children to Play: A Major Teacher
   Intervention   94
   Cynthia Uline

7 An Affective Education Program at Jowonio: Goals,
   Development, and Evaluation   120
   Rosalind L. Heiko

8 The Use of Music as an Integral Part of a Therapeutic
   Classroom   138
   Lyle Chastain

III Language and Communication   153

    9   Language Disorders in Autistic Children   155
       Sharon L. James

    10   Alternative Communication Methods   176
       Annegret Schubert

IV Developing Support Systems for Families and Schools   193

    11   Parent-School Partnership: The Essential Component   195
       Judy Kugelmass

    12   Sibling Support Groups   217
       Cindy Bodenheimer

    13   An Outreach Service Model: Beyond Techniques for
       Motivating Autistic Children   236
       Sheila Merzer

V Fostering Positive Attitudes toward Handicapped Children
and Teacher-Child Relationships   253

    14   Living Together: Teacher Behaviors That Promote
       Integration   255
       Ellen Barnes

    15   The Classroom Social Behavior of Children Labeled Autistic   275
       Carroll J. Grant

VI Evaluating Children and Programs   289

    16   Evaluating Peer Interactions in an Integrated Setting   291
       Ellen Barnes and Debra Isaacson

    17   Informal Diagnostic Assessment of Autistic Children   315
       Cindy Bodenheimer

Author Index   347

Subject Index   351

Contributors   359

Preface

This is a book about teaching autistic children in mainstreamed classrooms and schools. It is about teachers and parents working together to guarantee facilitative learning environments and a place for children who, not so many years ago, had neither schools nor communities that were aware of them and responsive to their short-term and long-term needs. To a large extent, this book describes the school program at Jowonio: The Learning Place, a mainstreamed setting in Syracuse, New York, for autistic children and their nondisabled peers. The majority of contributors to this book are staff members of that school and have been willing and able to take their valuable time to conceptualize their efforts with children so that others could profit from such experiences. In addition, other individuals not affiliated with the Jowonio School program have contributed chapters. This is in keeping with our belief that the mainstreaming movement can only move forward if diverse program patterns and points of view are communicated to professionals and parents.

Undoubtedly, the staff at Jowonio School has been involved in designing ways to mainstream autistic and autistic-like children longer than most, but none of us feel we have the only answer. What we have are our experiences, and it is those we share with you in this book. Each child, situation, and community is unique, and we hope you will read these chapters with your own situation in mind. In doing so, we also hope you are open to new possibilities for autistic children and their families.

Each of the following chapters stresses the point of view that it is necessary and possible to analyze the learning and social needs of autistic children and then design a daily program with interventions that respond to a functional analysis of their behaviors. The foundation of our responses grows from the humanistic belief that each is valued as an individual capable of learning from others and of giving to them. We are less convinced that there is one correct teaching methodology, and consequently we use a range of points of view. For some of our children, a developmental approach, using developmental milestones as a guiding frame of reference in observing their behavior and in designing interventions to foster growth, has been very helpful. For other children in our school, the severity of their impairment calls for specific behavioral training for acquisition of basic skills (such as self-help skills or acquisition of speech sounds). For all children, we strive to develop a highly organized and structured environment in which adults and children can learn to care for and respect each other.

I believe that each of us as a contributor to this book owes much to the children and families from whom we have learned so much. In turn, we can only hope that we have contributed in a significant way to autistic children's development.

Part I
Designing Mainstreamed Therapeutic Environments

1
Introduction to Teaching Autistic Children

Peter Knoblock

DEFINING AUTISM

The condition referred to as *autism* was initially described by Leo Kanner, a child psychiatrist at Johns Hopkins University (Kanner, 1943). He referred to it as *early infantile autism* and included a list of behaviors that qualified a child as autistic. These were:

- A profound withdrawal from contact with people.
- An obsessive desire for the preservation for sameness.
- A skillful and even affectionate relationship to objects.
- The retention of an intelligent and pensive physiognomy and good cognitive potential manifested, in those who could speak, in feats of memory, and in the mute children, in their facility with performance tests, especially the Seguin form board.
- Mutism, or the kind of language that does not seem intended to serve interpersonal communication. (Everard, 1976, p.2)

Since then, teachers and school psychologists, to name just two professions, have raised perplexing questions as to whether those behaviors adequately captured the complex nature of the disability they were seeing in classrooms and school programs. Other workers in the field of autism have attempted to improve upon Kanner's early effort. Margaret Creak (1964), a British psychiatrist, headed a British Working Party whose task was to specify the essential characteristics of autism. They concluded that autism is comprised of the following characteristics:

3

1. Gross and sustained impairment of emotional relationships with people; aloofness and/or empty symbiotic clinging.
2. Apparent unawareness of own personal identity; e.g., posturing or exploration of body parts, self-mutilation, echolalia, and never says "I."
3. Pathological preoccupation with objects without regard to their accepted functions.
4. Sustained resistance to change in the environment and a striving to maintain sameness.
5. Abnormal perceptual experiences (in the absence of discernable organic abnormality), excessive, diminished, or unpredictable response to sensory stimuli; e.g., visual and auditory avoidance and insensitivity to pain and temperature.
6. Acute, excessive, and illogical anxiety, especially precipitated by change.
7. Speech may have been lost or never acquired; echolalia and idiosyncratic words may be uttered.
8. Distortion in mobility patterns:
   (a) Excess as in hyperkinesis;
   (b) Immobility as in catatonia;
   (c) Bizarre postures or ritualistic mannerisms, e.g., rocking, spinning themselves or objects;
   (d) Tenseness shown by toe walking;
   (e) Peculiar gesticulations are not used to substitute for speech.
9. Background of serious retardation in which an islet of normal or near normal intelligence may appear.

In actuality, however, neither Creak's list nor the Kanner syndrome, as it has come to be called, respond to the differential diagnostic questions that keep arising, questions such as how many of those behaviors a child must exhibit to distinguish him (males diagnosed as autistic outnumber females by a ratio of 4 to 1) as autistic; whether there are degrees of intensity that characterize a child as autistic versus nonautistic or whether it is just necessary to demonstrate the behaviors in any degree of intensity.

The National Society for Autistic Children (Ritvo & Freeman, 1978) has prepared a more comprehensive definition that responds to some of these questions and takes a position on the cause and treatment of autism in children. Their short definition, reprinted below, clearly indicates that autism can be viewed as a brain disorder. The disorder is reflected in a range of behaviors. The National Society's position on causation is that psychogenic or emotional causes cannot be viewed as central but that autism may occur in conjunction with a variety of conditions, including mental retardation, viral infections, metabolic disorders, and epilepsy. The National Society believes that special education methods can significantly alter the behavioral pattern of an autistic person.

A SHORT DEFINITION OF AUTISM*

Autism is a severely incapacitating life-long developmental disability which typically appears during the first three years of life. It occurs in approximately five out of every 10,000 births and is four times more common in boys than girls. It has been found throughout the world in families of all racial, ethnic and social backgrounds. No known factors in the psychological environment of a child have been shown to cause autism.

The symptoms are caused by physical disorders of the brain. They must be documented by history or present on examination. They include:

1. Disturbances in the rate of appearance of physical, social and language skills.
2. Abnormal responses to sensations. Any one or a combination of sight, hearing, touch, pain, balance, smell, taste, and the way a child holds his body are affected.
3. Speech and language are absent or delayed while specific thinking capabilities may be present. Immature rhythms of speech, limited understanding of ideas, and the use of words without attaching the usual meaning to them are common.
4. Abnormal ways of relating to people, objects and events. Typically, they do not respond appropriately to adults and other children. Objects and toys are not used as normally intended.

Autism occurs by itself or in association with other disorders which affect the function of the brain such as viral infections, metabolic disturbances, and epilepsy.

On IQ testing, approximately 60% have scores below 50, 20% between 50 and 70, and only 20% greater than 70. Most show wide variations of performance on different tests at different times.

Autistic people live a normal life span. Since symptoms change, and some may disappear with age, periodic reevaluations are necessary to respond to changing needs.

The severe form of the syndrome may include the most extreme forms of self-injurious, repetitive, highly unusual and aggressive behaviors. Such behaviors may be persistent and highly resistant to change, often requiring unique management, treatment, or teaching strategies.

Special educational programs using behavioral methods and designed for specific individuals have proven most helpful.

Supportive counseling may be helpful for families with autistic members, as it is for families who have members with other severe life-long disabilities. Medication to decrease specific symptoms may help certain autistic people live more satisfactory lives.

*Adopted by the Board of Directors of the National Society for Autistic Children, June 27, 1977. This short definition is a working definition, and will be altered as indicated by the results of ongoing research. Taken from NATIONAL SOCIETY FOR AUTISTIC CHILDREN Newsletter, September, 1977.

Issues in Defining Autism

There are a number of professional workers who are critical of what seems to be a never-ending search for a list of distinguishing characteristics of autism. One of their issues is that such lists have little influence on actual programming. Bruce Balow (1980) is one of those raising this question. He states: "The issue, of course, is that we really are not clear about who we're talking about. In view of the definitional problem, unsolved after 35 years and unlikely to contribute much to programming decisions anyway, what is the point to focusing on narrow interpretations of signs and symptoms" (p. 2).

As with every issue, there are multiple viewpoints possible and it is important to acknowledge this diversity. For example, many parents would take issue with Balow's contention that the definition of autism bears little relevance to actual program development. Nicole Raaz, a parent and professional, responded to Balow by stating:

> Understanding the autistic child's disability gives the teacher more information to use in the problem solving that leads to programming which will be effective for that child. The label "autism" does mean something educationally. Each child's program will have to be modified to meet the child's individual needs, but knowing that the child is autistic will give the teacher more information with which to work. (1980, p. 6)

At this time, when special interest groups of all persuasions are lobbying for what they consider their fair share of the federal budget, her position is understandable.

Causes of Autism and Implications for Treatment

In addition to the question of whether a more adequate definition contributes to program decisions, parents and practitioners are grappling with varying approaches to understanding the cause or causes of autism. An underlying assumption held by some is that the nature of the disability and its causes have implications for program development and treatment. For example, in the 1940s and 1950s the predominant theory of autism, as espoused by Bettelheim (1967), focused on parental ineffectiveness, which was traced to certain personality characteristics (Kanner, 1949). Treatment approaches focused on the parents and the dynamics of the family. These beliefs led many professional workers to concentrate on changing parents and the nature of their interactions with their autistic children.

In the past decade, however, theories of parental causation have been adhered to by only a minority of researchers and practitioners in autism. In its place, theories focusing on body and brain dysfunctions have gained attention and credibility. Austin DesLauriers, a pioneer in the treatment of autistic children, highlighted the theory of a neurophysiological disorder in the arousal systems of the brain to account for the underresponsiveness characteristic of many autistic children's behavior (DesLauriers & Carlson, 1969). Similarly, Ornitz and Ritvo (1976) maintain that the symptoms of autism reflect an underlying neuropathological process. Such a defect can account for the autistic child's inability to process incoming stimuli and may also reflect a difficulty in modulating or controlling motor output and behavior. Folstein and Rutter (1977) have investigated the possibility of genetic influences accounting for autism. Their findings relating to the mode of inheritance and what is inherited were inconclusive, but they do make a strong case for continued systematic studies of genetic influences and for the possibility that "many cases of autism appear to result from a combination of brain damage and an inherited cognitive abnormality" (p.309). The next section discusses the usefulness of viewing autism as a learning and cognitive disorder. Menolascino and Eyde (1979) summarize a range of research supporting biophysical causes of autism.

Just as many parents and some professionals believe that a comprehensive and operationally defined set of behavioral characteristics leading to a definition (or definitions) of autism can contribute to program decisions, there is growing recognition that treatment approaches can be developed from many current theories. For example, DesLauriers and Carlson (1969) recommend intrusive adult behaviors designed to intervene in an autistic child's withdrawn pattern of behaviors. A set of procedures called *Theraplay* (Jernberg, 1979) were developed based in part on DesLauriers' theory of the need to be active when confronting passive and seclusive behaviors. Our focus on high intrusion approaches with autistic children was also encouraged by his work, as well as others'. Rimland (1976) and Feingold (1974) have developed therapies emphasizing biological processes to respond to central causative problems of autism. Rimland has long advocated megavitamin therapy as one way of responding to what he considers biochemical errors within the bodies of some autistic children. The Feingold Diet, stressing the elimination of chemical additives and other nonnutritive food qualities, is another example of a nutritional approach to the treatment of hyperactivity, a symptom of many childhood disorders, including autism.

Another broad set of interventions can be traced to sensorimotor theories of autism. The work cited earlier by Ornitz and Ritvo (1976) has led some practitioners to focus carefully on the kind of sensory stimuli that impinge on autistic children and to find ways to help them understand their sensory world and respond to it. Similarly, the sensory integration theory proposed by Ayres has led to a range of educational and psychomotor interventions by teachers and trained therapists who focus on the possible impact of vestibular dysfunctions in autistic children (Ayres & Heskett, 1972).

Autism Defined in Learning Terms

While the issues of proper definition and the efficacy of certain treatment approaches remain before us, there is growing belief that autism is a disability that can be defined or recognized by certain behavioral characteristics (see the National Society for Autistic Children definition). The search for biological or other complex causes will (and should) continue, but in the meantime the behaviors exhibited by autistic children demand a response. More and more professionals and parents are coming to view education as the treatment of choice for such children. This recognition is gaining acceptance because of the variety of theories that support the point of view that autism can be viewed as a problem of *learning* in the broad sense of the term (Baker, 1979).

Gallagher and Wiegerink (1976) have compiled a useful summary of educational strategies for teaching autistic children based on their learning needs. For example, they state:

> If we assume that the fundamental defect in the autistic child lies in the neural mechanisms controlling the short-term memory or in the complex reticular system controlling sensory input as Rimland suggests, then we might go back to the developmental beginnings of the child to see the implications that such a defect would have on early and subsequent development. (p.19)

Gallagher and Wiegerink describe the developmental learning problems autistic children may have in areas such as temporal sequencing, categorizing experiences, understanding affective and social experiences, and defects in memory functions. Atwood (n.d.) describes a range of behavioral characteristics associated with autism and offers suggestions for dealing with these behaviors. An example is the difficulty some autistic children experience in using more than one sense at one time. This is referred to as cross-modal information processing. Atwood offers these suggestions.

1. Autistic children often find matching two identical pictures (e.g., picture Lotto) fairly easy, but matching a picture with a spoken word very difficult.
2. In the first situation they are using only one sense—vision; in the second they are using two—sound and vision.
3. Autistic children find difficulty in integrating information from several sources.
4. The first teaching tasks are easier if they use only one sense, for example, picture Lotto, jigsaws, picture dominoes, etc.

Atwood offers suggestions for responding to hyperactivity, poor attention control, distractibility, kinesthetic learning, stimulus overselectivity, imitation learning and matching to sample, response to multiple clues, generalization and transfer of training, cognitive capacity, sequence and pattern detection, comprehension, learning sets and flexibility, and frustration tolerance. Each of these learning problems or learning dimensions may be manifested in a particular child's pattern of functioning.

This book heartily endorses the premise that teachers can develop teaching strategies and materials to respond to specific learning problems of individual autistic children. In addition, we are developing teaching approaches within the context of a mainstreamed environment in which a range of children—disabled and nondisabled—require responsive teaching.

The following sections present brief overviews of each part of this book. Embedded within each chapter are many important concepts of autism, teaching strategies, and approaches to mainstreaming.

DESIGNING MAINSTREAMED THERAPEUTIC ENVIRONMENTS

The first section of this book, beginning with this chapter, makes a strong case for both the learning potential of autistic children, including the role that teachers can play in their growth, and the possibility of designing mainstreamed settings that can facilitate that development. The message contained in each of the chapters of Part I is that teachers and school administrators (and parents) can design mainstreamed classrooms and programs that are viable and relevant to children's growth.

It is time, and it is necessary, to begin conceptualizing a variety of mainstreaming models for autistic children. Typically, the mainstreamed model considered most appropriate for autistic children is placement in a special class within a public school building. In the chapter on Models of Mainstreamed Programs, a variety of program designs are described. There may be many other designs, but to-date there are relatively few alternatives to special class placement. A new design created by the Syracuse, New York, City School district based on the Jowonio School model is of particular interest because it combines regular class placement with attention to the individualized learning needs of the autistic children.

Developing mainstreamed programs is not solely a matter of designing appropriate and responsive instructional procedures. Such programs only come about if they are valued and believed in by significant school and community representatives. Chapter 3, So You Want to Develop a Mainstreamed Classroom or Program?, asks you to explore your beliefs about mainstreaming autistic children. The questions are framed to include important ingredients of such programs. Thus you have an opportunity to explore your stand on actual content considerations.

Part I concludes with a detailed description of one mainstreamed classroom, Case Study of a Stage One Classroom. Sandra Mlinarcik has based her chapter on the classroom for youngest children at Jowonio School. She includes an analysis of what it means to implement a developmental teaching approach with autistic children. The implication is that autistic children can be viewed as seriously delayed learners and that developmental milestones translated into teaching objectives can be responsive to their needs. The author also lays the groundwork for one of our central teaching strategies at Jowonio School: a program for autistic children should be highly structured to include systematic teaching objectives and interventions that are responsive to those objectives with on-going record-keeping and evaluation procedures. In addition, she makes a strong case for implementing this teaching approach within the context of warmth and caring for the children and their families. This combination of structure and warmth is a central theme of this book and of our attitude at Jowonio School. It is both a belief and a strategy that can be implemented in many programs and by many practitioners, regardless of their theoretical persuasion (behavioral, psychoeducational, developmental, and so on).

CURRICULUM APPROACHES

In Part II several important approaches to teaching autistic children are described. Chapter 5, Case Study of an Autistic Child, by Ninno and Vermeulen details their work with a severely impaired child who presented many autistic behaviors along with severe mental retardation. Their chapter makes an important contribution to our understanding of the range of factors and teacher behaviors that can contribute to child change. They include such factors as designing a responsive schedule, using personnel and their specific functions, teaching generalization skills, designing a developmental curriculum that also includes behavior modification training to teach new skills, building home-school relationships, creating a low stimulus environment, building in ways for a child to respond with joy and pleasure, designing ways to involve a severely impaired child with others, and teaching self-control and communication so that such contact is possible. Their case study responds to many of the central questions that teachers have about teaching these impaired children.

The other three chapters in Part II describe curriculum approaches that are designed specifically to facilitate an autistic child's functioning within a mainstreamed classroom. Cynthia Uline's chapter, Teaching Autistic Children to Play: A Major Teacher Intervention, highlights the importance of giving these children a set of skills that will allow them to spend happy and productive time with their nondisabled peers. It is universally recognized that autistic children lack the skills to play without being taught in a structured fashion. It is likely that this deficit is due to their inability to deal with symbols and abstractions, for play is in many ways a highly symbolic task. This chapter documents a frame of reference for teaching dramatic play, with many examples included from her work with a range of children in her classroom. Thus we see the value of play to foster both cognitive and social skills. In addition, parents of autistic children look forward to the time when their child can function more independently, and the development of play skills can contribute to that independence.

Rosalind Heiko's chapter, An Affective Education Program at Jowonio: Goals, Development, and Evaluation, is important for two reasons. First, it describes a process that can create a sense of community within a classroom. That feeling of being part of another person's experience and coming to value individual differences is the objective of a mainstreamed setting. Repeatedly we have learned that placing children with diverse needs and characteristics together is not in itself sufficient. There is no guarantee that children will learn from each other and care about each other unless their time together is structured to provide them with meaningful ways to interact. Second, the affective education program described by Heiko teaches specific social skills to both disabled and nondisabled children and can therefore serve to foster more positive attitudes toward one another. Similarly, Lyle Chastain's chapter, The Use of Music as an Integral Part of a Therapeutic Classroom, describes a usually enjoyable way of bringing children together and at the same time building in the acquisition of skills and concepts. Her suggestions for songs and activities are both ingenious and simple enough for most teachers to incorporate into most classrooms. Chastain's approach and materials are of particular value in programs for autistic children because she stresses sensorimotor involvement. There is a growing recognition that autistic children's inability to organize their bodies in time and space is a central disability and that interventions should be designed to help them gain comfort with their bodies and control over them.

LANGUAGE AND COMMUNICATION

There is concensus that all autistic children show severe language and communication disabilities, although the nature and extent of the language disorder varies considerably. Sharon James, in her chapter Language Disorders in Autistic Children, describes a model for analyzing a range of language disorders. She makes suggestions for teacher interventions based on the specific nature of the disorder. Of particular value for classroom teachers is the discussion of children's language development and deviations from normal development. These variations are made clear by the use of many examples of children's language behaviors.

It is exciting to find an increasing number of teachers who are interested and skilled in understanding language development and who can design language intervention approaches for autistic children. One manifestation of this trend is in the proliferation of information regarding the use of alternative communication methods to teach autistic children to communicate without oral language. In her chapter, Alternative Communication Methods, Annegret Schubert, a language therapist at Jowonio School, describes a variety of methods that classroom teachers, parents, and language therapists can use to assist children to communicate. In addition to the broadening of the role of a classroom teacher to include information and skills on language acquisition and intervention, she implies that if a child is not communicating, it is our responsibility to find an alternative method that will teach and facilitate communication.

DEVELOPING SUPPORT SYSTEMS FOR FAMILIES AND SCHOOLS

In Part IV we turn to another of our strong beliefs: that the successful education and treatment of autistic children must take place in the context of a social system. This orientation recognizes that the child is part of a larger system, and each aspect of the system has an impact on the child and is affected by his or her presence. In Part IV, families, siblings, schools, and communities are all looked at as important aspects of the child's social system. Judy Kugelmass explores the importance of the parent-school partnership in Parent-School Partnership: The Essential Component. In her chapter, she points to the myriad ways in which parents and schools can reinforce each other's efforts on behalf of the children. She describes a parent support group meeting process developed at Jowonio and cites relevant literature that highlights other approaches. Of course, each program will need to design its own process to reflect the uniqueness of the parents. Our experience has been that providing parents with a range of support services puts them in a better position to respond to their children and to staff members and school initiatives.

The impact on the siblings of autistic children has been largely ignored in the professional literature. Cindy Bodenheimer, in her chapter on Sibling Support Groups, moves us to an understanding of what that impact is and how important it is to include siblings in any analysis of family dynamics that could contribute to our understanding of how a special child, siblings, and adults carry on their lives together.

Sheila Merzer's An Outreach Service Model: Beyond Techniques for Motivating Autistic Children provides a detailed discussion of how to involve schools and communities in the educational treatment plan for an autistic child. She has had extensive experience working with these children in clinical and community settings. In this chapter, she shares some creative approaches she has developed to assist schools in maintaining autistic children in public schools. Through the development of school organizational practices and creative classroom procedures, mainstreaming autistic children will become more prevalent and feasible.

FOSTERING POSITIVE ATTITUDES TOWARD HANDICAPPED CHILDREN AND TEACHER-CHILD RELATIONSHIPS

Part V has a long title, but the parts are intertwined in important ways. Carroll Grant discusses another central characteristic of autism: social aloofness and difficulty responding to the cues and behaviors of others. She describes her study of the relationships between teacher behaviors and the social responses of autistic children in their classrooms. Her chapter contributes to the growing recognition that autistic children can and do form relationships and can respond appropriately in social situations. Grant points to certain classroom conditions and teacher behaviors that foster positive behaviors.

Ellen Barnes, in Teacher Behaviors That Foster Integration, details an array of teacher behaviors, activities, materials, and classroom procedures that can bring disabled and nondisabled children together in mutually satisfying ways. The implication is uplifting—these efforts can come about if teachers are willing to work at daily programming. The techniques and strategies she describes are within the grasp of many teachers, if they are committed to problem-solving efforts to integrate children.

EVALUATING CHILDREN AND PROGRAMS

Part VI includes two chapters that offer many concrete suggestions for describing and measuring children's behaviors. Barnes and Issacson's chapter, Documenting Interaction in Integrated Settings, analyzes classroom observation data to support the contention that positive interactions between children are possible. Their chapter can be read as a research report, but it also contains classroom interaction categories that a teacher can keep in mind as he or she designs a classroom program to foster maximum social interaction. Bodenheimer's chapter, Informal Diagnostic Assessment of Autistic Children, is part of a growing body of literature that affirms the importance of finding creative approaches to assess the current functioning level of autistic children. One advantage of informal assessment procedures is that teachers can also administer those procedures. At Jowonio School we are constantly searching for ways to provide teachers with data about their children that can be translated into classroom practices. Bodenheimer's chapter contributes greatly to that teacher need.

REFERENCES

Atwood, T. *Some guidelines for parents and teachers to help autistic children to learn*. London: Eng.: National Society for Autistic Children, n.d.

Ayres, A.J., & Heskett, W.M. Sensory integrative dysfunction in a young schizophrenic girl. *Journal of Autism and Childhood Schizophrenia*, 1974, *2*, 174-181.

Baker, A.M. Cognitive functioning of psychotic children: A reappraisal. *Exceptional Children*, 1979, *45*, 344-348.

Balow, B. Current issues in programming for autistic children and young adults. *Iowa Perspective*, May 1980, 1-4.

Bettleheim, B. *The empty fortress*. New York: Free Press, 1967.

Creak, E.M. Schizophrenic syndrome in childhood, further progress report of a working party. *Developmental Medicine and Child Neurology*, 1964, *4*, 530-535.

DesLauriers, A.M., & Carlson, C.F. *Your child is asleep: Early infantile autism*. Homewood, Ill.: Dorsey Press, 1969.

Everard, M. (Ed.) *An approach to teaching autistic children*. New York: Pergamon Press, 1976.

Feingold, B. *Why your child is hyperactive.* New York: Random House, 1974.

Folstein, S., & Rutter, M. Infantile autism: A genetic study of 21 twin pairs. *Journal of Child Psychiatry,* 1977, *18,* 297-321.

Gallagher, J.J., & Wiegerink, R. Educational strategies for the autistic child. *Journal of Autism and Childhood Schizophrenia,* 1976, *6,* 15-26.

Jernberg, A. *Theraplay.* San Francisco: Jossey-Bass, 1979.

Kanner, L. Autistic disturbances of affective contact. *Nervous Child,* 1943, *2,* 217-250.

Kanner, L. Problems of rosology and psychodynamics of early infantile autism. *American Journal of Orthopsychiatry,* 1949, *19,* 416-426.

Menolascino, F.J., & Eyde, D.R. Biophysical bases of autism. *Behavioral Disorders,* 1979, *5,* 41-47.

Ornitz, E.M., & Ritvo, E.R. The syndrome of autism: A critical review. *American Review of Psychiatry,* 1976, *133,* 609-621.

Raaz, N. A parent responds. *Iowa Perspective,* May 1980, 5-7.

Rimland, B. Psychological treatment versus megavitamin therapy. In V. Binder, A. Binder, & B. Rimland (Eds.), *Modern therapies.* Englewood Cliffs, N.J.: Prentice-Hall, 1976.

Ritvo, E.R., & Freeman, B.J. National Society for Autistic Children definition of autism. *Journal of Autism and Developmental Disorders,* 1978, *8,* 162-167.

2
Models of Mainstreamed Programs

Peter Knoblock

The intent of this book is to present a convincing case for programs that educate autistic and nondisabled children together, and not to say that there is one correct program model. The application of the mainstreaming movement to autistic children is relatively new, and there are many advantages to conceptualizing and implementing a variety of models. Ideally, the program design adopted should respond to the needs of the children and parents involved and should represent the unique resources and characteristics of the school district. In this section I begin by describing the Jowonio School model in some detail, followed by a survey we conducted of mainstreaming efforts by school districts in our area. The chapter concludes with several other program designs and their advantages and possible limitations.

THE JOWONIO MODEL

Background

Jowonio* School was created by a small group of parents and educators in 1969. We envisioned an alternative learning environment that could respond to the emotional and cognitive needs of our own children, one in which they could learn as members of a learning community. All of the children were thought of

*In Onandaga Indian language, *Jowonio* means "to set free."

15

as normal, but each in his or her own way had begun to react negatively to school. These reactions varied from withdrawal and passivity to anger and hostile feelings turned inward or expressed to teachers or other adults. In time we began to receive referrals of children with special needs from parents and area school districts. Our high teacher-student ratio and individualized approach to the education of each child appealed to many referral sources. Those characteristics, coupled with a humanistic orientation, gave Jowonio high visibility (Knoblock, 1978; Knoblock & Barnes, 1979).

Graziano (1974), describing the evolution of a program for autistic and emotionally disturbed children, points to mental health programs operating on three major dimensions: (1) a practical, applied dimension of everyday operations, encompassing applied methods, facilities, staff, and clients, that draws its major rationale from (2) a conceptual dimension of abstractions, i.e., theory of human behavior, humanitarian-philosophical assumptions, that is supported by (3) a social-political, business dimension of finances and access to appropriate decision-making groups (p. 237). Jowonio School has operated along each of these dimensions since 1969, and the emphasis on each dimension has varied. Our beginning was marked by a heavy focus on the social-political and business dimension. As an alternative learning environment, we needed to establish credibility with the existing public school system and community and at the same time raise sufficient funds to pay our one teacher and to purchase supplies for the 10 original students. Once established, we focused on dimensions one and two—operating a complex learning environment day-by-day and finding ways to implement our philosophical position. We functioned as an alternative school connected to the public schools and the community, but with a high degree of autonomy.

In 1975, we began systematically planning the expansion of our school to include children labeled *autistic*. On a part-time basis, we worked with three preschool autistic children for whom there was no other available program. Parents of two of the children helped us gain access to area legislators and mental health agency personnel. These parents functioned on the political dimension and thereby facilitated a new direction for Jowonio. In 1976 we received a 3-year demonstration contract from the Bureau of Education for the Handicapped to aid us in further conceptualizing our point of view (dimension two above). As Graziano (1974) indicates, an agency or learning environment invariably continues to deal with one or more of these dimensions. That has been true of our experience at Jowonio School. The political realities of maintaining a mainstreamed school are always with us, and at times those realities demand major focus. In addition, the on-going operations and philosophical stance of Jowonio constantly undergo scrutiny and modification. Our experience shows that the development of a mainstreamed environment is evolutionary; that is, it can develop over a period of time and involves staff and parent involvement in all three dimensions.

Class Groupings and Daily Schedule

The basic grouping in the school is the "family group," based on the format used in the British infant schools, in which children of varying ages are placed together. Typical and handicapped children are assigned at the beginning of the year to a family group (located in a particular room); each group, led by 4 consistent adults, consists of 15 children, 5 of whom have been labeled *severely disturbed* or *autistic*. In addition, each group has an age spread of 3 or 4 years and as much balance of sexes as possible. Thus in each group there is a wide range of developmental levels among the typical children as well as the handicapped children. There is a lead teacher in each group with a teacher assistant and two university interns.

In addition to a range of ages, the family group contains a ratio of two typical children to one disabled child. The staff tries to plan the composition of each group to include typical students who are highly responsive and who have friendships with particular special children. Teacher styles and strengths are also matched to the styles and needs of individual children, with a major consideration being maintenance of consistent relationships with adults and peers.

Children remain in these groups for the majority of the school day, with some movement between groups for those children who can profit from additional contacts or experiences with other children and adults. An individual learning plan with treatment objectives is developed for each child, and this plan is acted upon throughout the day. We use a developmental curriculum approach using developmental milestones appropriate to each child (Wood, 1975). During the day, each special child is worked with individually or paired with one other child with similar needs several times each day. At other times, the children work along with the other children in group or individual activities in their room. For the most part, the class groupings and the daily schedule are designed to facilitate interaction between children of all developmental levels, whether they are typical or handicapped.

Naturally Occurring Interactions

A great deal of interaction between handicapped and nonhandicapped children occurs naturally in the daily life of the school. Some of the children ride together to and from school in a bus or in a carpool; they use materials within the same space in free situations which are not teacher-structured (e.g., block-play, climbing); they eat snack and lunch together, frequently sharing food (one parent reported her daughter kept asking for an extra apple for lunch, so she could share it with Larry, who seldom speaks but clearly loves apples). There is a great deal of touching and hugging modeled at the school, and the children frequently express this kind of caring with others as they proceed through the day—hugging in the hallway on the way to wash hands, sitting with an arm around another child in a group situation. In free play situations, nonhandicapped children often intrude upon others, offering help or attempting to engage a child in an activity. Since a teacher is frequently in close attendance to a labeled child, this child's activities may have higher attraction and visibility, and typical children join in whatever is going on. Interaction, when it occurs, is encouraged and reinforced by adults.

Interaction through Teacher Intervention

Teachers are very active in creating an environment which facilitates interaction through two major efforts: (*a*) the choice of activities and materials, and (*b*) the attention paid to social-emotional concerns of all the children.

Choice of Activities and Materials

In the family groups, materials made available and activities which are teacher-initiated reflect the need to accommodate a wide range of developmental levels in both typical and handicapped children. This may mean that the material or activity allows children to participate in different ways, with varying degrees of complexity; for example, blocks can be used to build very elaborate buildings or can be put end-to-end or stacked or used in sorting and matching exercises. Thus, an integrated group of children sitting around a table working with blocks can be working "independently together," can build on each other's work, can talk about what they're doing, and can offer feedback to each other. Teachers can interpret, reinforce, and guide not only the individual efforts but the interaction. In addition, teachers may initiate activities such as blowing bubbles, eating, singing games, paste, clay, and paint, sand, and water play, which all the children enjoy. Opportunities are available here for children to interact verbally and nonverbally, to cooperate, and to realize they can share interests and experiences. Lastly, teachers consciously set up activities which are joint and require several children to work together. The teacher may specifically ask some children to help others on particular tasks. Helping and teaching behavior is reinforced for all children.

Attention Paid to Social-Emotional Concerns of All Children

The teachers have a commitment to a therapeutic psychoeducational approach to focusing on the feelings as well as the cognitive needs of all the children in the school. This occurs constantly in the thousands of interactions in a day; it is also structured as a legitimate activity. Each family group meets each day for a discussion time; in one room this is called a "magic circle." The focus of the discussion is the feelings of individual children and adults or group inter-action. In these discussions, issues related to integration are raised. For instance, one group talked about "How I Feel When Harry Bites Me," at a time when Harry's biting, kicking, and hairpulling were creating tension in the group. These group experiences also offer an opportunity for all children to be seen as participants. Each child is encouraged to speak in the group, expressing a choice or a feeling, and the handicapped children are always included. For those children who do not speak, teachers and other children may interpret them. For example, a typical child says, "I know what song Harry likes us to sing. It's 'Hush Little Baby'!" The teacher responds, "You're right, I think, Martin. That's what Harry's mother says too." This group time is also a time for celebrations—birthday parties, holidays, special visitors; all children are included and celebrated.

Parents of typical children all chose this school knowing its integrated nature. They have been very supportive of what we are trying to do and have responded to their children's concerns and questions. Teachers have a crucial role in successful integration. Our teachers, by their words and behavior, demonstrate their respect and caring for each and every child in the school. The children seem to feel themselves valued and can in turn respond to others; the children imitate the teachers' words and behaviors with each other. Teachers offer explanations for behavior and suggest ways to deal with the behavior of others. They support the growth of all children at all different levels, so they congratulate and children clap when Harry first drinks alone from a cup just as they would when Michele, a typical child, writes her name. Teachers intervene often when children are upset, which demonstrates to all children that adult support will be there when they need it. The staff encourages realistic and appropriate feedback from peers about each child's behavior, while still offering explanations for why children may act as they do.

Children's Attitudes

Contrary to the myths that nonhandicapped children will make scapegoats of handicapped children, we have found a great deal of caring and responsiveness. Children have initial curiosity about unusual appearance or behavior. With young children, this curiosity may be expressed very directly. ("Why doesn't she talk?" "What does Sam's brace do?") Our teachers try to respond directly, to provide both reassurance and information. Children have concerns about frightening or aggressive behavior and how to deal with it; one child who pinches others without warning was avoided by many of his peers, although now they seem to know how to deal with him. For example, he was hugging one little girl very tightly and an adult headed toward them, fearful of a possible "attack." Sue (age 5) looked up at the adult and said, "No, I'm all right. I just tell him not to do it so hard and he stops."

The nonhandicapped children participate in parallel and cooperative play with the labeled children. They also function in a teaching capacity. As most of our labeled children are functionally nonusers of language, language stimulation is a major focus of the adults. Modeling this, typical children can be heard saying at lunch, "Larry, if you'll say 'apple,' I'll give you a piece." Many of the children have real relationships with each other—Robin reports to her parents that she plans to marry Harry; Rachel asks Larry and Robert to her birthday party; Ron says he likes Robert because he does his tasks real well. Some of the typical children have a deep capacity to care about others, and they express this in their words and behavior. A mother reports that her daughter dreams a frightening dream about what will happen to Larry when he grows up; another parent described her 3-year-old praying at night for Harry, who has had "a very bad day this week." This same small 3-year-old is utterly fearless when Harry approaches her at his most upset and aggressive times. She brings him food, talking to him softly as she sidesteps his kicking feet. A 7-year-old boy, himself a child of many emotions, approaches a teacher at a concert and out of the blue begins talking about Harry (as if he's been struggling with explanations), saying that maybe the reason Harry gets so upset at lunch is because he doesn't get enough to eat where he lives and he's afraid he won't get enough at school either. These are all small examples of the extent of concern that the children in the school express toward the labeled children. There is anger and avoidance as well, but the general environment seems to be one of warmth and responding.

Essential Program Ingredients

This school program is based on the following beliefs:
- That every child has the potential for growth and change;
- That schools should focus on social-emotional as well as cognitive growth;
- That children learn from each other as well as from adults; and
- That children should be responded to at their developmental level rather than at some predetermined notion about their chronological age.

These beliefs require the implementation of a highly planful environment that incorporates several essential components.*

Staffing Patterns

Staffing a school like Jowonio requires gathering adults with experience with both typical and special children. The teachers have trained and worked in

---

*These components are depicted in a slide presentation, "Integration Can Work: A Case Study of a Learning Environment," by Ellen B. Barnes and Peter Knoblock. Available from Human Policy Press, P.O. Box 127, University Station, Syracuse, NY 13210.

special education, elementary education, or early childhood settings. Teachers work in teams which meet each day for planning or inservice seminars. Adults must be learners, too!

In order to provide the individualized programming necessary in a setting where the developmental levels of children vary so, there must be a high adult-child ratio. So in addition to paid teachers and teacher aides, a number of other adults work in the school—student interns, volunteers, donated agency staff, and school support people. Graduate and undergraduate university interns are placed on both full-time and part-time bases. Settings with a commitment to teacher training can significantly increase the numbers and variety of human resources available through this means.

Specialized services are also provided to children and teachers through staff time donated by community agencies. For instance, at one point a pediatrician and physical therapist from the local developmental center provided referrals and evaluations of several children. A psychiatrist from a medical center saw two children and consulted with teachers on a regular basis.

Diagnostic Assessment

Good clinical teaching must begin with diagnostic assessment. After an initial period of observation, the staff of each family group establishes educational treatment objectives for each child. Parents are involved in this process. We use a set of objectives and curriculum suggestions from a teaching approach called *Developmental Therapy,* created at the Rutland Center in Athens, Georgia (Wood, 1975).

Children are rated on their skills and behaviors in four areas: Behavior, Communication, Socialization, and Pre-academic or Academics. An individualized program is developed by targeting several behaviors in each of these skill areas as treatment objectives.

The learning plan includes the selected treatment objectives, the activities and materials used to reach the objectives, and a checklist for teachers to use for record keeping. Children are periodically re-evaluated, and new objectives are identified when original ones have been met. A variety of other formal and informal assessment procedures are utilized, depending on the child's needs. Each special child, for example, has a thorough and on-going language evaluation with suggestions and materials made available to the child's teachers by the language therapist.

Classroom Programming

The next ingredient is classroom programming, which is based on the combined needs of the children in the room. Programming for children with a wide range of developmental levels is very complex. The end goal is that each child will have an individualized program appropriate to his or her needs and at the same time learn to participate with others in an integrated setting.

The first step is to think of a daily schedule that will foster as much contact as possible between disabled and typical children. This starts with busing in the morning. Many of the children come to school on the same buses.

Once together in the classroom, teachers must orchestrate their own time and children's activities to offer individual and group experiences, independent and teacher-directed work, in many skill areas. Early morning activities may include individual table work for children who can function fairly independently, while the adults give one-on-one attention to some of the special children in the same room.

With younger children, this early morning time involves relaxed free play with social interaction as an emphasis and one-to-one focus on children who need it. Later in the morning, children may be grouped for art, games, or movement activities. Many children need sensorimotor stimulation, and this time offers good opportunities to integrate typical and special students.

In some classrooms there are options of things to do, so that children can develop their own interests and get experience in making decisions and choices.

Midmorning in each group is a snack and meeting time where efforts are made to facilitate communication and a group feeling. Later in the day children are clustered for math and reading skills, readiness skills, play group, or language stimulation activities. Afternoon events may include dance, field trips, cooking, and art.

Children may also receive speech therapy, physical therapy, and counseling, if appropriate, all of which are integrated into the week's calendar. This complex schedule is based on children's needs, availability of adults, and an attempt by teachers to vary the tempo of the activities to provide variety and to arouse and calm children, depending on their needs.

As teachers plan the day's activities, they keep at least four questions in mind: Does the activity foster interaction, stimulate language, support positive self-concept, and seem appropriate to the child's needs?

Psychoeducational Curriculum

The program is based on a psychoeducational curriculum model which focuses on cognitive, psychomotor, emotional, and social growth. In each of these areas, the staff tries to meet individual needs and still promote integrated interactions between typical and disabled children.

Cognitive growth includes a focus on readiness skills, and problem-solving and symbolic skills like reading and math. The activities used to meet the cognitive goals for a child are designed to use a child's strengths and major learning modality, as well as to have high appeal, to allow a child to be active, and to foster interaction with others when possible. One child's need to work on body concepts can be incorporated into an experience relevant to and enjoyed by other children in the group. The materials used can be concrete, manipulative, and colorful.

Many of curriculum items used are flexible and open-ended. Cuisenaire rods, as a good example, can be used to teach basic and complex math processes, but they can also be used to sort by size and color, to match concrete objects to other subjects or to their symbolic representations, or just to build and "mess about" with. Using the same or similar materials fosters identification of all children with each other, even if the materials are used in different ways at different conceptual levels.

Cognitive skills are approached through individualized work assignments, completed independently or with the aid of adults or peers. Those children who need support and one-to-one instruction can often receive it within the family group. This promotes a more normalized view of special children by the typical children and presents opportunities for cooperative interaction.

Students also are grouped to work on particular skills. Efforts are made to include special children in these groups when appropriate; this is possible because of the range of development of the typical children. One major focus with many of the labeled children is the facilitation of receptive and expressive language. So while typical children are in reading groups, some children with language delays may be grouped for intensive language stimulation sessions.

Teachers also individualize the style of their approach to children. One youngster tended to function best when he could predict his daily activities. So he had a written-out schedule to check off as he completed each activity. This may be the first step toward helping a child function more independently, which is an important objective for special children.

In an integrated setting it is important to foster independent behavior for those children who can handle it. A significant area of teaching is self-help skills like toileting, dressing, and eating. While a goal is to increase a child's sense of autonomy, adults must recognize the degree to which a particular person needs direct psychological and physical support to function or just needs to know that someone is nearby.

One important measure of change is a child's increasing ability to play independently and to use materials appropriately. Play is evidence of and a means to a child's ability to symbolize. It is also an important step to integrating special children, by giving them ways to interact around play materials. The staff members teach play directly, developing units on cars and trucks, blocks, dolls, playdough, and so on.

Growth in Psychomotor Skills

Perceptual-motor curriculum materials are in wide use at the school. Many children develop proficiency in tangrams, pegs, and block designs as well as pen-and-pencil exercises. Fine motor development is encouraged through tracing, cutting, putting clothespins in a can, stringing beads, and similar activities.

A lot of children are physically tense and need to relax through gross motor activities, while other children need to be aroused physically before they function as active learners. Games and gross motor exercises are ideal ways of bringing a range of children together. Many children who have difficulty with verbal experiences can participate. These exercises also offer good opportunities for the development of imitation skills.

Children are encouraged to use their bodies to express themselves creatively, and many structured and nonstructured experiences can be developed to provide practice.

Emotional Development

In a therapeutic school, emotional growth is focused on as heavily as cognitive growth. Children learn through their relationships with others—first with adults, then with their peers. A child's openness to learning comes after the development of feelings of safety in the environment and trust in the significant adults who not only provide support but also set limits. One way the staff builds relationships and safety and security is to hold, hug, and make emotional and physical contact. This contact and relationship building may take place in the context of comforting a child, playing with a child, teaching a child, or being reflective with a child.

A truly complete curriculum responds to the feelings that are inside of all others. Expression of those feelings is encouraged not only through verbal and physical means and even through writing, but also in behavioral contracts between a teacher and child. The growth of a strong sense of self comes quickly for some children and slowly for others.

Feelings of mastery and being recognized help the development of a sense of self. Teachers facilitate this development through their moment-to-moment physical and verbal interactions with children and through consciously designed activities. For some children, having others imitate their actions creates a sense of power. This imitation process was built into a sign language time in one classroom; each child was asked to initiate a sign or movement that everyone else copied. A major purpose of this activity was to teach all the children the basic signs to be used with a nonverbal member of the class and also to give him visibility and importance in the group.

One teacher designed part of an obstacle course where each child had to stand on the top of the climber and shout, "I am somebody! I am Susie." Nonverbal children were helped in this activity by an adult or child who said their lines for them. The staff tries to model and facilitate nonsexist and nonhandicapist values, and to promote feelings of strength and confidence and worth in all children.

The personal way in which the adults respond to all the children is a model for the kind of caring they are encouraging on the part of children toward each other.

Social Development

Social growth is a major focus of an integrated program which seeks to facilitate interaction between children. The biggest problem for many of the labeled children is their lack of interest in other people. The central goal is to develop the children's awareness of others and to give them skills to participate in and enjoy human social interaction. Activities are purposefully designed to foster contact between special and typical children. The activity may initially be parallel or it may be more interactional—as when children share and utilize the same materials.

The staff is consciously seeking to create a sense of community among the children and adults, where each person is valued for his or her unique contribution to the group and there is a commitment to include all people in the group experience. They are consciously creating a climate which values cooperation and caring rather than competition. Where some children cannot initiate, others must reach out to them. When children in a classroom have a wide range of skills and abilities, there are opportunities everywhere for them to help each other.

A sense of community is developed in a number of ways—group games, singing, music, and daily meetings in which the focus is talking out loud about feelings and the group's life. These meetings offer an opportunity to encourage children to focus on other people, as well as to learn to express themselves. They can make children conscious of their part in the group as well as the ways in which they are special. One class has talked about how every person needs help in something and how others could respond to that need.

The meetings are also an opportunity to give input into the classroom's activities, and another way for adults to learn where the children are and build on it. One teacher had each person mention any problems or plans he or she would like to talk about. Then the children did a values clarification exercise about their fears. All children are urged to participate in their group, and verbal children may speak for nonverbal children. In this instance, several of the children mentioned that one labeled child was really a good swimmer, so of course he wouldn't be afraid of deep water.

Lunch and snack are good group activities for socializing; children share food, hear others talking, and are in close proximity to a range of children. Everyone can take an equal part. Food is also an excellent stimulus for language. "Juice," "cracker," and other food names are often words that are part of some children's limited repertoires.

Cooperative tasks are another way to promote group feelings. Children can work on a group block design created by the staff to encourage interaction and a sense of joint involvement. Another teacher intervention is to pair two children for an activity.

Focusing on each child's strengths and giving them recognition facilitates peer interaction. For example, one child, who is basically nonverbal, is adept at using tools and attracts other students because of this skill.

Integration is also fostered by experiences in which everyone can function and succeed at his or her own level. The water table is an example of this kind of developmental, high interest, low threat situation for play, learning, and social interaction. Teachers also use the attraction to their own presence and involvement with special children to draw the interest and participation of other children.

Creating Caring Attitudes

All of these strategies are aimed at creating attitudes on the part of children of caring about others. Initially many of the children observe and express curiosity about some of the special children—"Why doesn't he talk?" "What happened to her legs?" "Why does he bite himself?" These questions disappear as they have more contact with each other and they are given or develop for themselves satisfactory explanations, or as some of the problem behaviors change. Children need to learn things they can do; they need to learn ways to respond to the particular behaviors and needs of their disabled peers.

When the typical children were interviewed, most of them did not identify the disabled children as qualitatively different from themselves. This seems to be an adult view. Instead, they described each child matter-of-factly, as an individual with his or her own unique behaviors, which might include things such as not talking, not walking, or screaming when upset. In fact, a number of typical children chose labeled children as friends on a sociometric questionnaire.

Even young children have the capacity to share and care about others. In an environment which is set up to allow natural interaction to occur and which supports and facilitates giving behavior, caring and warmth are frequently expressed between children.

At first some of the children showed very aggressive behavior; they bit, pinched, pulled hair, or destroyed others' materials. Other children were afraid of them and tended to stay away. Teachers tried to deal with these feelings directly, as well as to give suggestions about ways to respond to the behavior. When children have some specific way to deal with aggression, they don't feel victimized by it and can respond to the aggressive child realistically and without fear. One child was often aggressive, and initially teachers sat with him at least an arm's length away from other children. As one group discussion was going on, a child of age 3½ turned to him and offered him something she had built from blocks. Even when this boy was at his most upset, she willingly approached him. In the midst of one tantrum, when he was being held by a teacher, she heard him and appeared in the hall to offer him part of her sandwich to calm him. It worked.

Children can function as teachers and can share the achievements. They are able to identify and take pleasure in the growth of others. They may announce at snack that a child "said 'tie shoe' today," or they may express interest in the progress being made in toilet training another boy.

Teachers work in different ways to facilitate peer teaching. For example, a poster lists the words that one boy can say. It was put on the wall to remind the verbal students what language they could ask him to produce. Many of the verbal children began on their own to use the controlled vocabulary, syntax, or sign language that teachers use with particular special children.

Relationships between special and typical children are quite possible. A child labeled as having difficulty in relating remembers his friend, says goodnight to him during his bedtime ritual, and still asks for his name in a writing lesson 6 months after he has moved away.

Parent Involvement

Parent involvement is a significant ingredient of our program. Each child has a teacher-advocate who is responsible for parent contact, including home visits and frequent phone calls and notes. Because the school is an alternative program, parents have been active in choosing it and they want to be involved in their child's program. A variety of means are arranged for parents and staff to interact—one-to-one conferences, classroom observations, open houses, group meetings.

Sharing information with parents is combined with formal and more social family and staff events, such as a day-long picnic. Many of the staff have developed personal relationships with parents, which facilitates good communication.

Parents contribute a great deal to the total school functioning. Some parents volunteer in the classrooms, serve as members of the advisory board, and serve on the hiring committee. Many parents have given time and energy to paint walls and build furniture—a necessity because of our limited budget.

One parent worker has been hired to help with the translation of goals and techniques between home and school. She will facilitate communication between parents and teachers as well as help plan child management programs with parents and run a parent group.

SURVEY OF MAINSTREAMING PRACTICES

In January, 1980, at the request of our Board of Directors, we initiated a joint planning process to develop mainstreamed programs for autistic children with all the school districts in our area. At the initial meeting, data were collected to show the types of mainstreamed programs that were available for handicapped children, including autistic children. The data indicated the following range of mainstreamed approaches in a metropolitan area of approximately

500,000 people, with school districts ranging from a few thousand pupils to 20,000 pupils.

- Autistic children, ages 9-12, mainstreamed into regular classrooms in a ratio of 3 to 15.
- Handicapped children mainstreamed in a readiness kindergarten classroom.
- Handicapped children mainstreamed into regular classrooms with resource teacher support and teacher assistant help.
- Handicapped children placed in resource rooms on the elementary and junior high school levels.

ALTERNATIVE MAINSTREAMING MODELS

Teaming Model

In 1979, the Syracuse City School District created a new program to mainstream autistic children in regular classrooms. The model was developed in consultation with Jowonio school staff members and was designed to respond to 9- and 10-year-old autistic children at Jowonio who needed to be placed in the public schools, as they had reached the upper age limit for attendance at Jowonio. The school district set up two classrooms adjacent to each other: a third grade and a fourth grade with 15 nondisabled children and 3 autistic children in each. One teacher is a trained special education teacher, and the other an elementary education teacher. The model calls for some movement between classrooms and joint teacher planning and support. Each classroom has an aide plus access to a speech therapist and school psychological services.

The teaming model is obviously a sophisticated one that requires careful planning and cooperation between school personnel. The model depends on the willingness and ability of the two teachers to work together to provide each other with their expertise, one in regular education and the other in special education. In addition, the school district must begin a long-range planning process to guarantee a continuation of mainstreamed programs as the children get older. In 1980-81, a fourth grade/fifth grade combination was established for the children who began in the program a year earlier. The challenge to a school district's creativity and commitment often comes at the junior high school level.

Transitional Program Model

A variety of program models for autistic children that function outside of the public school system have applicability within the schools. Jowonio's mainstreaming model is one example, and Project TEACCH in North Carolina is another. These programs face the challenge of finding ways to adopt their designs to fit within a larger system. One approach currently employed by the Jowonio staff is to place a classroom of autistic and nondisabled children in a public school building while maintaining some degree of administrative and philosophical control over the program. The Jowonio School Board of Directors, comprised of parents, staff, and community representatives, submitted a proposal to the Syracuse City School District in spring, 1981, for transferring one Jowonio class to an elementary school building.

The main components of the plan are:

1. A Jowonio class will be located in a Syracuse elementary school.
2. Jowonio will provide a teacher, a teacher assistant, speech services, and supervision of instruction and clinical programming. If one is available, a student teacher will also be provided.
3. In addition to the therapeutic program, Jowonio will provide parent services, including home training, support groups, regular school observations, and on-going communication.
4. The transitional class will provide an educational program for four or five children in the Syracuse district who have been referred for special educational services at Jowonio. The children will range in age from 6 to 8 years. In addition, 10 first-grade children from the Syracuse district will be included in the class.
5. The Director of Special Education will make the initial contact with the principals of potential building sites. Jowonio staff will then work jointly with the Director's staff in presenting the transitional program to the principals.
6. In the transitional program, the Jowonio teaching team will comply with the school policies as detailed by the building principals and will participate in school-wide activities.

In September, 1981, this program was implemented. It is considered a transitional program model because our long-term expectation is that the school district will assume increasing administrative and financial support for the program.

Teacher Plus Aide Model

One of the more prevalent models is the placement of one or two special needs children in a regular classroom with support provided by a full-time aide. As more parents of autistic children persist in their efforts to have their children placed in regular classrooms, the model of supplying an aide in the classroom is gaining momentum. Resource teachers and other support personnel are made available to the child and classroom teacher.

This model is highly dependent on the skill levels of the regular classroom teacher and aide, including their compatability in working together. The clarity of the aide's role is essential. Many program planners feel that the aide should respond to all of the children and not just the autistic child. The teacher must assume the leadership in planning for the special child and must not rely on the aide's keeping the autistic child occupied while business goes on as usual within the classroom.

Regular Class with Supplemental Services

There are some special children who can be placed in a regular classroom program in which there is a heavy reliance on supplementary services such as resource teachers, remedial reading, and language therapy. For this model to be effective, these resource persons must become an integral part of the classroom schedule and not be seen as mere appendages.

Tandem Class Model

In this design a resource teacher works exclusively with one or two classrooms in which special children are mainstreamed. This is a variation on models in which full-time aides are placed in a classroom. In this model, the teacher and resource person can form a support system for each other, but they must be willing to work closely.

Cluster Model

This is a variation on the tandem class. A special education teacher may work with a cross-age team (as in the teaming model) as a resource teacher. Special children are based in the regular classrooms and grouped for skill work with the special education teacher, who may work within the regular classroom or in a separate room. As is true with several of the models using resource personnel, its success is highly dependent on the way in which the teachers function together.

REFERENCES

Graziano, A.M. *Child without tomorrow.* New York: Pergamon Press, 1974.

Knoblock, P. An alternative learning environment: Its impact on prevention. In S.J. Apter (Ed.), *Focus on prevention.* Syracuse, N.Y.: Syracuse University, 1978.

Knoblock, P., & Barnes, E.B. An environment for everyone: Autistic and nondisabled children learn together. In S. Meisels (Ed.), *Special education and development.* Baltimore: University Park Press, 1979.

Wood, M.M. *Developmental therapy: A textbook for teachers as therapists for emotionally disturbed young children.* Baltimore: University Park Press, 1975.

3
So You Want to Start a Mainstreamed Classroom or Program?

Peter Knoblock

Many teachers and administrators are considering ways to place autistic children into classrooms and school experiences with their nondisabled peers. This chapter and its checklist is designed to assist you in asking some of the questions about program development that our experiences at Jowonio School and in the public schools have shown to be important. We hope the questions asked will not only help to put you in touch with your values and beliefs about mainstreaming, but will also alert you to approaches, techniques, and procedures that we at Jowonio consider important in the day-by-day running of a mainstream environment.

I hope that either now or at some point each reader will answer each question "correctly." While I recognize the existing diversity of opinion and practices in mainstreaming, the bias in each question is toward answering in the affirmative. What do you think?

VALUES AND BELIEFS

The debate continues as to whether the existing research supports the mainstreaming movement. It is likely that proponents and critics will be locked in battle for a long time. In the meantime, you and many of your colleagues are being asked to consider becoming involved as a teacher or administrator of such a program. Rarely do any of us act on the basis of published research, but we are propelled to action (or inaction) on the basis of our values and beliefs. Just how do you see yourself involved in a mainstreamed program? What personal and professional qualities do you have that could contribute to the success of a mainstreamed program? The following questions ask you to respond to several qualities that we have come to see as essential for effective teacher functioning.

Yes	No	
☐	☐	*Do you see yourself as a problem-solver who is willing and committed to work on a variety of curriculum and management issues that will inevitably arise?*

We tend to view such teachers with a repertoire of problem-solving skills as *clinical teachers*. This implies that you recognize that there are no certain solutions to complex problems, but that there may be new ways to look at persistent issues in the classroom. A clinical teacher is one who is committed to expanding his or her repertoire of curriculum and management skills and at the same time is willing to learn from children by engaging in systematic and accurate recording of their behavior. The following example highlights the problem-solving process engaged in by a teacher working within an integrated classroom.

> I suppose that the basic concept a teacher must remember, however, when attempting to encourage typical children to explore situations with labeled children, is that each child will need a different method of introduction and encouragement, according to their already formed individual values and feelings. So that, while with some children out-front discussions on the needs of specific children, and clear questions or answers on what specific actions a child could take would be the most appropriate way in which to help her understand her part in integration, others need more mild methods. With these others, perhaps only modeling and reinforcement for positive integrative activities will be necessary or accepted. It depends, I think, on the reason the typical child is responding; so that Molly, who is greatly in need of reinforcement and praise, will respond by modeling the efforts of those she will receive praise from. On the other hand, Rich will respond to Martin at lunch because whenever he does, Martin gives him part of his food. And also there is Kim, who generally seems to respond whether or not a teacher praises her, simply because she has decided for herself that it is a good thing to do.
>
> I do believe that a teacher needs to be very careful about overloading a child with both expectations of attempts at integration, and praise for those activities. I think that without limiting our urges to shout "Hurrah" everytime a typical child interacts with a special child, we can cause questions to appear that might never have come. For example, one time while telling Molly that I was really happy with the way she had responded to Martin, Ann (a typical child) said, "Well, y'know, she always says things like that to people."... And I realized that, even though I *believe* we should praise children for any positive interactions, I am far more conscious of doing so when it's labeled and nonlabeled children who are interacting.

Yes *No* *Do you see a learning environment as made up of diverse*
☐   ☐   *individuals and needs and do you not only accept this, but*
              value it?

For a long time I have been concerned with what we refer to as the "regular" classroom. Once we individualize our instructional approaches and in general move closer, psychologically and geographically, to each child, we begin to recognize the incredibly wide range of needs, skills, and personalities in each room. In mainstreamed classrooms, we quickly sense the need to respond to all children in specific and personal ways. The needs of nondisabled children, while different from those of autistic children, are nevertheless important and unique. This range of needs requires a teacher to construct a flexible daily schedule that will respond to each child, special and typical, and to make sophisticated plans as part of a team. These considerations are discussed in more detail in the sections on classroom organizational issues and classroom teaching behaviors.

Yes *No* *Do you believe that you can play a significant role in*
☐   ☐   *the improved functioning of an autistic child in a*
              mainstreamed setting?

We now recognize how important teacher expectation is in the implementation of a child's program. I am struck by the progress certain children can make when their teachers feel confident and behave that way with them. This does not necessarily mean that those teachers feel they have the answer, but it does mean that they feel good enough about who they are and what they know. It also means that they are willing to build on their existing skills. It may help you to acknowledge that you already bring skills to a teaching situation with autistic children. If you think of them as children with major learning and communication problems, then you can devise teaching behaviors and curriculum strategies to respond to their needs. Chapter 1 highlighted a range of types of teacher interventions developed to respond to specific learning problems of autistic children.

Yes *No* *Are you open and responsive to feedback from others?*
☐   ☐

I realize it is not enough to want and use feedback, but that one must work within an environment that is designed to foster feedback between adults, in a safe and trusting climate. More and more we are finding teachers who are making things happen because they want change—for themselves and for children. Developing a mainstreamed environment requires a commitment to stretch yourself in a number of ways. Teachers will need to plan academic and social experiences for a wide range of children; familiarize themselves with the available information on autistic (or other disabled) children; and consciously focus on ways to bring disabled and nondisabled children together. In order to avoid functioning in an isolated manner and to obtain assistance in accomplishing the complex goals mentioned above, you will need to include others in your planning. Efforts to involve parents and relevant school and community resource persons and agencies should be part of your agenda and the child's program.

SCHOOL ORGANIZATIONAL ISSUES

The initiation of the planning for a program to mainstream autistic children will immediately raise a variety of questions. The newness of the endeavor requires creative problem solving of organizational issues. Many of the questions raised in this section are ones that are frequently asked (or should be asked) when planning a new program for nondisabled or other special needs children. The universality of these concerns should help us recognize them and engage in whatever fine tuning is necessary to encourage the school's flexible response to programming for autistic children.

Yes	No	
☐	☐	*Is there a procedure for informing and soliciting the support of your school's parent group and your children's parents?*

When we began planning for the development of a mainstreamed public school program, the district Director of Special Education issued some press statements, and several newspaper articles appeared with brief descriptions of the plan. As planning in the particular school began, word spread. Once the teachers were selected, a number of parents requested to have their nondisabled children placed into the program, either because of what they had heard about the program (smaller number of children, higher adult/child ratio), their attitude toward an integrated model, the pull of the teachers involved, or some combination of these factors.

These voluntary, media, and word-of-mouth measures may not be sufficient to fill a classroom or two with nondisabled children. Here are some additional strategies that may be useful.

- Write up your program description and circulate it with a letter of explanation to families of children eligible for placement in the grade level(s) your program is geared toward.
- Follow up the letter with individual phone calls to parents, soliciting their children and their assistance.
- Invite parents to come to school and talk, to visit other integrated programs already in operation, and to meet with the prospective teachers.
- If you have a school Parent-Teacher Organization, present your plans to them and solicit their feedback and cooperation.

Yes *No* *Will you be seen as involved in decision making and*
☐ ☐ *policy decisions involving your classroom and/or school*
   program?

Ideally, you as a classroom teacher or administrator will be directly and intimately involved in the conceptualization and implementation of the integrated program. I say ideally, because very often the children for whom we are designing the program come to us from other settings and schools. Also, very often a new policy position may be made by the school district's central administration. Needless to say, when your classroom or school is involved, you should be part of the planning process. This may take some negotiating, and there are several areas you can focus on. If you are the teacher, you will want to *insist* upon inservice training opportunities for you and your staff (if you have any). This is particularly important if you are asked to respond to severely involved children or other groups with whom you have limited or nonexistent experience. You may need to determine if the child will have a period for transition into the program; this is important when considering the placement of a child after the school year has begun. Have you been guaranteed sufficient learning materials so your classroom is adequately provisioned? Do you have input into which materials are ordered? In an integrated classroom, you will be responding to children on many different levels, and it is important to have a range of appropriate materials available. In addition, more independent functioning is a goal for all children, especially severely involved children. A richly stocked classroom can allow and encourage children to interact with a range of materials and activities, thus gaining vital experiences and hopefully more skills and confidence in their own abilities. If you are the building administrator, all of the items on this checklist apply as they do for teachers, but the major item to negotiate at the outset is the degree to which you and your staff will have the planning responsibility for operating the program. Certainly, having access to the financial data often determines who runs the program. Since you may not see the actual dollars, you will, however, want input into the ways in which resources are put into your school's program. This can take the form of staff hiring, materials budget, or renovation to rooms such as the installation of a bathroom or the combination of two classrooms so children can move back and forth. We also know that negotiating may be a long-term process, but it is best to try to clarify who will be responsible for which decisions, especially those decisions affecting program funding and staffing.

Yes *No* *Can planning time be arranged on an on-going basis,*
☐ ☐ *either during the day or after school?*

This question has become crucial in light of more detailed, and in some instances, restrictive teacher union contracts. Our experience has shown that *some* after-school planning time is essential. On the other hand, if you are insisting on using after-school teacher time, it is *imperative* that whatever meeting time you have is well-organized and necessary. I say this for two reasons. First, teachers' time is valuable and at a premium once the children leave. Second, all of us need to release pent-up feelings of joy or tension or both, and many meetings are reduced to sharing of anecdotes. Some of that may be necessary, but with time so valuable unfocused talk should be minimized. There are a variety of strategies that can be used to design and guarantee teacher planning time.

- Many schools work blocks into a daily or weekly schedule to permit teacher planning time during the school day. This is usually accomplished by complex scheduling arrangements involving art, gym, music, and other special teachers. You can consider working into the same schedule. One advantage is that you will be part of the same process that other teachers are plugged into. It will be necessary, however, to work closely with the "special" teachers so they develop the confidence and skill to function with your group. In addition, it may still be necessary to provide additional volunteers or staff members to assist the special teachers.
- Some programs do not have children in attendance on Friday afternoon. That time is used as staff development for teachers and other program personnel.
- When planning for the implementation of the program, agreement should be reached on expectations for after-school meeting time. I am familiar with public school programs in which the teachers and other support staff meet on their own in the evenings or weekends. That should be an option, but not the sole opportunity for staff sharing and planning. One or more after-school meeting times are necessary for on-going planning to occur. These times should be protected, as much as possible, from incursions by other school-related events and activities. A central purpose of these meetings should be to foster team functioning. There is no guarantee that teachers and support personnel will effectively communicate and plan together. Meetings will need to make that effort a conscious focus. The assumption here is that there is a direct correlation between the communication between team members and the effective planning of children's programs.
- One integrated program for autistic children we know of came up with a meeting schedule that called for one after-school meeting of the team of teachers (head teacher, aide, student intern) and included the school psychologist and language therapist attached to the program. They strictly adhered to a time limit and came prepared in order to expedite their tasks. In addition, the classroom teachers met informally before the start of school in the morning and attempted to find time during the day when combinations of teachers could discuss children's programming.

Yes   *No*   *Is the classroom located in proximity to other classrooms?*
☐   ☐

For many years, special education classrooms were located in basement areas or in isolated sections of school buildings. Often teachers and administrators who were involved reluctantly accepted that placement because they wouldn't be "hassled" there and they could "do their own thing." Now that we are considering mainstreamed classrooms we no longer value isolation. Quite the opposite is true. We seek visibility for special children to support our belief that all children profit from being educated together. In selecting the location within a school building for a mainstreamed classroom or program, it is crucial to locate it where the action is. Ideally, it should be located in an age- or grade-appropriate area—essentially following the placement plan used for other classrooms. What we do should be visible and accessible to others so they can see our efforts and our children, and so other staff members have an opportunity to become involved. We know that proximity, while only one factor, can be important in fostering contact between neighboring teachers and children from adjacent classrooms. One mainstreamed program was made part of a team from other grades. The first year they were physically isolated from the other classrooms, thus making contact more difficult. The next year they requested and were placed in the same section with the other classrooms, which facilitated contact between teachers and children.

Yes   *No*   *As the teacher (or potential teacher) of a newly developed*
☐   ☐   *mainstream program, do you have a set of procedures for*
              selection of children and familiarizing yourself with
              teaching autistic children?

It is likely that, until there is an increase in university training programs for teachers of autistic children, regular classroom and existing special education teachers will be asked to staff new programs for autistic children. I believe it is important to involve regular classroom teachers, particularly when programs are designed around team-teaching models involving regular and special educators.

Table 3.1 outlines an orientation process involving selection of children, suggestions for reading materials on autism, and aspects of involvement in the planning process. These suggestions may be of more help to less experienced teachers of autistic children; but we assume that, for the time being, most of us are new to the development of mainstreamed programs for autistic children.

CLASSROOM ORGANIZATIONAL ISSUES

Our experiences in mainstreamed programs are teaching us how vital it is to orchestrate every aspect of classroom organizational structure. While this

Table 3.1 A Process for Teacher Orientation to Developing a Mainstreamed Classroom

Observation of special children in their present-setting.

Spend time observing the children and try to look at them in a variety of activities and situations.

Ask to talk with the child's teacher and to read the IEP and other current reports such as a Learning Plan (Implementation Plan).

➤ Do some guided reading about the kinds of children you will be working with.

If the focus is on autism, we recommend:
- *The Siege,* by Clara Claiborne Park (Little Brown-Atlantic, 1967).
- *An Approach to Teaching Autistic Children,* by Margaret Everard (Pergamon Press).
- *Developmental Therapy,* by M.M. Wood (University Park Press).

➤ Become part of the program-planning process.

This can and probably should include interviewing other new staff such as aides, language therapists, and other support services.

Help make decisions regarding the recruiting of typical children for your integrated room (if there are openings or if you are starting an entirely new grouping).

Meet with parents of special children to share your goals with them and learn of their expectations of the program.

BOOKS ON AUTISM FOR COLLEGE/UNIVERSITY LIBRARIES

The following collection of books is recommended by the Publications Committee of the National Society for Autistic Children as basic for the general library of a college or university:

- *Autism: A Reappraisal of Concepts and Treatment,* edited by Michael Rutter and Eric Schopler, Plenum Press, 1978.
- *Early Childhood Autism,* edited by Lorna Wing, Pergamon Press, 1976.
- *Autism: A Practical Guide for Parents and Professionals,* by Maria J. Paluszny, Syracuse University Press, 1979.
- *Autism: Diagnosis, Current Research and Management,* edited by Edward R. Ritvo, Spectrum Publications, 1976.
- *The Siege,* by Clara Park, Little Brown, 1972.
- *Label Me Jeff,* by Carolyn Betts, Living and Existing Publishers, P.O. Box 26275, Phoenix, AZ 84068, 1979.
- *Proceedings of the Annual Meeting and Conference of the National Society for Autistic Children,* published each year by the Society, 1234 Massachusetts Avenue NW, Washington, DC 20005.
- *Journal of Autism and Developmental Disorders,* published quarterly by Plenum Publishing Corporation, 227 West 17th Street, New York, NY 10011.

The books are also available from the NSAC Bookstore. Write Library Service, National Society for Autistic Children, 1234 Massachusetts Avenue NW, Washington, DC 20005, for price and ordering information.

undoubtedly places a burden on the staff, the results are clearly worth the effort. Considering the observation that autistic chidren do not necessarily profit from casual or incidental learning, it is necessary to structure classroom time and procedures. The following questions ask you about your routines and practices.

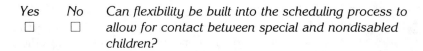

Yes   No   *Can flexibility be built into the scheduling process to*
☐   ☐   *allow for contact between special and nondisabled*
             children?

The therapeutic and systematic designing of a child's day is one of the most important interventions we have at our disposal. A child's schedule should grow directly out of the Individualized Education Plan (IEP) and fit into the structure and needs of the classroom group. Our experience has led us to focus on several ground rules in designing a schedule.
- It is useful to determine which learning and socialization needs can be met in a whole group situation and which ones have to be focused on in individual work with an adult. If possible, a child should be integrated with his or her peers.
- It is useful to analyze the impact of a special child's behavior on the rest of the group. If the behavior is unacceptable or disruptive to the group, it is important to work on both parts of the problem: assist the special child in modifying his or her behavior (aggression; messy eating that offends others; procedures for diminishing drooling behavior, etc.); and assist group and individual class members to change their behavior so that it is easier for others to fit in or to teach group members specific techniques and procedures they can use to respond more helpfully to their special peers. The range of ways this can be done is quite varied, but classroom time and energy should be allocated to interpersonal skill training for all children.
- In designing a schedule, you would do well to examine carefully the tempo needs of the child, the group, and your own teaching rhythm. When should academics or skills be taught? Are people most alert early in the morning? Does fatigue set in, making it necessary to vary the sequence of activities, interspersing more open play times following work times?

Yes   No   *Are you prepared to function as a member of a team*
☐   ☐   *along with other teachers and support personnel?*

Many of us might be *interested* in working directly with others in classroom programs, but few of us may be *prepared* for this in the sense that we haven't experienced very much team teaching, team planning, supervision, and support from others. Receiving assistance and responding to others may be skills we can develop. Here are some aspects to consider.

- Do you engage in active listening to what others are saying so that you are in a better position to understand their perspectives? The more clearly we listen and understand the messages directed at us, the better able we are to carefully choose and internalize those messages that have implications for our growth and change.
- Do you initiate with others, or do you wait and expect others to be active with you? If you were willing to take some risks in terms of giving others feedback, asking for feedback, or merely being social and active with others with whom you work, it is likely that an interactive climate could be fostered. Most of us are "waiters," hoping or even expecting others to do the initiating. Sometimes it happens that way, but it is a risk. If the goal is to create a team-like situation, then each member must assume some degree of responsibility for making it happen!
- Do you have authority issues or concerns with others in your group? Schools, as an example of a hierarchical social system, are notorious for "A over B" relationships, in which people are overtly or covertly kept in their place. Here is your chance to test out some of your assumptions about others. Given the reality that some people have been delegated more responsibility and authority, can we still find a common meeting ground with each other? In carrying out complex program structures like the ones we are discussing, it is necessary to work effectively with others for the short- and long-range benefit of the children. If you have issues with others, can you:
  - Talk constructively with each other about your differences and how you can function, recognizing those differences?
  - Set about to actively change the nature of the relationship so that it feels better to each person involved?
  - Actually test out whether your perceptions of the relationship are in fact shared by those involved?
- How comfortable do you make others feel when they visit, observe, or interact with children on a scheduled basis in your classroom? If resource personnel are to function effectively with your children, the kind of relationship you have will either enhance or minimize the child's progress. Very often a resource person may be doing a fine job with one of your children, say in language therapy. But if you, or the therapist, feel uncomfortable or resist each other's overtures, then it makes the translation of new information back into the classroom very difficult—if not impossible.
- Have you actually tested out and pushed against the boundaries with your school administrators? Our experience has been that much more could actually be done if teachers and administrators were direct with each other and did not make assumptions about what is or is not possible. Learn to check out some things out, and you might be pleasantly

surprised at what can happen—if not all of the time, at least some of the time!

- One of the skills that helps a team function together is to be prompt and thorough in record keeping and report writing. If each member does his or her share of observing and recording and writing, a norm of thoroughness is created. In turn, the team has more and better data upon which to talk and make decisions about a child's program.

Yes   No   *Are there provisions made for you to receive some form*
☐   ☐   *of on-going support from another adult or adults?*

If we assume that most teachers have not been exposed to teaching autistic children in a mainstreamed environment, it is doubly important to have access to other resource persons who can offer you technical as well as moral support. In truth, we feel strongly that all teachers should be connected to a support network. Here are some questions to ask about your situation.

- Will there be planning time available to me, either during the day or after school? In many school districts this is a complicated question for a number of reasons, including district policies on school day hours, teacher union contracts which encourage or restrict after-school meetings, school building norms which make it easier or harder for some teachers to put in long hours, and individual teachers' unique life circumstances. Undoubtedly there are other factors which impinge on all teaching staffs. The reality is, however, that planning time is an absolute necessity in the implementation of a mainstreamed program. The very presence of such a range of children with varying needs and abilities requires a lot of individualizing of instruction and thus a large teacher commitment to planning.
- Will the support person or persons actually observe in my classroom? Our experience leads us to believe that one of the most valuable contributions a support person can make is to function as a more objective observer and to then bring those observations into feedback and discussion sessions with the teacher or team involved in the child's program.
- Will I have access to a range of services and personnel should it be necessary to obtain new or diverse information about a child? Ideally, outside technical assistance should be located within or at least in close proximity to each program, but this is not always available. If this assistance cannot be obtained as an integral part of your on-going program, then you should insist on the use of outside resource persons. They may be psychologists, who can provide additional data on a child's educational and psychological functioning; social workers, who can help one of your families find home supportive services such as home aides, babysitting, or respite services; or other community agencies that can provide supplementary services such as physical therapy.

Yes   No   Is there a plan to re-people the classroom with additional
□   □   *paid and volunteer staff?*

Children with special needs, particularly more severely involved children, may require additional adult time, planning, and intervention. Classroom teachers interested in responding to these children will need, and should have, access to more adults in and out of their classrooms. Certainly the amount and kind of adult support needed will vary depending on the children involved and the size of the group. At the very least, when severely involved children are placed into regular classrooms an aide should become part of the staff. Some programs designate a teacher aide's time to be spent exclusively with the special child (or children). We recommend that an aide be used in a variety of ways: to respond to the rest of the class, thus allowing the teacher time with the special child; to function as a helper to the teacher with the entire class; to help to bring typical children in contact with the special child; to work with the special child in a small group of nondisabled children; and in a variety of other ways. The main point is that it is possible to isolate and segregate a special child in a regular classroom and that the use of additional adults should not contribute to that isolation. Their presence can help make the child more visible and his behaviors more functional in the classroom. In many classrooms, the use of a teacher aide is quite an acceptable design. It is less clear how others such as college student interns, volunteers, parent and community volunteers, foster grandparent aides, peer tutors, and other people find their way into the schools and then into integrated classrooms. At the heart of the issue, the school must develop a norm that allows, encourages, and values the use of "nonteachers" in classrooms. A related issue is the need to make a commitment to the training and supervision of others. This is not an easy issue; it ultimately falls back on whether teachers feel good enough about themselves to see themselves as teachers of adults as well as teachers of children.

Yes   No   Will the special children travel to school on the same
□   □   *transportation as other children?*

In the planning of a mainstreamed program, this issue of whether a separate school bus should be used for the handicapped children is invariably raised. The mixing of children on a school bus is a normalizing experience. It is much more stigmatizing for children and parents to use a station wagon bus, for example, rather than the full-sized vehicle used for other children. It may be necessary and desirable to have a bus aide available for particular children and to employ seat belt harnesses for those children who need that support for safety. Sometimes the decision to use separate transportation will raise the possibility of ending school early for those children. Neither decision should be encouraged, nor should the transportation department be allowed to exert such major programming control.

Yes *No* *Do the autistic children eat in the cafeteria with the*
☐   ☐   *other children?*

If the other children eat in a lunchroom, then you should seriously consider having your special needs children eat in the same space. Current wisdom on teaching autistic children speaks to their inability to handle noisy and overly stimulating environments. We should not assume, however, that all autistic children are unable to respond appropriately to the cafeteria scene. Again, it is normalizing to have all children eat together; and all children, autistic and nondisabled, can and should be taught appropriate lunchroom behavior. Normal peers can assist their disabled peers, and teachers can position themselves in proximity to the special children to be of assistance if necessary.

CLASSROOM TEACHER BEHAVIORS

Now that you have responded to the previous sections, you recognize that advance planning to design specific strategies for bringing a diverse group of special and nondisabled children together is needed. Each group of teachers and administrators working together may come up with unique plans to meet their individual situations. Since we have so few precedents to fall back upon, perhaps our experiences at Jowonio: The Learning Place will provide an initial frame of reference for you.

It took our teachers time to come to grips with the fact that they were dealing with an entire classroom and not just special children. In a mainstreamed program you truly end up responding to everyone. In working with a newly developing mainstreamed classroom in a public school, the Jowonio staff consciously focused on the types of questions that are included in this section. If you are looking for a way to plan a new program, just turn each of these questions into a statement and you will have a set of guidelines to follow.

Yes *No* *Is there a plan for focusing on the attitudes of typical*
☐   ☐   *children toward their handicapped peers?*

This is a central question and our conclusion is that the fostering of positive attitudes of nondisabled toward special children must be focused on by everyone in the classroom and should be worked at constantly, in a variety of ways. This belief reflects some teachers' aspirations and often includes concerns and questions as well.

> I think about this often. When first learning of mainstreaming, I found myself envisioning strong friendships between typical and special children, friendships of a different nature, perhaps, than between two typical children, but still involving the very crucial feelings of warmth, trust, and caring. In my

imaginings, I saw typical children growing completely nonchalant to differences of both a physical and emotional nature. I saw special children growing more quickly, through the trust and the ease of the environment. While the typical child learned of quality help, about responses and when and how to give them, in my vision the special child grew more caring about it all.

My vision is no less important to me now, after the year here in Jowonio and the half-year in the Gebbie Infant Clinic. No less important, but certainly more open to question. I suppose that my major feeling right now is that I DON'T KNOW FOR SURE. I Don't Know For Sure that all children are integratable at all times; I Don't Know For Sure that integration is a natural process; I Don't Know For Sure exactly what integration is to me; I Don't Know For Sure what my goals for it are exactly.

I do know that I get a good feeling from watching certain integrated situations. I do know that Debby (a nondisabled child) and others like her are far less afraid of differences than I was. I know, too, that after a time, special children and typical children become only children to me, with particular needs at particular times, and that I feel exceptionally good about that every time I think about it.

These statements reflect one teacher's growing awareness of her own beliefs and of the complexities involved.

Yes	No	Do you have a way of responding to the concerns that
☐	☐	will be raised about the teaching of academics to special and nondisabled children?

Schools and teachers are under increasing pressure to be accountable for children's academic progress. This concern cannot and should not be ignored in an integrated program, and teachers have developed a variety of ways to respond to the cognitive and learning needs of all the children in an integrated classroom. We hope this focus will be balanced by an equal emphasis on children's emotional and social development.

Here are some strategies you can employ to respond to the teaching of academics.

- You should clarify the issue with your building principal. Sometimes the pressure for skill training comes from within us, and we would do well to verify the level of concern of building administrators. This is an example of "checking things out," referred to previously.
- It is possible, and even desirable, to think about the inclusion and weaving in of skill development in every activity that you use during the day. By remaining conscious of the academic goals for each child, you can address them in a variety of ways throughout the day. For example, with an autistic child whose language development is delayed, you must create a communication environment throughout the entire day. You can ask him

questions, prompt the other children to converse with him by using a controlled vocabulary, help him label the objects that he comes in contact with, and so on.

- In conjunction with these points, it has helped us to designate specific time blocks throughout the day exclusively focused on skill development. These times may or may not be integrated times for the special child. This decision must be based on individual and group needs. One useful strategy employed by one teaching and resource staff is to have individual skill sessions, such as language therapy and individual tutoring, accomplished within the classroom and not in a separate room away from the others. This provides more visibility to the special child, so he is made to look less different, and provides the teacher with more opportunity to observe and hopefully model what a specialist is doing. On a long-term basis, this may help the teacher program for the child within the larger classroom group.

Yes   No   *Can the staff agree upon the use of one or more clinical*
☐   ☐   *teaching instruments that will allow for a common way of*
            looking at children's progress?

There are several good reasons for the systematic utilization of one or more clinical teaching instruments. First, they provide the entire staff with a common vocabulary they can use to describe the teaching objectives and interventions used. Second, they allow for a more systematic record-keeping process that can be used by a range of personnel working with the child. Third, some instruments have objectives that can be used by parents as part of a home training approach, thus coordinating the effort between home and school. Fourth, if one instrument is used and accepted by all the program personnel, then it is possible for team decisions to be made in planning a child's program and evaluating progress. For example, in setting teaching objectives in *Developmental Therapy* (Wood, 1975), a team of teachers and resource personnel meets together to reach concensus on the setting of objectives and recording of progress.

In *Developmental Therapy for Young Children with Autistic Characteristics* (Bachrach, Mosley, Swindle, & Wood, 1978), the same teaching objectives used in school are translated into procedures that parents can apply at home. Objectives fall into four areas: Behavior, Socialization, Communication, and (Pre)Academics. This instrument has a rating form that is completed at regular intervals by teachers and support staff. Record-keeping procedures can be devised to chart progress, and these are summary forms to monitor percentage of objectives achieved.

In dealing with autism, we are just beginning to see the development of teaching instruments with tasks relevant to the learning and behavior needs of autistic children. Martin Kozloff (1973; 1979) has written two books with detailed teaching objectives that provide teachers and parents with step-by-step interventions to use with severely impaired children. Schopler, Reichler, and Lansing (1980) have recently published their psychoeducational teaching approach for autistic and developmentally disabled children. That instrument also provides teaching strategies for parents as well as teachers. A more technical instrument is the recently published experimental edition of the *Autism Screening Instrument for Educational Planning* (Krug, Arick, & Almond, 1978). That instrument has five components: Autism Behavior Checklist, Sample of Vocal Behavior, Interaction Assessment, Educational Assessment, and Prognosis of Learning Rate.

Yes	No	
☐	☐	*In the planning for your mainstreamed classroom, have you obtained a commitment from your building administrators or central administration special education department for adequate learning materials and supplies?*

The usual standard of some set figure, for example of $75.00, for the entire classroom for 1 year is simply not adequate. Our experience has shown us that we can more easily reach the goal of fostering autistic children's exploratory and independent behaviors by richly provisioning the environment so that each child has access to a range of developmentally appropriate materials. After all, if we want children to be active, they should have materials, supplies, and objects with which to interact. This interaction of child, materials, and teacher is central to facilitating learning in any classroom. The next chapter, Case Study of a Stage One Classroom, places the use of materials within the context of a broader curriculum process in which the classroom schedule, the physical space, and the children and staff all contribute to an environment conducive to growth and social interaction.

One of our teachers had this to say about which materials are needed:

One last basic need for an integrated situation is the teacher's style of management of the physical room, and her activities and materials available. When planning an art activity, for both the special children and the younger children within the classroom, it is necessary to utilize materials that can be flexible enough to fit all groups. So that, as Ralph loves to paste, I might plan an art activity which would involve pasting. However, I would also need to provide challenges for the typical children, so I might make the activity based around a collage of "me's." Each child would make a collage, cutting pictures out of magazines that fit their likes or situations. Here, a teacher would be with Ralph, cutting out with him those items he recognized and mentioned. For Ralph, the focus would be on the actions of cutting and pasting, whereas for the typical children the focus would be on learning about themselves.

Around the room, there must be materials that can be versatile. Cuisinaire rods, blocks, dolls, books, marbles, cubes, puzzles, crayons, paste, and others like this all can be used by all children according to their own level. While Burt, then, might use a set of blocks to build a castle with a moat, towers, and windows, Martin might use those same blocks to sort colors, and Donnie might use them to practice fine motor control.

Yes	No	
☐	☐	*Is there an on-going plan for inservice training for you and building teaching staff and administrators?*

In considering a proposal to mainstream your classroom, you should insist upon initial inservice training. This should become part of a year-long, on-going inservice training approach for you and the others in your building.

At Jowonio we generally solicit input from teachers and other staff members as to topics or particular speakers they would like to hear. Some years we set up a committee comprised of teachers and administrative staff members to plan inservice topics, speakers, and formats. Inservice sessions were scheduled for full or half days (we adhere to the public school calendar), or they could be shorter after-school sessions. In other years, one of our administrative staff members assumes the responsibility for planning and scheduling inservice experiences, consulting with the school staff.

Over the years, our inservice training has reflected a range of staff needs and interests.

- We have scheduled a workshop day for the staff to focus on particular topics as a group, such as generating ways to design activities for Stage I children (Wood, *Developmental Therapy,* 1975). An example was the staff's generating activities to assist children in responding to objective B3 (Behavior), Respond with Sustained Attending. At that day-long workshop, small groups worked on separate topics and then shared their results with the entire group. These were recorded on dittos, and each person attending received a copy.
- Films such as Janet Adler's movement therapy film "Looking For Me" have been used as a springboard for staff discussion of teaching philosophy and interventions.
- In an effort to obtain content information and skills in areas in which we are not as proficient, we have scheduled speakers and workshops in behavior modification techniques, physical therapy, motor development of children, and emergency first aid procedures.
- Because of the integrated nature of our school, the teachers remain keenly aware of their need to maintain their skills in content areas such as reading, math, and science. Workshops have been scheduled in those areas, as well as sessions on cooking with children, block building, and effective transitions between activities—to cite only a few examples.

REFERENCES

Bachrach, A., Mosley, A., Swindle, F., & Wood, M. *Developmental therapy for young children with autistic characteristics.* Baltimore: University Park Press, 1978.

Kozloff, M.A. *A program for families of children with learning and behavior problems.* New York: John Wiley, 1979.

Kozloff, M.A. *Reaching the autistic child: A parent training program.* Champaign, Ill.: Research Press, 1973.

Krug, D., Arick, J., & Almond, P. *Autism screening instrument for educational planning.* Portland, Ore.: A.S.I.E.P., 1978.

Schopler, E., Reichler, R.J., & Lansing, M. *Individualized assessment and treatment for autistic and developmentally disabled children. Vol. II. Teaching strategies for parents and professionals.* Baltimore: University Park Press, 1980.

Wood, M.M. *Developmental therapy: A textbook for teachers as therapists for emotionally disturbed young children.* Baltimore: University Park Press, 1975.

4
Case Study of a Stage One Classroom

Sandra Mlinarcik

INTRODUCTION

An optimally designed learning environment for young children responds to the children's present levels of functioning, while providing opportunities for physical, social, emotional, and cognitive growth. Nursery, preschool, and day care programs may have widely varied services, educational philosophies, and physical structures. Yet as child-centered environments, many programs share numerous programming emphases:

- On play as a child's work.
- On self-acceptance and appreciation, as well as on successful participation as a group member.
- On the development of language and communication skills.
- On the development of fine and gross motor abilities.
- On awareness and appreciation of natural phenomena.
- On helping children develop confidence and delight in their ability to learn.

These traditional programming characteristics apply, as well, to the design of a therapeutic learning environment for young children who are identified as *autistic*.

Bachrach, Mosley, Swindle, and Wood (1978) maintain that every child has normal developmental traits, regardless of the severity of the impairment. These normal developmental traits must be used and strengthened in the learning environment. To effectively strengthen the normal development of young children with handicapping conditions, one additional programming characteristic is required: emphasis on integration with typical peers.

The benefits for the children in an integrated learning environment are readily apparent. It is easy to present theoretical rationales which support this approach: the powerful modeling of appropriate behaviors, an opportunity to develop positive attitudes toward human differences, a real consideration of all children's needs for individualized instruction. Underlying the theoretical advantages of an integrated learning environment, however, are issues regarding planning, implementation, and evaluation. Educators faced with putting the theory into practice must respond to these issues, which are summarized in Figure 4.1. These issues, and many others, must be addressed both in the initial stages of structuring a learning environment and whenever the children's growth demands changes in the environment.

The following case study of one integrated classroom for young children explores the process of planning the learning environment, implementing curriculum, and evaluating individual progress and total programming. The classroom described here is designed for children 3 and 4 years old. For some of the children, it is the initial school experience. For others, day care or nursery school programs have already provided an educational experience with peers outside of the home.

Figure 4-1

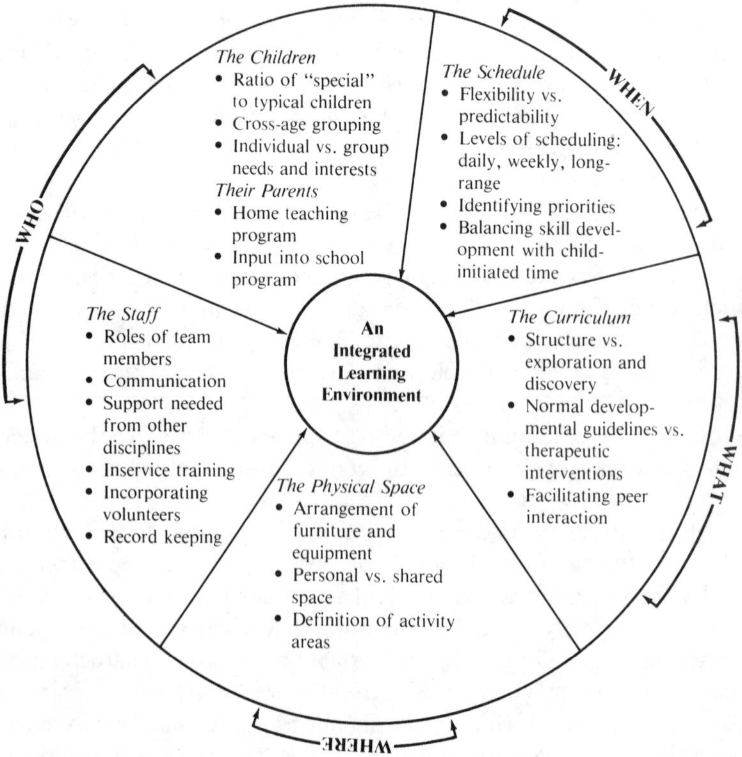

THE RAINBOW ROOM—JOWONIO: THE LEARNING PLACE

The Team

Jowonio begins each school year with a week of orientation for its staff. During this week, the teaching team of the Rainbow Room has a three-fold responsibility: to get acquainted with each other, to become familiar with the children, and to create an attractive classroom out of a somewhat motley collection of furniture and a wide assortment of materials. Lydia, the lead teacher, has a background in both early childhood and special education. As lead teacher, Lydia is accountable for the overall functioning of the classroom. She also has the responsibility for responding to some of the teacher-training needs of Bill and Diane, who comprise the rest of the classroom team. Bill, an undergraduate at Syracuse University, is spending a semester for state certification in special education. Diane is enrolled in a field-based master's program in autism and emotional disturbance. While she has taught for several years in an agency which serves adolescent girls, this is Diane's first experience working with young children.

During the school's summer session, Lydia had organized several afternoon play groups to which she invited small groups of children and their parents. The play groups gave Lydia an opportunity to observe the children's initiation of activity, interaction with peers, and current level of various self-help skills. In addition to laying the ground work for the teachers' early fall planning, the play group helped the children and their parents become familiar with the school environment. Lydia's anecdotal reports from the play group sessions, reports from other programs and community agencies, and forms completed by parents yield the initial data available to the Rainbow Room teachers during orientation week. The data will be supplemented at meetings with ancillary staff members, who also function as members of the team. The language resource teacher, parent worker, and school administrator can contribute information to the teachers from contacts with the children and their parents during the process of referral, assessment, and acceptance into the school's program.

Throughout the school year, the Rainbow Room teachers will work cooperatively with ancillary staff. The language resource teacher, who provides intensive language training for the children with special needs, participates in team meetings, as well as seeing children on a one-to-one or small-group basis. As a speech and language specialist, this resource person assists the teachers in setting language objectives, shows information from assessment and observations, and consults with the teachers regarding instructional methods which could be used to support language development in the classroom. If a child needs speech services which cannot be provided at Jowonio, the language resource teacher coordinates the referral to an outside agency and maintains contact with the agency for reports on the course of treatment and the child's progress. To remain consistent with the integrated model at Jowonio, the Rainbow Room teachers request the language teacher to implement individual language programs within the on-going classroom activities whenever possible.

The Rainbow Room staff is further supported by a parent worker who functions as a liaison between the classroom and families of the children who are labeled. During orientation week, the parent worker is a valuable source of information, which was obtained from developmental assesment and observations in the homes over the summer months. The parents were given an opportunity to show their priorities and concerns regarding their child's instructional program. Throughout the year, the parent worker maintains regularly scheduled contacts with the handicapped children at school. These contacts allow the parent worker to accurately translate the child's school experiences into a home training program.

The responsibilities of the teaching team extend from the Rainbow Room to the larger school community, to the children's families, and further to public school districts and agencies outside of Jowonio. The classroom teachers, language resource teacher, and parent worker receive support in fulfilling their responsibilities from a school administrator who identifies herself as a member of the Rainbow team. The school administrator helps coordinate team meetings, child conferences, and resources for the classroom, such as volunteers, instructional materials, and consultation with professionals from other disciplines. As a team member, the administator also assumes responsibility for acquiring firsthand knowledge of the instructional programs for the children who are labeled and for the class as a whole.

The team concept is an integral part of the learning environment at Jowonio. The expertise of each team member contributes to the functioning of the classroom and to the realization of intensive programming goals for all the children. The complexities involved in the team approach, however, are equal to its potential power. Therefore, the team in the Rainbow Room has an underlying responsibility to understand each member's role and to develop a workable format for problem solving as a team. Figure 4-2 charts the interactions between team members.

The Physical Space

The Rainbow Room occupies what had once been a traditional kindergarten room, equipped with child-size bathroom fixtures and familiar "cubbies" for clothing and treasures carried from home. A wall of windows provides both natural light and a vista for observing the weather, seasonal changes, and neighborhood happenings. The Rainbow Room teachers view the task of organizing and equipping this classroom as an opportunity to design curriculum and delineate general learning objectives.

Figure 4.2   Interaction between roles of team members

	Instructional Objectives	Daily Operation of Environment	Child Conferences	Commitments to Outside Agencies
Classroom Teachers	Collect available information Design activities to observe needs and interests of children Plan diagnostic activities to determine range of abilities	Create lesson plans Arrange activity areas Coordinate class and individual schedules Make written or phone contact with parents	Identify problem in child's program Contact other team members Prepare presentation of learning plan and current functioning Collect anecdotal records	Draft IEPs Attend staff meetings and inservice sessions Read reports sent to Jowonio for cumulative files Identify inservice needs
Language Resource Teacher	Assesses current level of functioning on language and communication Shares information regarding alternative language approaches	Provides one-to-one and small-group instruction Reports children's progress to teachers Shares materials and methods used in sessions	Models instructional strategies Provides additional information from language sessions	Coordinates speech referrals to other agencies Supervises speech and language interns Attends staff meetings and inservice sessions
Parent Worker	Communicates observations from home visits Relates parent concerns Reinforces school activities with home training program	Obtains first-hand information of instructional programs Coordinates parent visits to observe programming Records notes from home contacts	Observes child in classroom Arranges parent visit to school if necessary Provides information from home visits	Coordinates a monthly group for parents of handicapped children Writes school newsletter Attends staff meetings Coordinates IEP conferences
Administrator	Orders materials necessary to implement objectives Obtains first-hand knowledge of children Coordinates use of space and equipment	Coordinates transportation Arranges classroom coverage during teacher absence Coordinates visitors Responds to requests for information Handles conflicts	Arranges services from outside agencies, if needed Supports changes in programming with additional staff, schedule arrangements Provides additional information	Coordinates IEP process Organizes staff meetings and inservice training Attends Committee on the Handicapped meetings Coordinates tuition contracts

> The physical aspects of the classroom—the decor, the arrangement of furniture, the nature, variety, and accessibility of materials—are a statement about how the room is used and the way in which the teacher expects the children to be engaged in learning.... The order in the room, especially for the young child, is also a way of teaching. It should be logical and explicit; things are put together that go together, and the rationale is made clear to the children. (Shapiro & Biber, 1973, p. 697)

The physical organization of the Rainbow Room makes a "statement" which is responsive to the developmental needs of preschool children. The tremendous growth potential of young children, according to Smart and Smart (1973), demands a rich and varied environment in order to be realized. They propose that social growth is promoted by arrangements in the environment which facilitate cooperative play. In addition, Smart and Smart describe personality growth, especially building a sense of autonomy, as being facilitated by equipment which the children can manage. The Rainbow Room is an open, flexible space which invites exploration and discovery. Child-sized furniture, a rich assortment of materials, and storage which is both logical and accessible invites independence and child-initiated activity. Just as play is traditionally described as the *work* of young children, this classroom can be viewed as a child-centered *workshop*.

Wood (1975) describes the overriding developmental objective for children with severe emotional disturbance as "learning to respond to the environment with pleasure." This objective can certainly be generalized to the typical chldren in the Rainbow Room. The careful selection of equipment and arrangement of functional areas in the classroom is aimed at evoking pleasure through exploration, discovery, and accomplishment. For the four children requiring special programming, each functional area in the Rainbow Room must contain materials which lure the children into responding. These materials, for the most part, provide pleasurable sensory experiences and are introduced to the children during intensive, one-to-one instructional sessions. Figure 4-3 summarizes the activity areas in the Rainbow Room according to their purpose, necessary materials and equipment, and developmental objectives.

The Schedule

The design of a daily schedule in the Rainbow Room posed a challenge to the teaching team and ancillary staff. They attempted to create a balance between several competing factors:
1. High stimulation vs. low-key times;
2. Child-initiated vs. teacher-directed times;
3. Integration vs. intensive, one-to-one times;
4. Consistency vs. flexibility.

Figure 4.3 Functional Areas in the Rainbow Room

Area	Materials and Equipment	Potential Skill Development
Personal spaces	Coathooks, shelves, plastic bins which are accessible to children Name cards, photographs Mirror Display area on wall or bulletin board	Independence in self-help skills Recognition of name in print Strengthen manipulative skills; i.e., folding and hanging clothes Build positive self-concept
Expressive area	Assorted art supplies (easel, paint, large brushes, crayons, chalk, scissors, paste, paper) Materials for constructions and collages (pipe cleaners, cardboard rolls, texture samples, magazines) Washable floor surface Materials for sensory experiences (clay, shaving cream, rice, salt, macaroni) Shelves, containers, pegboard labeled by word, picture, or outline Provisions for clean-up (dust pan, whisk broom, sponges, small plastic bucket)	Exercise initiative and imagination Language development Integration of sensory and verbal experiences Strengthen fine motor skills Develop positive self-concept Develop an appreciation of beauty
Dramatic play	Housekeeping equipment (stove, sink, refrigerator, unbreakable dishes, table and chairs, dolls and doll clothing, grocery bags, food containers, broom and mop, clothespins and line) "Grown up" hats, shoes, purses, and clothing for dress-up Open-ended props (cardboard boxes, fabric scraps)	Recreation and practice of familiar experiences Exploration of various adult roles Problem solving with imaginative processes Language development
Blocks	Assortment of blocks which vary in size and construction (wooden, cardboard, foam) Accessories (vehicles, street signs, small dolls, dollhouse) Indoor/outdoor carpeting to cushion sound Shelf space with outlines of blocks to facilitate order and clean-up Open-ended materials (fabric scraps, boards cut to various widths, paper, markers, tape)	Develop fine and gross motor skills Cooperative play Recreation of familiar settings and experiences Develop eye-hand coordination
Gross motor and group activity area	An open space which serves many purposes Mat or mattress which can be stored against a wall Large wooden box with openings cut into it and several stairs attached Record player Balance beam Rocking platform	Increases gross motor development Explore shared space and cooperative movement Develop ability to follow directions Practice modeling and imitation behaviors

ecessary complicated manipulation of available time slots, the
ned a clear objective—to develop a schedule which allows young
ipate and successfully respond to class activities. A typical day
Room follows this schedule.

8:45- 9:00	Arrival and hello time
* 9:00- 9:45	Child-initiated activity
* 9:45-10:00	Meeting
*10:00-10:15	Movement activities
10:15-10:30	Snack time
*10:30-11:00	Small groups; teacher-directed activity
*11:00-11:30	Outdoor time
11:30-12:00	Sensorimotor activities
12:00-12:30	Lunch time
*12:30- 1:15	Rest and reading time
* 1:15- 2:00	Child-initiated activity and invitational time
2:00- 2:20	Music
2:20- 2:30	Goodbye time

Young children, either at home or in a total care program, are usually
allowed or, in some cases, required to nap for up to 2 hours following lunch
time. The Rainbow Room at Jowonio is not equipped for a formal nap time, nor
does the length of the school day permit a traditional nap. The teachers respond
to the children's needs for both times of high stimulation and energy release and
times of relaxation and quiet by careful juxtaposition of activities throughout
the day. An activity which requires gross motor response and large group
arousal is followed by a quiet activity which may involve fine muscle response
and allow the children to work independently. Attention to the children's individual needs is given through the choices available during activity times. The
child-initiated activity period opens up the entire room, and the children are free
to choose their activity level. A child who has had a long bus ride, therefore,
may initially choose a vigorous activity, such as crawling through an obstacle
course set up in the center of the room. Other children may initially choose to
spend time in the expressive area, quietly painting or cutting and pasting
magazine pictures. Throughout the day and within specific activity times, the
schedule provides a changing, responsive rhythm.

For the four children in the Rainbow Room who require special instructional methods, the teachers carefully considered how they might achieve maximum integration, while providing the intensive training which has been recommended. The teachers first identified the times during the day when all the children could be fully integrated. These times included arrival, snack, outdoor
time, sensorimotor activities, lunch time, and music. During each of these activity slots, the typical children were able to function independently, seeking only

*These are approximate time intervals. Their length can be regulated by the teachers in response to
the children's involvement and changing interests.

intermittent attention from a teacher, which allowed the teachers to focus on integrating the children with special needs. During snack, for example, a teacher planned on supervising the correct eating and drinking habits of one boy, while joining in the conversation of the other children at the table. This time was also used to practice the sign language which the boy was working on in his language sessions. Since all of the children may request "more" of a food item, the boy using signs was assisted in expressing his requests as well. Other activities during the day were identified as more structured and demanding more teacher input. During these periods, therefore, the language teacher and parent worker for the Rainbow Room scheduled one-to-one instructional times and structured play groups which took place outside of the classroom. When one of the special children was able to be integrated, with assistance, into one of the more structured or skill-oriented activities, an ancillary staff member or volunteer would be scheduled into the group at that time.

Maintaining a balance between consistency and flexibility is a factor which must be addressed in any early childhood program. Young children function more comfortably within routines which allow them to predict events and the expectations others will have of them. Consistency is especially important in an environment like the Rainbow Room, where some children have difficulty in drawing meaning from sensory stimulation. For these children, consistency provides many cues that guide them in responding. According to Bachrach and colleagues (1978), once the sequence of daily activities is established, it should be faithfully repeated each day. This repetition "builds security and trust in the child toward the adults, and toward the program itself."

While the sequence within a schedule must be preserved, flexibility in time intervals, in choices within activity periods, and in varied materials and settings can prevent the schedule from becoming a foreboding task master. If unusual weather conditions or an up-coming holiday arouse the children's energy to a level where they seem unable to focus their attention, the teachers may decide to shorten the child-initiated activity time and add a storybook to meeting. The art area may be moved outdoors on a hot day, or outdoor time may include a walk through the park. These changes within the schedule can enrich the children's experiences and provide opportunities to respond to new situations, without unnecessary threat to the routines and cues on which the children have learned to rely.

THE CHILDREN

The 13 children in the Rainbow Room range in age from "young" 3-year-olds, for whom this is an initial school experience, to "mature" 4-year-olds, who will turn 5 during the school year. The range in age is integral to structuring the learning environment in the Rainbow Room. The multi-age grouping provides a range of skill development, interests, and social-emotional needs which necessitates an individualized approach to instruction and facilitates integration of children with special needs. The ratio of nine typical children to four "special" children was chosen to maximize the possibilities for social interaction and peer modeling of appropriate behaviors. There was a conscious attempt to include a range in severity of impairment and developmental delay of the four "special" children, both to increase opportunities for their integration and to enable the teaching team to remain responsive to all the children in the class.

The four "special" children were referred to Jowonio from several school districts and a nonprofit service organization. The children were evaluated by ancillary staff and the lead teacher in the Rainbow Room. *Developmental Therapy (DT),* edited by Mary M. Wood (1975), provided the basis for evaluation and determination of curriculum objectives in four areas: Behavior, Communication, Socialization, and Academics. A short introduction to each of the "special" children and a summary of the initial behavioral objectives are given below.

Michael

Although Michael is already 5 years old, placement in the Rainbow Room was desirable for several reasons. He is functioning approximately 3 years below age-appropriate level in the area of receptive language. His expressive language is intelligible only when the listener has cues available or knows the topic of conversation. Michael needs to learn appropriate ways to play and interact with peers. Since language has not been a successful way to communicate, Michael resorts to aggressive interactions and tantrums. Michael has a very short attention span and strikes out at unwanted direction from adults. The initial *DT* goals for Michael are:

Behavior
4. To respond with motor and body response to complex environmental and verbal stimuli.
5. To actively assist in learning self-help skills.
7. To respond with recall to the routine spontaneously.
8. To use play materials appropriately.

Communication
2. To respond to verbal stimulus with motor behavior.
4. To voluntarily initiate a recognizable approximation to obtain a specific object or activity.
5. To produce a recognizable word to obtain a desired response from an adult.

Socialization
5. To engage in organized solitary play.
6. To respond to adult's verbal and nonverbal requests to come.

    7. To respond to single verbal request or command given directly to child.

  11. To exhibit a beginning emergence of self.

Academics

    5. To respond with rudimentary fine motor skill to manipulative tasks associated with 2-year level.

    6. To imitate words or action of adult upon request.

    7. To respond by simple discrimination of objects.

Diane

Diane is also 5 years old. She remained at home for a year after an unsuccessful attempt at participating in a half-day kindergarten. Diane's speech is delayed and incomplete. She does not use speech to express herself spontaneously, but her articulation is clear when she echoes words and phrases which she hears. Diane shows little purposive use of objects or toys, usually engaging in repetitive actions such as tapping a toy with her index fingers. During transition times, new situations, or in response to expectations from an adult, Diane covers her face with her arm and cries. In addition to making school a safe, pleasurable experience for Diane, the following *DT* objectives were outlined.

Behavior

    2. To respond to stimulus by sustained attending to source of stimulus.

    3. To respond with motor behavior to single environmental stimulus: object, person, sound.

    4. To respond with motor and body responses to complex environmental and verbal stimuli.

Communication

    2. To respond to verbal stimulus with a motor behavior.

    5. To produce a recognizable word to obtain a desired response from an adult.

    6. To produce a recognizable word to obtain a desired response from another child.

Socialization

    3. To respond to adult when child's name is called.

    4. To imitate simple, familiar acts of adults.

    5. To engage in organized solitary play.

    6. To respond to adult's verbal and nonverbal requests to come to him.

Academics

    5. To respond with rudimentary fine motor skill to simple manipulative tasks associated with 2-year level.

    6. To imitate words or action of adult upon request.

    7. To respond by simple discrimination of objects.

    8. To voluntarily initiate a recognizable verbal approximation to obtain a specific object or activity.

Patrick

Patrick attended an infant stimulation program and a full-day nursery school prior to entering Jowonio. He is currently functioning 2½ to 3 years below his chronological age of 4½ years. Patrick's behavior is characterized by a prolonged response time. He walks on his toes much of the time with an uneven gait, and his muscle tone is somewhat rigid. He makes a limited number of sounds but does not engage in true babbling. Patrick does not attend to other children's activities and withdraws from adult intervention by hitting his head with his fists. He prefers to wander about the room, occasionally stopping to look at the overhead lights or shiny objects. The following *DT* goals were outlined for Patrick.

Behavior
1. To respond to sensory stimulus by attending to source of stimulus by body response or by looking at object or person.
2. To respond to stimulus by sustained attending to source of stimulus.
3. To respond with motor behavior to single environmental stimulus: object, person, sound.

Communication
1. To attend to person speaking.
2. To respond to a verbal stimulus with a motor behavior.
3. To respond to verbal stimulus and single object with a recognizable approximation of the appropriate verbal response.
4. To voluntarily initiate a recognizable verbal approximation to obtain a specific object or activity.

Socialization
1. To be aware of others.
2. To attend to other's behavior.
3. To respond to adult when child's name is called.
4. To imitate simple, familiar acts of adults.

Academics
1. Same as Behavior #1.
2. Same as Behavior #2.
3. Same as Behavior #3.
4. To respond with motor and body responses to complex environmental and verbal stimuli.

Jay

Jay is 3 years old and is attending school for the first time. While nonverbal, Jay makes many vocalizations which vary in tone and inflection. His parents describe him as having many fears that he reacts to by crying loudly and flapping his arms. Jay observes all activities in his environment and responds to both children and adults who initiate interactions with him. Jay is not toilet-trained but has mastered self-help skills in the areas of eating and drinking. Jay's initial *DT* goals were:

Behavior

3. To respond with motor behavior to single environmental stimulus: object, person, sound.
4. To respond with motor and body responses to complex environmental and verbal stimuli.
5. To actively assist in learning self-help skills.
6. To respond independently to play material.

Communication

3. To respond to verbal stimulus and single object with recognizable approximation of the appropriate verbal response.
4. To voluntarily initiate a recognizable verbal approximation to obtain a specific object or activity.
5. To produce a recognizable word to obtain a desired response from an adult.
6. To produce a recognizable word to obtain a desired response from another child.

Socialization

4. To imitate simple, familiar acts of adults.
5. To engage in organized, solitary play.
6. To respond to adult's verbal and nonverbal requests to come to him.
7. To respond to single verbal requests or command given directly to child.

Academics

5. To respond with rudimentary fine motor skill to simple manipulative tasks associated with 2-year level.
6. To imitate words or action of adult upon request.
7. To respond by simple discrimination of objects.
8. Same as Communication #3.

Each of these four children will be evaluated by the teaching team according to *DT* objectives at regular intervals throughout the year. The initial *DT* objectives are used to write the children's IEPs. When finer breakdowns of behaviors are required, the teachers refer to a developmental sequence such as the *Behavioral Characteristics Progression* (1976). Detailed anecdotal records, ongoing observations, and a checklist of primary abilities, such as the Vallett checklist (1973), are used to compile information and progress notes for the typical children. Careful observation and documentation of all the children's activities and interests is necessary to maintain a warm, stimulating learning environment which responds to the children's growth.

The Curriculum

Curriculum in the Rainbow Room cannot be described merely in terms of content and skill development, nor can it be considered an isolation of the issues discussed previously. The curriculum may be thought of as a summation of many components such as the role expectations which the teachers have for themselves, the organization of the physical space, the sequence and content of daily activities, and the nature of the relationships formed with the children. The curriculum may also be thought of as a process of responding to the cognitive, physical, social, and emotional needs of the children. As a process, the curriculum would evolve through continuous, interpretational observations of the children's growth and changing interests. Finally, the curriculum, in an integrated learning environment like the Rainbow Room, may be viewed as a tool employed by the teachers to maintain a balance between normal developmental programming and intensive psychoeducational procedures. Each of these views is illustrated below with an annotated lesson plan. The lesson plans were designed for integrated activities, and each plan includes the instructional objectives for both the typical children and the special children.

Curriculum as the Sum of Many Components

Activity
> Block building; follow-up activity to class trip to the city zoo.

Objectives
1. To recreate a first-hand experience, within the classroom setting.
2. To discuss animal characteristics, habitats, and possible groupings.
3. *DT:* Behavior 3, 4, 6; Communication 2, 3; Academics 2, 3, 4, and 5.

Materials
1. Refer to "Physical Space," Figure 4.3.
2. Wooden blocks in a variety of shapes and sizes.
3. Oaktag, markers, and tape.
4. Assortment of plastic animals.
5. Accessories such as people figures, small cars and trucks, branches, stones, containers.

Procedure
1. Prerequisite: Class trip to the city zoo.
2. The teacher is seated on the floor with a small group of children in the block building area. "Where did we go this morning?... That's right. We went to the zoo. We saw many animals. Look at the animals in this box. Can you find one that you saw at the zoo?" The teacher arranges con-

tents of box in front of the children, who are encouraged to pick up, name, and talk about their zoo experience. The teacher has one of the "special" children sitting beside her, and she encourages the child to approximate the name of the animal he is holding.

3. The discussion continues. "The fences and cages keep the animals inside the zoo. Let's use our blocks to make cages and fenced-in places for the animals." The teacher pulls over several blocks and places them in front of the "special" child, "Give me block.... Good." The teacher takes the block and repeats the request. She starts lining up the blocks end to end. "Patrick and I will make a cage for the monkeys. Who will help us?... Thank you, Tim. We'll make the monkeys a big cage."

4. The other children are encouraged to make cages or fenced-in areas, independently or with a partner. The teacher elicits decisions from the children concerning which animals go together and what is needed in the animal home.

5. After the "zoo" is completed, the teacher takes out the oaktag, markers, and tape. "Let's make signs for our zoo." A sheet of oaktag is folded in half, and she prints "monkeys." "Tim, please choose a marker and trace our sign. It says *monkeys*." The children are asked for the words needed on their signs. Each cage or fenced-in area is given a sign. The "zoo" is left set up in the block area, and further play includes taking people figures on tours, making additional cages, or adding more details such as containers of water for pools or stones for climbing.

This teacher-directed block-building activity is but one example of the activities which were correlated with a field trip to the zoo. In addition to the block activity, the children were given opportunities to play with animal puppets, browse through a display of animal books available in the reading corner, and dramatize animal movements during exercise time. Correlated activities offer the children various ways to reconstruct reality and integrate their experiences at the zoo. The teachers offered the first-hand experience of the trip and designed the block activity which helped incorporate more content into the children's learning. Throughout the activity, the teachers attempted to facilitate the learning without interfering with the play.

The curriculum in the Rainbow Room is based on the decisions made early in the school year concerning organization of the physical space, scheduling, and relating to young children. The teachers designed the room as a child-centered workshop, where children's play is respected as work and where teachers function as resource people who encourage child-initiated learning and respond to developmental needs. Other units of work/play, in addition to the zoo, will be coordinated throughout the school year. The units originate with the children's first-hand, daily experiences—the vehicles they ride in, the foods they consume, their clothing, seasonal changes, buildings in the neighborhood, and the people who provide services. The classroom workshop allows the children to reconstruct their experiences and, as a result, grow in their understanding and trust in the people and events which surround them. For young children who have difficulty making sense out of the stimulation they experience, correlated activities in the curriculum both allow the necessary repetition of appropriate responses and pave the way to generalizing the response to situations outside the classroom.

Curriculum as a Process

Activity
Child-initiated activity time in the housekeeping area.

Objectives
1. To engage in symbolic play by taking on roles and inventing situations with actions and dialogue.
2. *DT:* Behavior 6; Communication 4 and 5; Socialization 4 and 5.

Materials
1. Refer to "Physical Space," Figure 4.3.
2. Props for bathing and dressing dolls; infant bath tub, small towels, cotton balls, baby powder, baby oil, small blankets, and doll clothes.

Procedures
1. The infant tub, containing water and several small bars of soap, is placed on the table in the housekeeping area. An extra small table has been provided for this activity, and it contains the oil, powder, and cotton balls. The dolls are dressed and sitting in the highchair and carriage. Towels and blankets are folded on the storage shelves.
2. A sign hangs on the back of a chair which has been placed in front of the housekeeping area. The sign reads "4 people," with four stick figures drawn on it.
3. One of the special children rides a bus which arrives ahead of the other children in the Rainbow Room. One of the teachers has planned to spend this time with the child in the housekeeping area this morning. The child is directed to the housekeeping area. The teacher sits down at the table with the tub and briefly observes the child's movements in the area. The teacher provides verbal cues, "Look! What is this?" and lightly splashes water to attract the child's attention and to elicit an approximation of "water" from the child. The teacher provides the doll, which is undressed and wrapped in a blanket. She initiates activity, "Let's wash the baby"; unwraps the doll and hands it to child; and directs the child to put the doll into the tub, if necessary.
4. As other children gradually arrive and enter the area, the teacher continues to observe the special child's solitary play and is available to respond to the other children, as needed.

In their on-going observations, the teachers in the Rainbow Room had noted several themes emerging: one of the children had a new baby brother, and his arrival had been a topic of conversation; the quality of play in the housekeeping area had been deteriorating, especially when more than four or five children were there; the children were quite attracted to "real" materials which were occasionally provided in the housekeeping area as props (e.g., dry macaroni for the play dishes and cooking utensils). Planning the "Bathing Babies" activity, described in this lesson plan, was an attempt to respond to the themes observed by the teachers.

The teachers had also noted that the activities in the housekeeping area seldom included any of the special children. Since so much of the play in this area is symbolic in nature and depends upon dialogue and cooperative planning, it may have been difficult for any of the special children to be integrated into housekeeping activities spontaneously. The teachers, therefore, employed the two-fold strategy of limiting the number of people in the housekeeping area to four at a time and of engaging one of the special children in appropriate solitary play in the area. As other children arrived in the morning and began selecting their initial activities, the special child in the housekeeping area was, in fact, modeling one of the available options.

As the "Bathing Babies" play continued, one of the teachers provided support to the special child by guiding her to use the powder and oil, by giving verbal cues, and by directing her to imitate what the three other children were doing. The water play and use of powder and oil made up a pleasurable sensory activity which helped sustain the attention and participation of the special child, as well as elaborating the play of all the children. Intermittent guidance was given by the teacher to all of the children, dabbing *small* amounts of oil on the dolls with cotton balls, keeping the baby powder on the dolls and away from the children's faces, helping fasten doll clothes and wipe up spills. Throughout the activity, the teacher noted the children's responses, listened to their dialogue, and looked for ways to expand their interests during the coming week.

Curriculum as a Tool

Activity
Integrated small group for teacher-directed water play (adapted from Watrin & Furfey, 1980).

Objectives
1. To explore the concepts of *boat, sink,* and *float.*
2. To practice color name and recognition.
3. To strengthen pincer grasp of small objects.
4. To engage in dramatic play.
5. *DT:* Behavior 1 and 2; Communication 2 and 3; Socialization 3, 4, and 5; Academics 1, 2, and 4.

Materials

1. Small toy boats or Styrofoam egg cartons cut into small sections. Each boat should be a different color.
2. Marbles.
3. Water table or large tub.

Procedures

1. Direct the children's attention to the boats. Handle the boats. Discuss the uses of boats, using the vocabulary words *boat, sink,* and *float.*
2. "Let's pretend we are captains of the boats. The captain has to make the boat go in the water. Which boat do you want to be the captain of?... All right. You be Captain Blue because you have a blue boat. I'll be Captain Green because my boat is green. The edge of the sink [touch] is the land where we live. Okay?... We have to get our boats from the land. Are you on your boats, Captain Blue [child responds], Captain White?... We are ready to steer our boats, then" (Watrin & Furfey, 1980).
3. Children sail the boats independently for a few minutes. The teacher is positioned next to the special child, guiding her attention and motor activity.
4. The teacher introduces marbles. "Let's pretend these marbles are people on the land who want to go for a boat ride." Each child is given a marble to put in a boat. "Have a nice ride, Captain White" [said to each child by given color.]... "Is the ride over? They have to get back on the land, you know."
5. The teacher distributes marbles across bottom of water table. "Look, what happens to the marbles?... Yes, they don't float. The marbles sink.... What can we do now with our boats and marbles, Captains?" The children are allowed to continue with water play, loading up the boats with marbles and watching the boats sink.
6. The teacher is available but withdraws from participating to observe interactions. Short anecdotal notes may now be made. Verbal cues and support with touch are used to sustain attending of special child.

This lesson plan demonstrates how curriculum can be used to maintain a balance between normal developmental guidelines and intensive, psychoeducational procedures. Water play is attractive and pleasurable to all children in the Rainbow Room. During child-initiated activity times, the water table and its wide variety of accessories is clearly one of the most popular choices for the children. At the water table, work and play are interwoven. Children can experiment with the properties of weight, volume, and composition of materials without being hindered by lack of vocabulary. Observing their own activities, as well as those of children nearby, contributes to their cognitive development, without teacher direction or interpretation.

For the child who needs intensive instructional strategies, the water activity described here was both a pleasurable experience and an opportunity to generalize skills which had been introduced in one-to-one training sessions outside of the classroom. Participating in the group experience gave the child repeated practice at following a single command, "Push boat"; at strengthening her pincer grasp, "Pick up marble"; at attending to the activities of others, "Look there." Since water play is so much fun, the teacher is able to fade out the structured input and allow the child to play freely along side the other children until the activity draws to a close.

The three perspectives of curriculum—as a sum of many components, as a process, and as a tool—are interwoven in the learning environment of the Rainbow Room. An observer in the Rainbow Room would see many activities typical of any educational program for young children. Underlying the curriculum in the Rainbow Room, however, there is an awareness on the part of the teachers of the "why" of any learning experience, rather than an emphasis on an activity as an entity in itself. According to Hodges, McCandless, and Spicker (1971), this awareness of "why" is an integral part of diagnostic teaching.

SUMMARY

The opportunities for cognitive, social, and emotional growth of all the children in the Rainbow Room are enhanced by the intensity and depth of the planning which the teachers undergo in creating the learning environment. Hunt (1961) proposed that there is a possibility of educating intelligence if we can find the proper match between an environmental encounter and the present status of the human organism. The design of an integrated learning environment for young children must be structured to maximize the opportunities for "proper matches" to occur. A broadened definition, as discussed throughout this case study of one integrated classroom, fits school experiences to the child's readiness to learn.

REFERENCES

Bachrach, A., Mosley, A., Swindle, F., & Wood, M. *Developmental therapy for young children with autistic characteristics.* Baltimore: University Park Press, 1978.

Behavioral Characteristics Progression, VORT Corporation, P.O. Box 11132, Palo Alto, California 94306, 1976.

Hodges, W., McCandless, B., & Spicker, H. *Diagnostic teaching for young children.* Arlington, Va.: The Council for Exceptional Children, 1971.

Hunt, J.M. *Intelligence and experience.* New York: Ronald Press, 1961.

Shapiro, E., & Biber, B. The education of young children: A developmental interaction approach. In S. Say & A. Nitzburg (Eds.), *Children with learning problems.* New York: Bruner-Mazel, 1973.

Smart, M.S., & Smart, R.C. *Preschool children: Development and relationships.* New York: MacMillan, 1973.

Valett, R.E. *A handbook of psychoeducational resource programs.* Belmont, Calif.: Fearon, 1973.

Watrin, R., & Furfey, P.H. *Learning activities for the young preschool child.* New York: Van Nostrand, 1980.

Wood, M.M. (Ed.). *Developmental therapy: A textbook for teachers as therapists for emotionally disturbed young children.* Baltimore, University Park Press, 1975.

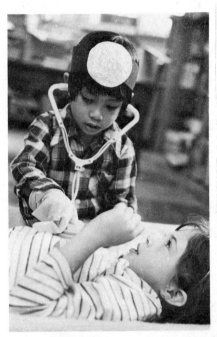

Part II
Curriculum
Approaches

5
Case Study of An Autistic Child

Margaret Ninno
Susan Vermeulen

BACKGROUND

Kelly is a 6-year-old girl in our class at Jowonio. She is the daughter of a professional couple and has a brother 2 years younger than herself. Her parents are separated, and Kelly and her brother live with their mother. She also spends some time in a state-run group home, to provide respite for her mother.

Kelly began having seizures during the first year of her life, and she has been taking phenobarbital ever since. She also demonstrated a great deal of hyperactivity which interfered with her sleep and other home activities from an early age. By the time she entered a school program at age 3, she still was not toilet-trained, had few other adaptive skills, and had no expressive language.

When she was 3, her parents enrolled her in a typical day care center for half the day and in a school for the retarded for the other half day. Kelly's parents also began counseling and training in behavior modification at this time, and they used their knowledge to set up programs in self-help skills. At the end of the school year, the people involved with Kelly felt that she would benefit much more from a full-day program in one setting, and so she was referred to Jowonio.

Kelly spent 2 years at Jowonio before coming to our class. In that time she developed many self-help skills and learned some basic pre-academic and attending skills. Her expressive language did not improve, so the decision was made to begin Kelly in a signing program.

LEVEL OF FUNCTIONING AS OF SEPTEMBER, 1978

Kelly was a child who would need a great deal of attention from our staff at Jowonio. The staff assessed Kelly's level of development in September, using *Developmental Therapy* (Wood, 1975). Along with the Developmental Therapy Objectives Rating Form (DTORF), the staff needed a brief descriptive picture of Kelly. The Behavior Rating Instrument for Autistic Children or "BRIAC" (Ruttenberg & Wolf, 1967) was also employed to evaluate Kelly's communication and to give the staff a larger picture of the whole child. At this time, the staff was interested in assessing Kelly's skills rather than searching for the underlying motivators of behaviors or causes of her disturbance (if there is one).

When Kelly arrived at Jowonio in September of 1978, she related across levels 1 and 2 of the section "Nature and Degree of Relationship to an Adult" in the BRIAC. Kelly made almost no eye contact with adults. She would gaze past the adults, seemingly fixating on some distant object. There was a lack of affective response, including such actions as smiling or frowning. Kelly's mother once reported that Kelly did not appear to recognize her if she was away for a few days. Kelly did not lift her head or respond to her name when called. She often displayed wild bursts of anxiety-produced behavior (screaming, physically moving to another part of the room, squirming) when approached or touched. If an adult entered the same room with Kelly, she would move away or jump around in wild excitement. Physical contact seemed to be a form of punishment to Kelly at this time. She seemingly preferred the company of objects with which she would self-stimulate. The staff felt that Kelly was, for the most part, oblivious to people; but at times she withdrew from others with more deliberateness, displaying some degree of awareness.

This picture of Kelly matched with the *Developmental Therapy* position. According to the scale on socialization, Kelly had not met the objectives B2, attending to other's behavior; B3, responding to name; or B4, interacting with an adult nonverbally.

It was determined that Kelly was a Stage 1 child and therefore needed to respond to her environment with pleasure. This included forming relationships with significant adults and learning to enjoy the pleasures of physical contact.

The BRIAC supplied a descriptive level of Kelly's communication. In September, 1978, Kelly related across levels 1 and 2 in the section on communication. The previous year, Kelly had begun to communicate in sign language. She had acquired one or two signs, but progress had been slow. When Kelly entered her new classroom, she did not use her signs with the new adults in her environment. Instead, Kelly showed undirected expression of affect, which took form in twirling, running, uncontrolled laughing, jumping, and panting. These behaviors did not appear to be directed towards a particular person. They were diffuse explosions of energy. In addition, it was almost impossible to form some ideas about what elicited these behaviors, as they occurred randomly throughout the day at first. The question of behavior control was a difficult one for teachers to deal with.

Kelly's behaviors did not appear to have communicative intent at this time. The staff assessed Kelly's communication in *DT* terms. Kelly needed to work on these objectives: C1, attend to speaker; C2, respond to verbal stimulus with motor behavior; C3, respond to verbal stimulus with a signed approximation.

After years of attempting to get Kelly to produce sounds, she had a very small repertoire of sounds. Her sounds were repetitive in nature, and they were developing very slowly. A total communication approach with sign language was implemented in the beginning of 1978.

This portrait of Kelly made it clear to the staff that Kelly would need a program which emphasized relationship building. The staff felt that, through consistent adult relationships, we might begin to get Kelly to communicate for such basic things as hugs, rides, and food. It was not so clear at this point about how to implement such a program.

One incident which occurred in the beginning of the year may help describe Kelly's behavior. Susan and Kelly were walking down the hall, which was decorated with streamers and pictures from other classes. Susan was taking Kelly to see the language therapist. Kelly was walking quietly with her head down. As Susan and Kelly passed the decorations, Kelly reached out and grabbed a streamer. She ripped it from the wall and began flinging it around. Kelly then began to jump in excitement. Susan took the streamer away, but Kelly continued to jump up and down. Susan removed Kelly to an empty room, where she sat with her for 15 minutes, holding Kelly in her lap. Kelly finally calmed down.

A lack of behavior control was apparent in Kelly. Objects in the environment would trigger wild bursts of energy. Kelly appeared to be ruled by her impulses. When we rated Kelly on the *Developmental Therapy* checklist, she had not met the following objectives: B2, react by sustained attending (attention span); B3, react to simple stimulus with a motor behavior; B4, imitate; B5, assist in self-help. These objectives would be the goals of her program.

Attention to behavior control will be given later in the chapter. However, as of September, Kelly was not fully toilet-trained. She would have accidents in school and at home. Kelly could dress herself with assistance in getting started, but she could not start a zipper, snap, button, or tie her shoes. Independence in dressing would be a long-range goal, broken down into small steps which Kelly could manage.

Pre-academics was also an area to be explored in looking at Kelly's skills. Kelly would have these objectives as part of her program—A4, imitates adults; A5, fine and gross motor at 24 months; A7, displays discrimination of objects; A8, approximates naming (signing) object.

The staff felt that Kelly would need time in the day to work on these objectives. We had seen some glimpses of Kelly's ability to use sign language and decided that all forms of communicating in sign language on the part of Kelly would call for high rewards from adults. The power of communication would be emphasized.

This written portrait of Kelly's level of functioning is meant to help you visualize her. It is not a complete picture, but the important information is there.

It will be used in the following sections to show *how* to program for such a child in an integrated setting.

FACTORS THAT AFFECTED CHANGE

After examining Kelly's past educational records, talking with her previous teachers and her mother, and observing her for the first 2 weeks of school, the staff found a number of factors that needed to be worked into the program. These factors are listed below and then described more thoroughly.

1. The schedule—This includes such things as the best time for Kelly to work at different activities, interspersing active and inactive activities, developing skills in all areas, providing pleasurable activities, maintaining Kelly in an integrated setting as much as possible, and providing activities to work on behavioral and social skills.
2. Responding to the environment with pleasure—High arousal techniques are designed to engage children and stimulate communication and social skills.
3. Personnel—This includes the number of people who worked with Kelly and what they did.
4. Low stimulus environment—This controls the stimuli that impinge on a child in order to enhance attention.
5. Generalization—This includes teaching Kelly to generalize skills she has learned to other people, to new settings, and to new situations. It also includes teaching her to generalize tasks to new materials.
6. Sign language—The development of a total communication program is described.
7. Curriculum and materials—This includes the curriculum developed for Kelly, based on *Developmental Therapy* academic goals, and the materials we used with her.
8. Home-school relationship—This includes the methods used to facilitate communication between home and school and how the parent-teacher partnership can work to foster learning.
9. Behavior modification—Techniques of behavioral management were used both to teach new skills and to change behavior.
10. Control—Teacher responses to a range of behaviors are described in this section.

The Schedule

In setting up a schedule for Kelly, the first thing we did was identify the skill areas we wanted to work on. These included fine motor, gross motor, self-help, and pre-academic skills; communication; and behavioral and social skills. Then we identified how much time and in what kind of setting each skill was best taught. For example, most of Kelly's signs are food signs, and so lunch and snack times seemed to be optimum times to work on communication skills. On the other hand, behavioral and social skills such as responding to her name and coming when called seemed to be best worked on throughout the day. Fine motor and pre-academic skills were considered other priority areas, and so times were scheduled for Kelly to focus on those areas.

The staff worked on Kelly's receptive vocabulary, building it into pleasurable activities and more table task time as Kelly's attention span was lengthened. Simple discrimination processes were reinforced through the day. Body coordination, including eye-hand and fine motor control and self-help skills, were a part of the Stage 1 therapy. Swimming was an excellent time to provide pleasurable experiences and body control awareness for Kelly. Many of these skills were integrated throughout the day in Kelly's activities, primarily with adults but also with other children.

One last factor that is an important part of a Stage 1 therapy program is providing the child with consistent outlines. At this stage, the child's concepts are fragmentary. Through routines and repetition, the child will be able to refine his or her skills. Routines also provide the trust and safety needs that the Stage 1 child has. With Kelly, we found routines and consistency to be extremely important for her learning of new information.

Responding to the Environment with Pleasure

Before beginning to outline the activities or materials used with Kelly in the beginning of the school year, it is important to state the position our school takes on the developing child and, particularly, the autistic child. We have adopted a developmental model for treatment of the autistic children in our setting. This model is *Developmental Therapy* (Wood, 1975), which was formulated from the wide array of literature written about children and their development. This model has become the foundation of the therapy at Jowonio and is used in implementing programs.

Developmental Therapy and other developmental models make some basic statements about the way children grow and change. One is that the process of growth follows sequential stages in both typical and disturbed children. Another is that each child's changes are unique and occur in relation to environmental conditions, prior and present experiences, and biological constitution. *Developmental Therapy* also believes that children's knowledge of the world grows out of experiences, and therefore therapy must be relevant to the child's experiences. The assumption that leads back to the topic at hand is that learning grows out of significant, pleasurable experiences. Success must be a part of a child's program and is best reached through pleasurable experiences.

Responding to the environment with pleasure is the first sequential stage in the *Developmental Therapy* curriculum. When Kelly's skills were first assessed, she was placed in Stage 1. Her level of functioning gave us a general idea about her specific needs. However, our more general goal for Kelly was that she begin to get in touch with her surroundings, the people, the objects, the feelings. This awareness stage was crucial for further development.

Responding to the environment with pleasure means more specifically learning to trust an adult and respond to him. Since Kelly was not capable of initiating, it was the adult's role to be an arouser and initiator. Simple attending and motor responses were goals for Kelly in the beginning of therapy. Kelly's therapy was confined to a few adults at first, as Kelly had to build trust slowly with consistent adults. This assumption comes from the developmental approach, which states that socialization (forming relationships) is a process which begins with awareness of a limited group of adults and peers and moves to more extensive group experiences.

Kelly spent time with adults in pleasurable arousing activities. She went swimming twice a week, where teachers were able to elicit pleasurable responses like giggling through tickling and splashing. Kelly also spent time in the gym on mats playing games like peek-a-boo with adults. The adults used many infant games to get Kelly to attend and react with a motor response. In the beginning of the year, Kelly was often lethargic to arousal. She would lie on the mat, gazing out the window. She also might attempt to run away. Another response to close contact from adults was a panic reaction, which often sent her into self-stimulatory oblivion.

These responses indicated Kelly's lack of control over her world. She had spent many years out of touch with people (for reasons we would like to have known, but only surmised at this time). Kelly needed to learn to respond to adults. Our staff also felt a strong need to keep up constant physical contact with Kelly, even though in the beginning of therapy she did not respond with much enthusiasm. For the teacher, this meant using the body to communicate with Kelly because we knew she had little comprehension of spoken language and little investment in it. It also meant continuing to provide stimulating activities.

The activities selected for Kelly at this stage emphasized pleasurable experiences in hopes of developing relationships with Kelly. They also emphasized body control and trust of one's own body. The activities that were selected were mutual games developed by adults. They were often particular to the adults involved with Kelly, but they were much like the games played with many young children—piggy back, row your boat, ring around the rosie. Activities were made to be as reciprocal as possible. There were also more informal times for contact like hugging and tickling.

Materials were selected to emphasize sensory experiences in all channels—tasting, smelling, seeing, hearing. Particularly effective materials were water, bubbles, sand, instruments, play dough, rice, and shaving cream. The teacher used these materials to establish contact between Kelly and himself and to acquire a response from Kelly. The teacher was interested in awareness and refining that awareness in Kelly so that she would begin to discriminate between materials and develop preferences for materials.

In the early stages of therapy, Kelly's impulsivity caused problems in the use of materials. She often tried to eat play dough or throw rice. The teachers used a process of guiding Kelly through the materials with their hands on top of hers to gradually let Kelly use the materials on her own, under supervision.

This problem with stimulating materials also appeared in the body awareness activities. A goal of therapy was to stimulate and arouse; however, Kelly would often become overstimulated. Her laughter from tickling would lead to uncontrollable laughter and occasional tantrums. The staff members were aware of this issue and had many discussions on the question of balancing pleasure and arousal with control. There appeared to be a fine line between arousal and overstimulation. For one period, the staff decided to opt for keeping the environment more controlled and safe, and some of the materials were put away. Quiet games of touching and whispering were substituted. Kelly responded well to the change, and arousing materials were gradually reintroduced with better success.

As stated before, the staff believed that, through relationships with adults, Kelly would begin to communicate. Many of the sensory experiences in which Kelly participated led comfortably to the incorporation of language. For example, playing with bubbles was something Kelly enjoyed. The teacher built in sign language and had Kelly sign for bubbles. The teacher would then blow some for her. Teachers used sensory experiences to teach Kelly new concepts for sign language. She learned to sign *ball, bubbles, up* (for ride), and *hug*.

A progression is evident here. Initially, the staff was interested in the pleasure of doing, of being involved. Interest in outcomes was implemented as Kelly could handle it.

Kelly learned to communicate for specific primary needs, such as food, pleasure, warmth, and touch. She began to directly express pleasure from satisfaction of the need—smiling when pleased and crying, for instance, when she had to wait for lunch. In the beginning, approximations of signed communication were accepted, and all communication was immediately reinforced. If Kelly spontaneously signed for potato chips, she was given them. As time passed and Kelly began to communicate on her own with adults and learned that adults would satisfy her needs, more rules and delay of gratification were applied. For instance, if Kelly signed for candy when we were out on a field trip, she was told to wait.

Kelly's awareness of the world expanded through relationships, communication, and academic work done individually with a teacher. Gross motor skills were taught both in a one-to-one setting and also in a regular classroom group. Self-help skills were again focused on throughout the day where appropriate (toileting, hand washing) and also at specific times (toothbrushing, dressing). There was less focus on skills at this time.

We also looked at Kelly to see when she was best able to focus on work, when she was tired, and when she seemed to have a hard time maintaining control. We found that first thing in the morning, Kelly had a hard time settling down after the long bus ride to school. However, once she calmed down, she was very alert in the morning and was able to attend to tasks for long periods of time. After lunch she was more tired and less able to focus on tasks for very long. Therefore, we scheduled more demanding work in the pre-academic and fine motor skills in the morning, and in the afternoon we scheduled less demanding activities such as gross motor skills, self-help skills, sensory play, cooking, and field trips.

We examined the schedule to be sure active and inactive periods were interspersed. We found that Kelly could work at table tasks in the morning for about 45 minutes at a time, and in the afternoon for not more than 20 or 25 minutes. Therefore, she had two 45-minute individual work periods in the morning which were separated by a group gross motor time. In the afternoon she had only one 20-minute work period.

We also looked at the schedule to be sure activities that were pleasurable to Kelly were included. She was not interested in most play materials or she perseverated with them, so that did not seem to be a pleasurable outlet. She did enjoy gross motor activities, and particularly liked playing on outdoor equipment, so some time was reserved for this. She also liked swimming a lot, so an extra swim period was scheduled for her. Kelly's schedule for the beginning of the school year is shown in Figure 5.1.

We wanted to include Kelly in as many classroom activities as possible. We found that most work sessions needed to be done individually and out of the classroom, but there were still many classroom activities she could participate in. These included field trips, swimming, outdoor play, art, music, gym, lunch, and cooking.

We made sure we included activities in the schedule that would develop behavioral and social skills. A major objective at that time was for Kelly to sit and wait, and we worked on this objective in a variety of ways. She learned to sit in the car (coming and going on trips), at the table at transitions, and on the floor for her turn in gym class. Another objective was to follow simple routines, so we made sure we had a routine for entering the classroom and beginning the day, riding in a car, eating lunch, using the bathroom, and leaving at the end of the day.

Because Kelly made progress in many skill areas this year, her schedule has changed. She can now attend to table work for longer periods in the afternoon. She spends more time with the group using the skills she has learned. She also is working on different behavioral and social skills, and so we have set up different opportunities for her to work on these skills. For example, she is now learning to walk holding a child's hand instead of an adult's. She is also learning to use play materials independently. She is learning more signs and to point to pictures, so

Figure 5.1

	Monday	Tuesday	Wednesday	Thursday	Friday
9:00	Come to school Morning routine Individual				
9:15	Indiv. play Follow direc-tions Gross motor Individual				
9:45	Pre-academics Fine motor Snack Individual	Swimming Self-help	See Monday	Swimming Self-help	See Monday
10:30	Gym, group Pre-academics		Gym, group		Gym, group
11:15	Fine motor Individual				
12:00	Lunch, group				
12:30	Toothbrushing Gross motor Sensory play Individual		Field trip	See Monday	See Monday
1:15	Art, group	Pre-academics Individual		Cooking, group	Outdoor play Individual
2:00	Fine motor Individual	Fine motor			
2:20	Get ready for home				

communication is worked on at times besides lunch. She is able to sit and wait for long periods of time, and so she now attends a library story hour with her class. At present, Kelly's schedule looks like Figure 5.2.

Specifically, the changes in the schedule include the inclusion of a 10-minute play period with the class three mornings a week, the addition of an individual pre-academic/fine motor session after lunch four times a week, and accompanying the class to the library for a story hour and movie every Friday in-stead of spending the time in outdoor play.

Figure 5.2

	Monday	Tuesday	Wednesday	Thursday	Friday
9:00	Morning routine Gross motor Fine motor Indep. play Individual				
9:45	Pre-academics Communication Fine motor Snack Individual	Swimming Self-help Communica- tion	See Monday	Swimming Self-help Communica- tion	See Monday
10:20	Play, group				
10:30	Gym, group				
11:15	Pre-academics Communication Individual				See Monday
12:00	Lunch, group				
12:30	Toothbrushing Fine motor Pre-academics Individual	Field trip	See Monday	See Monday	
1:15	Communication (outside) Individual		Music, group	Cooking, group	Library, group
2:00	Fine motor Individual		Outside play, group	Fine motor Individual	
2:20	Get ready for home				

Personnel

In our classroom, we have three teachers: a lead teacher and two master's students assigned full-time to the classroom. We also had available a resource teacher for 45 minutes a day, a language specialist for 45 minutes a day, and several volunteers from the university. The language specialist had worked with Kelly the year before, and the resource teacher had worked with her in another setting. The three classroom teachers had no previous experience with her.

The lead teacher became Kelly's advocate, and she was responsible for organizing Kelly's schedule, maintaining parent contact, writing reports, and gathering information from the other teachers about Kelly's progress. The language specialist was responsible for programming in the area of communication, and she also served as a resource regarding her pre-academic and fine motor program. As previously mentioned, Kelly's most difficult time of the day was first thing in the morning. Because the resource teacher already had established a relationship with Kelly, we agreed that she would be the most appropriate person to work with Kelly at that time.

We quickly became aware that Kelly had a difficult time forming relationships with her teachers and that the transitions when she changed teachers were very difficult for her. We also realized that Kelly needed an adult to be with her throughout the entire day, and so a teacher needed to be assigned to her even for group activities. Therefore, we decided to limit the number of adults who worked with Kelly to four teachers and one volunteer who had worked with Kelly the year before. We also lengthened the time each teacher would spend with Kelly to cut down on the number of transitions. We tried to make the teacher schedule as consistent as possible. Therefore, the resource teacher saw Kelly the first 45 minutes, the lead teacher the next 90 minutes, the language specialist the next 45 minutes, the master's student the next 75 minutes, the lead teacher the next 45 minutes, and the master's student the last 30 minutes. Kelly had the same volunteer for swimming and rode in the same car on trips.

Both the reduced number of adults to interact with and their consistent appearance seemed to help Kelly to be better able to form relationships with her teachers and to deal with her environment with more control. Naturally, when teachers were absent, substitutions in personnel and schedule were made. At first, Kelly had a great deal of difficulty with this and would engage in a lot of testing and acting out behaviors. She now is more accepting of changes and is able to deal with more people. She has two volunteers for swimming, both of whom she likes very much; and she does have occasional contact with the second master's student in the class. She is also much more accepting of the other children in the room and is able to walk with a child for a partner and sign to him.

Much time was spent throughout the year in meetings to plan Kelly's program, brainstorm and agree on intervention strategies, and report on progress. In the beginning of the year, progress was very slow and Kelly spent a lot of time testing us. These meetings were helpful both because they offered the opportunity to share successful techniques and because they allowed the teachers to be supportive of each other on especially difficult days. Another outcome of these meetings was that we realized that, in order to properly share information and chart Kelly's progress, we needed to keep very systematic records on her. Figure 5.3 shows some examples of record keeping we found useful.

Low Stimulus Environment

After observation of Kelly's behaviors and direct experience with her, the question of providing a therapeutic environment arose. Jowonio is an integrated

Figure 5.3

Signs used at lunch time

Sandwich	S S S S S S S
Juice	I V V V S S V S S
Yogurt	V V V V S V V S
Cookie	M M M M I I

S—Spontaneous
V—Verbal cue required
I—Imitation
M—Motor through

Week-long record of matching objects to pictures

	Monday	Tuesday	Wednesday	Thursday	Friday
Comb	+	+	+	+	+
Hat	+	+	+	+	+
Truck	−	−	−	−	−
Ball	+	+	+	+	+
Pants	−	+	−	+	+
Apple	−	−	−	+	+
Banana	+	+	−	+	+
Chair	−	+	+	+	+
Bed	−	−	+	−	+
	4/9	6/9	5/9	7/9	8/9

Record of toilet-training

Date	Time	Outcome
Feb. 3rd	9:00	W
	10:15	TU
	11:15	KU
	12:00	KU
	12:30	TN
	1:00	W
	1:45	TN
	2:15	TU
Feb. 4th	9:00	W
	10:15	TU
	11:15	KU
	12:00	KU
	12:45	TU
	1:30	KU
	2:15	TU

W—Wet
TU—Teacher takes to bathroom; Kelly urinates
TN—Teacher takes to bathroom; Kelly does not urinate
KU—Kelly goes to bathroom spontaneously and urinates
KN—Kelly goes to bathroom spontaneously and does not urinate

setting responding to the needs of a diverse group of children, ⅔ of which are typical children. Under those ratios, the environment of a typical classroom at Jowonio responded more to the needs of typical children. The classrooms are open, allowing for free periods for exploration and discovery learning. The atmosphere here is a warm one—conversation occurs between children and adults. However, to a stranger, the class might appear to be noisy. The classroom is also decorated with children's work, bulletin board displays, and a wide variety of materials. The classroom is organized in areas, each one a center which encourages independent work on the part of children.

Periods of the day are structured, and there are a number of rules governing behavior; but for the most part, the rooms are abundant with auditory and visual stimuli. For most typical children, this stimulation creates an atmosphere of active involvement in learning. But for some special children like Kelly, a classroom like this can be a hindrance to learning.

In the beginning of the year, Kelly displayed a lack of behavior control. We also found that Kelly was hypersensitive to certain sounds and hyposensitive to others. For instance, when she would flush the toilet, she would cover her ears. On the other hand, when a sudden loud noise occurred, she might not move.

Kelly did little visual attending to adults, nor would she look at materials at the beginning of the year. At the start of therapy, the staff found it difficult to integrate Kelly into the classroom. She was often distracted by others' movements and noises, which caused her to lose control of her body movements.

After deliberation, the staff felt that a low stimulus environment would provide the best conditions for initial learning. By a low stimulus environment, we meant one that had few auditory or visual stimuli other than those provided by the teacher. The language therapist's room was one such room where distractions were cut down to a minimum. This room was used in the beginning attending phase and later task situations.

A large motor room was also used for the more arousing activities. There were a limited number of materials there, which helped focus on building the relationship between the teacher and Kelly.

The low stimulus environment proved to facilitate learning, and therefore a section of Kelly's classroom was set up for that purpose. A divider (large bookcase) was put up in the back of the room, and the new area contained a table and two chairs. A shelf for materials was placed out of direct eye contact. The next step was to bring Kelly back into the room for short periods in the day.

Kelly was not taken out of the class all day long. From the very beginning, she was involved in group activities with the other children. However, these were more structured activities and were planned to meet the needs of a wide range of children's abilities. They often used sensory materials. Kelly was also involved in any meal time like lunch. Still, for many parts of the day, Kelly spent time in a low stimulus environment.

Kelly now spends more time in the classroom, but continues to work in the low stimulus environment. Her ability to handle distractions has improved, but she still appears to need the quiet of a room with one adult for more intense instruction. Other quiet spaces that were discovered (like the large motor room and the couch in the reading corner) are still used as places for Kelly to relax and for times when Kelly is more excitable.

Generalization

After reviewing Kelly's records and comparing observation information, we decided that one of the key skills we wanted to teach Kelly was generalization. We found that Kelly's skills were so segmented that she performed some tasks for some persons and not for others; she performed well in one room but not in another; she could use one set of materials well, but not a slightly different set. Also, each new task was something to be completely learned—Kelly could not seem to borrow from previous learning.

To generalize a particular skill to more than one person, we found it necessary to have more than one person teach that skill. For example, many of the skills the language specialist worked on Kelly would perform only for her. Therefore, the individual sessions Kelly had with the language specialist and the lead teacher were much the same. Her performance with the two teachers was nearly identical. Because the master's student worked with Kelly at lunch on signing, we found that she signed best and most spontaneously for her. Therefore, the other teachers found it necessary to spend part of their sessions eating little snacks to work on the food signs.

Similarly, we found that Kelly performed well when alone with an individual teacher, but not if she was in a group or being observed by others. Because gross motor activities are highly pleasurable for her, we placed her in a large gym class three times a week where she used the skills she learned in individual gross motor sessions. For example, Kelly learned to do sit-ups in an individual session, and she later performed them in the group gym class. The teachers for the individual and group sessions were different, which required Kelly to generalize the skill across people and settings. It also required the teachers to do quite a bit of planning so that the first teacher could teach Kelly individually what would be needed for the group session and the second teacher could know what to expect.

In order to teach generalization to new materials, we simply varied the materials as soon as the skill was mastered. For example, Kelly was able to sort objects by gross appearance and by length when she entered the class in September. However, each time new objects were provided for her to sort, she "forgot" how to sort. Therefore, we gradually introduced new objects to sort as old ones were mastered. When color sorting was introduced, we used a variety of materials right from the start. On Monday Kelly might sort red and blue inch cubes; on Tuesday, red and blue chips; on Wednesday, red and blue plastic firemen; on Thursday, red and blue beads; and on Friday, red and blue clothes pins. When objects were introduced in this way, Kelly had no problem generalizing color sorting.

Another aspect of generalization we stressed was varying the task slightly. For example, when we taught Kelly to match objects to pictures, we defined several ways in which Kelly could demonstrate this skill. These included:

1. Placing the object on the picture of the object. Direction: "Put it with same."
2. Placing the object on the picture of the object. Direction: "Put the hat on hat."
3. Touching the object when the picture of the object was held up. Direction: "Touch same."
4. Touching the object when the picture of the object was held up. Direction: "This is hat. Touch hat."
5. Touching the picture when the object was held up. Direction: "Touch same."
6. Touching the picture when the object was held up. Direction: "This is hat. Touch hat."
7. Using the object in a more active way when the picture was held up. Directions: "Give me same." "This is hat. Give me hat." "Pick up same. Put it in the box." "Pick up same. Put it on your head."

We found that varying the directions was important, so that we could be sure Kelly would transfer her skills to different language and different tasks.

Another example of this teaching of generalization was varying the commands to which Kelly responded in novel contexts and with new materials. For example, Kelly threw her paper towel in the garbage after washing her hands when told, "Throw it in the garbage." But she did not throw other forms of trash into the garbage when asked to, so we consciously asked her to throw away snack and lunch garbage, items found on the floor, and scraps left from art projects. Kelly also could open and close the door on command, but she needed to be taught that you could open and close jars, drawers, and boxes.

Sign Language

Kelly had begun a total communication program in the school year 1977–78. By the summer of 1978, Kelly had acquired a few signs—*soda, chips, up,* and *walk*—most of which she signed spontaneously or with a verbal cue from a teacher.

When Kelly entered her new classroom in September, 1978, she did not communicate in sign language with the new adults in her environment. It would be difficult to say whether she had forgotten the signs she had learned, whether she was deliberately withdrawing from all communicative contact, whether she was undergoing a period of adjustment, or whether there was another explanation. Nonetheless, she was not communicating.

One incident might help to explain the lack of communication. One afternoon at a table task time, Susan was working on a discrimination activity with

Kelly. Kelly was listless and had difficulty attending. She would gaze out the window. Susan attempted to direct Kelly's attention to the task by moving her head to look at the materials. Susan noticed that Kelly had urinated on the chair. Kelly had made no attempt to communicate that she had to go to the bathroom. She had shown no signals of distress either in facial or body language.

This is an extreme example of Kelly's communication deficit, but she displayed other similar behaviors. She did not communicate on the level of basic needs.

Kelly had not uttered many sounds in her life. Babbling and sound production was encouraged her first year, but there was little progress. Sign language was to be her form of communication, in conjunction with an imitation program for gestures. Kelly had some imitation skills that were worked on along with the sign language program.

The staff decided to plan the sign language program around objects or activities that would be motivating to Kelly. Food was a motivator, and Kelly learned new food signs more quickly than others, including *sandwich, cookie, orange, juice, yoghurt.* She uses these signs spontaneously. Gross motor signs like *up, jump,* and *hug* were motivating to Kelly, too.

Signs were selected with regard to their motor requirements, but teachers primarily tried different objects that would motivate Kelly and gave her the lead in selecting signs. Communication had to be as close to her own experiences as possible.

Kelly has begun to discriminate objects and has also been able to match objects to pictures for a limited repertoire of objects. We hope that she will be able to recognize pictures of objects she will have trouble with in signing (because of motor ability) and begin to point to desired objects from a board or cards.

Kelly's progress in acquiring signs has been slow, but her signs are becoming more refined all the time. Signs are always introduced with verbal language, so that Kelly begins to associate the sign with the verbal label.

Kelly is now communicating her basic needs to adults and is directing her communication for what she desires. She is beginning to learn signs for different activities like bathroom and work time. These are less concrete and will require more abstraction, but the staff will pair activities to adults, which may give Kelly more cues to learn the signs. The routine should help Kelly learn the activity signs.

Curriculum and Materials

In developing Kelly's academic program, we followed the Stage 1 objectives from *Development Therapy* (Wood, 1975). A brief description of her learning plan follows.

A4—To respond with motor and body responses to complex environmental stimulation given physical and verbal cues.

In the beginning of the year, Kelly responded to the commands *give me, throw away, come, sit, stand, jump, turn on water,* and *flush toilet.* We developed a list of other commands such as *open, shut, pick up, put on,* and with additional objects.

Imitation is also included in this objective. At first, Kelly imitated standing up, sitting down, hand on head, and pointing up, on the command "Do this." We used the motor imitation section of the Kent language program (Kent, 1972) to teach Kelly more imitation skills, and reinforcers were given at this point. Within 2 months, Kelly passed all items in the Kent imitation section, and we moved on to simple imitation songs such as "Open, Shut Them" and "Wheels on the Bus." Kelly became proficient in this type of imitative play, and she began to imitate the actions of others more spontaneously. At this time we felt Kelly had mastered this objective and began working on A6, to imitate simple, familiar actions of adult. This imitation takes place throughout the day and also includes imitation of other children. Kelly also mastered A15, to recognize several body parts, through this imitation training.

A7—To respond by simple discrimination of objects.

In the beginning of the year, Kelly could consistently discriminate 10 objects. She demonstrated this skill by responding to the command "Give me the _____" when presented with a choice of three objects. We chose additional objects for Kelly to discriminate based on their utility and interest. In addition to the "Give me" command, we also worked on identifying functions of objects. Thus presented with a hat, a comb, and a bell, Kelly might be asked to put on the hat, comb her hair, or ring the bell. By January Kelly could discriminate at least 25 objects and could use them appropriately, and we considered the objective met.

We then began working on identifying parts of the room such as the floor, door, window, and furniture such as the shelf, sink, table, and chair. Next we directed Kelly to place objects in relation to the room parts. "Put the comb on the floor." "Put the banana in the sink." "Put the shoe under the table." She was able to master these directions using the spatial relations *in, on,* and *under.*

Next we felt Kelly was able to begin relating to pictures so we began working on A14.

A14—To match identical pictures when presented with both identical and different pictures.

First we began by teaching Kelly to match known objects to pictures of those objects. Directions used were given in the generalization section. We then began working on matching identical pictures of objects. Again this was done in a variety of ways, with Kelly matching pictures on hookboards, on lotto game boards, and on cards. At the same time we began teaching the command "touch" instead of one which requires more movement such as "give me" or "pick up." We also began at this time to evaluate Kelly's picture vocabulary and discovered that it was more extensive than we thought.

A10—To demonstrate short-term memory for sound patterns, objects, or people.

To teach this, we began with hiding games using food. Kelly quickly became adept at the shell game when her favorite foods were used. We also showed her where a piece of candy was hidden each day, and then slowly increased the time she had to wait until she could get it. Short-term memory for people was taught by having a teacher hide and then having Kelly go look for her.

A11—To match similar objects with different attributes.

In the beginning of the year, Kelly was able to sort objects by gross appearance. We decided that Kelly could improve her skill in this area in several ways.
1. She would sort by color, size, or length. After these skills were learned, she could sort by more than one dimension simultaneously (for example, blue squares in one pile, red squares in another, blue circles in another, and red circles in the fourth).
2. She would sort objects into more categories. At first she sorted only into two piles. Now she can sort into six categories.
3. She would sort more independently. At first Kelly had to be handed each object and be directed each time to "put it with same." She now can pick up her unsorted objects from a box and work using only verbal cues.
4. She could learn to sort many different kinds of materials in different contexts. For example, she learned to sort pegs by color, placing them into different pegboards; sort paper clips by sizing them to cards; and sort legos by shape stacking them.
5. She could perform sorting tasks that would require a more difficult level of fine motor skill, thus incorporating A16, to perform fine motor coordination activities at the 3–4-year level. Therefore, she progressed from handling giant pegs to matchstick pegs to very small pegs. She also

sorted beads by color and learned to string them first on pipe cleaners and then on strings.

Puzzles are also included in objective A11, and Kelly was unable to complete one-piece puzzles. She did not look at the puzzle pieces at first, so all her work was trial-and-error. We found that to teach Kelly to do puzzles required much modeling and verbal direction from the teacher. To teach Kelly to turn the puzzle piece to make it fit, we had to first move her through the process. She now has the fine motor skill and the form discrimination to do a one-piece puzzle or form board with up to 5 discrete pieces. We are still working on handling smaller pieces and increasing the number of puzzle pieces.

A13—To perform body coordination activities at the 3–4-year level.

Many of the gross motor skills we taught were taken from the Portage Guide (Shearer, n.d.). We found Kelly's development in this area had many gaps, and so we taught some more basic skills such as log rolling, forward somersaults, pedalling a tricycle, and throwing and catching a ball. She also had many more advanced skills, particularly on playground equipment. She could climb and balance well and could keep her swing going for some time using a regular pumping motion with her legs. We found Kelly was a natural in the water and could already bob, float, and propel herself. She learned to swim a good combination breaststroke-crawl and to jump in the water and return to the side.

Home-School Relationship

At Jowonio, there are many ways in which teachers communicate with parents. There are social functions throughout the school year where parents and teachers can meet informally. Parents and teachers meet yearly to write the child's Individualized Educational Plan. Two formal progress reports are sent home each year. Meetings at home and at school are set up by both parents and teachers. Parents often visit school to observe their child or to volunteer in the classroom. There are usually frequent phone calls between parents and teachers. Many keep up daily communication through the use of notebooks which travel back and forth to school with the child.

We used many of these systems to communicate with Kelly's parents. In the beginning of the year, the lead teacher and the language specialist met with Kelly's mother to write the IEP. Kelly's mother had many ideas about specific skills which she wished Kelly would learn that year. Many of the skills were self-help and behavioral skills. She also was invaluable in helping us plan the techniques we would use in teaching Kelly. We also found out which specific skills we hoped to teach would be most helpful at home. For example, we drew up a list of signs which would have the greatest utility at home.

At this initial meeting we all determined that communication between home and school was of prime importance for these reasons.

1. The teachers needed to know which skills would prove more useful to Kelly at home and in other nonschool settings.
2. Kelly was not performing exactly the same at school as she was at home. For example, she put on her socks at school and not at home, but she flushed the toilet only at home. Therefore, we all had to learn from each other exactly what Kelly was capable of doing.
3. Kelly's progress was very slow and was measured in minute steps. However, we all needed to share in that progress and take joy in it.
4. Experiences at home often affected Kelly's behavior at school and vice versa. For example, she sometimes had sleepless nights, which usually resulted in her being more listless. If we knew of these experiences, we could plan for them accordingly.
5. Teachers and parents could share the techniques they had found most successful and those which did not seem to work. Activities that seemed to be more pleasurable for Kelly also could be shared, as well as those which failed miserably.
6. Teachers and parents needed each other's supplies and materials. For example, when we taught Kelly the sign for cereal, we asked her mother to send some in with her for lunch.

For these reasons, we decided that keeping a notebook between home and school would prove invaluable, and indeed it has. We can share positive and negative experiences every day, record accomplishments, and ask and answer questions. We also decided that we would meet several times throughout the year to review progress and to plan for future programming. A typical page from Kelly's notebook went something like this:

> Hi! Kelly slept well last night and so she should have lots of energy today. She used the sign for cookies last night when I was putting away a package of Oreos. Of course, I gave her some after that. How is she coming with her coat at school?
>
> Kelly's mother
>
> Yes, Kelly did have lots of energy—in fact, she swam 2 laps in the pool without stopping. Great news about the signing for cookie. We are beginning the sign for milk next week, so could you start sending milk in her thermos for lunch on Monday? Thanks a lot. Kelly is zipping her coat up by herself after we start the zipper and then say, "Zip up, Kelly." Have a nice evening.
>
> Kelly's Teacher

Behavior Modification

Because Kelly lacked the internal motivation to perform many tasks spontaneously, we used a positive reinforcement system to teach new skills and to elicit information from Kelly. Our first task was to determine what could serve as a reinforcer for Kelly, and we found that only edibles proved to be good rewards for her in the beginning of the year. She especially liked drinks such as juices and soda, salty foods, yoghurt, and candy, and these became the principal reinforcers.

We agreed that food reinforcers would only be used to teach pre-academic, communication, fine motor, and some self-help skills. Gross motor work was already intrinsically pleasurable for Kelly, so primary reinforcers were not needed. Next we determined a schedule to administer reinforcers. We decided that for teaching new skills, Kelly would be reinforced for each trial performed correctly. When she performed correctly over 50% of the time, reinforcers would gradually be decreased. The final goal would be to reward her only after the entire task was completed. We discovered that as long as the reinforcer was in view, Kelly was able to complete lengthy tasks.

One concern we had and still have is that Kelly learn to work for other types of rewards. We always pair edible reinforcers with much praise, hugging, kissing, and other social reinforcement. At this time, Kelly enjoys the social reinforcers very much, but they are still not powerful enough for her. We have also tried other rewards such as play with balloons, balls, bubbles, and musical instruments. Again, she enjoys the activities but they do not serve as reinforcers for her. The one exception to this has been the teaching of signs to obtain activities or objects she wants. For example, Kelly enjoys blowing bubbles, and she learned the sign for bubbles with the only reward being the activity of blowing bubbles.

We have used behavior modification techniques to change some of Kelly's behaviors. One technique that has proven useful is withdrawing a reinforcer. As previously mentioned, Kelly's reinforcers are always in view when she works. One behavior which interfered greatly with her learning and which we found unacceptable was throwing objects. Therefore, each time she threw something, we said, "No, you can not throw," and we removed one of the reinforcers. In addition, she immediately had to pick up the thrown object. Kelly soon learned that throwing was not acceptable to us and that it would result in the loss of part of her reward.

Control

At the beginning of therapy, Kelly required the teachers to do a good deal of intensive programming. To add to this, she also presented teachers with management problems which needed to be addressed. As described in the section on scheduling, Kelly spent most of her day in one-to-one situations with adults. Even in group activities, Kelly was always assigned to one adult. There were problems particular to groups which made it difficult to get Kelly to respond. (In group activities, the activity levels were very high, and Kelly frequently had difficulty controlling her behavior). However, throughout the day Kelly had problems controlling her behavior.

Teachers expressed the concern that there seemed to be very few things which motivated Kelly. Although initially much of Kelly's day was designed to provide pleasurable, nurturing experiences, our demand for contact and the stress of moving from activity to activity was often very grueling for Kelly.

Kelly's response to her new environment was confusion and resistance. Much of her behavior took the form of running away, anxiously jumping, and throwing herself, as well as self-abusive behaviors. Kelly's loss of control seemed to be a diffused type of acting out against the demands made by teachers in her environment, against the demands of forming relationships, and against the demands of experiencing new materials. Kelly was probably confused by all the stimuli bombarding her all day long. As a teacher, you could almost feel the anxiety building in Kelly. At other times, her release of energy and subsequent loss of control was more subtle. She would seem calm during a puzzle task, but then begin to lose control and scream. Teachers were often perplexed by this type of behavior. Kelly did not often give clues to what might have been an urgent unmet need.

The other response that teachers perceived in Kelly was one of more active, more aware resistance. Kelly was not interested in many activities or materials. She enjoyed most body games, but showed little interest in Stage 1 materials which are highly sensory. When teachers introduced new materials or activities to her, Kelly would display active resistance by throwing the material, eating it, or laughing and playing teasing games with the teacher. She was excellent at testing the teacher's patience. Teachers were forced to revise and re-evaluate some of their programs again and again, but persisted with others.

Within the *Developmental Therapy* context, permitting a child to participate with responses inappropriate to his developmental stage would perpetuate or extend the period of his disturbance. For this reason, great emphasis is put upon expecting appropriate responses, communicating these expectations clearly, and intervening to teach a response when it is not forthcoming (Wood, 1975, p. 111).

Kelly did not show positive responses to materials, activities, or even people. To wait for a signal for when Kelly was ready might have meant waiting a very long time. Therefore, we as teachers actively set out to teach Kelly new skills and alter her behavior patterns.

The use of physical intervention and body contact with Kelly was necessary to communicate our expectations as well as our support and warmth. Because Kelly communicated, at best, on the motor level, the use of verbal techniques would be beyond her comprehension at her stage of development.

Body contact was used as a technique in a number of ways. It was used as prevention in situations where it seemed Kelly was in the initial stages of losing control. A teacher's physical nearness was useful in communicating to Kelly that she had the teacher's support. Especially in group activities, Kelly needed the proximity of teachers.

A teacher's body could also be used to convey positive feelings. Hugging, rubbing, and holding were used to nurture Kelly and to establish the teacher's relationship with her. Kelly did not tolerate much touch at first, but her tolerance level increased to the point where she is now actively approaching adults.

The enthusiasm that a teacher conveys through touch can also be used to motivate children to learn. Teachers often physically moved Kelly through an activity or physically moved an arm or hand in response to materials. This helped to decrease the amount of resistance and battling that appeared to take place between Kelly and the teacher.

Body contact was also used a great deal in controlling a tantrum or intervening in a developing crisis. Initially, Kelly did not respond to verbal techniques or other changes in a situation which was creating her loss of control. Physical restraint was often necessary. Sometimes, physical restraint seemed to be the only way to protect Kelly from the consequences of her loss of control. It was necessary to hold her firmly, yet reassuringly, until she was able to calm down. Holding Kelly was always a supportive technique.

Kelly has progressed to the higher stage and is now more capable of controlling her behavior. She shows more awareness of others and responds to more verbal techniques. As teachers used physical intervention strategies, they were introducing the words and language communication skills necessary for impulse control. Kelly now responds to the words "calm down" and "relax" with help from teachers.

SUMMARY

Kelly remains a severely impaired little girl. However, under the intensive program described in this chapter, she has made a good deal of progress. She has mastered the specific objectives outlined in the section on curriculum. She has developed a small signing vocabulary which allows her to express her desires for toileting, food, and pleasurable activities. She has generalized these skills to a wide variety of settings and people. She is much less impulsive, and so is able to work and play in more stimulating environments and with fewer controls imposed upon her. She finds pleasure in more activities and in interacting with adults.

REFERENCES

Kent, L.R. A language acquisition program for the retarded. In J.E. McLean, D.E. Yoder, & R.L. Schiefelbusch (Eds.), *Language intervention with the retarded: Developing strategies*. Baltimore: University Park Press, 1972.

Ruttenberg, B.A., & Wolf, E.G. Evaluating the communication of the autistic child. *Journal of Speech and Hearing Disorders*, 1967, *32*, 314-324.

Shearer, D.E. *Portage guide to early education*. Portage, Wisc., n.d.

Wood, M.M. *Developmental therapy: A textbook for teachers as therapists for emotionally disturbed young children*. Baltimore: University Park Press, 1975.

6
Teaching Autistic Children to Play: A Major Teacher Intervention

Cynthia Uline

Children at play are the genuine creators. They are artists without preconception—operating at that point to which we, as adults, strive to return. Play is truly unsolicited behavior, perhaps the only unsolicited behavior of the human experience. It is the substance of childhood. It is motion and language and thought combined.

Play ranges from the most basic sensory motor level:

> 4-28-79
> Timmy has become very involved in water play this past month. Although he will sometimes lapse into perserverative behavior, his play, for the most part, is purposeful and varied. He fills cups, pours water from one vessel to another, drives vehicles through, and mixes sand. When he arrives in the morning, Timmy's routine often includes a trip to the sink. If he is provided a pitcher, he will fill it and then, in turn, he will use it to fill our "porto" water table (a plastic receptacle used for this purpose).
> Today Julie happened to be standing by the sink when Timmy arrived. She placed her hand on the faucet as Timmy positioned the pitcher.
> "What want, Tim?" she asked.
> No response.
> "What want, Tim?"
> "Wate'!"
> And he got some! Once Timmy arrives at the table, his play is largely solitary. He will tolerate an occasional parallel player, but as yet, there has been no real interactive behavior around this activity.

To highly complex sociodramatic play.

6-5-79
John: I'm the Daddy.
Julie: Mommies always sit in the front.
Nancy: Sit right here in the car, Baby, okay?
Rick: (Giggles)
Nancy: Get in the car!
Julie: And, do you know where my whole family is going? We're going to be in the Mickey Mouse Birthday Parade. I'm going to be Snow White and my husband and son...
Mike: I'm being Mickey Mouse.
Julie: Yes, and who will you be, husband?
John: Donald Duck.
Julie: Well, we're there, darling. We're in Florida!

Children's play experiences are a source of strength and power. Through play, they are able to stretch and test individual limits, potentials, and capabilities. For the teacher, as facilitator, play experiences provide a legitimate tool through which determined goals and objectives can be achieved. The way a child plays reflects his learning style, his development, and his coping skills. From structured and systematic observation can come diagnostic information and plans for intervention. Jerome Bruner, professor at the Harvard Center for Cognitive Studies, concludes that learning takes place most readily in an atmosphere of playfulness (Michelman, 1974, p. 179). Thus, from play can also come prescription for both cognitive and affective skills.

Theoretical and empirical support has been given to the assumption that play behavior and its components follow a developmental sequence from social behavior (Gesell, 1940; Parten, 1933; Piaget, 1951); to language acquisition (Garvey, 1977; Teece, 1976); to cognitive growth (Bruner, Jolly, & Sylva, 1976; Smilansky, 1968). This sequence is hierarchial and progressive in nature.

Given this hierarchy of play behaviors and its obvious application to the developmental approach to learning; given the determination that play is an effective tool through which learning, both cognitive-academic and social-emotional, takes place in children; and given the premise that play is essential to the childhood experience; it is the purpose of this chapter to present play as a legitimate vehicle for the successful integration, within a daily school program, of special and typical children functioning at very different developmental levels and to support the notion that play can and should be included as a significant part of the daily school curriculum for young children.

DEFINITION AND JUSTIFICATION

What is play? What distinguishes play from nonplay? Play is an intrinsically motivated behavior through which a child builds skills necessary to interact with peers and objects in his environment (Reilly, 1974).

2-28-79

During play group today, we played camping. Sammy has joined our group, lending new dynamics to our play. He is asleep in the sleeping bag by the "campfire." The rest of the campers are settled down for the "night" inside the tent... all except John. John is hiding out in the "woods," and, as he circles close to where I sit, he whispers—

"I'm going to pretend I'm a bear."

He then approaches the tent and lets go with a ferocious GROWL! Campers fly in all directions. There is laughter, accompanied by screams, hoots, and hollers. John is caught up in the excitement, which continues until I call everyone to the "campfire" for "breakfast" and "Pow Wow." John is still smiling widely, seemingly with surprise and pride in his successful effect upon the others.

Certain descriptive characteristics of play are widely accepted as basic to its definition (Garvey, 1977). Most would agree that:

1. Play is pleasurable, enjoyable activity.
2. "Play has no extrinsic goals. Its motivations are intrinsic and serve no other objectives" (Garvey, 1977, p. 4). It is means as opposed to end.
3. Play is voluntary. It is spontaneous.
4. "Play involves active engagement on the part of the player" (Garvey, 1977, p. 4.)
5. Play includes "certain systematic relations to what is not play" (Garvey, 1977, p. 5).

The desire to clarify the nature of these links continues to encourage research. The "systematic relationships" of play to what is not play are important to its definition.

> The very idea of play depends on contrast. The notion of contrast between play and nonplay and the fact that there are certain similarities between playful behavior and analogous nonplay behavior have influenced recent attempts to arrive at a working definition of play. (Garvey, 1977, p. 5)

This last quality is what makes play worthy of close consideration and research. Play behavior has been linked to problem solving, creativity, language learning, development of social skills, and many other cognitive and affective competencies. However, awareness of the importance of play has only come about in recent years. It has received only limited consideration from empirical research and textbook authors.

Yawkey (1973) concludes that, given this lack of knowledge, justification and rationale most often fall into two main categories. First, the nondescriptive level includes cliches, general comments, pat phrases, and trite statements. This reasoning has a purely personal basis and is often circular in nature. Second, the intuitive level is more sophisticated, gained after extensive experience with young children. It includes theoretical justification.

Yawkey holds to the notion that the main drawback to identifying and justifying play by these levels is their tendency toward "variability, broadness, lack of communication and misinterpretation" (p. 6). I would agree with Yawkey's stance. After considerable research in the area of play and play theories, in general, and play theories as they relate specifically to work with special children, I feel that the justification and rationale for the application of play to the school curriculum lie in its clearly developmental nature, as cited by Piaget (1951), Smilanski (1968), Takata (1974), and others. Close consideration of the implications for programming inherent in this developmental model, in addition to data compiled and their interpretation, will serve as justification for play as a legitimate educational and therapeutic intervention.

PLAY IN THE SUNROOM

Karen is learning the sign for "run." She LOVES to run up and down the hall and has begun to run the length of it—down and back—by herself on request. She smiles as she runs and will do it any time of the day with enthusiasm—fast and hard.

Now she is connecting the action with the sign, which is to rub palms together in a quick, up-and-down motion.

Today all the Sunroom kids join Karen for a run. Alice gives the sign, and they all run together. They laugh. They chase each other. They chase Karen. They run beside her—she beside them. They coax her, applaud her, themselves, each other. Everyone signs. Everyone runs together. Karen claps and smiles and dances. That, for Karen, says, "Im's excited!"

The Sunroom is a classroom of 10 children. I am one of the three teachers involved in the day-to-day planning and programming for these children, three of whom are labeled *special*, seven of whom are considered typical. The children range in age from 3 to 7 years old. Their development levels run a broad gamut.

Our daily routine is closely orchestrated in order to successfully meet such a wide range of individual needs. There is time for one-to-one attention, small-group instruction, and large-group activity. The daily schedule includes class meeting, skill building time, snack, reading, lunch, math, and special activities such as cooking, art, music, field trips, and library time, in that order. In addition to these activities, each day there is scheduled a variety of play situations as an integral part of the curriculum.

Although Karen (mentioned above) has recently turned 7 years old, her level of functioning in all areas is developmentally very low. She makes few word approximations and has learned several signs, but is nonverbal for the most part. Her gross motor development is in the 4- to 5-year range, and fine motor skills are a source of great difficulty for Karen. She self-stimulates. Her play is often perseverative and seldom purposeful; and although she is becoming more focused on other children and will now tolerate parallel and even some low level interactive activity, her main focus continues to be on the adults in the classroom.

> Alice and Timmy sat on the floor together with the mirror in front of them. With the can of shaving cream clearly visible, Alice asked,
>
> "What want, Tim?"
>
> "Shave!" Tim answered.
>
> Onto the mirror it went, and four hands worked to cover the reflective surface. Sometimes wipe it off and peek at the faces, sometimes write names, designs for Timmy to erase, sometimes squish fingers between fingers.
>
> Soon it was—
>
> "I want to try!"
>
> "Me too!"
>
> Julie sat down behind Timmy with her legs and arms about him and took over Alice's job (with some coaching). She held Jeffrey's hands. She pushed them into the cream. She talked to him. She asked him what he wanted. She pointed to his face in the mirror and directed him to look. For 15 minutes they sat together like that, both focused on the mirror, the cream, the activity.
>
> Meanwhile, the rest of the class was engrossed in covering another mirror placed close by.
>
> "What want, Mary?"
>
> "Shave!"
>
> "What want, Mike?"
>
> "Shave!"
>
> "What want, Bobby?"
>
> "Shave!"

Timmy's behavior tends to be what we might refer to as classically autistic in nature. He is very withdrawn. He exhibits some of the common behavior characteristics of autism, that is, arm flapping, perseverative hand movements, spinning objects. He is 4 years old, but delayed in speech, socialization, and cognitive-academic skills. Timmy is very much a sensory learner. He responds to auditory, visual, and particularly tactile stimulation. When he came to the Sunroom in September, his interactions were, for the most part, exclusively with his teacher, Alice. Over the course of the school year, they have expanded to other adults; and he has just begun, in the last month, to notice peers.

> Rick and John arrived at school early this morning. They were in the Sunroom before any of the others. Conversation started as they took off their coats.
>
> "We're the first ones here, John," said Rick.
>
> "I came first, and you came second, Rick Francis," replied John.
>
> I left the room for several moments. When I returned, the two had moved to the block corner.
>
> "John and I are building a castle, Cindy," offered Rick.

They worked on the structure together for 5 minutes or more, carrying blocks together, handing needed materials back and forth, reinforcing each other's additions. When the castle was completed, they set up block chair cars in the center of the room. Each carried a wooden block to be used as a C.B. radio. Conversation continued over the "air waves."

"It's raining out, John! John! John, switch on your radio!"

"Watch where you're going, Rick. Calling Rick. Calling Rick. Cars are crashing!"

The drive continues with C.B.'s tuned into conversation about road conditions, police, crashes, etc.—with added comments concerning the morning goings on in the room. Julie arrived and joined the twosome. Play continued, with John's involvement totaling 20 minutes.

John is 6 years old. When he arrived in the Sunroom in September, his behavior was very much withdrawn. His speech production was limited. He had an overwhelming need for structure and sameness and had virtually no tolerance for any change in his daily routine. John often responded inappropriately (cry, scream, completely withdraw) to frustrating, anger-producing, or high anxiety situations. Much of our work with John has centered around encouraging his interaction with peers, verbally and otherwise. Individual goals focus on socialization skills. John requires a great deal of support. He needs to be reinforced and assured that he is learning the skills he needs to be a part of the group. Low threat situations must be provided.

Because of these needs for language development and improved communication skills, motor development, cognitive growth, increased peer interaction, and improved socialization skills on the part of Karen, Timmy, and John; and because play situations so readily facilitate such growth in all children, regardless of their developmental level, we determined that a structured, purposeful play curriculum reflecting a developmental model be implemented as an integral part of the Sunroom program, to the benefit of all those children involved.

This developmental play curriculum includes a variety of play situations, including one-on-one play times for each of the special children, free play sessions for the entire class, and play group (which involves sociodramatic play situations for a group of nine children, two of whom are special children). One-on-one play times, play centers, and free play all occur within the daily routine. Play group occurs three times weekly for a period of 30 minutes each session.

While play is most often spontaneous, unplanned, and without externally imposed structure (Yawkey & Silvern, 1977); and, although we never want to lose this important component, it is necessary, particularly with special children, to planfully and purposefully create an environment conducive, responsive, and supportive of play *and* to integration and interaction within it.

How does a teacher create such an environment? How can play be planful, purposeful? What follows is an analysis of just such an environment, including a rationale with examples and pragmatic suggestions for classroom teachers who are interested in exploring the possibilities of a play curriculum.

PLAY AND THE DEVELOPMENTAL THERAPY MODEL

Wood's *Developmental Therapy* (1975) is a "psychoeducational approach to therapeutic intervention with young children who have serious emotional and behavioral disorders" (p. 3). It is a treatment process which (*a*) does not segregate the disturbed child from the mainstream and (*b*) uses normal developmental stages as guidelines within the therapeutic process. It recognizes "the sequential maturational process as a powerful force in therapy" and is built upon certain assumptions concerning this process. Included are two basic assumptions which have direct application to the concept of play curriculum. First, Wood assumes the "young child's knowledge of himself, his confidence in himself, his willingness to risk himself in new situations, grows out of significant, pleasurable experiences" (p. 4); second, that a "young child learns and grows by experiences" (p. 4). Wood's three remaining assumptions refer to the power and influence of the developmental process. This, too, is easily translated into a play curriculum model. "Play is an external expression of the developmental process, and the highly observable skills of play constitute a description of developmental, learning or adaptation process" (Reilly, 1974, p. 152). If play is to be used successfully as an intervention in the classroom, there must be some degree of structure and organization which will allow for planful, purposeful initiation and evaluation. With its four curriculum areas, Wood's model provides just such a structure.

The model we use (see Figure 6.1) is composed of the four basic curriculum areas: behavior, communication, socialization, and (pre)academic. There are three basic levels of play behavior within each of these four areas. This paradigm is built upon the basic assumptions that play behavior does, indeed, include all four curriculum dimensions; all four dimensions are interrelated, and behavior in any of the areas does not and cannot occur in isolation; and growth within each dimension affects growth in all other dimensions.

A child "winds out" through these developmental levels of behavior from highly egocentric to socialized, interactive play in all four curriculum areas. He or she moves from highly independent, nonverbal, solitary, concrete sensorimotor play through an intermediate stage of more self-sufficient, verbal, parellel, and symbolic play, to a highly independent, verbal interactive, cooperative, and complex sociodramatic level of play behavior. These three basic levels are by no means hard and fast. As with all other of the human experiences, a child's play is itself a continuous process. Actions are organic. New ones grow from old—each affecting and building upon the others. There are no clear-cut lines; often there is overlap. However, the stages presented here describe play behavior with some degree of clarity.

Figure 6.1

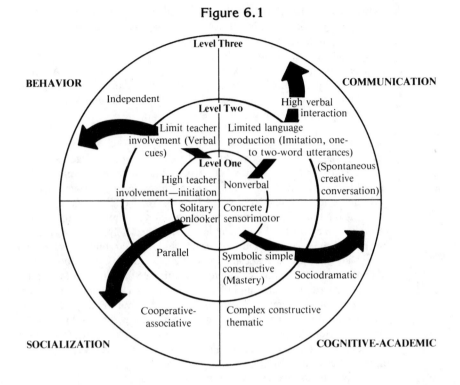

Behavior: Dependence-independence continuum

Behavior refers to the "physical adaptive responses which a child makes toward his/her environment" (Wood, 1975, p. 5). It is, most basically, being aware of where you are. It is attending to stimulus, motor response, and body control. It is organizing responses to environment "according to the expectations of other's involvement" (Wood, 1975, p. 5) in play. The child matures along a continuum, at the beginning of which play depends upon a high degree of adult initiation, moving out to more and more independent action on the part of the child.

Play incidents which involve John, recorded throughout the school year 1978-79, reflect this growth from high teacher involvement toward independent action, on the part of the child at play.

9-22-78

Today on the playground, I acted as "keeper of the gate" so that Karen could be free to roam around the area by herself. I watched John, who stood several yards from a group of chldren playing on the monkey bars. As he waved a stick, creating designs in the sand, he watched the others but did not move to become involved in their activity. Several moments later, he worked his way over to where I was sitting and crawled into my lap. We began to play our "rocking chair" game in which I become the chair and he the sitter. We rock, I sing, and when the momentum reaches a certain height, I pretend to lose my balance and *almost* fall backwards...."Whoa-o-o-o." We laugh and John yells for more. Today Mike looked on as we began our game. Asking if he could join us, he plopped himself down on the bottom part of my legs and leaned back on John. John proceeded to put his arms around Mike and say with a smile, "Rock with us, Mike," and we did.

10-11-78

We went camping today during the play group. The ladder house, draped with a blanket, became our tent. I built a campfire with blocks, spread another blanket on the floor, and made available pots, pans, a knapsack, and some camping hats. When John first arrived, he went directly to the scene but only checked things out briefly and then moved off to the table to draw. Mike and Bobby became involved immediately, along with Rick. We packed the knapsack and a paper bag and hiked around the tables and over chairs, arriving back at camp to build a fire and cook some food. I called to John that it was time for him to play with the other kids for a while. He skirted the area and ended up in his rocking chair—close enough to watch.

By this time, Tammy had also joined the group and was helping with the meal preparation—rice with rice. It came to me that perhaps John could be responsible for the dessert. I moved away to find play dough and paint brushes and then to John. He and I made "marshmallows" and placed them on the "sticks" for roasting.

"Give one to each camper, John," I suggested.

"Okay."

"Thanks, John."

"Don't burn them. Keep then turning," warned John.

After marshmallows, he made eggs and bacon. Everyone ate. Following the meal, Rick announced a bear approaching and everyone, including John, piled into the tent.

2-26-79

In the gym—

The game began when Bobby captured John and took him up to the "balcony." (The balcony is part of a brightly painted series of buildings, stairways, and climbables assembled on the stage in the gymnasium.)

"You stay here, John. I'll be back in a second with my friend." John grins and, as he waits for Bobby's return, he calls down to where I sit on the stage.

"Hello down there!"

Rick joins them. There are excited squeals. Following several minutes of this monster and spaceship game, the action switches to the gym floor, where trikes speed 'round and 'round the room. Bobby runs to John, who is riding one of the tricycles. He (Bobby) is pulling a four-wheeled cart.

"John, will you push me in this? I'm only four."

John does and after several times around the gym, they jump on a two-seater tricycle. They ride fast! John falls off and jumps right back on. Bobby falls off and John, wearing a mischievous grin, takes off peddling across the room, leaving Bobby sitting on the floor.

"Come back, John! What about me?"

John returns and they laugh and laugh as they fly around the gym on their two-seated trike, peddling together.

Communication: Nonverbal-creative conversation continuum

Play is an opportunity for language practice. Play situations "encourage imitation as well as creativeness" (Teece, 1976) in language development. There is a clearly definable sequence through which a child moves in this process. It begins with nonverbal responses on the part of the child and high involvement, imitation, and verbalization accompanied by sensorimotor bombardment on the part of the teacher. The child moves through this to the most primitive levels of verbal play—articulation and phonation—onto simple repetition play with syllables and monologue.

Because Timmy is so responsive to sensory stimulation of all kinds, this sensorimotor approach to fostering language production and communication is ideal for him. In September, Alice began at the most basic level, imitating his vocalizations and initiating tickling and peek-a-boo games which included repetition of simple syllables. Her approach was gently intrusive, involving extended periods of close proximity, touch, and physical contact. High verbal output on her part was characteristic of all play situations with Timmy.

This is followed by one and two-word utterances—those which are purposeful and communicative. Later Alice included the use of various sensory stimuli such as shaving cream, bubbles, powder, and hand cream. Initially, she would say the name of each specific item and then apply it to some part of Timmy's body. "Cream" would go to arm, "shave" to leg, "bubbles" to nose. Later she lined up the items and required that Timmy produce an approximation of each as he wanted them. Next he would request an item and point to the desired body part. Then, they generalized the activity to a baby doll, and so on.

10-30-78

Timmy loves to play with rice—run it through his fingers, drop it from one hand to the other, fill containers with it, mess about in it. This week, the rice was moved from atop the table to inside the plastic swimming pool. Plastic cups and containers, spoons, and boxes were added as play utensils. When Timmy arrived, he went straight to the pool and, soon after, climbed inside.

Mike and Rick arrived several minutes later. Taking a few minutes to investigate the situation, they, too, climbed in to join their classmate.

"Hi, Timmy!" said Rich and Mike in unison.

Nat held rice over Timmy's outstretched hands and, before pouring,

asked, "What want, Timmy?"
"RICE," called Timmy.
"What Timmy play with?" asked Mike.
"RICE," said Timmy.
"That's right Timmy. RICE!" repeated Mike in approval.

The final and most complex level involves spontaneous and creative conversation. Examples of this more sophisticated level of language practice are cited throughout the chapter where illustrations of dramatic play are included. As Teece states, "Interaction in activity is mirrored by interaction in language" (1976, p. 190). Conversation is cooperative. Conversation in play gives children practice in being social beings.

Socialization: Solitary-cooperative/associative continuum

Wood (1975) tells us that socialization involves the processes that lead a child into group experiences. These processes begin with basic awareness of first adults, later peers, and eventually parallel and cooperative play. "Theoretical and empirical support has been given to the assumption that social behavior as exhibited in play is developmental in nature" (Knapczck & Yoppi, 1975, p. 245.)

From the work of Parten (1933) and later Gesell (1940) and Barnes (1971), a developmental sequence of play has been defined. It begins with solitary and onlooker play and then moves through parallel to cooperative/associative play situations. (These theorists also include a competitive level. However, due to the age range of the children with whom I have worked and collected data, I will not address this level.) As the child grows in awareness and becomes more self-confident and self-sufficient as his language competencies increase, he moves out from himself to become more social in his play behavior.

If we reconsider the examples of John's play cited above, it is clear that his movement toward more social, cooperative play parallels his growth toward independence. As John grows in awareness, self-confidence, and competence, he moves from the solitary onlooker on the playground through parallel experiences, willing to share my attention with a classmate, to cooperative/associative activity with Rick and Bobby in the gymnasium. Each experience builds upon the next, until eventually he moves outside himself to become a more social being in his play with other children.

Cognitive-Academic:
Concrete/sensorimotor—complex sociodramatic continuum

There is much evidence to link play with cognitive development. Piaget (1951) concluded that play behavior is the natural matrix to learning (Reilly, 1974). Piaget, and later Smilansky (1968), viewed play as developing concurrently with a child's cognitive abilities. Although there is lack of agreement regarding the numbers of play periods in a child's cognitive development, the classification presented here closely follows the one recognized by Smilansky and others. Beginning at the most basic, concrete, sensorimotor stage, the child moves through simple symbolic and on to complex sociodramatic play. (Again, most classifications include games with rules and recreational play levels. However, because of age and developmental level, this chapter will not touch on these levels.) Play situations included in our curriculum span the levels from these most basic sensorimotor experiences (i.e., water play, rice, sand, shaving cream) through simple symbolic activities (i.e., pushing a truck across the floor, pretending to drink from a cup) to highly complex sociodramatic play situations involving sophisticated roles and spontaneous and creative conversation (i.e., camping, going on a trip, playing truckers).

It has become clear to me that not only can we move children through these developmental stages of symbolic functioning within a play milieu, but that it is also possible to integrate into the very same play activity children functioning on very different cognitive levels. Not only can tangibles that will attract and involve higher functioning children be included in sensory play, but it is also possible to create situations and alter the environment so that children functioning at very basic levels can be included and benefit from complex sociodramatic play activities. For example, consider adding a doll to water play.

3-15-79

Karen was involved in water play on the opposite side of the room from where the rest of the class was making macaroni jewelry. Nancy went over to watch and then went to the shelf and got a baby doll.

"Cindy, can I give the baby doll a bath?"

"Sure, Nancy."

The water table was filled with toys and cups, so I filled a plastic basin with water and placed it on the table next to where Karen was playing. She watched as Nancy and then Bobby washed their dolls. They left to dry their babies by the heater, and Karen moved to the basin. They returned and the babies went in the water table. Karen joined them, splashed some water on the dolls, and then went back to the basin. Babies joined her at the basin, and so it went until the babies were clean and Karen's pants were sufficiently soaked!

The teacher can instruct and isolate specific themes involved in sociodramatic play.

INTEGRATION INCIDENT

Sunroom
Time Begin: 10:30
      End: 11:00
Activity: Play Group
Observer's Name: Cynthia Uline

Children and adults involved: Christopher, Rick, Nancy, Bobby, Mike, Mary, Julie, John, Sammy, Cindy, and Judy.

Interaction

Sammy, age 8, has begun to join us for our structured play group. His teachers determined that he needed play time with younger children in order to encourage symbolic play and peer interaction. It was decided that the Sunroom play group had potential for meeting that need. We began 2 weeks ago. Themes for these weeks have been first camping and then going on a trip. Sammy seemed to grow more comfortable with each session. His withdrawal to explore other toys in the room, flights out of the room, and attachment to Alice diminished with each visit. Judy and I observed Sammy watching the other children, focusing on the group, and modeling behavior. He smiled for most of the half hour.

During our "take a trip" theme, chairs were set up as cars and a gas pump supplied for fuel.

Sammy was given the job of station attendent and, at one point, pumped gas into Mike's car. Mike helped him to find where to insert the hose. He motored his hands to the correct location.

"Put the gas right here, Sammy."

Sammy smiled wide.

"Mike's car. Put the gas in Mike's car!"

For the week following, Mike became a focus for Sammy. He talked about him to his teachers. He wrote about him in his reading stories. He snuck into the Sunroom to see him.

"Mike, Mike!"

We felt good about Sammy's apparent adjustment to the situation, but both Judy and I were concerned that the level of complexity presented to him by the dramatic play might be too high and too confusing. I decided that perhaps several basic themes presented repetitively throughout each larger theme might provide Sammy with a more manageable structure—something on which to focus. For the first of these themes, I chose sleeping and eating. This week we tried it out.

The overall theme for this week's group was "truckers." Tangibles included a road constructed from blocks and a large pillow hill, a "truck stop" with plastic dishes, and a C.B. base station (a miniature replica of last week's gas pump was presented, too). Each trucker was given a hat and a truck and we're off!

Sammy pushed his car along the road. He pumped gas into it at the gas station. He lined up to participate in a "convoy." He ordered food at the diner and pretended to drink from his cup.

"What want, Sammy?"

"Orange juice and french fries."

When the lights went out signaling night and time for sleep, Sammy laid down and put his head on the pillow hill along with Julie and Mike. When it was time for play group to end and everyone was to "go home" to the rug, Sammy went without cues from Judy!

It is time to leave the Sunroom. Everyone says, "Bye, Sammy!"

"Good bye," with a smile.
"We will come again on Friday, Sammy," says Judy.
"Friday, Sunroom, Mike!" and Sammy leaves.

PLAY AS A MEDIUM FOR INTEGRATION

It has been determined that:

1. In the case of the autistic or developmentally delayed child, there is "generally very little interaction with the environment or objects in it. If the child plays at all, it is alone and he frequently uses play object inappropriately" (Black, Freeman, & Montgomery, 1975, p. 363).
2. This inability to play appropriately further hinders the impaired social and cognitive development.
3. Play is the business and the right of *all* children. (Froebel, James, Dewey, and others have promoted the principles of learning through play, and the right of each child to a joyful childhood.)

Thus the necessity for devising interventions to stengthen and enhance play skills in these children is clear.

Several studies have shown, and my data supports the notion, that models are important in building imitation. Nondelayed children provide appropriate models for relevant play (Guralnick, 1976). The typical child models the adult world, thus building upon his or her undertanding and competence. The special child, in turn, models the typical child modeling the adult world.

There is evidence to support a substantial increase in both quantity and quality of play in handicapped preschoolers when nonhandicapped children act as models (Guralnick, 1976).

> Modeling of a more informal, dynamic, and interactive type...was actually an essential component of the process.... Specifically, the nonhandicapped children often demonstrated a play activity and then encouraged the handicapped child to duplicate it. (Guralnick, 1976, p. 241)

Thus, the adult provides an environment that encourages play, specifically spontaneously interactive play, provides the necessary structure, and then steps back to observe and to allow peers to teach each other.

Figure 6.2 translates the developmental spiral of Figure 6.1 to grid form. The grid allows us to analyze compiled data from incidents when integration occurred between special and typical children within play situations in the Sunroom between September, 1978, and April of the following year.

A total of 100 interactions between special and typical children within the Sunroom were recorded. Interactions could be at any level, could be positive or negative, and could include any or all of the children or adults in the Sunroom population. Of the 100, 63 occurred within play situations.

Figure 6.2

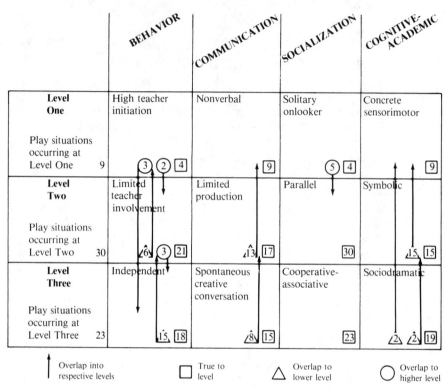

Overlap into respective levels

True to level

Overlap to lower level

Overlap to higher level

These situations spanned the clearly developmental levels of play behavior and showed evidence of activity which could be placed into Wood's four curriculum areas. On the grid, behavior combinations within the four curriculum areas at each of the three major levels are depicted horizontally. Sequential development through these levels is depicted vertically. Overlap is noted through the use of arrows.

I have analyzed the incidents according to levels of play—9 occurring at the most basic level, 30 occurring at level two, and 23 occurring at level three. I have also broken them down in accordance with the specific behaviors characteristic of each curriculum area, noting overlap where appropriate. Thus, for example, of the 30 interactions that occured in play situations at level two (that is, play requiring limited teacher involvement, exhibiting limited language production on the part of the child, parallel and symbolic in nature), specifically in the realm of communication, 17 of the interactions showed limited language production, true to the behavior expected of level two play. Thirteen of the interactions overlapped into level one behavior in the realm of communication in that no language production on the part of the child was noted. To further illustrate, the following is an incident involving Sammy, eight of the other Sunroom children, and two adults.

INTEGRATION INCIDENT

Sunroom
Time: Begin: 10:30
         End: 11:00
Activity: Play Group—"Circus"
Observer's name: Cynthia Uline
Children and adults involved: Sammy, Julie, Nancy, Mike, Rick, Christopher, John, Mary, Bobby, Judy, and Cindy.
Interaction:
Christopher and Nancy suggested circus as a theme for play group. I took them up on it and today the Sunroom kids and Sammy became clowns. We had hats and old shoes, baggy shirts, and colored chalk for faces.

"I Love a Clown" played from the record player, and everyone sat before the mirror to put on his make up. Sammy watched through the mirror and modeled. A little on each cheek, some on the chin, a little around the eyes—a huge smile looked back at him from the mirror.

I had taped three circles on the floor and broke the group up into threes.

"Dance, sing, be silly. Do what clowns do. Be whatever kind of clown you wish!" I said. "When the music stops, it will be supper time for clowns. When the lights go out, it will be time for all circus clowns to sleep!"

Sammy danced in a circle with Nancy, Mike, and Judy. "Mike, clown," said Sammy. He tossed his head back and forth. When Mike fell to the floor, he sat down, too. He ate with the clowns, and when the lights dimmed, he lay down in his circle to sleep. "Clowns go to sleep," from Sammy. He moved with very few cues from Judy. Most he took from the clowns around him!

I placed this interaction at level two. On the grid it is noted as one of the 30 occurring at this level. It reflects limited teacher involvement and limited language production on Sammy's part. The clown dancing, eating, and sleeping was largely parallel activity and was symbolic in nature (lying down is symbolic of sleep; the play cup is symbolic of juice to drink; make up and music are symbolic of a clown), perhaps reflecting the beginnings of sociodramatic play for Sammy.

Each interaction was so analyzed and is noted on the grid. Children functioning at any and all of the developmental levels have a place on this matrix of play activity. Therefore, it is possible that children functioning at all these levels can be integrated within play situations. It becomes the responsibility of the teacher/facilitator to provide play situations that can and do respond to these varying levels, simultaneously. Some specific examples of such activities have already been presented. The final portion of this chapter will suggest a workable process for creating others.

PLANNING FOR PLAY

What of the day-to-day mechanics—the scheduling, the pencil-and-paper planning, the generating of novel ideas, the creating of a physical environment that is conductive, responsive, and supportive? How do you plan for play? How do you encourage interaction within that play?

It is the responsibility of the teacher/facilitator to match the abilities and goals of each child to the environment and the activity, responding to individual needs according to developmental differences. At the same time, he or she must offer novel experiences and provide for some method of continuing observation and assessment. This is a large order, but it is clearly workable with some degree of forethought and organization.

Physical Environment

The physical environment for play should be neither overstimulating or understimulating. It should include a variety of settings, both indoors and outdoors—classroom, gym, playground, and so on. Areas should be spacious enough that they readily lend themselves to a variety of activities, both highly active and more passive. Play equipment should be applicable to a variety of purposes, "to more than one child and more than one developmental level" (tricycles, ladder house, water table) (Michelman, 1974, p. 194).

Play materials should also meet the needs of children functioning at varied developmental levels and play stages. They should be as open-ended as possible in order to facilitate their use in many different play situations. For example, a wooden block becomes material for road building, castle construction, a C.B. receiver, a loaf of bread. There are published lists which include a myriad of specific examples of play materials available to the classroom teacher (Michelman, 1974; Wood, 1975).

The environment should structure time so that activity is consistent and predictable. The daily schedule should include a balance of play, work, social interactions, chores, and rest. This will allow for a sense of order that will eventually become internalized. This understanding allows for better adjustment to change. Figure 6.3 shows a sample schedule of a child in the Sunroom. Scheduling is of particular importance when planning for a child like John, a child with little tolerance for change or ambiguity.

The environment should be oriented toward success. Each child should feel accomplished and secure in his or her play—regardless of the level of functioning. Time to solve problems and time for reflection on and rewarding of those problem-solving efforts should always be provided.

Figure 6.3 Daily schedule for John

	Monday	Tuesday	Wednesday	Thursday	Friday
8:45- 9:00	Bus arrives (time alone)	Bus arrives (time alone)	Bus arrives (time alone)	Bus arrives (time alone)	Bus arrives (time alone)
9:00- 9:15	One-on-one play time with Cindy	Greeting and play with kids	One-on-one time with Cindy	Greeting and play with kids	One-on-one play time with Cindy
9:15- 9:30	Skill time	Skill time	Skill time	Skill time	Skill time
9:30- 9:45	Free play	Free play	Free play	Free play	Free play
9:45-10:15	Meeting	Meeting	Meeting	Meeting	Meeting
10:15-10:30	Snack	Snack	Snack	Snack	Snack
10:30-11:15	Structured play group	Open play	Structured play group	Open play	Structured play group
11:15-11:50	Reading	Reading	Reading	Reading	Reading
11:50-12:30	Lunch	Lunch	Lunch	Lunch	Lunch
12:30- 1:00	Play centers—choice of two activities	Language instruction with Nancy	Play centers—choice of two activities: one active, one sit down	Language instruction with Nancy	Library
1:00- 1:30	Math	Math	Field trip	Math	Library
1:30- 2:00	Trip to store for cooking supplies	Music	Field trip	Art	Library
2:00- 2:30	Reading/story/rest	Reading/story/rest	Field trip	Reading/story/rest	Library

Play Experiences

When generating possible ideas for integrated play, you should keep in mind that an important goal is the inclusion of children who are at many levels on the play curriculum. Therefore, it is important to provide play experiences that follow closely the normal play stages. They should, wherever possible, encourage imitation and allow for repetition. "Imitation...helps children learn group awareness.... Play activities performed over and over again lead to success through trial and error learning" (Michelman, 1974, p.202).

They should respond to different levels of readiness, cognitive capacities, and motivation. Whenever possible, there should be provisions for both verbal and nonverbal interactions. They should be novel, stimulating, and exciting.

Adult Involvement

After the planning and the initiation is over, what role should the teacher/facilitator assume? This depends upon the nature and level of activity. At one level, the adult must be the pursuer and maintain a high level of active involvement. On the other end of the continuum, it should be the adult's responsibility only to observe, record, and perhaps interject an occasional comment or cue.

Whatever the level, adults should always present themselves as appropriate models who stimulate and encourage an atmosphere of interactive playfulness.

THE PROBLEM-SOLVING PROCESS

My purpose here is not to present a step-by-step plan of action for developing an entire play curriculum. If one were to make a complete list of play activities, including all the developmental levels of play, the result of the effort would indeed be prodigious. Because of the magnitude of such an undertaking, and because my own personal involvement in the Sunroom was directed more to the specific area of sociodramatic play, it is this level on the continuum that I will address.

What follows is the problem-solving process through which I moved in order to provide a dramatic play situation responsive to the particular needs of one child in the Sunroom—in this case, John—and to the more general needs of the group as a whole.

Again, John is a child who needs encouragement and support in interaction and socialization skills. When John came to the Sunroom at the beginning of the school year, his behavior was so withdrawn that it was necessary to provide specific programming within his school day in order to assure his involvement with the other children. If left to his own devices, John would choose a seat alone at the table and paper and pens with which to draw. Verbal cues from an adult were necessary, along with visual reminders in the form of schedule charts, in order to remind him that it was time to "play with the other kids." Even when involved, his play tended to be more onlooker, more parallel, and less interactive.

For these reasons it was determined that John should be involved in a dramatic play group that would meet three times weekly for a period of 30 minutes each session. The purpose would be to create a safe, structured environment within which John could be comfortable to take risks and increase the amount of his interactive play.

My responsibility, at this point, was two-fold. First, I needed to develop novel and exciting play themes that would attract and capture the interest of the class as a whole; second, I needed to keep the theme, materials, and props at a level responsive to John's particular needs. The process for this has been a generative one, through which my knowledge and sensitivities have sharpened over time. It has included time for thought, for simple generation of ideas, for brainstorming with the other teachers in the room, for listening carefully to the children themselves—for they provide a wealth of ideas for play situation, if we only listen with interest to their "let's pretend...."

Once an idea is firmly planted, the next step is the paper-and-pencil planning, the cut-and-paste production, and the trash and treasure search for materials and props. Through all this, specific objectives and goals (goals that will no doubt change over time), should be clear and at hand. Thus, it is best to begin with the paper-and-pencil planning. Figure 6.4 shows one suggested planning form used to keep clear those specific goals and objectives for John specific to play group over the course of a week's time. These are taken directly from his Developmental Therapy Objectives Rating Form (Wood, 1975). This form then records material and interventions used and the outcome of each. Thus, not only are we attending to prescription but also assessment.

With three specific goals in mind, a play activity centered around the theme of "airport" was devised. The result was positive for John and for the other children, as well. Along with John, they were captured by the energy and the excitement of the activity and became involved in its completion. "Airport" as an activity provided opportunities for movement, for creative expression, for leadership, for role taking (as the control tower person and as pilots), and for some degree of interaction—partnered flights, "dancing planes," and so on. Where it lacked strength, however, was in encouraging verbal interaction and creative conversation. Part of the on-going process to develop appropriate dramatic play situations is to remedy these shortcomings as they arise.

Because interactive play is such a high priority, consideration of how to facilitate interaction between children is most important. Whether it is the partnered roles of doctor/patient during hospital play, or customer/barber duos during barber shop, or two in a sleeping bag during camping play, the objective of the teacher must always be to find ways to encourage interaction and conver-

Figure 6.4 Weekly planning form

Child: John
Activity: "Airport"

Teacher: Cynthia Uline

Day	Objective(s)	Materials and Interventions Used	Outcome
Monday	S. 17: John will participate in cooperative activities or projects with other children during play time indoors or outdoors.	John will be involved in a play group with other children centered around the theme "Airport." Props will include plastic planes and helicopters, a rug "runway," an airport constructed from blocks, and a control tower consisting of head phones and a blinking light bulb. Play will be	John became involved in the airport activity with enthusiasm (smiles, expressed desire to have a certain plane, excitement about being control tower person—"When will it be MY TURN?"—It is the responsibility of the control tower person to give
Wednesday	S. 15: John will initiate appropriate minimal movement toward another child.	open-ended, for the most part, with initial involvement on the part of the adult, fading to observer, providing only verbal cues to the group. "Now fly quietly. Now	the signal, with the blinking light, for take off). My involvement was limited—mostly verbal cues from the control tower table. John's physical investment was maximum. He ran, he jumped, he swooped high and
Friday	B. 21: John will spontaneously participate in activities previously avoided: in this case, high energy, movement activity.	be trick pilots," etc. John will maintain involvement for 25 to 30 minutes with at least three specific interactions, verbal or otherwise, with other children.	low, he "crashed." He made authentic engine sounds.
			Because the activity was high energy and physically active, the amount of verbal interaction among the kids was reduced. John's interactions with other kids totaled two per day. He maintained involvement for the entire activity.

sation. He or she may do this through the use of props; it may be inherent in the experience and roles; or she may encourage it with her own presence as a model and dispenser of suggestions and cues.

In this particular situation, when I was to initiate "Airport" play again several months later, specific props were added to stimulate more verbal exchange. These props included four large colored clouds constructed from poster board and a flight schedule with the children's names and names they chose for their planes written on a large piece of chart paper. I could then direct certain planes to land on certain clouds, or children could chose to do so spontaneously, always, of course, allowing time for conversation once pilots were adrift on the paper clouds. Perhaps now John would have more opportunity to practice his verbal, along with his motor, skills.

The outcome was surprising and illustrates one of the problems and risks involved in planning for integrated play. (See Figure 6.5.)

> Well-informed adults are sensitive to children's changing needs, incentive, and moments of readiness. They will neither expect things too soon,...nor will they miss the moment of a child's readiness. (Michelman, 1974, p. 199)

This is a delicate balance to strike. In this case, an error in the calculation of John's readiness at that particular time resulted in a difficult experience for both him and the other children involved. At some times when problems arise in various play situations, the problems can be exploited as teachable moments and issues worked through on the spot. In this particular instance, however, John was much too upset and threatened to work through his difficulty with the other children. There was no other choice but to withdraw attention and leave him alone.

As can be seen, even play as an intervention is not without its problems. Not only must the teacher strike the delicate balance between risk and readiness, he or she must also consider the issue of management. The teacher must somehow maintain interest and energy and, at the same time, assure some degree of structure and security for all those involved. With each problem, however, will come new insights and strategies.

There is also the complex role of the adult as initiator, observer, facilitator, and monitor to consider. It is no easy task to keep abreast of the actions and interactions of 9 to 10 children at play, particularly when some of these children have special needs. It takes practice to become attuned to the constant ebb and flow and to be confident and ready to make a judgment to step in when necessary. Fortunately, with practice, this skill does develop.

Planning and preparation are time-consuming at first. Generating a backlog of materials takes hours, energy, and input from others. Once the initial investment is made, however, and themes are established and materials created and collected, it is helpful to have at your disposal "prop" boxes (Cherry, 1976) that may be used and reused (i.e., a box filled with menus, hats, aprons, pots

Figure 6.5 Weekly planning form

Child: John
Activity: "Airport"

Teacher: Cynthia Uline

Day	Objective(s)	Materials and Interventions Used	Outcome
Monday Wednesday Friday	S. 17: John will participate in cooperative activities or projects with other children during play time indoors or outdoors. S. 15: John will initiate appropriate minimal movement toward another child. B. 21: John will spontaneously participate in activities previously avoided: in this case, high energy, movement activity.	John will be involved in a play group with other children centered around the theme "Airport." Props will include plastic planes and helicopters, a rug "runway," an airport constructed from blocks, and a control tower consisting of head phones and a blinking light bulb. Play will be open-ended, for the most part, with initial involvement on the part of the adult, fading to observer, providing only verbal cues to the group. "Now fly quietly. Now be trick pilots," etc. John will maintain involvement for 25 to 30 minutes with at least three specific interactions, verbal or otherwise, with other children.	John has been having a difficult week—low frustration tolerance, numerous outbursts, limited interaction. During "Airport" he kept his distance. He flew alone. He avoided contact. He was rigid in his play ("I won't land on the red cloud, only on the GREEN cloud"). When everyone gathered around the blue cloud for conversation, John flew to the green cloud and sat alone. He watched the group but made no move to join them. Alice and I watched from across the room. "Does anyone have a C.B. on their plane? Someone needs to call John," said Alice. "He's lost on a cloud all by himself."

Julie made a microphone with her fist and, speaking into it, said, "Calling John! Calling John! Come in, John!"

This served as cue for everyone to jump up and "fly" to John's cloud. "Come on, John!"

"Go away! Go away, everyone! You bug me!" yelled John in a loud, angry voice.

Everyone looked toward Alice and me with surprise, eyes big, mouths open.

"I guess we need to give John some space. It seems he's not in the mood to play with us right now," I said.

The activity continued as before, with John on the fringe; and now, the others avoided interaction with him.

and pans, and play food for "Restaurant" play; one with toy doctor kits, nurses' caps, doctor's hat, and signs for "Hospital" play, etc.).

It is a challenge to create play themes that respond to a variety of children, with a variety of needs, functioning on a number of developmental levels. Being sensitive to how these needs change over time increases the complexity of the task. The task is not an impossible one, however. Over time, as you become familiar with the children, their likes and dislikes, what motivates them to become involved, what encourages them to talk and be creative in their play, ideas evolve naturally and the job becomes easier. The total experience never ceases to be an exciting, moving, growing one for both the children and the adults involved.

SUMMARY

This chapter has presented a model for a play curriculum to be used in teaching specific play skills to developmentally delayed children. Included are a rationale for the application of play to the school curriculum, a developmental model for the teaching of specific play skills, and examples of how a play curriculum, responsive to a wide range of developmental levels, was successful as an intervention in order to encourage social, emotional, and cognitive growth in both special and typical children in an integrated classroom setting.

REFERENCES

Barnes, K. Preschool play norms: A replication. *Developmental Psychology,* 1971, *5*(1), 99-103.

Black, M., Freeman, B.J., & Montgomery, J. Systematic observation of play behavior in autistic children. *Journal of Autism,* 1975, *5*(4), 363-371.

Bruner, J., Jolly, A., & Sylva, K. (Eds.). *Play: Its role in development and evolution.* Harmondsworth: Penguin, 1976.

Cherry, C. *Creative play for the developing child, early lifehood education through play.* Belmont, Calif.: Fearon, 1976.

Garvey, C. *Play.* Cambridge, Mass.: Harvard University Press, 1977.

Gesell, A. *The first five years of life.* New York: Harper, 1940.

Guralnick, M.J. The value of integrating handicapped and nonhandicapped preschool children. *American Journal of Orthopsychiatry,* 1976, *46*(2), 236-245.

Knapczyk, D.R. & Yoppi, J.O. Development of cooperative and competitive play responses in developmentally disabled children. *American Journal of Mental Deficiency,* 1975, *80*(3), 245-255.

Michelman, S.S. Play and the deficit child. In M. Reilly (Ed.), *Play as exploratory learning: Studies of curiosity behavior.* Beverly Hills, Calif.: Sage Publications, 1974.

Parten, M. Social play among preschool children. *Journal of Abnormal and Social Psychology,* 1933, *28*, 136-147.

Piaget, J. *Play, dreams, and imitation in childhood.* London: Routledge, 1951.

Reilly, M. (Ed.). *Play as exploratory learning: Studies of curiosity behavior.* Beverly Hills, Calif.: Sage Publications, 1974.

Smilansky, S. *The effects of sociodramatic play on disadvantaged preschool children.* New York: John Wiley, 1968.

Takata, N. Play as a prescription. In M. Reilly (Ed.), *Play as exploratory learning: Studies of curiosity behavior*. Beverly Hills, Calif.: Sage Publications, 1974.

Teece, C. Language and play. *Language and speech*, 1976, *19*(2), 179-192.

Wood, M.M. *Developmental therapy: A textbook for teachers as therapists for emotionally disturbed young children*. Baltimore: University Park Press, 1975.

Yawkey, T.D., & Silvern, S.B. *Play and play processes of the young child in early education programs: A Piagetian analysis*. Chicago: Spencer Foundation, August, 1977. (ERIC Document Reproduction Service No. ED 144 717).

Yawkey, T.D. *Play of the young child and day care workers: A Piaget justification*. 1973. (ERIC Document Reproduction Service No. ED 107 366)

7
An Affective Education Program at Jowonio: Goals, Development, and Evaluation

Rosalind L. Heiko

Many of the programs which focus on affective education for children (Bissell & Palomares, 1972; Simon, Howe, & Kirschenbaum, 1972) have been rigidly implemented by teachers and other professionals in classrooms (Hunter, 1977). Individualized and flexible goals and teacher skills within the classroom setting are not taken into account in designing these programs. The suggested curricula are often inflexibly followed (for instance, exercise #5 must follow #4), even if not appropriate for a particular group of children. Other important educational goals for children's cognitive, as well as affective, growth (e.g., problem-solving and reasoning techniques, understanding concepts such as responsibility and self-esteem) often remain undiscussed and unresolved. A more reasonable affective education program useful to both teachers and students would be one in which individual as well as group concerns and ability levels were incorporated with personal and interpersonal skill development.

In my role as a school psychologist at Jowonio during the year 1978–79, my classroom observations revealed that there appeared to be a need (in two classrooms in particular) to structure a weekly time to explore many of these affective concerns. During a conversation, one of the teachers disclosed that she wanted such a program "to be a time to focus on feelings and to focus on problems that the kids in the class were having."

As a consultant, I could offer my services to these teachers to help them organize an affective education program for their students. As one of the teachers stated,

> And one thing I'm very aware of is that in a group you can't possibly deal
> with kids to the affective degree that you would like.... So I'm much more
> aware of setting a tighter structure, but also if a kid has a problem within a

group like that...and it involves ten other kids...you can't quite do it. It depends how I'd handle that; sometimes I can only handle it behaviorally because it wouldn't make sense to put it off to a later time...sometimes it may even be put at the end of the day, if it's really to talk about what happened so I might settle it with the kid...so I might...get back to the kid later in the day and say, "Remember when I did that? Well, let's talk about that for a few minutes"...because my situation is so much more group oriented.... Sometimes it seems it's almost automatic to go to the way you've dealt with it before, and I have to remind myself that if I have the time, it's more optimal to deal with it [later].

The difficulties with discussing feelings and individual student problems (self-control, anger, self-confidence, and so on) during a tightly scheduled day are many, particularly if children have certain academic goals to pursue in the course of a day. Even so, for almost all of the teachers at Jowonio, a focus on affective concerns of the children is a primary educational and personal goal. As one teacher says,

Like sometimes [a particular child] will get mad and he'll throw something, or he'll turn and hit you, or something. And we talk about how you're feeling. He knows labels, he knows *mad,* but he doesn't always know why he's feeling that way, so I try and help him clarify why. And with him it gets as basic as giving him suggestions of why he's feeling that way because he just hasn't acquired that skill yet, and then what are we going to do about it, what's going to make you feel better...how are we going to get this "mad anger" energy out of you, and he does it, push on the pillow, stamp the feet, run up and down the hall kind of stuff.... He's learning those options. He never even had those before.

Many of the teacher goals for emotional growth are alike, as this teacher states:

My biggest one is the children learning how to express their feelings, especially the little ones. They have a really hard time with that, labeling their feelings and being able to express them freely and knowing what they are and why they are feeling that way...then what to do about it, thinking up answers for that, how to get over it, or how to use it, making sure they know it's okay to feel that way, but we'll have to do something about it.

The *Developmental Therapy* objectives incorporated into the Jowonio educational program support the teachers' emotional and cognitive goals for the students. As a consultant, I believed that an awareness program might be of value to Jowonio teachers who requested assistance in planning an affective education program, to focus upon certain issues, concerns, and objectives they had developed for their students. The pupils ranged in age from 5 to 11. The organization of this awareness program would involve meetings with the teachers to define goals, define specific problems, discuss past interventions in terms of affective issues within the classroom, delineate the teachers' roles within such a program, develop strategies for the program, and finally evaluate the effectiveness of the program (both in terms of short- and long-range goals).

Two of the lead teachers decided that they wanted to meet and share information concerning the development of what I termed an "awareness program." Throughout the following discussion of these programs, please bear in mind that all of the final presentations and strategies were the result of collaborative effort between the teachers and me. The success of a consultation service delivery model is contingent upon the understanding that the teacher is the most direct and perceptive judge of student needs. The resources within the teacher are therefore invaluable; his or her information about the class as a whole, and individual students in particular, is a requisite component of any program organization.

DEFINING GOALS

The most important aspect of setting up an affective program—or any program, for that matter—is first clarifying the "what," the underlying values and beliefs of such a program, which will affect both the students and the teacher. The "how" of implementing plans and techniques will logically and more easily follow a concise understanding of the nature and reasons behind the program's development.

One of the teachers stated her goal for an awareness program.

> A lot of times things happen, we have issues in the room that need to be dealt with immediately, and sometimes we have meetings during the day [to do this].... Well, one day...by the end of gym, about half of the class was crying, not ever wanting to go back to gym again, mad and that kind of thing, so obviously there's a time we had to spend time immediately to talk about what was going on. Another day we had a real hard time on a field trip with kids just not paying attention, actually being very rude, and so the next day, instead of doing what we planned, we talked about behavior on the field trip. So there are other times when we problem-solve about things in the room, but I think that we kind of identify with continuing issues, and things that are not just immediate crisis problems, but that seem to be recurring, that we can work on in those meetings once a week. That's why we set them up, and because I don't feel that I have a lot of expertise in math or that area [affective education].

The other lead teacher expressed the following goals.

> An expectation is that people see themselves and their own growth not necessarily compared to others, but as compared to themselves and where they're going...that all kids see all the other kids as part of the group, as not different but similar in some way...that there's some sense of belonging to a group,

that there's part of family kind of attitude, helping.... Another one [expecta-tion] would be talking about feelings.... I feel like that also changes with re-spect for particular kids, so I would ask some kids to talk more than others,...and another one is just respect for people in the group. Some of these I think do become structured by rules because the kids need them bro-ken down at times into steps, concrete steps that they can follow.... Another expectation [is] that kids would take some responsibility for not just their ac-tions...but for making the situation better.

These discussions about expectations and values concerning students formed the basis for further planning. It was necessary to set up several meetings with the teachers to clarify their perceptions about the value of an awareness program apart from their daily activities and interactions with their students. For one of the teachers,

I'm a strong believer...that kids need a forum, somewhere in the day on a daily basis, to deal with things that they feel, whether it's home-related, school-related, or thinking-related. I think it's important because I think kids need a forum to deal with other kids, to work out some of the problems they have with other children...with some of the things they have difficulty with, whether it's talking about feelings, whether it's competition, whether it's be-ing able to take pride in something that's theirs; and I also see it as a time to develop a group sense, as well as to work on certain skills.... Two [days a week] are used very definitely for discussions of feelings, how kids feel, how they deal with things, problems they have with each other...(also) as a prob-lem-solving meeting where, if there's a problem in the room, kids talk about it and suggest solutions. We do a lot of group decision making, which I see as important, both for kids to feel like they have input and are responsible...for their own behavior; but also in a group sense to just get kids to realize that certain things that might be good for themselves are not always good for others.

I developed a Group Behavior Survey (see Appendix B), and I asked each of the three teachers in the two classrooms to fill it out before the first planning meeting. As a result of time restrictions, only during the early goal-defining meetings could both the lead teachers and the two student teachers in each room attend discussions, although both the lead teachers and I kept advised of the stu-dent teachers' reactions to the program. These surveys were designed to examine individual and group behavior within the classroom (both positive and negative), teacher reactions to specific students, and teacher perceptions of chil-dren's affective skill levels. The information was placed on a graph to more clearly delineate teacher perceptions. In addition, in one classroom children were asked whom they liked best and least, and a sociogram of the data was devel-oped. Another handout (see Appendix A) was given to the teachers to delineate program objectives. The information obtained from these methods was shared directly with each classroom teacher, either in group or individual meetings. The results of these last discussions formed the framework for future planning of strategies for the awareness program.

As a result of these meetings, I was able to compile a list of objectives and assumptions concerning the projected programs. This information was presented in the form of a ditto to each teacher using the following format.

How is learning accomplished?
By structuring the environment:
• Sharing
• Clarity
• Responsiveness
• Facilitation of openness/disagreement/constructive confrontation
• Receiving and giving feedback

OBJECTIVES in an Awareness Program:
• Students can develop a postive self-concept.
• Students can become aware of differences/similarities which distinguish individuals.
• Students can recognize that each person has a contribution to make to the group—whether that be in class, with family or in a group of peers.
• Students can learn the value of working cooperatively and supportively with others.
• Students can become sensitive to the desires/feelings/needs and problems of others.
• Students can learn to accept competition/weaknesses as steps toward positive growth.
• Students can come to appreciate the efforts of others on their behalf.
• Students can learn to recognize and accept feelings and understand the relationship between feelings and their consequences in terms of interpersonal events.

ASSUMPTIONS need to make clear in any group interaction:
• Can only use "I" or "me"—not "we" statements.
• Don't have to participate but can't stop others.
• Talk about feelings, not "I think" statements (this is the difference between opening up an interaction and closing it off).
• Nothing is "right" or "wrong" in feeling statements.
• Trust feelings as being real and trusting the group to support the expression of feelings.
• To identify and express feelings can lead to their not being bottled up inside.
• Change can be positive; it isn't necessarily painful.
• We make judgments all the time but what's important is what we do with those judgments (grow into new ones, use them constructively, etc.).

PROBLEM DEFINITION

Teachers discussed many of the positive and negative interactions within the classroom. Some examples of these are:

Every day during job time the typical kids are highly supportive and helpful with the special kids. Yesterday [Tyler] sang to [David] to help him take off and hang up his coat.

At attendance time several [typical] kids...help [the special kids] say "here".

At meeting, [Kirstin] was describing her fear of swimming and that she felt badly that she was in this big group and not able to do things as well as some other people. [Tanya] chimed in that she understood that and that she sometimes put an F on her math and reading papers when she made even one mistake because she felt badly that she made the mistakes at all. [Sarah] then commented that she knew [Tanya] did that and wasn't that a bit hard on herself. When I asked if anyone would help [Kirstin] talk to her swimming teacher about being afraid, [Nova] volunteered.

[Tanya] refused to call on [Nova] when we made hand shadows, even though [Nova] was the only one with her hand raised.

Following a play period involving [names of children], it was clean up time. [Nova] had not felt well so she lay down and fell asleep. The kids would not clean up without her. We discussed how she didn't feel well and since she was so sound asleep, let's do her part for her. They were very insensitive, accused her of "faking" and tried to make noise to wake her. They left things for her to do when she woke up and complained as they completed clean-up.

Several meetings with teachers were devoted to discussing both their written and verbal descriptions of skill and interactional levels of their children. The following is a list of issues and concerns which summarized the teacher assessments (this is a condensed form of each teacher's classroom handouts).

Awareness program

Below are some issues and concerns which may possibly be underlying some of the interactions of classroom members.

- Acceptance of differences (typical/special children).
- Power issues (manipulation as well).
- Self-image concerns.
- Authority issues.
- Self-control.
- Need for assertiveness and identification of wants and needs.

- Need for acceptance.
- Supportiveness within the group (this means warmth, caring, genuineness).
- Competition issues.
- Expression and identification of feelings.
- Individual and group decision making/problem solving.
- Choosing from several alternatives.
- Criticism/nonsupport of group members.
- Possession of materials/sharing.
- Home/family concerns.
- Fears of risking/fear of new things.
- Problem solving.

Questions to ask students or to recognize in student interactions:
- How do you feel? What made you feel that way?
- Do you feel people listened to you? Who did in particular?
- Do you really share your feelings or are you screening them before you talk about them?
- Do you worry about talking too much? Saying too little?
- Do you have any strong feelings that were different from those of the group? Do you express those feelings? What happens when you do?
- Are you being treated the way you want to be treated?
- Who do you like to listen to?

One of the major concerns of the teachers was the integration of special and typical children in the development of an affective education program. As one teacher reflected,

> Aside from looking at kids' individual needs and looking at the group's needs and looking at when are optional times...you also want to make sure you're integrating kids to the degree that they can be integrated, and that's tricky sometimes...because the age groups that we have are not homogeneous.... While we [could] split the typical kids to teach more optimally, we [don't] want to segregate the special kids.

We realized that often the special children cannot join the planned activities as participants. However, many of these children can gain in awareness through exposure to a group of children by being observers in a group activity. For one teacher,

> One day a week we have a signing meeting for kids to all learn how to sign things, because we have two kids in the room who sign, and we thought it was important for the kids to learn the signs, and also that the kids respect it as a good way to communicate.

When this teacher was asked if all of the special children were integrated with typical kids at meeting times, she stated no.

We don't have [Charlie] at meeting because he really doesn't have either the ability to sit at meeting for that long, and he wouldn't profit from it and understand what was going on, but [Mark] is there and [Dawn] is there, and both of them we've found need a lot of extra support...and also we wanted to have time during the day, during the week where [Mark] would shine.... Kids are finding out that there are signs, and he gets excited by it, and he's definitely very grateful for that time.... They're walking up to him and saying, "sign this," "sign that," and they talk to him a lot more, and it's really promoted a lot more friendship between the kids and [Mark].

This teacher also decided that:

There are two special kids that are at the meeting; we do look at them as really having different goals for being at that meeting.

So in regard to the integration issue, we decided to structure the children's groups by incorporating most of the special children. It was felt that they could best profit from watching other children during the program sessions. We would insure that an adult was present for those children to guide them through the group activities and to aid them in being as involved as possible with the other children. For example, one child (Mark) was not a verbally communicative child. His teacher's goals were to get him to tolerate his peers, since he had little awareness of other children. During program planning meetings, the goals for his participation were to encourage nonverbal expressions of feeling and to pair him with a typical child using activities he enjoyed (such as drawing) in order to get him more involved with other children. In addition, the typical children's acceptance of and respect for special children's needs was a goal throughout the program.

PAST INTERVENTIONS

Discussions of the teachers' past efforts to handle affective classroom and personal issues was included in order to better plan program activities and goals. The teachers had handled many of the interactional and individual problems of the children in a variety of ways. Meeting times were scheduled daily so that children could learn the ground rules.

What it was a lot in the beginning of the year was establishing schedules and rules and routine for our class.... So we do a lot of setting up rules and talking about what our day was going to be like and what we were going to be doing, and what kinds of expectations the teachers had for the kids, what kinds of expectations the kids had. A lot of just getting to share interests, and the other thing that we did was introduce materials in the room, how it was going to be used...introduction to routine...(also one meeting a week was devoted to "Show and Tell"). The kids listen to each other and are really interested in each other and not always just listening to teachers, so that's been really nice too.... [Also] we are doing dramatic kinds of things, like using bodies to express emotion and not problem solving or role playing, but just using your body and your wits to show different expressions and feelings, and again one of the reasons we've done that has been to integrate the other kids, the special kids, because it's something that they can do.

Meeting times were a place were children were encouraged to interact with each other and to discover positive experiences and emotions, not only related to self, but concerning other children as well.

In one of the classrooms, the lead teacher tried to help the students develop a sense of responsibility towards others through a problem-solving process.

A lot of kids had come up to me with complaints about "this person is knocking this down," "this person is using all of the blocks"; and it just got to the point where I said, "There are this many complaints and it looks like something we should look at and try to define more clearly how people are going to be acting." But they went along with it very easily.... There had clearly been some problems, and though none of the kids stated it, they clearly recognized that something had to be worked out.... [They did this] by setting up a process where one by one we defined what the problems were and thought of rules that...would govern kids' behaviors.... I think most of them did [understand that process]. There are some kids who have more of a difficult time relating to a group process because they are still egocentric, but for the most part I think kids did take part in the process.

On the whole, the teachers felt very positive about the children's capacity to learn about expressing feelings appropriately and to develop problem-solving skills. There were areas of concern which seemed to be on-going problems for individual children as well as for the class as a whole (for example, the development of cliques; competition issues). The teachers felt that a more structured and individualized program would best fit their students' needs—1 day a week for 30 minutes for one classroom and 2 days a week for approximately 45 minutes in the other room.

THE FACILITATOR

The two lead teachers agreed to lead the groups together during the week, with my aid as program consultant. Our goal was to share planning and structuring the group's activities, as well as to facilitate the children's responses within the framework of the program objectives. My belief, shared with these teachers, was that they had within them the ability to process group, as well as individual, dynamics and to teach interactional skills to their students. Our end goal for this program was for me to phase out my role as consultant in program planning with the teachers. In fact, as a result of scheduling difficulties in one of the classrooms during the latter part of the year, I was only able to act as a consultant. This teacher was still able to depend upon my support and resource help and yet feel competent to continue with the program as a group leader.

For a facilitator in an awareness program, the goal is to focus upon what is happening in terms of dynamics, both within the group as a whole and in individual students. The difficulty here is in not losing sight of either of the two concerns. This task was made easier by the fact that two group leaders were available; both could feel comfortable sharing participant/leader/observer roles at different times within the meeting.

Using both verbal and nonverbal (e.g., facial expression, body attitude) information presented by students during the sessions, the facilitators tried to observe and explore both the content (the stated meanings) and the process (the underlying issues, the nonverbal messages) of the group's presentation during the sessions. The objective for the group leaders was to clarify what the students said and begin to check back consistently (through statements and questions) to see if individual children were understood by both the facilitators and the group. Peer interactions were encouraged and praised whenever they occurred. Another dimension of the facilitators' role was to summarize what happened during the session at the end of the allotted time and ask for student questions or comments. This helped to draw together whatever conclusions or learning the students had experienced during the meeting.

At first, the teachers felt uncomfortable with such a large share of the group leadership role during those sessions with the children. It was helpful and positively encouraging to share perceptions of the group's process and behavior with the consultant. Both the teachers and I were able to see how we as group leaders affected the group's learning and expression, both positively and negatively. We discovered this through our discussions of how we engaged the attention of, and responded to, the students. We wished the students to gain a better perception of how their behavior with others was related to certain consequences (such as expressions of feelings or positive or negative actions on others' parts). We also hoped to learn whether the way we stated expectations or feelings would have an impact upon the students, in the regular classroom setting, as well as during the program meetings.

In accordance with the literature, all of us made efforts to feed information back to each other concerning our processing skills. Amidon and Flanders (1971) report that, in many of their studies, student teachers who were taught interaction analysis skills were found to (a) take more time to accept and use student ideas, (b) encourage a greater amount of pupil-initiated talk, (c) use less criticism, (d) use less direction, (e) be more accepting and encouraging in response to student ideas, and (f) have a more generally indirect teaching style. When a second person participated in verbal feedback (Morse, Kipilka, & Davis, 1970), self-approval techniques were found to be more effective. In addition, Carkhuff (1969) reasoned that practice and feedback from a competent trainer were requisite to the learning of specific humanistic teacher behaviors.

PLAN IMPLEMENTATION

The lead teachers and I decided to use resource material from the Jowonio library as well as my own references (see Partial Resource Bibliography). As the program continued, we decided to expand our sessions to include such materials as transactional analysis for the children's activities and more body-oriented awareness exercises. For these ideas and materials, the resource teacher in the school was also helpful. Even browsing in a large bookstore near the university area produced some materials. For information concerning family histories, both the teachers and the parent worker provided invaluable comments. The lead teachers and I were careful to share some of our decisions and material regarding the program planning with their classroom student teachers.

Both classroom teachers decided upon a framework to cover several months' program planning. This structure was very similar: an initial focus on Self-Awareness (self-image and identification of feelings), moving to Group Awareness activities, which would, we hoped, lead to topics of Fostering Cooperation and Group Interactions.

Individual as well as overall group exercises were devised during our planning meetings. For instance, in one of the classrooms, many of the children had great difficulty with expressing themselves and attending within the confines of a group task. Yet other children in that same class were verbally fluent and very responsive to group activities. Pairing high- and low-functioning children for specific activities became a viable method of solving the difficulty of unequal levels of response abilities. In the planning sessions, many hours were spent in initially discussing individual needs, not just particularly for the special children, but for every child. The blending of those individual and group goals into viable activities came more easily after we reached an understanding of children's functioning. The teachers were often very clear about their expectations for each of their students; this familiarity with a personal, family, and social history was crucial to the program's development. They were able to keep in focus individual problems as well as group issues to an extent which often was remarkably perceptive. Our combined knowledge of appropriate child behavior was also important in planning activities: to expect children who are accomplishing only parallel play with peers to quickly learn to interact in a more sophisticated way, in terms of participating in group decision-making and cooperative activities, was unrealistic. We kept a record of what activity we planned to do; how we were going to divide up the group (e.g., individually; with partners); whether the task required different goals for some students (e.g., for some who couldn't draw, to be guided through a drawing activity); and what roles we would take within the group (e.g., who would introduce the activity or topic, whether we would summarize what was accomplished during the session).

In one of the classrooms, both student teachers were able to cofacilitate at least one session with me. Their consistent participation was precluded by the need of several of the special children for one-to-one attention. It was felt they could more profitably interact with an adult in an individualized situation, rather than in the awareness program.

Both teachers introduced the program to the children by discussing the special nature of the time set aside for the meetings. The lead teachers explained that is was important for children to get to know themselves and the other children in their class better, and also that we as teachers felt this was a good time to try to understand children better. With the lead teachers, I explored the "Here and Now" (present-oriented) focus of the program and what was meant by focusing on content and process in children's interactions—in short, to try to help the teachers develop their analysis skills and to explore interpersonal dynamics within the group context.

Many of the exercises and activities which we developed used newsprint sheets and crayons. Other materials included puppets, blackboard, dittos, and drawing paper. The following is a partial list of our program content.

- Drawing a picture of what each child could do best (in school or at home), and sharing the drawings and comments with the group.
- Drawing a picture of what each child believed he or she could use some help with (from an adult or child) in terms of school or home activities, and sharing the drawings with the group.
- Drawing different expressions on face models for different situations and feelings; then acting out, with partners, some of the situations and stating how they would feel.
- Reading the "Warm Fuzzy"* story in *T.A. for Tots* (Freed, 1979) and drawing pictures of how each child would feel if he or she was a child from that story.
- Developing a large oak tag chart, on which children gave "warm fuzzies" to someone else in the classroom. Each child would be responsible for writing when they received a "warm fuzzy" and why they think they deserved it.
- Drawing self-portraits and sharing them with the group.
- Interviewing other children using a dittoed form (e.g., what is your favorite color or thing to learn about; what are you best at; what are some things you enjoy doing; what makes you mad) and compiling a "Newspaper" on a ditto with summaries of the children's interviews to hand out to the class.
- Having the children divide into partners and blindfold one of each pair; the other child leads the blindfolded one around the room. At the close of the activity, when all have participated, discuss the issue of trust.

---

*"Warm fuzzies" are the good feelings you get when someone does something nice for you.

- Role playing various situations using puppets or the children themselves. The situations included needing and giving help to others in a variety of situations (from opening lunchboxes to helping another child with a difficult math problem); losing one's temper and the consequences of that (hurting another child physically or emotionally); competition problems of group members which arise out of team game playing and discussions of feelings and alternatives.
- Brainstorming solutions to problems other children have, both at school and home (e.g., when feelings of frustration, disappointment, or anger arise).
- Generating a list of things which made the children feel good and placing the items on newsprint; then acting out some of these nice activities.
- Drawing pictures of the children's families and discussing what things each child likes to do with family members and what things the children don't enjoy as much within the family structure (e.g., taking care of infant siblings, performing chores); asking children to find more appropriate ways of adjusting to family life.

PLAN EVALUATION

Weekly meetings with the lead teachers to discuss how each session progressed were scheduled for at least an hour. These sessions were also a time for us to try to evaluate what was most effective in terms of statements to, or activities with, the class. We shared our perceptions of how students reacted to the exercises and discussions, what was said at meetings, which children participated the most and least and why that might be so, and how we might improve our presentation for the next session.

Often meetings did not run as smoothly as we had planned. We hadn't taken individual problems or responses into account as much as we might have, and some children felt hurt or angry when difficult issues (such as competition, jealousy, or cliques) were mentioned. Many times there was not enough time left at the end of the session to fully process children's feelings about more complex problem-solving or emotional issues. The teachers or I would then try to work out the unresolved feelings of that child individually or the next time the group met, with the help of individual group members. Another difficulty was with scheduling; particularly during the holidays and at the end of the year, it was difficult to meet regularly. Special programs, trips, and illness were the main impediments to a regular schedule. In addition, the very complex issues of failure, competition, anxiety, and team building remained extremely difficult to attempt to discuss or process with the children as a group.

The lead teachers were asked to evaluate the program's effectiveness. One teacher stated, "I think that it's been real successful; we've done a lot of difficult kinds of things." She continued to reflect on the program.

I think I've been very, very influenced in particular by [Susan—one of the student teachers in her classroom] and maybe you about how to get across different ideas and help kids problem-solve more and actually even what should be the focus of meetings. And it's kind of interesting because before I came to Jowonio I think maybe I have focused as much on kids, by helping kids problem-solve, help the kids identify their feelings; but I never thought about doing it at a meeting. I never thought about formally setting up any program; it was just something that naturally worked into the day; that when things happen you talk about them, that the staff who are available talks about them either in groups or individually.... I think in some ways it's good because it makes you look at the problems and it makes you not ignore them, and that's good. And in some ways it's bad because I think that dealing with things when they happen is preferable and I also think that things can become forced.... I think that's one thing that we've found is that the level of under-standing the kids have and what they can verbalize is not what adults...and other children verbalize, and it's hard to know what you can expect. But I guess I do like it and I'm glad I did it this year because it did force me to look at it a little more closely, a little more systematically. I think that I've gotten more ideas of how to do things, that there are a number of ways to introduce ideas...and if one thing doesn't work, you don't stop doing it, you try a dif-ferent way. But what I'm still not sure of is what level to expect with the kids and how to pull some things from some kids and not from others and how to individualize that.... But just bringing the kids together and asking them to help decide...how a problem should be solved or how something should be run was very successful, almost always successful. Also helping the kids to identify good things, I think, identify happy times and happy feelings, was pretty successful and it was something that I don't think we do focus on enough in general.

The other lead teacher commented:

I would say that some of the most helpful have been...group problem-solving times that have happened and also some of the meetings that have focused on kids' listening skills. I think they've gotten a lot over the year of just what the rules are for listening to someone else and responding. And in fact I find the kids reminding other kids, "Now, raise your hand," "Wait your turn!" "You're butting in," whatever.... One of the ones that I remember that was really good was one the kids brought up on friends, and it was a good discus-sion on problems kids have about friends they didn't have or what their friendships were like out of school. A couple of others that I remember as be-ing helpful were the times that we talked of things that people were best at. The self-concept nature of the meetings has been helpful. I feel like there are a number of kids in that room with not very good self-concepts, and I feel like they've definitely improved over the year, and I feel like meeting has been helpful in that.... I remember a really good [meeting] was the day we drew pictures on things you were good at. Kids obviously liked it, did a good job. I think in some ways it's hard to say that there's a lot of improvement in self-concepts directly tied to meeting, because the self-concepts move so slowly in terms of how much progress is made with them.... But I feel like it's been a real development in the goals we've been working on.

The children had this to say about the program meetings:

Like a big group gathers up to talk...well, [about] problems like [Nova] and me are going to have the same problem pretty soon. My mother's going to have a baby and her mother is going to have a baby.

Well, sometimes meetings are like sit down and talk things. And we talk about your feelings, what other kids do.... I love em.... Now that I have someone to sit down and talk to, I feel good.... We could tell your feelings, and maybe you'll find someone to help you. That's what's good about it.

[They're] fun. We play games...twenty questions and role playing. I would just rather have it the way we have it.

It's like a good time and we get to tell out all our stuff...if we're happy or sad or what's going on around us.

Meetings with you [consultant] are different. They're more exciting...because you have us do things like draw pictures, and I like to draw pictures.... Well, sometimes I'd like to go out and find some animals to bring back and some other things too...talk about them, everybody get one thing and then we'd tell everybody what we know about that one thing.

Future program planning should include a pre- and postanalysis of the program's effectiveness. We used the Group Behavior Surveys, data on the children's understanding of different emotions, and sociogramic information concerning the most popular and least liked students to provide teachers with valuable information as a guide to program planning. By administering these surveys and questionnaires after the program's end, the children's progress could be measured. Further research into the effectiveness of this type of program is strongly recommended.

This affective education program was a successful one from many points of view: the students', teachers', and consultants'. The lead teachers' remarkable energy for and commitment to program planning and implementation attests not only to the uniqueness of Jowonio as a teaching facility, but to the individual lead teachers' skills. The program proved to be enjoyable, stimulating, and educational—certainly ample reward for our efforts.

REFERENCES

Amidon, E., & Flanders, N. *The role of the teacher in the classroom: A manual for understanding and improving teacher classroom behavior.* Minneapolis: Association for Productive Teaching, 1971.

Bissell, H., & Palomares, U. *Methods in human development.* La Mesa, Calif.: Human Development Training Institute, 1972.

Carkhuff, R.R. *Helping and human relations* (Vol. 1). New York: Holt, Rinehart & Winston, 1969.

Freed, A. *T.A. for tots.* Sacramento, Calif.: Jalmar Press, 1979.

Hunter, C.P. An interpersonal relations and group process approach to affective education for young children. *Journal of School Psychology,* 1977, *15,* 141-151.

Morse, K., Kipilka, M., & Davis, O., Jr. *Effects of different types of supervising feedback on teachers candidates development of refocusing behaviors.* Report series No. 48. Austin: The University of Texas, The Research and Development Center for Teacher Education, 1970.

Simon, S.B., Howe, L.W., & Kirschenbaum, H. *Values clarification: A handbook for practical strategies for teachers and students.* New York: Hart, 1972.

PARTIAL RESOURCE BIBLIOGRAPHY
(Used in Awareness Program)

Gram, R.K., & Guest, P.M. *Activities for developing positive awareness (Grades K-7).* St. Louis: Miliken, 1977.

Kirschenbaum, H. *Advanced values clarification: A handbook for trainers, counselors, and experienced teachers.* LaJolla, Calif.: University Associates, 1977.

Palomares, U. *Magic circle books.* LaMesa, Calif.: Human Development Training Institute, 1975.

Satir, V. *Peoplemaking.* Palo Alto, Calif.: Science and Behavior Books, Inc., 1972.

Simon, Howe, & Kirschenbaum, 1972. See above.

APPENDIX A

Setting Up an Awareness Program

1. *Defining Goals*

   What can you identify as your main concerns for setting up a program? Who can you target as your main focus—group problems or individual ones? Both?
   - For the Teacher: One goal could be to get to understand the students in other ways (emotional, familial, etc.) or in other perspectives.
   - For the Student: One goal could be to get to know themselves and the other students better.

2. *Problem Definition*

   On what issues would you like to work? Which students can or can't successfully and/or effectively handle each issue at present?
   - For the Special Students: What special needs/concerns do they have, above and beyond those of the typical students? Presently how are they handling these problems?

3. *Past Interventions*

   How have these main issues or problems been handled to date? Did you have time to discuss/evaluate these conflicts with resource teachers or others? Did you discuss them with the student? Did you ignore the conflicts? How did you resolve them successfully?

4. *The Facilitator*

   The teacher role:
   - Facilitator: To focus on both what is happening within the group and the individual (but not to lose sight of either group or individual goals).

- Focus: Look at both the content (what is said by students; the stated meanings) and the process (the underlying issues, the nonverbal communication) during the program times.
- Use: The verbal and nonverbal information presented by students during the program times; remain in the "Here and Now."
- Clarify: What the students say and try to consistently check back to see if the other students (and you) understand.
- Summarize: At the end of the program time just what has occurred and ask if there are any questions or comments.

5. *Plan Implementation*
- Resources: From what resources (people or materials) can you ask for information or help (school psychologists, resource teachers, catalogs, etc.) in your school? In the community? Is there an education library nearby that specializes in source materials?
- Search for Alternatives: What alternatives can you think of to try to solve some of the problems?
  - Can you locate materials (values clarification exercises, successful role play instructions from books, etc.) to use? (Sometimes crayons, paper, and newsprint will do well.)
  - Can you brainstorm ideas for strategies of handling each issue? Think of role plays, drawing exercises, discussion topics, and small-group activities.
  - Work on a few weeks/months of planning at a time so that you can change your activities to better meet the group or individual needs.

6. *Plan Evaluation*

Try to sit down with a resource person or another teacher regularly (preferably on a weekly basis) to discuss how the program went and try to evaluate what was effective with the students and what wasn't. How did the students react to discussions? What did they comment about? Who takes most of the responsibility for talking? The least? How can you get more people to participate next time? Try to be flexible about changing your list of goals and problem areas to work on if you see that other needs or conflicts arise.

APPENDIX B

Group Behavior Survey

Name: _____

Date: _____

Please answer the following questions with the first names only of any group members who best fit the description of behavior(s). Base your answers on interactions within the group in the school and classroom.
1. Which members can most easily influence others to change their opinions?
2. Which are least able to influence others to change their opinions?
3. Which have clashed most sharply with others in the group?
4. Which are most highly accepted by the group?
5. Which are most ready to support members of the group?
6. Which try to keep themselves in the limelight?

7. Which are most likely to put personal goals above group goals?
8. Which have most often introduced topics not directly related to the group tasks?
9. Which have shown the greatest desire to accomplish something?
10. Which have wanted to avoid conflict in group discussions?
11. Which tend to withdraw from active discussion when strong differences begin to appear?
12. Which have sought to help in the resolution of differences between others?
13. Which have wanted the group to be warm, friendly, and comfortable?
14. Which have competed most with others?
15. Which have done most to keep the group lively?
16. Which would you choose to work with?
17. Which have formed cliques?
18. With which have you interacted least?

Using whatever available space is needed, please write down whatever incident most comprehensively answers the question. Thank you very much for your time and cooperation!

1. Describe a situation in which the class members participated in a way you would categorize as positive and supportive (sharing, aware, encouraging, etc.).
2. Describe a situation in which the class members participated in a way you would categorize as negative and destructive (unhelpful, holding back, tense).

8
The Use of Music as an Integral Part of a Therapeutic Classroom

Lyle Chastain

When group music sessions are recommended as a component of an educational program, teachers often say "I'm not a good enough musician" or "I'm not trained in that area" or "We need a specialist to do that." Actually, a teacher does not have to be a musician or a specialist in music therapy in order to use music as a teaching medium. It is much more important that a teacher be a good observer of behavior, be flexible, and be willing to experiment with new approaches to learning.

Basically, the same kinds of things can be taught during music time that are taught during the rest of the day. Music is simply a different medium to use in working on various skills such as positive social interaction, constructive group experiences, fine and gross motor skills, and pre-academic skills such as color, letter, and number identification.

We have found music to be an effective intervention medium for working on such varied skills as:

- Learning names of body parts;
- Enjoying touching and being touched;
- Developing imitation skills;
- Following directions;
- Attending to tasks for extended periods of time;
- Tolerating a group setting;
- Cooperating in a group setting;
- Enjoying group activities;
- Using appropriate and spontaneous speech;
- Learning to help or tolerate help from others.

In this chapter, I would like to describe some of the ideas concerning the use of music in the classroom that we discovered while trying to design a music program for a small group of autistic-type children.*

Our music program began in a small, self-contained classroom for severely multiply handicapped, autistic-type children. There were eight children ranging in age from 4 to 10 in the class. Each child had an individual teacher who was a graduate student in special education. The class met daily from 9:00 to 11:30, and each child had a totally individualized program based on his or her unique combination of needs. Since most of the teaching was done on a one-to-one basis, our daily music session was originally one of the few times the children were all together in a group.

Most of the children participated in afternoon public school-based programs, where they had a larger teacher-child ratio and where the children had the opportunity to be exposed to more "normal" peer models. In the process of meeting with the teachers from the afternoon classrooms and other teachers who taught classrooms with very different populations of children, we also discovered how very adaptable the basic music program was.

When our music program began in September, 1974, it might best have been described as pure chaos. Two of our eight children refused to sit in the circle. They screamed and fought to get away from the group. The other six children appeared to be totally unaware of anything that was going on. Despite this inauspicious beginning, we gathered our teachers and children together every day for 20 minutes of music time, in the belief that eventually something would come of it if we kept at it long enough. Surprisingly, it was not nearly as hopeless as it had seemed. Within 2 weeks the children who were so resistant began to stay in the group, and the other six children began to show signs of interest in what was going on.

Most of the concepts and procedures we now use were learned directly from the children—from observing their reactions and responses to the things we tried. In other words, we added, subtracted, and modified various songs as a result of the children's behavior rather than modifying the children's behavior to fit precisely into our preconceived ideas of how they should respond. This is not to say that we did not have specific goals in mind for each song; rather, we designed our goals so that there was considerable flexibility in the way each song was used.

For example, one day while singing the "Name Song" (described in detail later in the chapter), Ken was happily swaying back and forth in the center of the circle during his turn. Suddenly he went up to another child, Greg, and held out his hand as if to invite Greg to join him. This was the first time to our knowledge that Ken had initiated any peer interaction. Although the song was designed for each child to participate *one at a time,* the group leader changed some of the words and immediately incorporated Greg into the activity. (Exactly how this

---

* For more information, see L.D. Chastain, *A handbook on the use of songs to teach autistic and other severely handicapped children.* Goodhue, Minn.: White Oak Press, 1979.

was done will be described later.) This spontaneous action on Ken's part also led to the realization that some of the group was ready for songs where two children could participate together, and one of the teachers came up with the song "Two by Two," which will also be described later.

Getting up the courage to attempt a live music session in the classroom is probably the most difficult aspect of the entire procedure. Once you muster the courage, the rest of it is relatively simple.

The instrument we use for group music sessions is the autoharp. It is an extremely easy instrument to play—you push a button with one hand and strum across the strings with the other. It requires no special musical skills. The chord names are printed on the buttons and, when you push the button, felt dampers block out all the strings you don't want to sound. All you have to do is push the right button and you *can't* get a wrong note! To make it even simpler, most children's songs have only three chords in them, so you only have to learn to use a total of three buttons!

Once you have mastered the simple techniques involved in playing the autoharp, you can lead live music sessions and avoid all the problems involved with records, including songs that are too fast for your group, songs that are too slow, activities that are too difficult, and words that are not meaningful for your particular population. You can create your own pace and have total control over the skill level required to participate. You are also free to make the words or activities relevant to the specific children in your classroom. As your children change and their abilities change, you can adapt your songs accordingly. With this kind of flexibility, music time can become a real teaching experience for the entire class.

There are many different kinds of songs that can be used during music sessions, each focusing on specific developmental areas. We have arbitrarily grouped songs into categories.

- Individual songs—These songs are usually used at the beginning of the music session to give each child an opportunity to receive positive attention for an action performed in the center of the music circle.
- Group activity songs—These are usually "stand up songs" where the group is following directions which involve various gross motor activities. These very active songs are usually interspersed with songs where the group is seated. This way the music leader has control over the activity level of the group.
- Social interaction songs—In these songs two or more children are required to participate together in a specific activity. Individual songs are also interspersed with group songs so the children alternate between active participation and learning to enjoy watching others participate.
- Pre-academic songs—These songs involve the use of colors, shapes, instruments, letters, name tags, and fundamental concepts.
- Passing songs—These songs help develop social skills such as waiting for turns and name identification. Some require fine motor or gross motor skills.

- Quiet songs—These songs are used to end the music sessions. They help prepare for transition and are used to help facilitate teacher-child interaction and attending skills.

The next section of this chapter details one specific song in each category.

INDIVIDUAL SONGS

If the group is small enough, it is helpful to begin each music session with a song that identifies each individual child and gives each child an opportunity to do something special. If the group is too large, it is possible to adapt most songs so that two children at a time can participate.

The following is a rather detailed description of the "Name Song," a song we often use to start our music sessions. It illustrates some typical objectives, procedures, and ways to vary the songs to accommodate growth in the children. Since the group of children in our classroom were multiply handicapped and most were nonverbal, we began with a very simple version of this song.

Almost everyone is acquainted with some variation of a song that is sung to the tune of "Where is Thumbkin?" Our version is as follows:

Where is Kenny?
Where is Kenny?
Here I am.
Here I am.
How are you this morning?
Very well I thank you.
Please sit down.
Please sit down.

The children and teachers sit in a circle. Each child stands up when his or her name is sung and then sits down at the end of the verse. Often, in the beginning, the teachers must prompt or even totally assist each child in getting up, staying in the circle once standing up, and sitting back down.

During each child's individual time, the other children sing (if possible), clap their hands, and with teacher assistance, anticipate their turn and follow the actions of other children. The initial objectives for this song include:

- The child remains in the group situation during the song.
- The child shows recognition of his name.
- The child stands unassisted when his name is sung.
- The child stands in the center of the circle during his verse.
- The child sits down when asked.
- The child attends to what is happening around him.

When a child begins to show recognition of his name and shows some recognition that it is his turn to participate (for instance, looks at the song leader, smiles, or changes posture or facial expression when his name is sung), we assume that he is ready for less direct assistance. At this point, the teacher might place his hands on the child in the way previously used to get the child up, but this time let the child use more of his own body strength to get up. Later, a touch on the shoulder might be sufficient. This change is gradual, depending on the child.

If a child has a tendency to leave the group, the teacher can hold her hands and swing them back and forth while the child's name is sung. When the child begins to show less desire to leave the circle, the teacher can hold only one hand. Then, keeping in mind the goal of having the child stay in the circle, the teacher can let go *just before* the child is to sit down. In case the child begins to leave the circle, a touch can indicate that it is time to sit down, not that she had been unsuccessful in staying in the circle.

The same kind of techniques can be applied to sitting down—first, total assistance, then a touch to help the child, then verbal and visual cues with no physical contact, then only verbal cues, and finally the child needs only the words to the song in order to participate independently. The teacher tries to always be prepared for the child to respond independently instead of getting into the habit of seating the child automatically after each turn.

Variations

When a child is standing and spontaneously begins to move his or her body or jump or sway to the music, a second verse can be added. This verse can be tailor-made to fit the physical abilities of any individual child. Instead of singing "Please sit down" at the end of the verse, the group can sing,

- Dance for us, or
- Sway for us, or
- Jump for us, or
- Turn for us.

and so on. The second verse continues:

Kenny's dancing [turning, jumping, etc.].
Kenny's dancing.
Good for you.
Good for you.
How are you this morning?
Very well I thank you.
Please sit down.
Please sit down.

Once these variations are added, new goals become possible.

- The child can participate positively on his or her own to gain attention from the teachers and other children.
- The child is able to follow more complex directions in front of the group.
- The child chooses the way he or she wishes to perform for the group.

Procedures

When the child shows that she can stand during her verse, the teacher can often help her sway back and forth and then slowly remove this active guidance, leaving the child to sway independently. Since there is apt to be a wide variety of abilities in any group, the song leader and other teachers should be prepared to alter the second verse for each child, always keeping in mind that the child is progressing toward a new stage of development. If a child is swaying back and forth alone, she might be able to jump or turn around if asked. If she does, she could then, at a later date, make a choice between jumping or swaying. The teacher must always be thinking ahead to new goals and never assume the child has reached some ultimate performance level.

Other Variations

On occasions when a child's behavior is "inappropriate," and he is screaming or refusing to stand up on a particular day, these actions can sometimes be incorporated into the song. The action then automatically becomes "appropriate," and the child is participating, even though the behavior might appear to be unacceptable in other circumstances. For example, if a child decides he doesn't want to stand up and hides his face in his hands, you can sing:

Ken's hiding.
Ken's hiding.
Good for you.
Good for you.
How are you this morning?
Very shy I thank you,
Please sit still,
Please sit still.

An occasional verse of this sort when the situation arises can be very successful. Using this technique, the child is not allowed to remove himself from the group, but instead, has engaged in the behavior of his choice and remained within the group setting.

If a child is really enjoying his turn, a third verse can quickly be added by changing "Please sit down" to "Dance [jump, sway, etc.] some more." This additional verse is also useful if a child had a slow start and is just getting into his activity as the second verse ends.

If a child spontaneously chooses another child or teacher (as was described earlier), this initiation of social interaction is spontaneously incorporated into the song by singing:

Kenny's dancing.
Greg is dancing.
Good for them.
Good for them.
How are you this morning?
Very well I thank you.
Dance some more.
Dance some more.

Spontaneous improvisation capitalizing on opportunities presented by the children is very important to the successful use of this song.

GROUP ACTIVITY SONGS

Songs in this category include songs that emphasize group participation, knowledge of body parts, direction following, and gross motor skills. One song we use frequently which can be sung to any simple melody helps teach names of body parts. The words are as follows:

If you know where your hands are clap them,
If you know where your hands are clap them,
If you know where your hands are clap them,
Clap your hands.

There is no end to the variety of verses you can make up using this simple format. Some of the children's favorites include:
- If you know where your nose is wiggle it.
- If you know where your feet are stand on them.
- If you know where you stomach is rub it.

You can also vary the song to include verses such as: "If you know where Matthew is, point to him."

The initial objectives of this song include:
- The child listens to the song and focuses attention on the specific action requested.
- The child recognizes the body parts mentioned in the song and can perform the actions independently.

When a song such as this is being sung, the music leader can often pick up an action that a child is already doing and sing about it (i.e., "If you know where your head is, shake it"). When this is done, the leader can sign, "If you know where your head is, shake it"—and add in a speaking voice,"like Pat," bringing the attention of the group to the specific child's behavior.

Verbal children may be encouraged to give suggestions for other verses. Nonverbal children often can make choices by demonstrating an action to the group, thereby having the opportunity to initiate an action that the entire group will follow. This leads to additional objectives such as:

- The child uses his or her imagination to create new actions or chooses preferred actions.
- The child learns to imitate the actions of a peer.

SOCIAL INTERACTION SONGS

As a result of a child's attempt to involve another child in a dancing activity, we came up with a very simple song which we call "Two by Two." The words are sung to the tune "Skip to My Lou" and are as follows.

Kenny and Greg two by two,
Kenny and Greg two by two,
Kenny and Greg two by two,
Skip to my lou my darling.

The objectives are similar to those of the "Name Song," with the addition of:

- A child participates in a dance situation with another child—first parallel dancing, and later dancing while holding hands with another child.
- A child chooses another child with whom he or she wishes to dance.
- A child responds to being chosen by another child.

It is also possible to sing about three by three or four by four by simply slowing down the section of the song where the children's names are sung. It can become quite a tongue twister to sing, for example, "Ken, Greg, Suzie, and Matthew, four by four"—but it can be done!

Other ways the children enjoy varying this song include singing "march to my lou" or "jump to my lou" instead of "skip to my lou." This way each pair or group of children can individualize their participation.

PRE-ACADEMIC SONGS

One of the songs we often use is "Old McDonald." We use a big wooden barn and wooden farm animals to provide the children with the opportunity to actively participate in the song as well as sing it.

When the song is first introduced, the teacher usually hands out one animal to each child. After the song becomes familiar, a variety of procedures can be introduced.

- Children can come up individually and select an animal.
- Children can name the animals they want, and one of the children from the group can pass out the animals.
- The teacher can have children name animals that start with certain letters ("who wants an animal that begins with C?" "What animal name begins with C?") The children then get animals they name.

Variations like these can be geared to the specific skill level of the classroom.

When the song is sung, each child brings the animal he or she has to the center of the circle and places it in the barn when the group is singing about that animal.

Objectives for this song can be extremely varied, depending on the children's skills. They can include:

- The child holds on to the toy animal.
- The child is able to make a choice as to which animal he or she would prefer to hold.
- The child learns the names of the animals.
- The child has the opportunity to participate in a group activity.
- The child learns to follow directions and attends to his or her turn.
- The child learns first letter sounds.
- The child learns to participate independently in a group activity.

Putting away the barn and the animals after the song can also provide an opportunity to work on direction following, turn taking, and cooperation.

PASSING SONGS

These songs usually involve the children sharing various materials with each other. We usually sing this song to the tune of "Farmer in the Dell." The words are as follows.

Oh, Johnny has the car.
Oh, Johnny has the car.
Hi Ho the Derry-O,
Oh Johnny has the car.

He gives the car to Kelly.
He gives the car to Kelly.
Hi Ho the Derry-O,
He gives the car to Kelly.

Now Kelly has the car.
Now Kelly has the car...

and so on around the circle. Although this seems like a very simple procedure, it incorporates many concepts in social development.

Various objects can be used for this song. For example, if a child has a fondness for teddy bears, he can get the favorite teddy bear and share it during the song. If one child has difficulty in being separated from a favorite possession (a specific toy car, a blanket, etc.), her possession can be used during this song. If it is used *after* the child is familiar with the song and its actions, the child will be aware that the favored possession will go around the circle and will *return to him*. This song can be very helpful during the early stages of a program designed to help a child separate from a most favored possession.

If a specific object is used during a lesson one day, it can be passed during the song to add extra reinforcement to that day's lesson. This can be anything from a shoe to a specific letter of the alphabet. It is also possible to use a ball and roll it from child to child across the circle. This is a more complex activity and is especially fun for more advanced children. The objectives for this song include:

- The child recognizes his or her name and the names of the other children in the group.
- The child focuses attention on a specific object in his or her possession.
- The child develops the necessary physical dexterity involved in receiving, holding, rolling, throwing, or passing an object.
- The child learns to accept the necessary physical contact involved in exchanging an object with another person.
- If a child has a specific attachment to an object, he or she learns to accept separation from it.
- A child learns to allow others to touch, hold, or play with a most favored possession.
- A child learns to anticipate his or her turn and to reach out to another child physically.

QUIET SONGS

Quiet songs such as "Twinkle, Twinkle, Little Star," and "You Are My Sunshine" are used at the end of each music session. Folk songs or popular songs that the children particularly like can also be used. This time provides an opportunity for a close, quiet relationship for the students and teachers. It also creates a quiet setting for transition into the next activity.

In our setting, these songs have repeatedly led to a nonverbal child's first attempt at humming or at speech. It is important for the teachers to listen carefully. If a child makes an attempt to sing or hum a tune, the teacher should give praise for the attempt. These favorite tunes can also be used during individual activity time to stimulate language development. However, there should be no strong demands placed on the children to sing these songs. If a child begins to sing or hum, it should be acknowledged, but singing or humming should not be required. One of the reasons for this is that all other demands made on the child during music can be prompted or guided. However, speech itself cannot. The teacher can ask the group to sing, but specific children should not be singled out to sing unless the teacher is very sure of getting a response and sure that it will be a positive experience for the child.

Since snack time usually follows music time in our classroom, we often end music time with a transition song that goes like this.

It's time for snack.
It's time for snack.
Let's go to the table now,
It's time for snack.

Songs are often an excellent way to help create a smooth transition from one activity to another and can be easily written about any of the daily activities. Songs about time to go home, time to go outside, time for math, nap time, and so on are fun to create and often help children accept transitions more easily.

When you are exploring songs to use with your own population of children, keep in mind that every word and every note in every song is always changeable! Any song can be adapted to fit specific needs, and it is relatively easy to do.

Here is an example that may help prepare you to think creatively. A song we call "Picking up Blocks" resulted from one particular incident. Two music students wanted to use the song "Way Down Yonder in the Paw-Paw Patch" with the children. The words are as follows:

Where, oh where, is dear little Sally?
Where, oh where, is dear little Sally?
Where, oh where, is dear little Sally?
Way down yonder in the Paw-Paw Patch.

Picking up paw-paws, put them in a basket.
Picking up paw-paws, put them in a basket.
Picking up paw-paws, put them in a basket.
Put them in a basket and go home to your Ma.

These words were to be acted out. As we discussed the song, it became clear that "Way down yonder in the Paw-Paw Patch" were not very relevant words for our particular children. However, the words "sitting in the circle right next to Greg" (or whomever) did fit the rhythm and seemed much more logical. Also, the children's names and the concept "next to" can be taught in this way.

Pretending to pick up paw-paws could be changed to actually picking up blocks and putting them in the basket; here again a real skill could be incorporated. Instead of ending by going home to your Ma, a verse could be added.

That's enough blocks, your turn's over.
That's enough blocks, your turn's over.
That's enough blocks, your turn's over.
Your turn's over, now go back to your place.

Now the song is:

Where, oh where, is dear little Sally?
Where, oh where, is dear little Sally?
Where, oh where, is dear little Sally?
Sitting in the circle right next to Ken.

Picking up blocks, put them in the basket.
Picking up blocks, put them in the basket.
Picking up blocks, put them in the basket.
Put them in the basket in the middle of the floor.

That's enough blocks, your turn's over.
That's enough blocks, your turn's over.
That's enough blocks, your turn's over.
Your turn's over, now go back to your place.

The group can sit in a circle; and each child can go into the center, pick up some blocks that are on the floor, and put them in a basket in the center of the circle. It gives each child a chance to receive praise for following directions. If a child has difficulty leaving tasks unfinished (in this case, is upset by not getting to put *all* the blocks in the basket), it is a good song to use to help that child learn to share a task with others.

With this simple modification we went from imaginary paw-paws to real blocks, from abstract paw-paw patches to sitting in an actual circle, and from music solely as entertainment to music as both entertainment and instruction.

MUSIC AND CLASSROOM INTEGRATION

Music activities such as the ones just described can be most useful in facilitating a variety of different kinds of integration in the classroom. A music setting is often a less threatening environment in which to begin integration because of the "nonacademic" yet structured atmosphere created. "Backwards integration," a term we have used to describe bringing nonhandicapped children into classrooms for the handicapped, was very successful in beginning integration in our own multiply handicapped classroom setting. In the last section of this chapter, I would like to describe several different kinds of integration situations we have incorporated into our music sessions over the past few years.

Several years ago, during the school year, we made contact with an open school whose director had shown interest the preceding summer in figuring out a way to get some of her students involved with special children. We were a little skeptical at this point because we were serving a population of severely multiply handicapped, nonverbal children. We therefore asked the teacher to carefully select only six of her best students to come over to our school. We decided to let them observe our classroom through a one-way mirror, select one student to work with, and then have these pairs (one open school student and one special student) participate together in a group music session.

As the open school students watched our classroom, it became apparent that they really were excited about the opportunity to participate. They began making comments about the children, and we realized the comments were all positive! They ranged from remarks such as "Isn't that little blonde girl cute?" to "I'll bet he could really kick a soccer ball far."

The open school children easily selected specific children to pair up with, and we brought them into the classroom and introduced them to our students and teachers. We all sat down in a circle, and music time began. We began with an individual "Name Song" to give each child a chance to be introduced and then proceeded with our regular repertoire.

The thing that astounded us the most as we watched and participated that first day was that (as we interpreted it), the open school students did not have limited expectations because they did not know our children. They *expected* the children to be able to get up and dance, for example, two by two, and hold hands. They expected that the children could clap their hands or imitate touching their ears. This high level of expectation resulted in some astounding (from our perspective) achievements on the part of our handicapped population! The music session ended with spirits high, and the open school students wanted to know when they could please come back.

The open school had a list of activities their students could choose if they successfully finished all their academic work. During the course of the year, they added "Attend the program for autistic-type children one morning during the week." As the open school students became more familiar with our students during music time, we began to find ways to incorporate them into other aspects of our program as well.

During our 6-week summer program we often have 20 or more students who are autistic-type, multiply handicapped, or emotionally disturbed. In the last 2 years, we have made an effort to incorporate the brothers and sisters of these children in our summer program. We have found that, again, music time is the perfect time to get the brothers and sisters involved in activities with their handicapped siblings. This also provides an environment to observe the interactions between siblings and is often an excellent stepping stone to working on interactional difficulties between siblings. It also has provided the siblings of the special children with opportunities to meet or talk to other children who are also attempting to deal with a difficult brother or sister. One of the most beneficial aspects of involving normal siblings in the music sessions is that they have an opportunity to observe their "handicapped" brother or sister participating *successfully* in a group activity. Children have often used our games and songs to help establish meaningful activities and relationships with their handicapped sibling in their own homes. This particular integrational aspect of our summer program is one we hope to explore further in the coming years, since it appears to have positive effects and carry over in the family setting.

We have also used group music sessions as a part of a parent participation program. We have found that inviting parents to participate in music, not necessarily with their own child, but with someone else's child, has often helped build that parent's confidence in his or her own skills. When the parents "discover" that they can successfully manage a different difficult child, they often are able to translate this successful experience into better management and understanding of their own children. Again, the nonpressured, "fun" atmosphere created by a group music session provides a nonthreatening environment in which to practice interacting with a child.

Part of our present hospital-based program includes an outreach service to public schools. (See chapter 13 by Sheila Merzer.) In the course of helping establish programs for difficult children in public school settings, we have had the opportunity to introduce the use of group music sessions into a large variety of classrooms.

As mentioned earlier, several of the children attending our morning program (which presently is for preschool-aged children) go to public programs in the afternoon. Often they are involved in classes for developmentally delayed children or small classes for children who need extra help before beginning kindergarten. This sometimes means that the child from our program is more severely involved than the other children in the afternoon class. Because of this fact, we are often looking for ways to help our child "fit in" to a higher functioning group of children.

One of the ways we have found to help facilitate integration is to use music. We often teach the afternoon teacher the songs that we use in the morning. This way, when they have music time in the afternoon setting, the child we are trying to incorporate into the group is already familiar with some of the songs.

When one of the preschool children in our classroom begins to show signs of being able to be involved in play or of imitating other children, we try to arrange for the child's teacher to take the child to a "normal" nursery setting for a short period each day. Often, for starters, we like to include the child in the nursery school music time. Again, we offer to teach the nursery school teacher some of our songs, so that we can make the transition into a normal setting less traumatic for special children by having familiar songs be part of the new setting. We have found that nursery school and kindergarten children delight in many of the songs we use and can come up with delightful variations.

In public school settings we have also used older, sometimes "behavior problem" children as "aides" during music. Often hyperactive children, or children who simply can not find enough quiet things to keep themselves occupied in a normal class, will thrive as helpers in group music sessions. These children as well as older handicapped children can be used to help in music classes and can benefit greatly from the opportunity to be helpful and needed. At the same time, the children who need assistance to participate in a group music setting are getting help. These mutually beneficial situations can be established throughout a school building by classroom teachers who are willing to experiment with group music sessions.

In closing I wish to reemphasize that the same things are important in music time that are important in any other aspect of teaching the autistic-type child— flexibility, caring, creativity, intuition, good management, good teaching, and sensitivity. The success of a music program depends on the individual teachers involved. The children will pick up on either the teachers' high spirited enthusiasm or on their apathy. If the teachers are willing to invest their time and energy and be aware of the stage of development of each child during the music session, it can be a very rewarding experience for teachers and children alike—rewarding in the sheer enjoyment of music, in the shared experience of fun, and in the development of additional skills by the children.

Part III

Language and Communication

9
Language Disorders in Autistic Children

Sharon L. James

Children diagnosed as autistic are likely to show deficits in oral language development (Baltaxe & Simmons, 1975; Churchill, 1972; Cunningham, 1968; Doherty & Swisher, 1978; Ricks & Wing, 1975; Shapiro, Chiarandini, & Fish, 1974). These deficits may be receptive (understanding language) as well as expressive (speaking or producing language). They may range in severity from the apparent absence of receptive and expressive language to mild difficulties with certain words, speech sounds, or grammatical structures. The literature on the communication and language deficits of autistic children indicates that a broad range of problems, involving all aspects of language, is possible. Among those problems which have been described are idiosyncratic use of words and phrases and use of inappropriate or purposeless remarks (Cunningham, 1968; Ricks & Wing, 1975; Wing, 1969); a high incidence of echolalia (Cunningham, 1968; Shapiro, Roberts, & Fish, 1970; Wing, 1969); failure to use language to provide information (Cunningham, 1968); omission or incorrect use of prepositions, conjunctions, auxiliary verbs, verb tense markers, and other function words (Bartolucci & Albers, 1974; Ricks & Wing, 1975); deviant pronunciation or articulation of speech sounds (Cunningham, 1968; Shervanian, 1967); and distortions in pitch, rhythm, intonation, and stress patterns (Goldfarb, 1961; Rutter, 1965; Wing, 1969).

These investigations and descriptions of autistic children provide considerable information about the variety of their language and communication deficits. However, this information is of little help to a professional responsible for designing a language intervention program for such a child. One reason for the lack of clinical and educational utility is that the information provides a very fragmented picture of the child's language abilities and deficits. For example, we know that many of these children have difficulty with grammatical words or markers like prepositions, conjunctions, and verb tense endings, but we don't know if these grammatical difficulties are inappropriate in relation to the development of other aspects of the language, such as vocabulary or use of different types of sentence structures. The information available from the literature does not provide that sort of profile. As Baltaxe and Simmons point out, "Investigators from different disciplines have looked at isolated linguistic phenomena, and language data have mostly been dealt with in general terms without attention to language as a system" (1975, p. 443). In order to make appropriate intervention decisions, we must describe the child's entire language system, not just isolated aspects of it.

In our attempts to assess the language of and plan intervention programs for autistic children, we became very aware of the need for a model which treats language as an integrated system. One model which fits this description was developed by Bloom and Lahey (1978) for describing children's language development and disorders. The model treats language as an integrated system made up of three major components: content, form, and use. Figure 9.1 is a schematic representation of these three components and the way they fit together to form the language system. Each of the components will be described briefly.

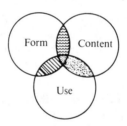

Figure 9.1   The intersection of content, form, and use in language
(from Bloom & Lahey, 1978)

A MODEL OF LANGUAGE

Content

Bloom and Lahey (1978) define language *content* as "what people talk about and what they understand of what other people say" (p. 98); it is the meaning or the semantic aspect of the language system. The content of our language is based on our knowledge of objects* and events in the world and our

---

*Throughout this discussion, the term *object* is used in the broad sense to refer to something that can be seen, touched, or otherwise sensed. Thus, people and animals, as well as inanimate entities, are included in the term *object*.

feelings and attitudes about those objects and events. Bloom and Lahey (1978) discuss three categories of content: knowledge about objects, knowledge about relations among objects, and knowledge about relations among events. Object knowledge includes knowledge about particular objects (e.g., words like "Mommy" and the name for a favorite stuffed animal) and about classes of objects (e.g., words like "girl" and "doggie"). Knowledge of object relations includes knowing that an object exists ("this cookie"), can disappear ("all gone cookie"), and can recur or reappear ("more cookie"); that objects have different attributes or properties, such as size ("big dog") and color ("red ball"), which distinguish among objects in the same class; and that objects can relate to other objects through location ("cookie in tummy"), possession ("my cookie"), and action ("eat cookie"). Finally, knowing about relations among events includes knowledge of ways in which different events are related in time ("You wash your hands *before* you eat") or in causality ("Mommy's mad *because* I made a mess").

To summarize, language content is *what* we talk about—the meaning or semantic component of the language system. It is "the linguistic representation of what persons know about the world of objects, events, and relations" (Bloom & Lahey, 1978, p. 14).

Form

The *form* of language is the means by which we connect sound with meaning, allowing us to convey our message through speech. Form can be described in terms of the linguistic units involved, both phonological (sound) and morphological (meaning), and the rules for combining those linguistic units.

Phonology refers to the sound system of our language. Thus, phonological units are the individual speech sounds (vowels and consonants) and the prosodic features, such as intonation, stress, and rhythm. *Morphology* refers to the meaningful units in our language, including words for objects, events, and relations, and grammatical markers such as noun plurals and verb tense markers. The rules for combining grammatical markers with words and for combining words to make phrases and sentences are referred to as *syntax*. Thus, in order to express our language content, we must know about phonology (sound units), morphology (meaning units), and syntax (ways to combine meaning units).

To summarize, language form is *how* we convey the content we wish to express. It is "the means for connecting sound with meaning and consists of linguistic units and the system of rules for their combination" (Bloom & Lahey, 1978, p. 19).

Use

The *use of* language refers to the ways in which we actually use our language code to communicate. Use has two major aspects: (*a*) the communicative functions or purposes for which we use language and (*b*) how we choose among different forms to express a particular function.

Among the major communicative functions are giving information; describing an event; getting the listener to do, believe, or feel something; expressing one's own intentions, beliefs, or feelings; indicating a readiness for further communication; solving problems; and entertaining (Rees, 1978). The particular form that we choose to express our communicative function will depend on several factors, including the person to whom we are talking; whether the objects, people, or events we are talking about are present or absent; the actual physical situation in which the communication is occurring; and whether we are initiating or simply maintaining a conversation. For example, if your communicative function is to get your listener to close the door, you may choose to express the function in several different ways, such as "Shut the door"; "Could you please shut the door?"; "I think the door should be shut"; or "It's rather breezy in here" (as you look meaningfully at the door). All of these forms have the potential to get the listener to do something, and the form that you choose will vary with the listener and the situation.

Knowledge of all three components—content, form, and use—must be acquired in order for a child to become a competent language user. In some children, one or more of these language components does not develop adequately, resulting in a child who has trouble communicating effectively. Using this integrated model of the language system, let's look at the language deficits of autistic children.

DISORDERS OF THE LANGUAGE COMPONENTS

Children with autism may have deficits in all three of the language components. However, our clinical experience with one group of autistic children leads us to suggest that the greatest deficits are likely to show up in their language content and language use. Although deficits in form are often present also, they appear to be secondary rather than primary problems. This pattern contrasts with what we frequently see in children whose only problem is that of oral language development (i.e., the child labeled "language disordered" or "language impaired"). The majority of these children show major deficits in development of language form. They have the basic content necessary and they use what language they have in appropriate ways, but they have difficulty with the forms for conveying their message. This is not to say that language disordered children never show disorders of content and use. They do. However, the majority seem to show the greatest deficits in development of form. Other investigators have reported similar observations about the nature of the problems in language disordered children (Freedman & Carpenter, 1976; Leonard, 1972; Morehead & Ingram, 1973).

To further elaborate on the language deficits which seem to be most characteristic of autistic children, I will discuss two major patterns we have noted and provide examples from some of the children we have worked with. First of all, the autistic children we have seen can be divided into two general groups based on their language production: those who are preverbal and those who are verbal. By *preverbal,* we mean children who are producing no words that anyone is able to identify as meaningful (consistently referring to an object, place, or event). Children who are identified as *verbal* include those who are producing meaningful single words as well as those using phrases and sentences. These two groups—preverbal and verbal—can be described, respectively, as children who demonstrate primarily content deficits or primarily use deficits.

Preverbal Group: Disorders of Content

One of the major characteristics of the preverbal children is their seeming lack of awareness of their immediate environment. These children do not seem to "tune in" to the people, objects, and events around them. They have little, if any, eye contact with others; few, if any, appropriate behaviors with toys; little indication that they understand the speech addressed to them. Many of the behaviors observed seem to correspond to those associated with infantile autism (Wing, 1969). I do not mean to suggest, however, that all of these preverbal children are autistic, but simply that they have some autistic-like behaviors.

In normally developing children, acquisition of knowledge about objects, people, events, and the relations among these objects and events begins in infancy. Piaget (1951, 1954) has described in great detail the infant's development of this knowledge during what he calls the *sensorimotor period* of cognitive development. In the sensorimotor period, which runs approximately from birth to age 2, children actively explore and learn about the environment. They see, hear, taste, touch, and smell the world around them; they act on objects and with objects, moving them, dropping them, mouthing them, hiding them; they observe that people do things with and to them, to objects, and to other people. All of this exploration and observation provides children with information about the world. Several investigators have suggested that the development of this sensorimotor knowledge is strongly related to—perhaps even necessary for—early language development (Bates, Benigni, Bretherton, Camaioni, & Volterra, 1977; Bloom, 1973; Corrigan, 1978; Ingram, 1978; Kahn, 1975). Bloom and Lahey propose that the development of sensorimotor concepts underlies the child's development of the content component of language.

Since our preverbal autistic-like children did not seem to have even basic language content, we wanted to determine if they had the prerequisite knowledge for developing such content. Using the Infant Psychological Development Scales (Uzgiris & Hunt, 1975), we assessed the children's knowledge of some of the basic sensorimotor concepts. For example, we looked at the children's ability to find an object when it was removed from sight; this ability to search for and find an object indicates that a child realizes that objects are permanent and constant and that they still exist even when you can't see them or touch them or hear them. We also assessed the children's ability to figure out what causes something to happen (e.g., what causes a mechanical toy to move). This knowledge is necessary for understanding causal relations between events. A third ability we were interested in was problem solving—the child's ability to discover the means to an end and to use that means intentionally (e.g., to use an instrument, such as a stick, to obtain an out-of-reach object). We also observed how the children manipulated or played with familiar objects or toys. Their characteristic pattern of object manipulation tells us about their awareness of what objects are used for and about their abilities to play and pretend (both symbolic behaviors). According to Bloom and Lahey (1978), knowledge of these sensorimotor concepts is necessary for the development of language content, that is, knowledge about objects, relations among objects, and relations among events.

We found that six of the seven preverbal children we tested, ranging in age from 3 years to almost 7 years, were performing these sensorimotor tasks at or below the level expected for a 12-month-old infant. These results indicate that the children lacked the cognitive or conceptual knowledge for the production and comprehension of language. Their major deficit, therefore, was primarily one of language concent. Without the language content, the form and the use components failed to develop also. Thus, these preverbal children had no systematic means for communicating with other people. In order to give you a clearer picture of these children, a description follows of the information obtained in our initial evaluation of one of the preverbal children.

At the time of initial testing, Terri was 5 years, 8 months old. She was observed performing tasks from the Infant Psychological Development Scales, testing her knowledge of object permanence, causality, the means to achieve an end, and schemas for manipulating or relating to objects. In addition, her comprehension of words for familiar objects was assessed.

To test knowledge of object permanence, the examiner hid a toy Terri was interested in under a cloth while Terri watched. She did not attempt to pick up the cloth, nor did she look for the toy elsewhere once it had disappeared under the cloth. The same lack of interest after the toy disappeared was observed on three different trials. The examiner then partially covered the toy of interest with the cloth so that a small part of the toy was visible. In all three trials with the partially hidden toy, Terri immediately pulled the cloth off and picked up the toy. Her level of performance on the object permanence tasks is typical of an infant about 6 months old (Uzgiris & Hunt, 1975).

Terri's knowledge of causality was examined by activating a toy top and then observing behaviors with the top when it ceased to spin. On all three trials, Terri picked the top up and looked at it briefly, but did not try to activate it herself, nor did she give it back to the examiner to activate. This process was repeated with a toy wind-up radio because Terri loved music; the same behaviors were observed. By about 12 months of age, normally developing infants will try to get an adult to reactivate a mechanical toy (Uzgiris & Hunt, 1975). Terri did demonstrate some knowledge of the relation between a cause and an effect, however, when she attempted to get the examiner to take hold of her hands and sway back and forth (this is a game the teacher plays with Terri while singing "Row, Row Your Boat"). Attempts to reinitiate a familiar game like this are typical in children around 10 months of age (Miller, Chapman, Branston, & Reichle, 1978).

Terri's development of the ability to use a means to achieve an end was observed also. She demonstrated several behaviors indicating that her knowledge of means-ends relations is similar to that of a normal 8- to 9-month-old infant (Uzgiris & Hunt, 1975). Among these behaviors were the following: she walked over to get an object or toy she wanted which was out of her reach; she let go of an object to reach for another one; she pulled a cloth to pull an out-of-reach object close enough to grasp it. She did not perform any behaviors which indicate a higher level of means-end development.

Terri's development of schemas for relating to objects was assessed by presenting several toys or objects familiar to her, including a cup, hairbrush, a ball, a music box, a doll, and some blocks. The majority of Terri's behaviors (over 90%) with these objects consisted of mouthing, shaking, and visually inspecting the objects. All of these behaviors are the predominant ones engaged in by infants under 6 months old. However, she also demonstrated two later-developing behaviors: she picked up the cup and went through the motions of drinking from it, and she put a block in the cup when given both objects at the same time. These more conventional behaviors with objects are typical of children around 9 to 10 months of age (Uzgiris & Hunt, 1975). However, Terri engaged in very few of these sorts of behaviors.

Terri was observed to produce no vocalizations that could be defined as referring to a specific object, person, or event. She vocalized very infrequently during the observation sessions, and these vocalizations appeared to occur randomly rather than in response to specific stimuli or events. The vocalizations included humming with a rising and falling inflection and production of an "uh" sound. She did not produce any consonant sounds during the observation. The absence of words was confirmed by her teachers.

Terri's comprehension of names for familiar objects was tested by placing a set of five objects at a time in front of her and asking her to point to the object named. The objects included a ball, block, toy car, spoon, cup, brush, and book. The objects were rotated, so that there were only five at a time, and moved around so they were not always in the same position; each object was named three different times. Terri correctly pointed to the cup two out of three times. She did not correctly identify any of the other objects, and her response appeared to be random.

Terri's performance of the IPDS tasks indicated that cognitively she was performing at the level of 6- to 10-month-old infant, with a few behaviors (schemas for relating to objects) falling below the 6-month level. Her level of language production was very low. She did not babble and she did not appear to use her few vowel-like vocalizations for communicative purposes. It is difficult to draw conclusions about her language comprehension. She did not seem to understand the names for the majority of the familiar objects used.

In summary, Terri's cognitive and language development were severely delayed. She did not appear to have developed the necessary knowledge of objects, relations between objects, and relations between events to even have a rudimentary comprehension or production vocabulary. Since she had failed to respond to previous attempts to teach her either oral or sign language, we designed an intervention program to help facilitate sensorimotor concept development before working directly on language content. We wanted her to learn that objects are permanent entities, that events have a cause, and that objects can be used as a means to an end. Many of the specific activities used to develop these concepts are described later in this chapter.

Once Terri's development of these sensorimotor concepts had reached the level expected for a 12- to 18-month-old infant, a basic sign language program was begun, along with continued sensorimotor concept training. Signs were presented simultaneously with the words for familiar objects and events, and Terri quickly learned to imitate some basic signs. After a few months of sensorimotor concept and sign training, she was able to produce 12 signs and was beginning to use many of these signs spontaneously and purposefully. For example, she used the signs for *juice* and *gum* when she wanted these things. She sometimes produced the appropriate word with the sign. She also began to answer questions, although by no means consistently. Terri's acquisition and use of signs was accompanied by increased nonverbal and verbal interactions with teachers and other children. She still has a lot to learn, but her overt awareness of and interaction with the world around her has increased tremendously since the initiation of the sensorimotor concept training.

Terri's performance pattern at her initial evaluation is very similar to the patterns we found in our other preverbal children. Not all these children have progressed as quickly as Terri has; however, there has been an increased awareness of objects and relations between objects and events in all of the children involved in sensorimotor concept development activities. The one preverbal child who did not fit the pattern was a child who appeared to have a fairly good receptive vocabulary. He would, on occasion, point to objects, animals, and pictures in books and pictures when asked "Show me _____"; none of the other preverbal children demonstrated this level of understanding. His performance on the IPDS tasks was above the 2-year-old level, and our impressions were that his language deficits involved a lack of knowledge about the forms for conveying content or an unwillingness to use these forms, rather than a content disorder. For this child, then, sensorimotor concept training was neither necessary nor appropriate. He was the only one of our preverbal children who demonstrated this particular pattern; however, this may be another pattern found among a significant number of children labeled *autistic*.

Verbal Group: Disorders of Use

The verbal children have something to say (content) and some ways of saying it (form). Their development of both content and form usually is delayed in comparison to normal age-peers; however, their biggest language deficit appears to lie in language use. Many of these children do not seem to realize that they can use their language for various communicative functions such as getting their needs met, interacting socially, and learning about their environment. In cases where the children do use their language for different functions, they seem to have difficulty choosing the most appropriate form for the situation. Examples will be given from various children's communicative interactions to illustrate the deficits in their development of language use.

Limited Use of Different Communicative Functions

Some children do not seem to realize that their language can be used to serve a variety of different functions or purposes. Thus, we see some children who use their language almost exclusively to label or describe people, objects, and events. For example, one child initially produced a lot of sentences like "That's a big truck. It's red and it has black wheels." But when you asked the child if he liked it or if he wanted to play with it, he would give you another descriptive statement like "It's a dump truck."

The following descriptions of situations involving two different children illustrate the failure to use language for a very basic communicative function—requesting an object or action to satisfy some need.

George, a 7-year-old child, had a vocabulary appropriate for his age and sufficient syntactic forms for expressing himself. His greatest language deficit appeared to be his failure to use his language to manipulate his environment. Here is an example illustrating this failure during an interaction with his speech/language clinician.

> The clinician brought in a bottle of soap bubbles which George was very eager to play with. The clinician deliberately kept the bubble pipe hidden. George opened the bottle, looked in, and then looked briefly around the table. He made some blowing motions with his mouth, but did not say anything. After several minutes of just sitting there, the clinician asked the child if he needed something and he replied, "Yes, a bubble blower."

George used language to get his needs met only after he was prompted. He failed to initiate a request for the necessary object, even though he enjoyed and was eager to blow bubbles. This pattern is found among many of the verbal autistic children we've worked with. Interestingly, there is increasing evidence that normally developing infants intentionally use their vocalizations and gestures to get people's attention and to request out-of-reach objects, food, and so forth, as young as 9 to 10 months (Bates, Camaioni, & Volterra, 1975; Bruner, 1975).

An even more extreme example of this failure to use language to request an object or action was demonstrated by another child who has sufficient language content and forms for doing so. The child's mother had been instructed to omit a necessary item at mealtime to try to stimulate requesting. Here is what she reported.

> Mitch's mother gave him his usual cereal for breakfast, but put no milk on it and did not give him a spoon. Mitch sat looking into the bowl and after 10 minutes still had not asked for, or in any way indicated that he needed, either milk or a spoon.

Another communicative function that was notably missing from many of the verbal children's language was initiation of conversation. When someone else addressed a question, statement, or request to them directly, these children frequently would respond verbally or nonverbally. However, they rarely started a conversation on their own, especially with other children. If they did initiate a verbal interaction, it was usually with a teacher or other familiar adult. This tendency to address most utterances to adults rather than other children is quite typical of children under 3 years of age (Schachter, Kirshner, Klips, Fredericks, & Sanders, 1974; Wellman & Lempers, 1977); however, by 4 to 5 years of age, children talk to peers more than adults in natural communicative situations (Schachter, et al., 1974). The autistic children I'm describing were all well over 3 years of age and could have been expected to have initiated many conversations with their peers.

Inappropriate Use of Language

In addition to limited use of communicative functions, another problem is the inappropriateness of the language used. Sometimes the children's language was inappropriate because the content appeared unrelated to the preceding questions or statements. At other times it involved the use of inappropriate forms for the situation.

An example of inappropriate content is found in a couple of children who frequently responded to the questions with answers unrelated to the content of the questions. Results of other testing and observations led us to conclude that these children were capable of understanding and responding appropriately to *wh-* questions such as *what, who, where, why,* and *how.* However, in conversational interactions, both children frequently responded with inappropriate content. Here is an example from our observations of each of these children.

Mike and his mother were looking at a puzzle he had made for her. The mother asked, "How did you make it?" Mike responded, "The mouse is licking the cheese."

Brian had been discussing his day with his teacher. The teacher asked, "What did you eat for breakfast this morning?" Brian said, "My new car got broken."

These examples were not isolated instances where the child was momentarily distracted and, therefore, gave an inappropriate response. They illustrate a consistent pattern of inappropriate responding in relation to the content of the previous speaker's utterances.

The use of forms which are inappropriate to the communicative situation was demonstrated by one 9-year-old child we observed. This child's development of the content and form components was at age level; however, he had failed to learn what sorts of questions are appropriate to address to an unfamiliar adult listener. Thus, upon seeing me appear in his classroom for the first time, this child asked in rapid succession, "What are you doing here?" "How old are you?" "Do you have any brothers or sisters?" He waited for each of my answers before firing the next question to me, but he did not respond to any of my replies. After my third reply, he just wandered off. This child used his language to initiate interactions, but his forms for doing so were not socially appropriate for the situation. Another child's favorite conversational opening consisted of "Welcome to Jowonio. Let me kiss your hand"! Unfortunately, such inappropriate language use tends to mark these children as "different."

In summary, the autistic children we have observed and worked with at Jowonio: The Learning Place had major deficits in language content (the preverbal children) and in language use (the verbal children). Obviously, the preverbal children hd not developed the form and use components either, but we believe that their major deficit is their lack of knowledge about the world of objects and relations between objects and events (that is, the content component). The verbal children we worked with frequently had some problems in language content and form; however, these problems were secondary to their deficits in language use. The next sections includes some suggestions for what classroom teachers can do to help facilitate development of language content and use.

FACILITATING LANGUAGE DEVELOPMENT

The suggestions I am going to make regarding input and activities to facilitate language development are simply that—suggestions. They are meant to provide some ideas for helping children develop language content and use. Select those activities that seem appropriate for different children, try them, modify them whenever necessary, and develop new and more creative activities as the need arises. As you use some of the suggestions made in this chapter, you will undoubtedly think of new and better ways for facilitating various aspects of your children's language development. The most important thing is to be sensitive to the children's communicative needs and to try to help them meet those needs.

Nature of Your Language Input

As a classroom teacher, you are one of the most important sources of language input for the children in your class. You constantly are serving as a language reinforcer for the children. The kind of language you use is, therefore, very important. Your language must be appropriate for the language level of the children you're working with. This means using simple words and simple short phrases and sentences with children who are preverbal or in the early stages of language development. It means that your words, phrases, or sentences should refer to objects, people, and events in the immediate environment. Talk about the activities the children are involved in or about what they talk about. For children who are producing longer, more complex sentences, you can increase the length and complexity of your sentences. Always be sensitive to both verbal and nonverbal cues indicating that a child is not comprehending what you say to him or her. You may need to simplify your sentences, repeat instructions more frequently, and make your message very clear. For example, adults often say things like "It's time to get our coats now." If a child does not go and get a coat, it may be because he or she wasn't listening or attending, in which case you would need to get the child's attention and repeat the sentence. Another possibility—one that we've often found to be the case—is that the child does not understand indirect commands like the one above and needs to be told directly to get the coat. Try to be aware of the nature of your language input and how it may be influencing whether or not the child understands.

Facilitating Development of Language Content in Preverbal Children

Since the major problem among the preverbal children we've described involves language content, I will suggest some activities that help children develop the underlying concepts assumed necessary for language content. Some of the children you work with will need little help in some of these areas and perhaps a lot in others. You, the speech/language pathologist, and the other resource personnel in your setting will need to determine each child's strengths and weaknesses and plan the program accordingly. With the kinds of preverbal children I've described, our first goal is to help the child learn about objects, about relations among objects, and about relations among events. As you remember from the discussion of the language model, these are the major aspects of language content. The activities described to help facilitate development of this knowledge will have to be tailored to the particular child you're working with. One child, for example, may need to begin at the first level of the activity, while another may be ready for more complicated or complex forms of the activity.

The Hiding Game

One basic concept in object knowledge is object permanence. The development of this concept can be facilitated through hiding games. Find an object (favorite toy or food) that the child is very interested in, get his attention focused on it, and then cover it up while he watches. Start by covering it only partially with a cloth or pillow so that he can see a little bit of it. If the child does not try to get the object, guide him through the process. As the child's ability to search for and find the object improves, the hiding game can become more complex. The next step, for example, would be to completely cover the object. You would then progress to successive hidings, so that you're moving the object from one location (cloth, pillow, piece of furniture) to another while the child watches. In the last stage of this hiding game, the child should be able to find an object which he didn't directly observe being hidden. You set up this situation by putting the object in a topless box or container and then, without exposing the object, dump it out under a pillow or cloth. Once the child can find the object following the invisible hiding in one location, you can move the box with the object from one location to another, pretending to hide it at each location. These hiding games should be done on a carpeted or padded surface to prevent the child from responding strictly on sound cues.

In addition to hiding games in which the child is the seeker, Bloom and Lahey (1978) suggest that children be encouraged to do their own hiding. You first demonstrate by dropping objects in a container and putting the cover on, or by hiding objects under or behind something, and then have the child imitate these activities. Our experience has been that as children become proficient seekers, they spontaneously begin to hide the objects. They don't always wait for you to find them, however, especially if the object is food!

These hide-and-seek games are designed to help the children learn that objects exist independently of them and their actions upon them—that objects have a permanence all their own. According to Piaget, the child is acquiring a mental image of the object as a permanent, constant entity, and that mental image or representation is thought to be necessary for the acquisition of stable verbal symbols (words) for objects. In addition to gaining knowledge about the permanence of objects, the hiding games will help the child see the relation between himself (as seeker and hider) and the object. He will also be learning that he can be the cause of an event; he causes the object to reappear when he finds it. Thus, he is developing knowledge about objects and about relations among events, both of which are necessary for development of language content.

Object Manipulation Game

Another part of object knowledge is learning about relations among objects. The child needs to learn, for example, that one similarity among different objects is that they can be acted upon in the same way. The hiding game will give the child some opportunity to grasp this concept because she will have learned that different objects can be hidden and found (disappear and reappear), and that all of these objects, no matter how different, are permanent entities. You can facilitate knowledge of the relations among objects through a variety of activities. For example, you can take several different objects, such as a block, a ball, a toy car, a doll, and a piece of crumpled aluminum foil, and do the same activities with them. They can all be banged together, thrown, and dropped. They can be put into a box or container and then dumped back out, a popular activity at about 12 months of age in normally developing children. Demonstrate the same activity with the different objects and then have the child do it. If the child's daily behaviors indicate that she's already aware of this relation among objects, you won't need to work on these kinds of activities. The children who benefit most from these sorts of activities are those who show little awareness of objects and how objects can be acted upon.

Children also need to learn that specific objects are usually acted upon or used in specific sorts of ways. For example, we drink from cups, eat apples, and brush our hair with hair brushes. We cannot drink from hair brushes, brush our hair with apples, or eat cups. In order to teach the children conventional use of objects, you can demonstrate and have them follow your model. It is best to begin with objects they may encounter frequently, such as cups, spoons, and brushes. We've found that the objects first used appropriately tend to be eating and grooming tools. Helping the children learn how to act on or play with toys is more difficult and may take considerable time to teach. However, this ability appears to be an especially important prognostic indicator for language development. Play is related to the ability to use symbols, and language consists of a set of symbols.

Thus far I've been suggesting activities to help the children see how single objects can be acted on in the same and in different ways. Children also need to learn about how two or more objects can be brought into relation to one another (Bloom & Lahey, 1978). For example, they need to learn that objects can have spatial relations to each other. The best way to introduce this concept is to have each child experience these relations between himself or herself and an object. Have them get into a big box, on top of that box, and under the box. The same concepts can then be worked on using objects (blocks, toys, dolls, etc.) and having the children put these in, on, and under. You should demonstrate first; some children need to be led physically through the activities.

Object manipulation games can also be designed to help each child understand that both she and others can cause an event to occur. Toys, such as mechanical toys and wind-up radios, are excellent for working on this concept. You
can demonstrate how to make the toy move and then encourage the child to
reactivate it when it stops. Initially, a child may simply return the object to you
to reactivate; this indicates that she is at least aware that something has caused
the movement. The next step is to help the child realize that she can be the causal
agent.

There are several object manipulation activities that can be used to help a
child learn about means-end relations among objects. You can, for example, tie
a string onto something the child wants and then encourage him to pull the string
to get the desired object; a similar activity involves placing the object on a cloth
so that the child cannot reach the object unless he pulls the cloth closer. Once he
is able to get objects by pulling the cloth and string, introduce a tool, such as a
toy rake or back scratcher, as a means for retrieving an object. Place the object
out of reach on a table or other flat surface and show the child how to use the
tool to get the object within reach. As in other activities, you may need to physically lead some children through the actions. Use daily activities to set up situations in which the child will be able to discover a means for achieving an end.
For example, put his lunch box on a shelf out of his reach and place a step stool
nearby. He then has two possible solutions to the problem of getting the lunch
down: he can stand on the step stool and get it down himself, or he can get someone taller (you or another adult) to lift it down. Either way, he is making use of
one object as a means to obtain another object. The final goal is the child's use
of nonverbal and verbal language as a means to achieve an end.

The sorts of activities described thus far are designed to help develop concepts underlying language content. These activities are summarized in Table 9.1.
Once the child is beginning to grasp these underlying concepts and perform the
sorts of tasks and activities suggested, it is appropriate to begin directly working
on facilitating production of words for objects and relations between objects.

Introducing and Encouraging Production of Single Words

Normally developing children begin talking in single words, which is
what you can expect from preverbal children when they begin talking. The
kinds of words that should be introduced first are names for objects and
events that the child is involved with or engaged in—words that are related to
the here and now and are oriented toward the child's activities. The first
words you encourage the child to produce should grow out of the developing
knowledge of objects and relations among objects. For example, once the
child is beginning to search for and find objects in different locations, he
should be encouraged to use the name of important people and objects in his
environment. He can be taught that these single words can be used to get
someone's attention (e.g., calling "Mommy"), to get a desired object (e.g.,

Table 9.1   Activities for facilitating sensorimotor concepts underlying language content

Activity	Purpose

1. The hiding game
  A. Child as seeker
    1. Object completely hidden
    2. Object partially hidden
    3. Object hidden in successive locations
    4. Object hidden invisibly
	To facilitate the development of object permanence, awareness of the relation between objects and their location, and knowledge that objects can be acted upon.

2. Object manipulation games
  A. Acting on or manipulating different objects in the same way
    1. Banging, throwing, dropping objects
    2. Putting in and dumping objects out of container
  B. Acting on specific objects in specific ways
    1. Use of common familiar objects (eating and grooming tools)
    2. Manipulating or playing with toys
  C. Spatial and causal relations among two or more objects
    1. Location of child in relation to an object
    2. Location of one object in relation to another
    3. Others as the cause of an event
    4. Child as the cause of an event
  D. Means-end relations between objects
    1. Using a string or cloth
    2. Using a tool
    3. Creating problem-solving situations involving daily activities
	To facilitate learning about similarities and differences among objects, about spatial and causal relations among objects, and about using objects as a means to achieve an end.

saying "ball" while reaching for it), and to simply name the person or object. All of his attempts, spontaneous and imitative, to use words for objects and people should be rewarded by attention, the desired object, or repetition of the intended word ("Yes, that's a doggie").

Words like "all gone" and "more" code awareness that things disappear and reappear (sensorimotor concepts). These concepts were developed on a nonverbal level through experience with the hiding games. These words are good ones to introduce and work on at snack and lunch times. The word *no* can easily be introduced in classroom situations where the child has a need to let someone know he does not want something or does not want to do an activity.

One other type of word which should be introduced into a child's early vocabulary are words coding action. The object manipulation activities helped the child learn about acting on objects. This concept can be coded in words for common actions, such as *turn, push, go, open,* and *eat.*The words should be introduced when the child is engaged in that particular action or when you and the child are performing the action together. The child also can be encouraged to use words for locative actions (Bloom & Lahey, 1978), such as *in* as he gets in or puts an object in another object; *on* as he puts his jacket on or puts one object on another. Again, these are words coding relations among objects which were acquired nonverbally in the object manipulation games. Table 9.2 summarizes the major characteristics of the types of words that should be introduced first.

Once the child has a basic vocabulary of words for objects and relations among objects, you, the speech/language clinician, and the other resource personnel will be ready to sit down and plan a comprehensive program for facilitating the development of multiword utterances. Many of the activities and approaches will be the same and, therefore, will not be described in this chapter.

As you work with preverbal children such as we've described, you'll constantly discover new situations and methods for facilitating development of language content. Your own ingenuity, creativity, and willingness to experiment will be the greatest facilitation tools you have.

The next section deals with some ways in which you can facilitate development of language use in children like the verbal children we've described. These are children who seem to have sufficient language content and form to communicate, but do not use their language for effective communication.

Facilitating Development of Language Use in Verbal Children

The children who fell into our verbal group demonstrated the greatest language deficits in language use. As described above, some of these children were quite limited in the functions for which they used their language, and many of them rarely used language to initiate conversational interaction. Some children

Table 9.2   Characteristics of the first words to introduce

1. Refer to the here and now
   A. Names for objects and people present in the situation
   B. Words that code events as they occur, such as the disappearance and reappearance of objects
   C. Words for familiar actions which the child is performing or observing
2. Used to serve different functions
   A. Getting attention of others
   B. Requesting an object or activity
   C. Naming an object, person, or event

initiated interactions and used their language for varied communicative functions, but the content or the forms used were socially inappropriate. First of all, let's consider some of the ways that you could facilitate the development of communicative functions in a child with problems in this area.

Situations to Elicit Communicative Functions

Bloom and Lahey (1978) suggest that children use their language for four basic functions: establishing contact with other people, manipulating or regulating other people's behaviors, getting desired objects, and obtaining or giving information. In the case of children who fail to use one or more of these communicative functions in situations where you would expect them to, it may be necessary to design specific situations to teach that function. For example, a child who fails to use language to establish interaction with others may need specific demonstrations of how to initiate an interaction verbally. You can set up a program where the child is taught to approach and greet a classmate or another teacher every morning when arriving at school. You will need to model this for the child at first, then encourage the child to imitate your model, and finally do it on his or her own. Be sure that all of the child's attempts at verbal interaction are reinforced with a verbal response from the other person. You also can use dolls or puppets and role-play situations in which the child's doll or puppet must initiate a conversational interaction. Playing "store" is another activity that encourages the interactional function.

Children who fail to use language to obtain a desired object can be placed in a variety of situations where they need to use language to get an object. For example, a child's lunch box can be placed out of reach. If the child fails to ask for it in any way, you can model the appropriate form and encourage him or her to imitate your model. The model you provide must be appropriate for the child's level. Thus, if the child is using single words, encourage him to use the name of the object or a word like *more* or *mine* to accomplish this function. As soon as he produces an utterance that indicates he wants the desired object, reward him by giving it to him.

In addition to setting up specific situations designed to elicit different communicative functions, be sure to capitalize on the natural situations in the classroom to model the use of various functions for the child. It may require a lot of modeling and encouragement before children begin to use language for the desired function; but once they do, they will quickly discover that language is an effective way to accomplish many things. Using language then becomes inherently reinforcing.

Situations to Encourage Socially Appropriate Language

A variety of conversational interaction situations can be used to help children learn how to maintain a conversational topic and to interact appropriately.

It may be necessary to begin with some situations where the message to be conveyed is highly constrained. For example, you may talk with a child about something she is doing or an object she is acting upon right at the moment. Talking about present objects or on-going events constrains the amount of information to be dealt with and will help the child stay on the topic. For some children, these constraints may not be enough. In our example of Mike, who said "The mouse is licking the cheese" when his mother asked how he made the puzzle they were looking at, these constraints did not result in appropriate language use. You may find that a child like Mike needs to have appropriate responses to statements and questions directly modeled.

For children who frequently fail to provide enough information for the listener to understand the message, you may want to try some games where the child has to describe an object or situation to a listener who cannot see that object or situation. Krauss and Glucksberg (1969) designed a communication situation where the speaker and the listener sit on opposite sides of a table divided by an opaque screen so they cannot see one another. The speaker's task is to describe a series of nonsense forms so the listener can select the appropriate ones from a set which matches the speaker's. You can modify this task in many different ways. Berko-Gleason (1972) describes a form of this game used with preschoolers in which the teachers put M & M candies under different containers and then modeled statements like "The M & M is under the box that has the mitten on it" (p. 104). After about only an hour of training, many of the children began using similar statements when they were placed in the speaker role. It may take considerably more training for some of the children you work with, but such communication games give the children excellent practice in conveying adequate amounts of information to a listener.

In addition to needing direct work on providing appropriate information in a conversation, some children also need help in developing appropriate forms for conversational interactions. You may encounter children who do not know the appropriate forms for opening a conversation or how to take turns in a conversation. We found that some children needed to be taught the appropriate forms for greeting another person, for reqesting attention, for asking to share an activity or object. Many of these forms can be modeled for the child in the course of daily classroom activities. Demonstrate the appropriate models, have the child imitate your models until he or she seems to have the idea, and then set up some situations where the child can use the forms spontaneously with other adults and children. The positive responses the child will get from these communicative interactions will increase the probability of using these forms in the future. Using dolls or puppets and setting up various role-playing situations so that child can practice use of the appropriate forms may sometimes be helpful. With one older child who could read, we successfully used written scripts to work on appropriate conversational interactions. Scripts were written for different conversational interactions like those the child was likely to be involved in. The child then switched roles so he gained experience as both a speaker and a listener.

Again, be sure to capitalize on all of the natural communicatve situations that occur every day. Use modeling, role playing, and communication games to facilitate appropriate language use. Encourage conversational interactions not only between you and the child, but especially between the child and other children. Our ultimate goal is to help each child use whatever language he or she has to communicate effectively with all of the people in the environment.

SUMMARY

This chapter presents a model of the language used to describe the major patterns of language deficits we observed among the autistic children at Jowonio: The Learning Place. Two major patterns are described: deficits in the development of language concepts in a group of children who were preverbal and deficits in the development of language use among the verbal autistic children. Based on the areas of language deficit, suggestions are made to facilitate development of language content and language use.

REFERENCES

Baltaxe, C., & Simmons, J. Language in childhood psychosis: A review. *Journal of Speech and Hearing Disorders,* 1975, *40,* 439-458.

Bartolucci, G., & Albers, R. Deictic categories in the language of autistic children. *Journal of Autism and Childhood Schizophrenia,* 1974, *14,* 131-141.

Bates, E., Benigni, L., Bretherton, T., Camaioni, L., & Volterra, V. From gesture to the first word: On cognitive and social prerequisites. In M. Lewis & L. Rosenblum (Eds.), *Interaction, conversation, and the development of language.* New York: John Wiley, 1977.

Bates, E., Camaioni, L., & Volterra, V. The acquisition of performatives prior to speech. *Merrill-Palmer Quarterly,* 1975, *21,* 205-226.

Berko-Gleason, J. An experimental approach to improving children's communicative ability. In C. Cazden (Ed.), *Language in early childhood education.* Washington, D.C.: National Association for the Education of Young Children, 1972.

Bloom, L. *One word at a time: The use of single-word utterances before syntax.* The Hague: Mouton, 1973.

Bloom, L., & Lahey, M. *Language development and language disorders.* New York: John Wiley, 1978.

Bruner, J. The ontogenesis of speech acts. *Journal of Child Language,* 1975, *2,* 1-19.

Churchill, D. The relation of infantile autism and early childhood schizophrenia to developmental language disorders of childhood. *Journal of Autism and Childhood Schizophrenia,* 1972, *2,* 182-197.

Corrigan, R. Language development as related to stage 6 object permanence development. *Journal of Child Language,* 1978, *5,* 173-189.

Cunningham, M. A comparison of the language of psychotic and non-psychotic children who are mentally retarded. *Journal of Child Psychology and Psychiatry,* 1968, *9,* 229-244.

Doherty, L., & Swisher, L. Children with autistic behaviors. In F. Minifie & L. Lloyd (Eds.), *Communicative and cognitive abilities—Early behavioral assessment.* Baltimore: University Park Press, 1978.

Freedman, P., & Carpenter, R. Semantic relations used by normal and language-impaired children at stage I. *Journal of Speech and Hearing Research,* 1976, *19,* 784-795.

Goldfarb, W. *Childhood schizophrenia.* Cambridge, Mass.: Harvard University Press, 1961.

Ingram, D. Sensorimotor intelligence and language development. In A. Lock (Ed.), *Action, gesture and symbol: The emergence of language.* New York: Academic Press, 1978.

Kahn, J. Relationship of Piaget's sensorimotor period to language acquisition of profoundly retarded children. *American Journal of Mental Deficiency,* 1975, *79,* 640-643.

Krauss, R., & Glucksberg, S. The development of communication competence as a function of age. *Child Development,* 1969, *40,* 225-266.

Leonard, L. What is deviant language? *Journal of Speech and Hearing Disorders,* 1972, *37,* 427-447.

Miller, J., Chapman, R., Branston, M., & Reichle, J. *Language comprehension in sensorimotor stages V and VI.* Paper presented at the annual convention of the American Speech and Hearing Association, 1978.

Morehead, D., & Ingram, D. The development of base syntax in normal and linguistically deviant children. *Journal of Speech and Hearing Research,* 1973, *16,* 330-352.

Piaget, J. *Play, dreams, and imitation in childhood.* New York: W.W. Norton, 1951.

Piaget, J. *The construction of reality in the child.* New York: Basic Books, 1954.

Rees, N. Pragmatics of language: Applications to normal and disordered language development. In R. Schiefelbusch (Ed.), *Bases of language intervention.* Baltimore: University Park Press, 1978.

Ricks, D., & Wing, L. Language, communication, and the use of symbols in normal and autistic children. *Journal of Autism and Childhood Schizophrenia,* 1975, *5,* 191-221.

Rutter, M. Speech disorders in a series of autistic children. In A.W. Franklin (Ed.), *Children with communication problems.* London: Pitman, 1965.

Schachter, F., Kirshner, K., Klips, B., Fredericks, M., & Sanders, K. Everyday preschool interpersonal speech usage: Methodological, developmental, and sociolinguistic studies. *Monographs of the Society for Research in Child Development,* 1974, *38*(no 3).

Shapiro, T., Chiarandini, I., & Fish, B. Thirty severely disturbed children: Evaluation of their language development for prognosis and classification. *Archives of General Psychiatry,* 1974, *30,* 819-825.

Shapiro, T., Roberts, A., & Fish, B. Imitation and echoing in young schizophrenic children. *Journal of American Child Psychiatry,* 1970, *9,* 548-567.

Shervanian, C. Speech, thought, and communication disorders in childhood psychosis: Theoretical implications. *Journal of Speech and Hearing Disorders,* 1967, *32,* 303-313.

Uzgiris, T., & Hunt, J.McV. *Assessment in infancy.* Urbana: University of Illinois Press, 1975.

Wellman, H., & Lempers, J. The naturalistic communication abilities of two-year-olds. *Child Development,* 1977, *48,* 1052-1057.

Wing, L. The handicaps of autistic children—A comparative study. *Journal of Child Psychology and Psychiatry,* 1969, *10,* 1-40.

10
Alternative Communication Methods

Annegret Schubert

INTRODUCTION

In recent years, reports of using "alternative methods of communication" with autistic-like children have increased greatly. One of the reasons for the increase is the greater acceptance (among professionals and parents) of the central role that a specific communication deficit may play in development of these children (Fay & Schuler, 1980).

Most of the reports deal with the use of **sign language.*** In most cases, signing is used in combination with spoken English. The combination of spoken communication with signing (or any other **alternative communication system**) is frequently called **total communication.** For many children the first signs learned are the first socially acceptable means of communicating their needs. Some children learn sign as a supplement to vocalizations and are expected to communicate orally as well as manually. Sone studies find that spoken communication may grow as a result of teaching signing, hoping that signs can be faded out as spoken communication increases. For *all* children, the highest goal is that their communication system (be it manual only, manual and spoken, or spoken and faded manual) can develop beyond the level of basic needs communication and become a true language (that is, used to respond to and make statements, ask and answer questions, refer to events outside the here and now).

Often as a second alternative—possibly because a child's motor ability is not adequate for signing—**communication boards** are introduced. Autistic-like children often display visual discrimination skills far superior to their auditory discrimination skills, which are needed for **oral communication.** Displays of pictures may provide basic communication skills for some children. Others may

*Words appearing in **boldface** are defined in the glossary at the end of this chapter.

176

recognize written words, yet be unable to speak. The use of written words on a communication board or of spelling and writing is a theoretically unlimited, though slow, communication system, which will provide for basic needs communication as well as higher levels of communication. **Symbol** communication **systems,** such as **Non-SLIP** (NonSpeech Language Intervention Program, Hollis & Carrier, 1978) or **Blissymbols** (Bliss, 1965), allow children to refer to meanings other than those we can easily picture (e.g., actions, feelings). Non-SLIP symbols are arbitrary shapes which are assigned a meaning. Unlike pictures, they can be combined to form sentences. The formation of Blissymbols is primarily meaning-based, where symbols ($\sim$ = water, $\downarrow$ = down) are combined to form new meanings ($\leftthreetimes$ = rain). Blissymbols are always combined with printed words, making their meaning accessible to most untrained persons communicating with the child.

This short description of systems which have been used with autistic-like children is only an overview. Table 10.1 lists the most important characteristics of each of the alternative communication systems used with autistic-like children. A list of other sources of information can be found at the end of this chapter. In-depth descriptions of each system, its uses, applicability, and range, should be reviewed by professionals and parents making a decision on alternative communication.

REVIEW OF RESEARCH ISSUES

The most frequently raised question related to the use of alternative communication systems with autistic-like children appears to be what specific strengths or deficits account for the successes with alternative communication systems as opposed to the failures with spoken communication (see Fay and Schuler's 1980 review). There is no general agreement in the literature on this question. Some authors (Bonvillian & Nelson, 1976; Carr, 1979; Casey, 1978; O'Connor, 1971; Tubbs, 1966) attribute the success with sign language to the dominance of visual/spatial characteristics as opposed to auditory dominance in speech. Fulwiler and Fouts (1976), Simon (1975), and Bryson (1972) suggest that specific deficiencies in auditory-visual **cross-modal association** are responsible, as this type of transfer is not needed in the use of signing or communication boards. McLean and McLean (1974) claim that communicaton via tangible pictures, words, or symbols may be more effective because their processing or use does not require short-term memory retrieval (they are **nontransient**). Hermelin (1976) supports this suggestion with her findings that autistic-like children are deficient in both visual and auditory modalities when a task requires **temporal sequencing** (ordering in time, as is needed in speech and signing). This, again, suggests that the spatial/visual aspects of communication boards and signing are essential to their success.

The relative ease of shaping the movements required for communication boards (McLean & McLean, 1974; Premack & Premack, 1972) as well as for

Table 10.1

Systems	Visual	Auditory	Transient	Nontransient	Can be used by untrained persons	Needs to be learned	Limited vocabulary, meanings	Creative potential	Can make sentences	One/two word limitation	Simple motor output	Complex motor output	May hinder mobility (bulky)	Other
Spoken word	x	x	x		x			x	x			x		
Sign language	x		x			x		x	x			x		Need to differentiate between sign systems (ASL, signed English, etc.); need to be proficient user as teacher
Combined sign and spoken language	x	x	x		x	x		x	x			x		Some researchers think inter-modal transfer (auditory–visual combined) may be difficult for autistic-like children.
Picture board	x			x	x		x			x	x		x	Least symbolic mode, short of simple gesturing
Blissymbols	x			x	x			x	x		x		x	Need to adhere to Blissymbol system and be familiar with system to teach it
Non-SLIP	x			x	x	x	x		x		x		x	Symbols arbitrary and not widely known
Written word board	x			x	x			x	x		x			Useful with those who read, but don't speak
Writing/typing	x			x	x			x	x			x	x	Slow, but less limiting than a board; need sophisticated spelling and reading skills

178

signing (Creedon, 1973) may also contribute to learning. The importance of nonverbal, nonvocal, facial, and gestural expression in communicating with autistic-like children underlines the advantage of using larger motor movements (Pronovost, Wakstein, & Wakstein, 1966; Ruttenberg & Gordon, 1967). Motor action itself may facilitate growing body awareness (Creedon, 1973) as well as speech production (Luria, 1966).

Much of the reported work with signing and autistic-like children indicates that increased **vocalizations** or **verbalizations** may accompany increased use of signs (Cohen, 1981; Fulwiler & Fouts, 1976). However, some dispute this claim (Carr, 1979; Salvin, Routh, Foster, & Lovejoy, 1977). The differences appear to be due to *individual* differences in children (some were **echolalic,** some vocalized, some were mute at onset), as well as differences in treatment programs (Carr, 1979). Much success is reported using a total communication approach (Benaroya, Wesley, Ogilvie, Klein, & Clarke, 1979; Benaroya, Wesley, Ogilvie, Klein, & Meany, 1977; Brady & Smouse, 1978; Cohen, 1981; Fulwiler & Fouts, 1976), which here means stressing spoken and signed input and output simultaneously. Success of total communication may indicate, again, that the language deficit is not auditory/visual modality specific; that **multisensory input** aids processing and attending, and that the cross-modal association difficulties which may exist are ameliorated by intensive intervention.

Studies report a variety of effects of signing on general adaptive behavior: increased spontaneous communication (Benaroya, et al., 1977; Schaeffer, Kollinzas, Musil, & McDowell, 1977), reduced self-stimulatory and severely disruptive behavior (Casey, 1978), and an increase in complexity of social behavior (Benaroya, et al., 1977; Konstantenareas & Leibovitz, 1977). In all of these cases, it is difficult to state that signing *per se* caused the progress, as it is usually part of a complex educational program. Carr (1979) isolated the effects of signing on self-stimulatory behavior by increasing and then extinguishing and found that the more signing the child does, the less self-stimulatory behavior is seen.

The reported uses of communication boards (LaVigna, 1977; McLean & McLean, 1976; Silverman, 1976) have been limited to very basic communication needs (up to 25 prompted symbols). Considering the disadvantages of the communication board (limitation of options, mobility, expression of concepts) and our limited knowledge about its applicability to autistic-like children (especially with symbol systems), the simple response mode (pointing) and elimination of the need for retrieval seem to be the two most important variables in selection. More reported use may show growth beyond the limited scope evidenced so far.

In summary, many questions related to the use of alternative communication systems with autistic-like children remain disputed or unanswered. From our experience, however, a review of available reports *does* aid teachers and parents in the difficult and inevitable decision-making process.

USE OF ALTERNATIVE COMMUNICATION SYSTEMS

As you will see, many individuals are involved in each child's communication development: classroom and resource teachers, administrators, parents, the child, his or her peers, and the speech/language clinician. Each contributes in a unique way to the process of communication development; each has individual perceptions and feelings about the communication system used.

At Jowonio, we are presently using alternative communication systems with three 6- to 7-year-old boys. Classroom and resource teachers, administrators, and parents were asked to provide feedback about the initial decision to use an alternative system, the system itself, changes in communication and behavior, future communication, and the speech/language clinician's role in supporting them. This feedback has helped me truly represent as many aspects of teaching an alternative system as possible.

The Children

Jimmy (7 years) uses a variety of vocalizations ("z," "ba," "o-o") to communicate. We have combined many of his vocalizations with signs in order to make them intelligible to more people. Jimmy's weakness is his poor oral and manual motor ability (little imitation and shaping possible) and poor visual discrimination (responses to picture difficult to obtain). His strength is his desire to communicate with people. It often happens that Jimmy approaches an adult and says "mama," which means "say 'mama' " and "give me more"!

Jeff (6 years) uses some vocalizations ("ha," "gaga") for particular needs in combination with a picture-Blissymbol **communication book.** His book is a ring binder with 20 individual pages. Each page represents a category: self-help, food, outside, play, and so on. Common words are always visible. A color coding system helps people find appropriate pages. Jeff's pattern has been regular appearance-disappearance of vocalizations over years, with good constant picture discrimination as early as 2 years of age. His motor activity level and control does not allow Jeff to sign. Thus symbols were added to a previous picture book for inclusion of action, feeling, and other, less concrete concepts that are outside of Jeff's known vocalization repertoire. Jeff's symbols and Jimmy's signing/speaking repertoire (April, 1981) are summarized in Table 10.2 below.

Mark (7 years) uses manual signing to communicate about events and things present or absent. Mark has never relied on vocalizations for communication; rather, he uses gestures and pulling. After 3½ years of signing, he is just now using sign creatively as a language. He is hard to keep up with!

The Decision

All of the children at Jowonio have one common characteristic: their initial education programs did not include an alternative communication system. There are a variety of reasons for trying the "speech" route first.

1. Spoken language has most potential for generalized use and acceptability.
2. No obvious physical disability (i.e., hearing impairment, cerebral palsy) points to alternative approaches.

Table 10.2 Jeff's and Jim's vocabulary

Jeff's first symbols

(In addition to his extensive display of object pictures)

more	go	toy	run	hug	mad
all gone	Jeff	messy stuff	up	toilet	downstairs
yes	hi/bye	help	spin	outside	happy
no	food	love	sad	open	drink
play	tickle	upside down		Jeff's room	

Jeff has used almost all of these symbols in totally spontaneous, meaningful ways. Many times, however, we have to prompt and model for him.

Jimmy's words

sign and vocal.	vocal. alone	sign alone
more /mɔ/	milk /mɔ/	run
	go	yes, no (gesture)
zip /z/	"z" (swing)	toilet
all done "a"	open "a-a"	gym

Jim has used all of these words in spontaneous, meaningful ways. Often, he will wait for a model and then repeat. But who waits longest?

3. The complex decision-making process *and* the unfamiliarity of an alternative system may create apprehension which needs to be overcome.

Frustration or failure on everyone's part—child, teacher, parent—appears to trigger the search for an alternative system. Yet before an "alternative system" is formally introduced, teachers and the speech/language clinician need to assess and observe the child's communication skills so that implementation can be rationally based. Mark gestured frequently, Jeff showed good picture discrimination skills, Jimmy showed social approaches to adults. Alpert (1980) suggests "pretraining assessment," which includes comparing progress in *two* alternative systems before making a formal decision. Whether such a procedure is used or not, a predecision assessment period should answer the following questions.

1. What is the level of prelanguage skills? (attending, imitation, play, social approaches)
2. Are any vocal skills present? If so, are they meaning-based? What is communicated with the vocalizations? Can they be shaped? Does child imitate vocalizations?
3. What kind of meaningful gesures does the child use? Can hand movements be imitated or shaped?
4. Does the child show good visual discrimination skills? Of pictures? Of shapes? Of letters? Does he attend more to pictures than other objects and actions?
5. How do the child's parents perceive and accept him or her? What are their long-range expectations for the child? How much support can they give to an alternative system?

Jeff started to use Blissymbols just 8 months ago. The decision process we followed will illustrate the type of observation and discussion that is necessary. Our teacher-clinician team observations led to the following answers on the questions outlined above.

1. Some attending, gestural imitation, social approach; mainly limited to prompted efforts.
2. Vocal skills sporadic; not easily shaped.
3. No meaningful gestures; very quickly moving hands.
4. Good picture *and* letter discrimination.
5. Parents concerned about limitations of a picture board; expect him to speak; need support in acceptance.

After consultation with the parents to obtain their input (in this case, much concern that "the book" might be a "crutch" and prevent vocalization; that "options are limited" in a communication book), the team of teachers, resource teacher, speech/language clinician, *and* administrative support persons met formally. Our observations along with our recommendation to expand Jeff's present picture board system by using Blissymbols were presented by the speech/language clinician. The discussion led to further recommendations:

1. To combine pictures and Blissymbols.
2. To keep stressing vocal/verbal skills simultaneously.
3. To include the parents' recommendations in the expansion process.

Following the process of observation and expanded team discussion seems to be a viable approach for evaluating the feasibility of the many options. At this point, there are no proven methods for choosing one alternative method over another. We have found that the team observation/discussion approach provides the subtle input needed when weighing the advantages each method might offer the child.

The Participants: Adults

The main issues which dictate our individual involvement with a child are difficulty in generalization from setting to setting, as well as the need to learn about communication in its total and real context. Athough the speech/language clinician may see a child in one-to-one therapy (in Jeff's case, to introduce shape and location of new symbols), her main responsibilities are to:

1. Observe the child and collect information from teachers and parents regarding possible communicative needs (new functional words).
2. Provide information about the system and teach important aspects to users.
3. Pinpoint opportunities for meaningful and frequent use of the system.
4. Support parents and teachers; unfamiliarity creates much apprehension.

The teachers' responsibilities are to:

1. Consistently implement recommended procedures; create opportunities throughout the day for use of the system.

2. Observe new needs and new spontaneous uses of communication.
3. Discuss problems regarding the system or communication with the speech/language clinician.
4. Learn the system (e.g., sign language).

The parents' responsibilities are to:

1. Provide frequent opportunity for use of the system at home.
2. Become aware of and point out communication needs not yet met by the system.
3. Respond to and report successful spontaneous use.
4. Learn the system.

Weekly team meetings serve as a forum to evaluate and plan. These meetings are successful when all participants are open to input and discussion. In Jim's case, a team meeting might address the following items.

1. The speech/language clinician pinpoints specific opportunities (after having observed) throughout the day when Jim could meaningfully request "help" (signed and vocalized).
2. The teacher points out that Jim may have difficulty because he doesn't like us to shape his hands, that maybe we should model only at first.
3. We jointly decide that we would model "help" in some situations when Jim takes someone's hand for help. This should lead to imitation. We plan to discuss this approach with his parents.

Other Children

Beyond all the adults, peers at home and at school play an essential role in programming for alternative systems. They are as unfamiliar with the system as teachers and parents. From the beginning of developing an alternative system, we need to establish a community of people around the child who can communicate with him. Thus the effort involved in teaching such systems as sign language to large numbers of people is an important consideration in the initial decision.

Weekly signing lessons for the whole class have stirred enthusiasm for sign language in Mark's classroom. Some of Mark's classmates can now independently communicate with Mark during play or lunch. Since Mark's signs are not accompanied by any vocalizations and since he is creatively using signs, signing skill is required to understand him. Mark is just now beginning to seek out a variety of people to talk to rather than just his teachers. Involving peers has been a most important step in socialization and generalization for Mark.

A word of the week had been the vehicle to raise the interest of peers in Jeff's and Jim's communication. During a group meeting, Jim's word (e.g., *open)* will be discussed (when and how Jim could say it) and posted for everyone. This is followed up by giving peers opportunities to elicit "Jimmy's word" from him. Pride and sharing of responsibility and success result for the peers. High levels of intrusion and opportunities for generalization are the direct benefits for Jim and Jeff.

Jeff's book arouses everyone's interest. We let his classmates flip through it. We show them how to use it and make up games they can play with "Jeff's words." We post symbols around the classroom as labels for objects (e.g., *food, toilet*). We have mentioned often that Jeff's symbol-words could be an opportunity for *all* his classmates to learn sight words!

IMPLEMENTING A SYSTEM

Initial Stage

The introduction of a system requires many decisions on "what to teach" first. Although *most* programs take into account the children's interests, many continue to teach labels of objects (such as body parts) or to reinforce the production of *any* word (spoken or otherwise) with the same tangible reinforcer. An example will illustrate best how an initial phase is crucial for much more than mere word production.

> Jeff was learning his first symbols: *more, he, food, drink*. We wanted to teach him that his words are powerful. When Jeff pointed to *more,* he got more of the same; when he pointed to *food,* he got food. He learned about meaning and control. We wanted to teach him that he could express his needs; that he needn't cry and get upset. So when Jeff seemed to want more and cried, we'd model appropriate communication for him by pointing to *more.* We wanted to show him that we valued his choices and feelings. Therefore, we have always used symbols as tools for Jeff to express his feelings and control others.

Parents are the most important source of information at this stage. They know best what their child loves and needs. Continuous contact, including frequent home visits, can help the speech/language clinician identify first words to teach and later verify that the child has begun to use them as intended.

With both a communication book and signs, the apprehension created by unfamiliarity needs to be turned into excitement at the prospect of new productive communication avenues. Parents and teachers need to *learn* about the system quickly; they need to see the system used proficiently by the speech/language clinician. Parents may need to express their doubts about the system, and they need teachers or speech/language clinicians to help them find those countless opportunities to practice communication effortlessly.

Middle Stage

Even in our approach, which is meaning-based and self-reinforcing, a point may be reached when all the words you believe the child can handle have been introduced. You see that the child is using these words with your prompts, but rarely on his or her own. You feel that this is a time to make sure the child knows and appropriately uses what has been introduced.

Assessing what the child really knows is more than asking him to point to certain symbols or keeping track of spontaneous vocalizations or signs. It means we have to change our behavior to let the child tell us more frequently what he or she does know. For example, Jeff points to *spin*. In the initial stage, the teacher or parent would respond immediately, saying, "Jeff want spin?" and then spinning Jeff around. In the middle stage, the teacher or parent responds, "Okay, come on," but waits for Jeff to get into an appropriate position before spinning him around.

Waiting is an essential component of this stage. We wait for the children to indicate that they understand the meaning of their own utterances. We also hold our "What want?" and give them opportunities to initiate. We let them walk down the hall to other rooms and wait for them to say "Hi" first. We also give them opportunities to respond to us the way we respond to them (that is, to ask them for "more shaving cream!").

In Jeff's case, the middle stage has been a time for him to become more independent in the use of his book. With some prompting, he can now flip to appropriate pages in his book. He also seems to be much more familiar with all the pages in his book; he is beginning to choose which category he wants. By changing the positions of some pictures and symbols in the book, we have helped Jeff refocus on the actual symbol/picture, which appears to aid his attending to "what he points to."

As an aside, I'd like to mention that a communication book is an individually created instrument for a particular child. The practical aspects of arranging pictures/symbols, of finding sturdy materials, of expanding and re-arranging, and/or repairing should not be underestimated. The tool itself needs to be assessed by all its users, with the speech/language clinician as the coordinator of changes.

Later Stage

It is exciting to read that some children have used sign phrases up to seven signs (Carr, 1979) and that sign language has become a true language for them. That the same can happen with communication boards is known for other populations (for example, cerebral palsied children), but not yet for autistic-like children. At Jowonio, Mark is the only child who has reached this later stage of development. Therefore, all of the examples in this section are drawn from our experiences with him. As with oral/verbal children, we set our communication goals according to normal developmental sequences. Among Mark's goals this year have been subject-verb-object phrase structure and responding to where, what, and who questions. As with all autistic-like children, unusual language patterns may develop. **Echopraxia** is observed in signing (Creedon, 1973). For example, Mark started all his sentences with "I want...," although that was only appropriate sometimes. He echoed parts of questions and did not respond to them.

As with all other autistic-like children, individual communication assessments (especially *contextual* language samples) are necessary to guide the team's way to the next level of communication. Priorities chosen do not generally differ from those we choose for spoken communication. Often use of language (pragmatics) is a large consideration. In Mark's case, we wanted him to initiate conversation, to respond to questions, and to speak of things outside the here and now. Sentence structure development (syntax) and further vocabulary growth (semantics) are approached as well, with the emphasis on appropriate contextual use.

In this stage, the children may begin to pick up structures and vocabulary incidentally (though planned by us—there has to be time and plenty of opportunity for talking every day!). Typical language learners are surrounded by competent users of their language. One of the most important components of Mark's program has been a total communication environment. Teachers sign whenever they speak to him or the group. This increases Mark's attending, as well as causes him to "practice" new signs. Much of our conversation time with Mark is spent extending his utterances and ideas and getting him to use more complete phrases.

Teachers and the speech/language clinician continue to provide support for the parents. This stage of signing requires much dedication from everyone to truly learn the language. Mark's parents are excited about his constant meaningful signing, but "it can be frustrating." For instance, Mark used a sign for *dome* to tell his mother where he went on a field trip. She didn't know that he was talking about the field trip, that they had gone to the dome, or that Mark had learned a sign similar to *balloon* to mean *dome*. The teachers were surprised in this instance that Mark remembered the sign and tried to relate the event! Fortunately, communication about events between teachers and parents is steady; signing is practiced at frequent parent-teacher meetings; and Mark's mother has become proficient at guessing what Mark is signing.

LONG-TERM CONSIDERATIONS

There are considerations with long-term implications that separate programming of alternative communication from spoken communication.

First, there are a variety of sign languages, including American Sign Language, Signed English, and Pidgin Signed English. In order to teach a child a true language, we need to choose *one* of the systems. Using several at one time or in sequence is like teaching French and English in the same lesson. Some of the questions that need to be considered are:

1. Does the child comprehend spoken English structure input—or does he mainly use sign input?
2. What is the child's reading potential? Will he need to know English sentence structure to read or will he be limited to some sight words?

3. What is the child's potential future community—Ameslan users or hearing signers?
4. What system do possible future teachers use?
5. What system dominates in the local education community?

One obvious requirement is that we, as teachers and speech/language clinicians, need to become totally familiar with sign languages. Our knowledge and long-term perspective is likely to have the greatest influence on what system is chosen.

Second, growth with a communication board (or book) requires us to consider the expansion potential of the tool we are using. The heavier and larger a tool, the less likely is its generalized use in settings outside home and school. We need to address whether:

1. The child can learn to use the system on a smaller scale (perhaps ¾ " squares on an "apron").
2. An extension system, such as spelling or classifying, can be taught. (For instance, Blissymbols may have a symbol for *dirty*. The child would point to *opposite* + *dirty* to describe *clean*.)

Third, another limitation of sign language is lack of universality (few people sign). A limitation of communication boards is their restricted space—for mobility and additional concepts. Concerns over those limitations are foremost in the minds of parents and teachers. With Jeff and Jim, we continue to push for verbalization to overcome those limitations. If verbalization is not a prospect, other alternatives may need to become part of long-term planning. Alternatives such as spelling, writing, typing, or using a **voice synthesizer** could possibly become supplemental to a primary mode such as signing. Those long-term considerations need to be part of early programming, however. Mark, for example, seems to be showing a growing potential for reading. This potential might lead to greater than ever priority given to his reading program. Such a program, if planned in coordination with the speech/language clinician, can from the beginning be communication-based and -motivated.

Educational/Vocational Placement Considerations

When a child using an alternative system changes schools or becomes part of a vocational program, teachers, parents, and the speech/language clinician need to assure that the new environment can provide for continued growth in communication.

With sign language, an interpreter may be necessary for effective communication. In many cases, new teachers need to take sign language courses. When a child becomes proficient in sign language use, as Mark has, an introductory course will not suffice. Practice in using and understanding sign language is essential. We hope to provide this experience for Mark's new teachers before they need to communicate with him without our support.

Communication books are not as complex to learn. Yet continuity will be assured only if teachers and the speech/language clinician are familiar with the system, trust its usefulness, and can expand on it. They also need to learn how to use the communication book most effectively throughout the day.

Observation of the child and initial communication with the child in his or her present school and at home are essential components of continuity in using an alternative communication system. It is the teachers', parents', and speech clinician's responsibility to provide *all* of the information to new individuals involved. Follow-up visits by the previous teacher or speech/language clinician would facilitate continuity.

FINAL CONSIDERATIONS

The use of an alternative communication system has had undeniable positive effects on overall behavior in the three children in our program. Mark almost never self-stimulates any more and prefers signing to silence. He attends more readily when signed to. He expresses some feelings by signing instead of tantruming or self-stimulating. He makes us aware of his thoughts by communicating about them. He has just learned the meaning of "like" and now compares things: "blue like Mommy's car."

Jeff gets frustrated less often, and his scratching has almost disappeared. He seems to be becoming aware of his emotions, of his own body and actions; all of these are expressed in his book. He shows pride about *his* book. And he appears to enjoy the control he has over us when he communicates with us. We also know more about his conceptual skills. He consistently answers yes/no questions with his book and we can have conversations.

Jimmy also gets frustrated less often; head banging has become rare. He enjoys control over his environment and the independence we give him now that he didn't have before. He uses sounds and motions just to "connect" with us (saying "boom-boom" and wanting us to repeat it), enjoying the contact more than isolation.

Thus, all three children have grown emotionally, behaviorally, and in demonstrating their cognitive skills. Yet all three continue to need extensive programming for their growth in *all* areas—emotional, social, academic, and communication. Some skills—such as spontaneity, initiating language use, creating sentences and ideas independently—may be just as slow to appear with alternative systems as with spoken communication. Some tendencies—such as echoing, roteness, failure to initiate language—may be just as prominent. But with some children (and they must be carefully selected and planned for), the alternative system may provide a better vehicle for overcoming obstacles that these particular children could not overcome with oral communication alone.

Finally, let me quote one of Jimmy's teachers describing the effect of growing communication on his behavior:

> We have given him a system which responds to his active involvement in the environment. He is talking and acting with much more precision and focus....The beauty and the challenge of the system is to use it to give him appropriate and satisfying ways of dealing with himself and others.

REFERENCES

Alpert, C. Procedures for determining the optimal nonspeech mode with the autistic child. In R.L. Schiefelbusch (Ed.), *Nonspeech language and communication: Analysis and intervention*. Baltimore: University Park Press, 1980.

Benaroya, S., Wesley, S., Ogilvie, H., Klein, L.S., & Clarke, E. Sign language and multisensory input of children with communication and related developmental disorders: Phase II. *Journal of Autism and Developmental Disorders*, 1979, *9*(2), 219-220.

Benaroya, S., Wesley, S., Ogilvie, H., Klein, L.S., & Meany, M. Sign language and multisensory input training of children with communication and related developmental disorders. *Journal of Autism and Childhood Schizophrenia*, 1977, *7*, 23-31.

Bliss, C. *Semantography*. Sydney, Aust.: Semantography Publications, 1965.

Bonvillian, J.D., & Nelson, K.E. Sign language acquisition in a mute autistic boy. *Journal of Speech and Hearing Disorders*, 1976, *41*, 339-347.

Brady, D.O., & Smouse, A.D. A simultaneous comparison of three methods for language training with an autistic child: An experimental single case analysis. *Journal of Autism and Childhood Schizophrenia*, 1978, *8*, 271-279.

Bryson, C.Q. Short-term memory and cross-modal information processing in autistic children. *Journal of Learning Disabilities*, 1972, *5*, 81-91.

Carr, E.G. Teaching autistic children to use sign language: Some research issues. *Journal of Autism and Developmental Disorders*, 1979, *9*(4), 345-359.

Casey, L.O. Development of communicative behavior in autistic children: A parent program using manual signs. *Journal of Autism and Childhood Schizophrenia*, 1978, *8*, 45-59.

Cohen, M. Development of language behavior in an autistic child using total communication. *Exceptional Children*, 1981, *47*(5), 379-381.

Creedon, M.P. *Appropriate behavior through communication: A new program in simultaneous language for nonverbal children*. Chicago: Dysfunctioning Child Center Publications, 1973.

Fay, W.H., & Schuler, A.L. *Emerging language in autistic children*. Baltimore: University Park Press, 1980.

Fulwiler, R.L., & Fouts, R.S. Acquisition of American Sign Language by a noncommunicating autistic child. *Journal of Autism and Childhood Schizphrenia*, 1976, *6*, 43-51.

Hermelin, B. Coding and the sense modalities. In L. Wing (Ed.), *Early childhood autism*. London: Pergamon Press, 1976.

Hollis, J.H., & Carrier, J.K. Intervention strategies for non-speech children. In R.L. Schiefelbusch (Ed.), *Language intervention strategies*. Baltimore: University Park Press, 1978.

Konstantenareas, M.M., & Leibovitz, S.F. *Auditory-visual vs. visual communication training with autistic children*. Paper presented at the annual meeting of the American Speech and Hearing Association, Chicago, 1977.

LaVigna, G.W. Communication training in mute, autistic adolescents using the written word. *Journal of Autism and Childhood Schizophrenia*, 1977, *7*(2), 135-149.

Luria, A.R. *Higher cortical functions in man*. New York: Basic Books, 1966.

McLean, L.P., & McLean, J.E. A language training program for nonverbal autistic children. *Journal of Speech and Hearing Disorders*, 1974, *39*(2), 186-194.

O'Connor, N. Visual perception in autistic children. In M. Rutter (Ed.), *Infantile autism: Concepts, characteristics and treatment*. Edinburg: Churchill Livingstone, 1971.

Premack, A.J., & Premack, D. Teaching language to an ape. *Scientific American*, 1972, *227*, 92-99.

Pronovost, W., Wakstein, M.P., & Wakstein, D.J. A longitudinal study of speech behavior and language comprehension of fourteen children diagnosed atypical or autistic. *Exceptional Children*, 1966, *33*, 19-26.

Ruttenberg, B.A., & Gordon, E.G. Evaluating the communication of the autistic child. *Journal of Speech and Hearing Disorders*, 1967, *32*, 314-324.

Salvin, A., Routh, D.K., Foster, R.E., & Lovejoy, K.M. Acquisition of modified American Sign Language by a mute autistic child. *Journal of Autism and Childhood Schizophrenia*, 1977, *7*, 359-371.

Shaeffer, B., Kollinzas, G., Musil, A., & McDowell, P. Spontaneous verbal language for autistic children through signed speech. *Sign Language Studies*, 1977, *17*, 287-328.

Silverman, H. *The educational applications of the Ontario Crippled Children's Centre (O.C.C.C.): Symbol communication program for other groups of exceptional children*. Toronto: Blissymbolics Communication Institute, 1976.

Simon, N. Echolalic speech in childhood autism. *Archives of General Psychiatry,* 1975, *32,* 1439-1446.
Tubbs, V.K. The type of linguistic disability in psychotic children. *Journal of Mental Deficiency Research,* 1966, *10,* 230-240.

SOURCES OF INFORMATION ON ALTERNATIVE COMMUNICATION SYSTEMS

1. Signing

Fristoe, M., & Lloyd, L.L. Manual communication for the retarded and others with severe communication impairment: A resource list. *Mental Retardation,* October, 1977, 18-21.
Wilbur, R. *American Sign Language and sign systems.* Baltimore: University Park Press, 1979.
Local Association for the Hearing Impaired

2. Blissymbols

Hehner, B. (Ed.). *Blissymbols for use.* Toronto: Blissymbolics Communication Institute (350 Rumsey Road, Ontario, Canada M4G 1R8), 1979.
Silverman, H., McNaughton, S., & Kates, B. *Handbook for Blissymbolics.* Toronto: Blissymbolics Communication Institute, 1978.
Local Cerebral Palsy Association

3. Written Word

LaVigna, G.W. Communication training in mute, autistic adolescents using the written word. *Journal of Autism and Childhood Schizophrenia,* 1977, *7*(2), 135-149.
Marshal, N., & Hegrenes, J. The use of written language as a communication system for an autistic child. *Journal of Speech and Hearing Disorders,* 1972, *37,* 258-261.

4. Non-SLIP

Hollis, J.H., & Carrier, J.K. Intervention strategies for nonspeech children. In R.L. Schiefelbusch (Ed.), *Language intervention strategies.* Baltimore: University Park Press, 1978.
McLean, L.P., & McLean, J.E. A language training program for nonverbal autistic children. *Journal of Speech and Hearing Disorders,* 1974, *39*(2), 186-194.

5. Information on All Systems

Lloyd, L.L. (Ed.). *Communication assessment and intervention strategies.* Baltimore: University Press, 1976.
Schiefelbusch, R.L. (Ed.). *Nonspeech language and communication: Analysis and intervention.* Baltimore: University Park Press, 1980.

GLOSSARY OF TERMS

Alternative communication system: Any nonoral system of communication (signing; picture, symbol, or word boards; writing; voice synthesizer) used to replace or supplement oral-verbal communication. Mainly used with handicapped persons with auditory problems (deaf) or motor problems (cerebral-palsied). Recently, use of alternative systems with other populations (mentally retarded, aphasic, autistic) has been explored.

Blissymbols: Ideographic ($\bigcirc$ = house), meaning-based ($\downarrow$ = down), and arbitrary (+ !! = yes) symbols used in combination with printed words to create a language of symbols. Charles Bliss (1965) invented the system with the idea of creating a "universal language." Blissymbols have been increasingly and successfully used with cerebral-palsied individuals. The Blissymbol Foundation (see *Sources*) attempts to keep it a uniform visual language. Although the symbols can be creatively combined by the user, they are always on display. Thus it is a nontransient system and need for retrieval is nearly eliminated. Little motoric skill necessary.

Communication board: Display of pictures, words, symbols, or letters on a board to be carried by the user at all times. Size, durability, and options for adding to the board are considerations in choice of materials. Often the display is organized by the Fitzgerald Key or coded in some manner to make it faster to use. Since the display never disappears (nontransient), the need for retrieval is eliminated.

Communication book: A communication board which is divided into pages for better mobility (small size) or less distraction by large number of pictures or symbols.

Cross-modal association: Used when information from two or more modes (auditory, visual, tactile, etc.) needs to be processed or related at the same time.

Echolalia: The exact repetition of a phrase someone else has spoken. In normal development, echolalia is a well-known behavior of 3-year-olds, who repeat things without "understanding." Autistic children may echo phrases immediately or after a delay and have little or no self-structured spontaneous language. However, detailed analyses of an autistic child's speech show a variety of intended meanings of echoic utterances, often not just empty repetition (see Fay and Schuler, 1980).

Echopraxia: Echolalia accompanied by movements of the extremities. In communication, echopraxia refers to sign language.

Multisensory input: Use of several modalities (auditory, visual, tactile, etc.) simultaneously to convey the meaning of a single element. For example, using a real apple to demonstrate the meaning of the word, you can touch, taste, and see the apple, hear and see the word spoken, see the word written, trace a picture or letters representing it, and so on.

Non-SLIP: These arbitrary plastic or wooden symbols were first used to teach a chimpanzee, Sarah, limited communication skills (Premack & Premack, 1972). Hollis and Carrier (1978) then began to use a set of 20 nouns, 5 verbs, 3 prepositions, and 2 functors with severely retarded individuals. It is a nontransient system, requiring little motor ability and no auditory processing.

Nontransient system: A multiple-choice type system where pictures or symbols remain, so that short- or long-term storage and retrieval are not essential. Communication boards are nontransient because (*a*) they are stored on a permanent display for all to see, and (*b*) a sequence of pictures or symbols can be easily retraced with pictures and symbols present.

Oral communication: Spoken/heard communication. Often used synonymously with *verbal* communication, although technically the use of an alternative system is *verbal* as well.

Sign language: Gestural language used mainly by deaf individuals. There are many forms of signing, including American Sign Language (ASL or Ameslan), Signed English, and Pidgin Signed English. The manual movements, though complex, are easier to shape than oral movements. Signing is transient.

Symbol systems (Includes Blissymbols and Non-SLIP, among others): System used to express meanings which may or may not be easily pictured (e.g., "more") by a visual configuration. Letters and Non-SLIP symbol shapes never relate directly to their meaning, whereas some Blissymbols directly represent an object. In comparison to pictures, symbols can represent a broader, more generalized meaning (compare a picture for *open* with an "open box," the Blissymbol $\underline{\bigtriangleup}$). The association of symbols with their meaning requires higher cognitive ability than association of pictures with objects.

Temporal sequencing: All communication occurs over time, usually in a special (sentence) sequence. Spoken words are ordered in time and need to be memorized (because they are transient) for processing. Signs are ordered in space and time and also transient. Communication board pointing is also spatially and temporally ordered, yet is nontransient because the display is permanent.

Total communication: In this chapter, used to describe the combined use of manual and spoken communication, either receptive or expressive.

Transient systems: Systems in which initial portions of a statement are not preserved—except by the listener's memory—as the statement continues. Speaking and signing are transient and require good short-term retrieval for comprehension and use.

Verbalization: The use of a conventionally accepted approximation of a word. Often limited to *spoken* communication. Many autistic children may verbalize without recognizable meaning or intention.

Vocalizations: Making sounds either in sound play or babbling *or* to communicate meaning. The sounds are not close approximations of words.

Voice synthesizer: Recently developed instrument which is operated by push buttons and produces audible, intelligible words and sentences. Beginning to be used with disabled individuals.

Part IV

Developing Support Systems for Families and Schools

11
Parent-School Partnership: The Essential Component

Judy Kugelmass

The staff manual for our school defines the approach taken with parents: "At Jowonio, we approach parents with respect, trying to respond to their concerns and, with them, developing a consistent program for their children." The belief in the value of parent involvement in the education of their children has led to important programmatic practices which have as their goal the integration of the child's home and school life. Jowonio's history reflects the desire of parents to bring their children's school experiences closer to the values and attitudes of their homes. Parents were the originators of this setting. Although only two of the original "founding parents" remain, family involvement continues as a key component in programming. In a private school, parents have chosen to send their children here and are therefore committed to truly integrated education and the individualized, psychoeducational approach used with all the children as well as to the concept of family involvement. This commitment certainly facilitates an active role by the families of both our typical and "special" children. This chapter describes both the formal and informal practices that have been developed at Jowonio to foster parental involvement. Each approach, however, should not be seen as a separate program plugged into the school to deal with our concern for families. They are aspects of a milieu which has internalized a commitment to each child's family.

Both the structure of the school and its programs are continually evolving. The program description is that which existed during the 1979–1980 school year. Since then, the school's response to parents has continued to change. The importance of describing what we have done during this one year lies not in our ability to replicate our practices from year to year or to have others do the same. Rather, the goal of this chapter is to present some approaches towards parental involvement that we have found to be successful and from which you may take concepts which fit best into your setting. These concepts can then be translated into practices that best fit the needs and resources of your school and families.

It is not essential for a school to have role designated Parent Worker in order to carry out the practices that I describe. Having the funds available to establish this position is not always feasible. During the 1980–1981 school year, the various roles that our Parent Workers have taken, as described here, were divided among several of our school staff, inclding classroom teachers and assistants, supervisory personnel, and administrative staff. We recognize the advantage of one person coordinating all parental activity, but feel that the most important aspect is that the work get done, regardless of the staff position. Teachers can, therefore, integrate many of our practices into their approach toward parents, as can social workers, psychologists, supervisors, and administrators.

The concepts which underlie the development of our parent groups are likewise applicable to programs which may not have the resources to establish formal group programs. Group discussion by parents at a classroom level or social events sponsored by an individual teacher can accomplish many of the same goals as those described in this chapter. Teachers, in the same way as many parents, often feel intimidated by the "expert" role of other professionals. We must keep in mind that teachers and parents occupy most of the child's waking hours. A true partnership between parents and teacher, those adults who know the child best, will assure optimal programming for all children.

THE SCHOOL-FAMILY PARTNERSHIP

The nature of the commitment to their child's education is different for each parent. Parents of typical children have learned about the school from friends and relatives and vary in their expectations about the total program as well as in their need for involvement in their child's program. Our "handicapped" population is referred by other agencies in the community, pediatricians, and school district committees on the handicapped. These families vary as much as all others. Over 50% of our children live in single-parent families, which both necessitates an increased supportive role on the part of the school and complicates the parent's ability to play an active role in school activities. In these instances, as in circumstances faced by other families, the parents who are most in need of support are often least able to obtain it. We do not approach this situation with the often-heard attitude that "those parents who become involved are those who need it least," but rather we believe that each family is in a unique situation at any given moment and needs to be responded to accordingly. Basically, the approach towards parents has the same underlying philosophy as the rest of the program; it is highly individualized and recognizes that parents, like everyone else, are at different stages of readiness to learn and integrate new skills. Both the affective and intellectual aspects of parenting are approached in our programming, as we recognize the need to integrate both in order for learning and growth to occur.

Recent research substantiates the strong relationship between home variables and school achievement and validates the emphasis Jowonio places on home-school partnership and its approach toward parent involvement. Nedler and McAfee (1979) summarize into six categories those variables shown to have the most significant influence over a child's performance in school. They are family structure, family attitudes, family process, home-school interactions, cognitive factors, and affective factors. Family structure includes the number of children in the home, the occupations of the father and mother, the educational backgrounds of the parents, family income, religion, and language of the home. These factors, although important in relationship to school achievement, are not as important as attitudes and practices within the home. Family attitude relates to the parents' feelings toward their child's education, their ambitions for their child, and the child's own aspirations. They report that positive parent interest in the child is correlated with higher school achievement. Family process variables are identified as press for achievement, language models, academic guidance, family activities, dominance patterns, independence training, work habits and order, and stimulation and reinforcement practices. Coleman (1966) and Jencks (1972) are cited as evidence that both the home and social system have a greater influence than the schools on achievement and that, therefore, home-school interactions are essential.

Both the cognitive and affective behaviors of parents have been shown to exert a strong influence over school achievement. Nedler and McAfee (1979) identify positive parent behaviors in each domain. The cognitive factors they list include:

1. Parents who see themselves as teachers of their child.
2. Parents who talk *with* their child rather than *at* him or her.
3. Parents who consistently provide some sort of academic guidance for their child.
4. Parental behavior that consistently reflects praise and reinforcement.
5. A high level of verbal interaction within the home.
6. Homes that have a variety of books and materials for the child.
7. Parents who provide information and feedback to the child about the environment.
8. Parents who listen to, share, and plan with the child.

The affective factors correlated with the child's development are identified as:

1. The parent's sense of self-esteem and confidence.
2. Consistency in managing the child.
3. Discipline that reflects rationality and explanations.
4. A willingness to spend time with the child and devote efforts to child rearing.
5. Parental feelings of control over the events in their lives.
6. Parental ability to work within the social and economic system and operate within the framework of established institutions (pp. 31-32).

The implications of these factors for programs developed for parent involvement go beyond the teaching of effective parenting skills and reach into the need to understand the total life-space of the child and his or her family. Although a school can do little to alter a family's "structure," it can provide an environment where all families feel comfortable enough to want to become involved in its functioning at whatever level seems feasible. Jowonio offers many levels of involvement for all the school's families. Involvement may range from attending one of the many social functions arranged either by the school or by an individual teacher to a more active role in programming and hiring as a member of the Board, 50% of which is made up of parents. The key to it all, though, seems to be that an environment has been created in which all parents feel that they are an important part of the program. The effect of the staff's openness to parents is described by one parent.

> I don't know what they do at Jowonio but you can just go in and feel like you can talk to them. They are not threatened by our presence. They say, "Come on in. We are doing dancing now. Watch." That is one of the real keys that, for whatever reason, we as parents are not threatening them and in return they are not threatening us by setting themselves apart. I always feel that when I go in at any time I am really welcome and they are pleased that I am there. It makes me feel good and it certainly makes me feel like coming back. With other experiences that we have had, I really felt very much the intruder; and I was not only taking up mental time with the teacher but physical space, "If you could just move outside the door, I'd be able to deal better." That attitude is not at all at Jowonio; otherwise I don't think I'd be skipping up here [25 miles away] all the time.

As a result of this feeling of "belonging" to the school, parents are frequent visitors either informally, as is the case with the father above, or in more formalized roles as parent-volunteers, party givers, guests, or occasionally as entertainers or instructors of those skills they have which are of great interest to children. Parents' active participation in the school helps reinforce the attitude and process variables essential to positive achievement. The openness of the school to parents gives them the opportunity to observe our teachers and their classroom space. Each classroom presents a model of the eight positive parental behaviors cited by Nedler and McAfee (1979) as highly correlated with cognitive development in children. In addition, positive affective growth is fostered by the parents' feeling a part of the program and thereby having more control over this significant part of their life, which, in turn, enhances their confidence and self-esteem. A model of consistent management of the child and rational discipline is also presented.

The many social events held by the school add to the spirit necessary to sustain positive feelings throughout the school year. For some of our parents, these may be the only social events they are able to attend because of the many other demands they face in their lives. It is essential that parents have the opportunity to come together and share some of the joys of raising their children. In the past, the large extended family served as a gathering place to share holiday festivities, birthdays, family picnics, pot-luck suppers; but for many of our families, these kinds of gatherings no longer take place because of distances, circumstance, and changing family structures. Jowonio offers these occasions to our families and thereby tightens the connection they feel for each other as well as for their children.

FAMILIES WITH SPECIAL NEEDS

Although these social events and the sense of openness to families are essential to the operation of the entire school, these aspects are of particular importance to the families of our special needs children. For many of these families, particularly those in which the child is severely handicapped and may therefore exhibit bizarre behaviors, large social gatherings are to be avoided or attended with a good deal of anxiety because the family members anticipate others' reactions to their child or sibling. As Barsch (1968) points out, the attitudes of relatives are often viewed by parents of handicapped children as a negative factor added to the other problems of raising their child. This has been the case for several of our families. Although it is important for relatives and family friends to learn to support and accept the handicapped child and his or her parents, it is equally essential that parents and siblings have the opportunity to share a joyous social occasion without the anxiety that may accompany an extended family or community gathering. Integration and its benefits extend beyond the classroom and into the social events of the school. One parent expressed the effects of these events in this way: "I feel like I'm a parent at these things, not just a parent of a handicapped child." Participation in these events reduces the sense of isolation many of our parents experience. The following suggestion is offered by the same mother.

> I think one thing that is really important for all of us to realize is that a child isn't just a child with a handicap but a child within a family and that there are a lot of other things going on. And the same is true for parents. Teachers and other kinds of people working with children and families need to see that those parents have needs besides the needs that focus on the child. That is one way we can say, yes, okay, go ahead and go out for the evening. We can refer them to ways to get babysitters and how to get information.

Not only does integrated programming directly benefit each child, but it also presents many opportunities for positive growth among their parents, which in turn has positive effects upon the children. Parents have the opportunity to observe their child interacting with both typical and handicapped peers and therefore can get a better perspective on the child's strengths and weaknesses. An issue often raised by parents of special children, particularly if their child is an only or a first child, is that they do not know which of their child's problems are the result of the handicapping condition and which are a function of normal development. A 3-year-old nonverbal child may refuse to share his toy or relinquish a favorite blanket, as might any 3-year-old. By observing the other children and talking with other parents, this child's parents may be able to put the behavior into better perspective. Likewise, unrealistic expectations are often tempered by a parent's painful, first-hand exposure to the competencies of typical peers. This awareness can occur here often because of the support given to the parent both by the professional and by other parents. All our parents are able to share the pride they have in their children's accomplishments, whether they be learning to subtract or learning to sort shapes.

The parents of our special children are thus able to see their child from a perspective other than one which focuses on the disability. They are afforded the opportunity, as are all parents, to view the developmental aspects and positive growth of their child's behavior. In this way, it becomes somewhat easier to sort out those aspects of the child's disability which have been magnified by cultural bias. This awareness reduces the psychological devastation they may feel, which in turn results in an increased capacity to cope and therefore help their child.

While the basic philosophy at Jowonio focuses on establishing a normalized environment for all the children and their families, we recognize that the families of handicapped children have needs for support which are often more intense than those of other families. The stress they encounter has been repeatedly documented (Auerbach, 1968; Barsch, 1968; Love, 1970) and reported by parents themselves (Greenfeld, 1978; Kaufman, 1976; Park, 1967). The handicapped children at Jowonio have been labeled as *autistic* or *severely emotionally disturbed* and, as is characteristic of many such children, are often nonverbal or have severe language disorders. These handicapping conditions create certain pressures on our families that are often different than those encountered by parents of children whose condition is considered to be, by its nature, a physical disability. In the past, the dominant school of thought regarding the etiology of autism and severe emotional disturbance was that these children were the victims of improper parenting. The psychoanalytic approach, which saw the "refrigerator" or "schizophrenogenic" parent, particularly the mother, as responsible for the child's condition, invaded the culture as well as the medical profession. It left in its wake scores of guilt-ridden parents. The treatment of choice was, according to this theoretic position, to remove the child from the family and place him or her into a residential "therapeutic environment." Parents, because they were seen as the cause of the condition of their child, were kept away and received individual psychotherapy (Bettelheim, 1967).

The approach taken at Jowonio regarding the cause and treatment of autism is dramatically different from this psychoanalytical approach and agrees with experts who feel that the autistic child's strange behavior is the result of improper sensory processing (Rimland, 1964; Ritvo, 1976; Rutter, 1971). The precise organic condition underlying autism continues to be investigated; but to those of us who have worked intimately with autistic children and their families, it is clear that parental behavior cannot be held responsible for the dramatic condition of their children. Studies cited by Love (1970) point out similar findings. Although some studies found certain statistical tendencies, a sizeable amount of variance in child behavior remains unexplained.

> We still found families in which the parents appeared maladjusted, evidently didn't get along, and exhibited the most abhorrent kinds of attitudes toward their children, but those children appeared to be getting along beautifully. We saw parents whose attitudes and other characteristics were in nearly perfect congruence with the stereotype of the "good parent" but whose children display problems of the most severe order (Peterson, 1967).

In addition to the children who exhibit classic autistic behaviors and histories, we have several children who have had extremely deprived and traumatic early experiences, which have certainly contributed to their current disability. In either case, the position taken toward the parents of our children is that they are not to blame for their child's condition. Inappropriate behavior on the part of the parents can often be seen as a reaction to the child's handicapping condition and can, in fact, intensify the child's problems. It is our belief that parents can develop the skills and self-confidence required to help minimize their child's problems and at the same time make life for the entire family more pleasant.

It is important to point out that children and their families come to Jowonio on a voluntary basis, which in itself demontrates that the parents have a level of awareness of their child's problem and a commitment towards working with the staff. The severely disturbed or abusive parent is not represented in the population of parents with whom I have worked at Jowonio. I do believe that the techniques employed at this school are equally applicable with "disturbed" parents, though I recognize the greater difficulty presented by parents who are overwrought by their own psychological disturbances. The disturbed parent cannot be seen in isolation from a child and the rest of his or her environment. By providing for parents a supportive program which focuses both on the needs of their children and on their own needs, a good deal of the pressure facing the adults can be alleviated.

FOSTERING COMMUNICATION

The importance of open communication between the parents and the school cannot be too strongly emphasized. For many of our parents, the informal structure of the school is not enough to assure that two-way communication will flow throughout the school year. We have developed several programmatic approaches to help assure that parents are aware of the activities and events that will occur. All our families receive a monthly newsletter and calendar which inform them of significant events that have happened in the school and community which may be of interest and importance. In addition, these newsletters and frequent dittoed notes tell of activities which can be anticipated for the coming month. All children need to have some degree of predictability in their life. With autistic and disturbed children, the slightest change in daily routine can be a devastating experience. By informing our parents far in advance of school holidays or special events, we can better prepare both the parents and the child for these occurrences.

For a family with a typical child, the events of the day at school are most often communicated by the child. Of course you have the classic dialogue, "What did you do in school today?" "Nothing." But often even a 3-year-old will tell of a special trip to the library, a birthday party, an argument with a best friend and the resulting hurt feelings, or just that he or she is feeling particularly tired after playing tag all afternoon at the park. This type of communication is lost to the parent of a nonverbal or language impaired child. Often our children cannot relate a sense of the continuity of the events of the day to their current state of mind. It is frustrating, to say the least, to be faced with a child who is upset at the end of the day but cannot communicate the source of his or her upset or may not even know. "Is my child sick or hurt?" "Has someone said or done something to him on the bus?" "What can I do to help?" We try to answer these questions either by a phone call that explains that, in fact, Billy didn't want to leave the swimming pool and has been crying ever since or by the use of a small notebook accompanying each child in his or her lunchbox. Any messages which need to be communicated, if a parent cannot be reached by telephone, are jotted down by one of the teachers. This is done for all the children at least once a week, so that the parents can get an idea of what the week has been like for their child. The notebooks have a reciprocal purpose in that parents can tell teachers of events that have occurred at home which may be significant for a particular child, such as the birth of a new sibling, a lost tooth, or a visit to Grandma's. The importance of the notebook for both the parents and teachers of the language impaired child is especially obvious. Parents see it as a useful device not only as a means to communicate problems their child may have had or to inform them of coming events but as a major step towards normalizing the child's and family's experience of schooling.

> Billy got really upset because they put too much jelly on his sandwich; I wouldn't ever have known. It is a simple thing, but it's not. He got really upset. Then if he had a bad day, I can write and tell or they can tell me he got upset about swimming or something. But even simple things, a simple thing upset him that I would never [have] guessed or known.

> I find it helpful in the sense that Alex will not volunteer information. If I say, "How was your day today at school?" he will say, "Fine." Even if it was

probably a disaster, that would be his programmed response. But if I look in the notebook and there is a listing of a couple of activities that he did, I can say, not specifically maybe, "Did you go swimming today?" but "Did you have a good time when you went swimming?" or "Did such and such happen today?" or maybe bring something out that he might be willing to talk about. If I didn't have that almost day-to-day cueing, I wouldn't be able to ask those questions and I wouldn't be able to get him to start to talk to me about it, which I think is one of the most helpful things. And from my standpoint, sending the notebook back is to feed information to them and say, "Look, he really had a bad night. He slept only an hour and a half. That may take its toll on you today." They are prepared in that way.

PARENT WORKERS

The best form of communication is certainly face-to-face contact between our staff and parents. In addition to the frequent meetings between parents and teachers both at the school and at the child's home, two parent workers, one full-time and the other half-time, are in constant contact with the child's family and teachers. This role has evolved over the past few years from one which was a social worker position, where the parent worker spent time with the family in a counseling relationship, to one which is a liaison between home and school. The parent worker may become involved in a counseling relationship with a parent or family, if that seems to be needed. For the most part, however, our parents want assistance with concrete suggestions regarding how to handle certain behaviors that their child may be exhibiting and, at the same time, expressing the feelings they may have about the situation they currently face.

The position of parent worker was first given to a woman who was a special education teacher with extensive experience in working with preschool children. During her first year, she worked exclusively with families and found herself to be experiencing a good deal of frustration when called upon to offer concrete suggestions. She did not know the children as well as she felt she needed to in order to offer the assistance the parents were seeking. The next year the role was changed to one where the parent worker divided her time equally between the child and the parents. Another half-time parent worker was added to the staff as it became obvious that one worker would not have enough time to deal with all the children and their families in any depth. The second parent worker is also a special education teacher, currently working on a degree in family counseling.

The parent workers are involved only with the handicapped students and their families. This relationship does not take the place of their communication with the teachers and other staff members, which is open to all our families, but rather helps facilitate communication around the many issues that these families must face. In the fall, before a new special student formally joins the program, the parent worker goes to the home and meets the family. This initial meeting, on the child's turf, helps smooth the way for the development of a positive and trusting relationship between the home and school. The parent worker is able to observe the child in a familiar environment and as a part of the family constella- tion as it is reflected by the relationships in the home as well as by the child's physical environment. The parent worker will return with the child's teacher for a second visit. In this way, both the parents and the child have the opportunity to meet the teacher before that first, sometimes traumatic, day of school; and the teacher can get a more direct understanding of the child he or she is to live with during the coming school year. There has never been any difficulty with a family feeling that their privacy is being invaded. In fact, all the parents I have spoken with see the home visits, in particular the initial home visits, as very posi- tive events, relieving a great deal of their anxiety and greatly improving the com- munication with the school.

> The very first contact we had with the school after that was when the teacher, parent worker, and language person all came to the house. We sat down and the whole purpose of that was to find out how our child's performance is in a setting where he is comfortable, where he knows what is going on. I should say that the teacher and the speech pathologist were particularly interested in the particular language we used, unusual words that we used, special things that we said, things that we worked with him on. They were also getting a feel for the house, I think, and the kind of life style we lived, which they had to get in our house.

Because so many of our children have severe language disorders or are non- verbal, consistency in the approach used towards communication with the child is essential. As our father just stated, many families have their own idiosyncratic expressions for events, foods, common objects, and toileting. Where most chil- dren can be flexible and quickly discover synonomous language, this is certainly difficult for our children. It is one of the important aspects of their idiosyncratic language development which the parent worker must communicate to the family and back again to the teacher. One parent told of a time when he lifted his child into the air and said "whoops." From then on, "whoops" meant "Lift me into the air." The teachers were baffled by the child's constant calls of "whoops," and his subsequent frustration over their lack of understanding. A phone call from the parent worker quickly cleared up the matter.

Many of our nonverbal children are given signs to help facilitate their com- munication. The use of signing and other alternative communication systems, such as Blissymbols or communication boards, varies with each child. We have children who may use only one or two signs and one who now uses over 200 signs. The decision to sign or not to sign is one which is carefully made in consul- tation with the parents. Alternative communication cannot be considered suc- cessful unless the child is able to use these techniques in the home as well as in school. Facilitating this carryover is a major role of the parent worker.

The method used by the parent worker to help the parents use alternative communication systems at home illustrates the manner in which various other skills are reinforced. Since the parent worker has spent a good deal of her time working with the child on a one-to-one basis both in the school and at home, as well as spending some of her time with the child in the classroom, she is continually aware of the child's program and progress. She and, of course, the parents have been an instrumental part of the IEP planning and are very much aware of the goals that have been set for the child. The teaching of alternative communication techniques has often been discussed at the IEP conference, as is the necessity of carry over into the home. At times, the decision to teach a new skill, whether it be signing or any other skill, is made midyear, because of a child's progress or lack of it using the techniques which the staff and parents had earlier thought to be most appropriate. These decisions are made at a "team meeting" attended by the child's head teacher, teacher trainees, team supervisor, parent worker, speech and language teacher, and any other staff personnel who may be involved with the child. All aspects of the new approach are discussed in depth. The parent worker is able to offer valuable insights as to the feasibility of family involvement in the use or reinforcement of the program at home. In some cases, it may be unrealistic to expect a family to be able to sit down with the child every night and work on practicing certain skills. The parent worker may know that the parent has a low frustration tolerance for the child's inability to grasp a particular concept and may therefore suggest an alternative approach. In the case of signing, the parent worker may know that a particular family is still holding on to the belief that their child will talk very soon. Although the staff feels that this is unlikely to happen and that the child needs to develop alternative methods of communication, if only to reduce his or her frustration, it is obvious that the family needs to be worked with before they are asked to teach these skills to the child at home.

Often the skills or issues on which the parent worker focuses are those which are of greatest concern to the family, although they may not be issues in the classroom. Because the parent worker has had the opportunity to observe the child in both the home and school as well as to work with him or her in both settings, she is better able to determine whether or not the child's difficulty is a function of the particular environment or is a consistent problem. In addition, she has first-hand experience as to how difficult it may be to work with the child in the various settings. Some of the issues that concern parents may not be directly relevant to "schooling" in the traditional sense. Our recognition of the value of integrating a child's home and school experiences leaves few, if any, parental concerns beyond the scope of the parent worker's involvement. Our parent workers talk about the variability of the roles in the following ways.

We maintain contact with the families and try to find out what they want for programming. For Tommy, for instance, we have done a lot of self-help things at home and some play things. With Matt, it has been an eating program. It has been a big thing, as has been playing with his brother and sister. It varies a lot from child to child but "going places" is sometimes something real hard with special needs kids. So, sometimes we go to the grocery store or to a playground with the family; and the mother and I or the father or brother or whoever is there do it together and try to get new ideas for making it a more constructive time. It is real different from one to another.

I guess my role with each family has been very different, and it depends very much on the family. There is a parallel to how one deals with kids in an individualized program. That is how I thought about my working with families. I know that some families needed a lot of support and some situations had developed into getting the mother in the home involved in a work situation and finding things for her to do where she would feel better about herself. That, in turn, would make the family situation a better place for the child to be.

Several of our parents have expressed appreciation for being approached by the parent workers as individuals, not just as parents of a handicapped child.

Parent workers have helped us to become our own person besides just being the mother of a handicapped child or a father of a handicapped child. You have your own person, too, and these people help us to be that. We probably wouldn't have done it if we hadn't had contact with people that can deal with our problems besides the kid's problems or beside the teacher, too. It's a bridge to say something....It is nice to be able to be honest. That is the part I like about a lot of this.

It is odd that parent workers mostly concerned with the child helped us to get over the fact that we are not just a parent of a handicapped child. We are a person first. I laid my biggest fears on them. I told them that I was really worried about this and we could talk about it, whereas before, it was hard knowing where to go with it. At least they know a little bit more about where we can go with it.

ESTABLISHING PARENT GROUPS

An additional role played by the parent workers has been facilitating parent groups held at the school, each for 2 evenings a month. I have been involved, during this past year, in the organization and coleadership of both the group for the parents of our handicapped children and a single parents' group. Like many of the programs at Jowonio, these two groups have been established as a part of the school's evolution and its experience with families and their needs. One major logistical problem to be faced in setting up any type of parent group is finding a time that is most convenient for the majority of parents. The year before, two groups were established, a day group and an evening group. The day group consisted entirely of nonworking mothers and so issues which concerned fathers and the coordination of parenting roles were never addressed. Single parents and working mothers find it very difficult to go out at night and leave their children after they have been away all day and the children have been left in the care of a babysitter. One helpful technique is to offer free child care at the school and hold the meetings early enough in the evening that parents may bring their children. In the case of a severely handicapped child, it is often difficult, if not impossible, for our parents to arrange for a babysitter at home. Thus we often help make such arrangements when necessary. This year we decided to hold both groups in the evening as that seemed convenient for most parents and would help insure the presence of fathers.

A group for siblings of our handicapped children was run during the previous school year and found to be very helpful to the children who attended and their families. It is certainly recommended. We were unable to run a similar group this year because of time pressures on our staff as well as a lack of interest on the part of many of this year's siblings. It is often very difficult for children to conceptualize the benefit of a "talking" group without having had similar previous experience. It would be helpful to plan activities in which the children can participate actively and around which discussions can arise. A good deal of the success of a sibling group depends on the amount of involvement encouraged for the entire family throughout the year.

In determining the type of group that we were to run, we were faced with several options. Both of the parent workers and I believe in the value of parent groups as means for parents in special situations to give each other the emotional support they often need and to help relieve the isolation they feel. We decided to limit the groups to one for the parents of handicapped children and another for our single parents, as we felt that these two groups were most in need of support and would be helped by talking to each other about shared concerns. This may appear to be counter to our philosophy of integration; but we felt that all our parents are offered many opportunities to interact on many other occasions. By giving these parents the chance to meet together in a group made somewhat homogeneous by the similarity of circumstances, the content of the discussions would turn towards issues that members of the group felt to be most significant. This understanding is based on research in group dynamics, as well as our own experience, which has shown that pressure towards uniformity and unanimity are ever-present in the functioning of groups (Cartwright & Zander, 1960).

The procedures we followed in the initial organization of our parent groups can be followed in establishing any type of group program for parents. The first step must be determining the greatest needs for a group program. The realistic limitations on staff time and on the availability of group members only on specific days and at specific times makes the setting of priorities essential. There is no limit to the numbers of groups for parents that a program could organize, all of which might be highly beneficial to its members and, therefore, of benefit to the children in the school. From previous experience with the parents of special children who had been in the school and their discussions with new parents, the parent workers felt that priority should be given to the need of this population to connect with each other to share concerns and offer support and information. The value of group discussion by parents, and in particular, by parents of handicapped children, has been documented by other writers who have explored approaches taken in working with parents (Auerbach, 1968; Hereford, 1963; Nedler & McAfee, 1979; Schopler & Reichler, 1971). Auerbach (1968) points out that, in the past, many agencies have been reluctant to establish parent groups for children labeled *emotionally disturbed* other than in the form of group psychotherapy. She goes on to point out that there has been a shift in this attitude among many professionals, which has brought about a change in the attitude about the services they require.

> But today there is a wider understanding of the many factors, both constitutional and environmental, that may cause emotional disturbance in children. This knowledge has brought about a shift in attitude towards the parents of these children. They are no longer automatically stereotyped as being seriously troubled themselves and are approached much less dogmatically and consequently with less prejudgement and condemnation. There is also a growing appreciation of the effect on parents of having an emotionally disturbed child and living with him day to day. The burden of meeting the constant demands of children of this kind together with the feelings of guilt because they feel they have been responsible for the child's condition may well contribute to the emotional difficulties for the parents. Thus their disturbances may be the result and not the cause of the child's difficulties.

The second group of parents at our school who appeared to have the greatest need for a support program was single parents. Over 50% of our children live in single parent families, and many of the concerns expressed by both the children and their parents are directly related to this status. In several cases, single parents have been attracted to Jowonio because of its concern with affective issues in the child's education and overall development. Parents are assured that their children will receive the emotional support they may need to help smooth out some of the uncertainties they may be experiencing. Several of our single mothers requested the opportunity to meet together to discuss their concerns. These factors, added to our awareness of the potential value of support groups for parents in special situations (Auerbach, 1968; Hereford, 1963), led to the decision to offer a group for our single parents.

Our next concern was one which is the second step taken in setting up any type of group program, that is, establishing a specific plan and structure for the group. In doing this, you must establish when and where the group will meet, what the size and composition of the group will be, and the purpose of the group. As stated earlier, single parents are generally not available for day-time meetings, and it is often difficult for parents to leave their child in the evening after they have been gone all day. We therefore arranged our meetings for mid-week, early evenings, at our school, with child care available when needed.

Primary custody for the children in our school has in just about every situation been given to mothers. The parent worker and I discussed at length whether or not our group would be open to all single parents or just mothers. We realized that the nature of the group would be altered dramatically by this decision. We wondered if men and women together would feel open to discuss issues related to sexuality, for example, and the pressures it brings to single parenthood. We decided that we felt confident enough in our skills as group leaders that this issue could be approached and might even offer benefits to both sexes. Our final decision on this matter and on the issue of the size of the group and the frequency of meetings was made by the parents who attended our first few sessions. This practice is consistent with the philosophy of giving parents as many decision-making opportunities as feasible. Parent programs often fail because the professionals feel obligated to make many of the logistical decisions. A great deal of group cohesiveness and commitment occurs when the decisions about frequency of meetings, size, and composition of the group are left open for discussion among the members. Certainly, a leader may have to place limits on the final decision, based on his or her preference for group size, which should be determined both by the composition of its members and the purpose of its meetings. Both groups were announced in the school newsletter and flyers sent home to all our parents. In addition, teachers and parent workers made phone calls to those parents whom they felt would particularly benefit from attending the groups.

The evolution of both groups followed from the needs that each set of parents expressed. In the case of the single parent group, it became readily apparent that this would be a group for single mothers. On our first meeting, six women attended. This later changed to four regularly attending members. The initial focus of our discussion was informal, introducing ourselves and discussing the possible organization and functions of the group. Some of the women expressed their feeling that the presence of men in the group would inhibit their frankness, and others recognized their lack of assertion in the presence of men. This, then, became a topic for discussion by the group. This informal selection of the group's focus for the evening became the pattern throughout the year. The mothers in this group saw that their greatest need was to have support from each other for the issues they faced as single women raising children. Often these concerns centered directly on their children. They involved issues of discipline, joint custody, individual differences among their children, and their reaction to divorce. There was a great need to determine which aspects of their child's behavior were the result of being from a "broken home" and which were a function of the child's development or temperament. Several of the women arranged to have their children play together after school and on weekends, which helped ease their child care expenses and left one or more mothers with a few hours of free time.

The strong need that each of the women had to spend more guiltless social time or be by herself became more apparent as the group evolved. We spent a good deal of time helping each other to work through the emotional and practical aspects of these situations. The group began to evolve into a place where the mothers could spend a social evening and talk less directly about their children and more about their personal concerns for their own futures. Each person took turns in supplying refreshments, and on two occasions the group met in a local restaurant for drinks, dinner, and conversation. The parent worker and I became concerned about our role as group leaders as we felt ourselves becoming members of the group, particularly because of the social aspect it began to have. We recognized the possibility that the group members would interpret each other's nods of support as reinforcement for destructive patterns and made a conscious effort to facilitate the flow of discussion and offer insights into the situations that many of the women faced. After several months, the group became cohesive enough and trust had become firmly enough established that we were able to provide feedback to the members as to the patterns that we were observing in their behavior and concerns. This seemed to serve as a model for the group, and they were soon able to offer excellent insights to each other. The effect of the group was most dramatic for one mother for whom our bimonthly meetings were the primary social connection. She was able, through our support and discussion, to make some major changes in her life and consequently in that of her children, which were the beginning of movement in a positive direction.

Giving parents the opportunity to determine the nature and functioning of a parent group does not eliminate the group leaders' responsibility to keep the group flowing smoothly and protect its members from others' unconscious insensitivity. Jowonio parents are, for the most part, a highly sensitive group of adults, particularly with regards to the emotional needs of others. It is possible that the parent workers and I were able, in the case of both groups, to take a more passive role with our members than we might take with another population. I strongly believe that, regardless of the individual characteristics of parents in any school, they can better determine their needs than most professionals. The group leader can help facilitate the meeting of these goals by his or her knowledge of group dynamics and the possible options and resources available to families in a given community, but the direction of the group should be determined by what its members see to be their most pressing needs. The group leader's primary role is to help the members arrive at a consensus as to the group's needs and to present the options available in meeting them.

PARENT GROUP FORMATS

Auerbach (1968) describes several forms that parent discussion groups may take and proposes a type which she feels is particularly suited to the needs of parents of children with handicapping conditions. She calls this last group "Parent Group Education." The determination of which type of group is run for parents should result from the needs of the population with which you are working, each group being suited to a different purpose. The first group approach described is "Formal Academic Teaching." Focusing on child development and family relations, its purpose is to enlarge parents' intellectual understanding. The "Group Dynamics" group focuses the members on the functioning of the group itself and uses this understanding as the means by which its members change and grow. The purpose of this type of group is to have its members develop a sense of validation for their beliefs and opinions. "Group Counseling" focuses on having individual members of the group solve specific problems and may therefore rely on many of the techniques employed in a "Group Dynamics" approach. "Group Psychotherapy" has as its purpose the removal of "pathological blocks that stand in the way of the continuing acquisition of knowledge and understanding needed to enable the growth process to continue" (Auerbach, 1968, p. 37). This last approach was, until recently, considered the only appropriate group approach for parents of emotionally disturbed children.

If we were to enter into a parent group program with a fixed notion as to which of these approaches to use, it is quite possible that we would be missing the needs of some, if not all, of our parents. The "Parent Group Education" approach integrates all of the other group practices into a form that most resembles the parent group that we ran last year for our parents of handicapped children. The "Academic Teaching" on specific issues occurs as the parents present those topics that are of greatest concern to their current experiences with their child. Unlike formal academic training, no specific curriculum is set by the leader; rather, it emerges from the needs of the families. The substance of the meeting is not presented in a formal teaching sense, although an expert may present information on a specific topic, but rather encourages the parents to participate and present real circumstances and the emotional implications for their child and family. Rather than perpetuate the student-teacher relationship with parents, the leader deliberately sets out to encourage independent thinking which will help the parents arrive at solutions which will be best suited to the unique situation that each family faces. This process should teach an all-important skill that our parents can apply after the group experience has passed. In this way, "Parent Group Education" can be seen to employ the dynamics of group process but has as its goal the development of individual decision making and independent thinking.

"Group Counseling" is, in many ways, similar to "Parent Group Education," particularly if it takes the form of a client-centered group. The difference is that the focus and assumption of our group was not that any parent had a specific problem but rather that as a group our parents would come to a better understanding of their unique situation and that of their child. By experiencing other family's situations, each member might gain a clearer understanding of him or herself and support one another.

"Parent Group Education" is more unlike "Group Psychotherapy" than any of the other approaches. Auerbach (1968) points out that the primary difference lies in group education's focus on developing the ego strengths of parents and on presenting ways to master the demands and stresses they face. Our group was opened to all parents of our special students, where in group therapy, the leader selects particular members so as to create a particular atmosphere which is felt will benefit the therapeutic purpose of the group. The assumption is made as to which parents can benefit from the group; in contrast, our assumption was that any parent who attended the group meetings would benefit to some degree. We explore a parent's history only as he or she sees fit and most often for the purpose of illustrating a situation. This information is often used by other parents as a frame of reference from which to compare their own child's development. It became apparent that this was a strong need among our parents, because many of our children defy the traditional developmental sequence spelled out in the literature.

The group of parents of our handicapped students was initiated with each of these approaches as a possible format. In taking the same initial approach towards this group as we had towards the single parents group, we hoped to best suit the needs of the parents who would attend. On our first session, 14 parents attended. Attendance varied throughout the year, from as many as 16 parents to as few as 3 one evening. We held our meetings regardless of attendance and found that on those evenings when attendance was low, a good deal was accomplished. These became very informal "rap" sessions where parents were able to verbalize more of their emotional reactions to their child than when they were in a larger group. This reinforced our belief that, by letting parents take the lead in an ambiguous situation, we would be best able to meet their needs.

We presented to the parents our feeling that we wanted these group meetings to address those issues that were of primary concern to them. Their immediate response was that they wanted to get information regarding their children's conditions and methods of dealing with their experiences. One parent later pointed out that this was very different from the way he had been approached by other professionals.

I had some problems with professionals in that parents vary in what they need. I, as a parent, needed some very different things than some other parents. I was treated as though I needed emotional support at the time, which I did not need. I needed information. I needed technique. I needed skills, more than anything else under the sun. I didn't need emotional support....People just did not perceive that. They started blaming the parents right off. We didn't need any of that because we were fairly convinced that we didn't have anything to do with our adopted son's problem. The only point that I want to make, very commonly, parents really do have difficulty handling exceptionality and handling exceptional kids and feel guilty and really do need support. Parents really do need different things. We wasted an awful lot of time with people trying to therapeutize us.

At that first meeting, the parents generated a list of topics they would like to see covered during the year. The list included early speech development, issues and approaches to nonverbal children, autism, how to use the medical profession effectively, how to get away with or without your special child, local school board issues, assertiveness training for parents, labeling, siblings, the Committee on the Handicapped, appropriate toys and gifts for our children, future planning, bed-wetting, medication, and special diets. They also expressed the desire to have "experts" come to the meetings when possible, to address many of these issues, and asked if we could get films that might do the same thing.

It was our role as group leaders to determine the best method of addressing the issues that were of primary concern to our parents. It was apparent that Auerbach's "Parent Group Education" was the most suitable format to follow. Certainly our parents needed information, but it needed to be presented in a manner that could be integrated into their lives and would take into account the emotional implications and everyday realities that they must face. They want and need factual information about their child's disability and to be able to predict, to some degree, the implications of this condition on future development. With other handicapping conditions, professionals may be able to offer a prognosis with some degree of certainty. Our parents have, for the most part, learned to become extremely cynical about the medical profession and to live with the reality that there is still a good deal to be learned about autisim. I am certain that living in this state of uncertainty has added to the upheaval many of our parents expressed during the year. It also explains each parent's intense curiosity about other children's development. The parent of the nonverbal child needs to know when someone else's child finally began to talk and the sequence that he followed, as well as the language therapist's present methods of facilitating the child's use of language at home. However, I found it necessary to point out, when parents would compare their child's progress with that of another who exhibited similar behavior, that each child is unique. Behaviors which may appear to be quite similar often are the result of very different sets of circumstances and, therefore, respond quite differently to varied approaches. For example, one child's echolalic speech could be seen to diminish as his home environment became more stabilized, his school program focused on his affective needs, and he received intensive language work. Another child's speech pattern would most likely not respond as rapidly to similar treatment because of the probable organic nature of his pathological language.

We were very pleased that, on most evenings, fathers were well represented in our group. They played an active role in our discussions, even though the parenting role each had in his home was quite different. Our planning and communication with the families was carefully thought out so as to maximize the possibility of fathers' attendance. The consistent presence and participation of fathers in a parent group was a new experience for me, as most other groups with which I had been involved were essentially "mothers' groups." We feel that the more active role taken by many men today is a positive development in the evolution of the family in our culture. In the situation of a family with a child with a handicapping condition, this participation is essential not only because it relieves some of the enormous pressure placed on the mother but because of the benefits offered to the father as well. Active involvement not only lets the man know his child on a more intimate level, but gives him a greater sense of control over the events that may shape his child's future. The fact that many men in our culture have a good deal of difficulty verbalizing their feelings has been stated repeatedly. Our group's initial focus on concrete things to do with children at home as well as our offering specific information requested by our parents offered an attractive format for our fathers. Discussions around specific topics offered fathers the opportunity to discuss their emotional reactions to specific situations. One of our group members expressed her appreciation of the men's participation.

> One of the things that I noticed about the groups that I belonged to before was that they were separated by sex. Jowonio is great because we have husbands and wives coming. It is not just all the wives. A lot of the groups that I belong to are just women, and women are more conerned about their feelings and men are more concerned about, "What can I do to help my kid?" They really don't want to go through this whole feeling process. They want concrete things. When we have these planning things where we are picking things, you will notice the men will pick, "Let's talk about what we are going to do about this," and then the women will say, "Okay, let's have a meeting. We are going to talk about our feelings." Somewhere along the line as a parent you grow in your feelings and there is not such a big gulf any more. You can share this, men and women. You are through with your feeling problem. You are all over that. Now you can go on to, "Let's talk about what concrete we can do." A lot of the things I like about Jowonio is that we do have a nice mix of men and women. It doesn't just get to be a women's group where we are always talking about feelings. I think it gets to be too much.

We can see from this woman's comments that both fathers and mothers can be at different stages in the development of their understanding of their child, both intellectually and emotionally. It is incorrect to believe that group meetings will meet all the needs of all our families or accomplish everyone's goals. Our hope has been to move with parents along their continuum of growth and facilitate this growth with our various programs. It was apparent to both parent workers and me that on several occasions some of the parents who were new to our program were not ready to deal with the issues that were being addressed by our "older" parents. Their silence was often a reflection of this mismatch. Fortunately, the parent worker would be able, if appropriate, to address the group interaction with the reluctant parent at one of their individual meetings. By having the parents themselves generate those issues they wished to address, this problem is minimized. Although each set of parents may not be at the same stage of readiness to deal with certain issues or may never face the same concerns that are primary for another family, each parent's presence seems to assure the others a kind of support and understanding that those of us who are not parents of a handicapped child can only begin to appreciate. The parent group serves as a means of facilitating the connecting of parents with each other.

CONCLUSION

The following statement by one of our mothers illustrates the reality that there is more parents can do for each other than many professionals might imagine. We hope they can continue to teach us.

> I think a lot depends on where you are with a handicapped kid. In the beginning you really search out for people who are in the same shoes. You want to know that you aren't alone in the world. Some of us have closer contacts than others. We know the other person is going to understand. There was this woman who would call me. I knew when she called me that she was in trouble. One time she called me and she felt like committing suicide and killing her child also. It is pretty scary. So we talked for about 2 hours. You still reach out as your child gets older.

The notion that parents can best assess their needs at a given period of time and that we, as professionals, can learn from parents can be integrated into any program, regardless of staffing patterns or funding. Given both the research that has emerged showing the influence of the family on a child's intellectual and emotional growth and our awareness of the impact of a handicapped child upon the family, it is essential that programs for handicapped children incorporate programmatic practices that will most effectively address these concerns. It is my belief that establishing a strong school-family partnership is not an auxiliary service to be attached to special education programming but rather should be perceived as an integral part of each child's program. We hope that some of the specific approaches we have used at Jowonio can be incorporated into other settings. A more realistic expectation is that you, the reader, will be able to take the concepts I have explored and create an environment, at the classroom level, where parents can feel themselves to be an essential component of their child's education.

REFERENCES

Auerbach, A.B. *Parents learn through discussion: Principles and practices of Parent Group Education.* New York: John Wiley, 1968.

Barsch, R.H. *The parent of the handicapped child.* Springfield, Ill.: Charles C Thomas, 1968.

Bettelheim, B. *The empty fortress.* New York: Free Press, 1967.

Cartwright, D., & Zander, A. *Group dynamics: Research and theory.* Evanston, Ill.: Row, Peterson, 1960.

Coleman, J. *Equality of educational opportunity.* Washington, D.C.: U.S. Office of Education, 1966.

Greenfeld, J. *A place for Noah.* New York: Holt, Rinehart, & Winston, 1978.

Hereford, C.F. *Changing parental attitudes through group discussion.* Austin, Tex.: Hogg Foundation for Mental Health, 1963.

Jencks, C. *Inequality: A reassessment of the effect of the family and schooling in America.* New York: Harper & Row, 1972.

Kaufman, B.N. *Son rise.* New York: Harper & Row, 1976.

Love, H.D. *Parental attitudes towards exceptional children.* Springfield, Ill.: Charles C Thomas, 1970.

Nedler, S.E., & McAfee, O.D. *Working with parents: Guidelines for early childhood and elementary teachers.* Belmont, Calif.: Wadsworth, 1979.

Park, C. *The siege.* Boston, Little, Brown, 1967.

Peterson, D.R. Parental attitudes and child adjustment. In G.R. Medinus (Ed.), *Readings in the Psychology of parent-child relations.* New York: John Wiley, 1967.

Rimland, B. *Infantile autism.* New York: Appleton-Century-Crofts, 1964.

Ritvo, E.R. (Ed.). *Autism: Diagnosis, current research, and management.* New York: Spectrum, 1976.

Rutter, M. (Ed.) *Infantile autism: Concepts, characteristics, and treatment.* Baltimore: Williams and Wilkins, 1971.

Schopler, E., & Reichler, R.J. Parents as cotherapists in the treatment of psychotic children. *Journal of Autism and Childhood Schizophrenia,* 1971, *1,* 87-102.

12
Sibling Support Groups

Cindy Bodenheimer

Proponents of the ecological view of childhood disturbances cite the importance of dealing with the total environment of the disturbed or disturbing child. As related to autism, this view leads us to recognize not only the maladaptive behaviors of the child, but also the reactions of those persons close to the child whom those behaviors affect. Parents, teachers, classmates, friends, and siblings of autistic children must learn to respond to the special child's needs, to intervene in disturbing situations, and to find their own ways of relating to this special person who touches their lives.

A review of relevant literature reveals a surprisingly small number of attempts to either counsel siblings of exceptional children regarding the extra stresses and responsibilities their handicapped sibling is likely to bring them or to train them to be effective helpers and teachers. However, several sources, including Parfit (1975), delineate the need for information and emotional support of siblings of handicapped individuals. In those instances where sibling programs have been systematically attempted, encouraging results have been reported.

Weinrott (1974) trained 18 siblings of retarded children as behavior modifiers in conjunction with a therapeutic summer program. Siblings were exposed to learning theory classes, observed behavior management techniques, and practiced what they had learned in closely supervised situations. Evaluation of the experience indicated that, after the program, siblings spent more time with the handicapped children, expected more of them, and gave them more encouragement in learning situations. An added benefit of the program was that some of the children gained a new perspective on their own family situation by meeting other children who shared many of the same difficulties, although this was not an explicit goal of the program.

Other instances where small numbers of siblings have been trained in behavior modification techniques with their behaviorally disorded siblings (Colletti & Harris, 1977; Lavigeur, 1976) have also reported relative success. They suggest the use of siblings as behavior modification aides in treatment procedures.

Therapeutic programs concentrating on adjustment and emotional support, rather than training, of brothers and sisters of retarded children have been described by Kaplan (1969), Grossman (1972), and Schrieber and Feeley (1965). These groups explicitly dealt with issues such as the etiology of retardation, fears siblings have regarding their handicapped sibling and themselves, the extra stress often present in an exceptional family, and in general with the sibling's reactions to and questions about the handicapped child. Success was generally reported in terms of an increased knowledge and a healthier emotional reaction on the part of the siblings. Berg (1973) and Klein (1972a, 1972b, 1972c) also cite the beneficial effects of family and group situations in which issues regarding handicapped children were freely discussed with siblings.

This chapter describes a sibling support group offered in conjunction with Jowonio: The Learning Place's therapeutic program for autistic children. In answering the needs of not only our special children, but their special families as well, we decided that a support group based on a combination of the goals of the previously mentioned programs would be most appropriate. We aimed to provide a program which would both help the children accept and deal with their feelings about their handicapped sibling and would also assist them in becoming more effective helpers and teachers. With this type of group, we hoped to have primary therapeutic effects on the group member and indirect benefits for the special sibling in the form of encouraging better relationships and more fruitful helping situations.

Since there is so little written about groups like this in general, and virtually nothing recorded specifically on groups for brothers and sisters of *autistic* children, we depended heavily on defining and answering the needs of our specific group of youngsters, improving when we had to and learning as we went along. We hope that the following descriptive account of our sibling support group will be able to be used and built upon by others.

DEFINING THE NEED

The need for contact with the siblings of our special children was originally made apparent to us through parents who had informed us of their children's questions and concerns. Several children had asked about explaining a brother or sister's handicap to their friends. Others had wanted to learn new ways to help their sibling in the home. Still others were upset by the extra responsibility implicit in caring for a handicapped sibling. Parents brought these concerns to us, wondering if we could suggest books or information that they could share with their families. Upon seeing such a similar need in several of our families, we decided it would be most efficient to share our resources directly with the groups of children themselves. Thus our idea of a "siblings support group" was formed. Our first step was to obtain an accurate idea of exactly how many children wanted or needed such a group. We decided to run the following notice in our monthly school newsletter.

> **Brother/Sister Support Group**—We have been thinking lately of the brothers and sisters of our special children. It is not uncommon for them to have many questions and feelings about why their brothers and sisters are the way they are. There may be a problem in how their friends react to their sibling's handicap or in learning how best to help their special brother or sister. We would like to know how many parents think a support group for kids would be useful. We're thinking of meeting several Saturday afternoons to help the kids share their experiences, problems, and information. Talk it over with your kids and if you think your child could benefit from such a group, please call us at school within the next two weeks. We can be flexible about dates and times.

The response to our offer was encouraging. Parents and kids definitely wanted a forum for sharing their concerns and questions. Our next step was to specify goals for our group, based on the major concerns parents (and several siblings) had brought to us. We were careful also to take into consideration the age and sex of the siblings we were to include as active participants. We decided to include in the group children who ranged from 9 to 13 years. Luckily those children interested included approximately equal numbers of boys and girls. Several younger (4- to 5-year-old) children had been brought to our attention as also struggling with the concerns of understanding a special sibling, but we decided in those cases that it would be most helpful to work with the children through their parents rather than include them in our group with the older siblings. If we had had more than three young children, we would have considered running a separate group directed at their level of understanding.

Through informal contacts with both the siblings and parents, we ascertained that the major needs of the group were in the areas of needing specific information and a place to share experiences. These contacts helped us to specify the following goals.

1. To raise the children's awareness of handicaps in general. We hoped to be able to increase their ability to empathize with and more fully understand their handicapped sibling.
2. To provide a forum for children to share experiences in the hope that this would reduce feelings of isolation with their problems.
3. To encourage group problem solving around specific issues brought up by the children.
4. To impart information in answer to questions raised by the group members. We hoped to include a visit to Jowonio as part of this effort so that the children would have first-hand experience in understanding how their siblings learned in school.
5. To provide specific skill training around interventions and teaching.

SCHEDULING AND STRUCTURE

After our goals were well-defined, we turned our attention to the nitty-gritty problems of scheduling. Lest our well-laid plans fall victim to such problems as timing or transportation (as described by Grossman, 1972), we carefully arranged a Sunday afternoon time when all six of the children could be dropped off via a car pool.

For those families who had responded to our newsletter notice, we followed up with a phone call to the sibling, and discussed the group, the child's specific interests, and a convenient meeting time. This served as introduction to the one child (of the six) we had not met personally and helped to encourage an interest and commitment on the part of the others. On the Friday before the first meeting, we sent home the following "lunchbox reminder" with the handicapped child to remind the sibling of our meeting that weekend.

BULLETIN!!

What?:   Brother/Sister Support Group
When?:   Sunday, Nov. 20th
Time?:   2:30 P.M. till 4:00 P.M. (We'll call parents if it
turns out to be longer or shorter than anticipated)
Where?:   Jowonio: The Learning Place
See you there. Snacks to be served. All you need to bring is
yourself!

It is noteworthy that we were interested in having the child decide whether or not to join the group. That was the reasoning behind suggesting that parents discuss it with their children, making the phone call, and sending the lunchbox reminder to the sibling. We felt strongly that a free-choice situation would lead to a stronger commitment on the part of the sibs who did choose to participate. In fact, this was the case in all but one family. In this family, the parents, concerned about their children's reaction to their handicapped sibling, required their two children, against their wishes, to attend at least the first siblings group meeting. Predictably, these were the only two children who dropped out of the group. It was obvious from the first meeting that these children were not yet comfortable enough with their own feelings about their brother to be able to share them in a group situation. It was recommended that the facilitator meet with these children alone and that they come to visit their brother's class. In light of this experience and a similar one reported in the literature (Lavigeur, 1976), it would seem appropriate that, once children are informed of the purpose and existence of a group of this nature, their wishes as to whether or not to join be respected. Certainly other types of support can be found for children unwilling or unable to share experiences of this type in a group.

We found it helpful to divide our 2-hour sessions into two parts, the first being activity/experience focused and the second centering on discussion, problem solving, and information giving. This split, we felt, suited the age level and attention span of our group. We anticipated having 4 to 5 monthly meetings of this sort, depending on a continuing need expressed by the group.

INTRODUCTION

We planned an introduction which would enable the children to get to know each other in an informal situation. At the first meeting, facilitators and the children told the group their names and interests and shared anything else about themselves that they cared to. We had also asked each sibling to bring along a picture of their special siblings and to tell the group a little bit about him or her. This allowed for a common interest and less personal introduction to the group for any children who were not comfortable sharing much about themselves at first. It also served as a terrific ice-breaker as children quickly found out who had brothers or sisters in the same class and what their interests and problems were. This type of exchange served the purpose of immediately setting the tone of the group as one of comradery and giving all the children the experience of knowing at the very beginning that they and their families are not alone in their problems. Another issue which we brought up at the very beginning was confidentiality. As a group, we decided it would make it easier for everyone to share ideas and concerns if we all knew that no one would repeat what anyone said by name outside the group. All decided that it would be helpful to be able to discuss the general issues of the group with parents and friends, but agreed not to reveal specifically who had said what. This knowledge also helped form a cohesive group and encouraged trust among the members. It allowed us to respond to a parental concern that children would share "family secrets" with the group. We assured parents that we would let them know in general what topics were discussed, which was obviously reassuring to several nervous parents. (As it turned out, most children were more than anxious to share the group's information at home, and parental feedback to us was positive and encouraging from the first meeting on.)

EXPERIENCE/AWARENESS ACTIVITIES

In order to help the children better understand their sibling's handicap, we devised a number of exercises designed to simulate a disability and the frustration involved in being handicapped. These are similar to the experiences Bookbinder (1977) suggests using to sensitize typical children to the special needs of mainstreamed youngsters. Listed below are the exercises the children found most helpful.

Write Name in Mirror

The children were given a pencil and directed to write their name looking only at the reflection of their paper in a mirror. They quickly became frustrated by this simple experience. Several of them gave up, threw the paper or pencil, or refused to try upon seeing how much difficulty the others were experiencing. (Several of the older children had to be reminded to use the *mirror*, rather than their kinesthetic memory, to write their names.) For those children who did not really feel a great deal of frustration in writing their names, we prepared a large star for them to trace in the mirror. This proved to be more frustrating, probably because they could not count on memorized kinesthetic cues. It was helpful to hold a piece of cardboard over the children's hands so that they could *only* view their progress (or lack thereof) in the mirror. It was very helpful to later process this experience with the children, explaining that these, their own reactions, are the same or very similar to those of their special siblings in a frustrating situation. It was also helpful to ask several of the children for examples of when their brother or sister had acted so frustrated.

Dizzy Balance Beam Walk

In this exercise, the children were spun around about five times and then immediately directed to walk a balance beam raised about 6 inches from the floor. (It is important to have someone help the child to insure his safety in this exercise.) Needless to say, these normally well-balanced children found their bodies suddenly uncooperative and unable to perform a usually simple task. Following this experience, the children discussed how different their bodies felt when they were dizzy and how unsure of themselves they became on the beam. This exercise was easily related to the apparently abnormal perceptual experiences of autistic children.

Taste/Smell Identification

In this experience, each child has a turn to be blindfolded while they examine through taste and smell a series of everyday foods, such as carrots, honey, salt, sugar, oregano, coconut, coffee, and cheese. The ease of identification of the foods should vary. The other children know the identify of the unknown food, which often increases the blindfolded child's frustration. The discussion following the exercise centered on how common, everyday items can appear strange in a situation where you do not have the benefit of all the usual information, as with a child with a short attention span, which does not allow him to take in all the usual cues.

Blindfold Walk

The children were divided into pairs. In turn, each member of the pair wore a blindfold and was directed around the room by the other. Discussion afterwards centered on the guide's impatience and the blindfolded subject's fearfulness. We talked about how important and difficult it is to be a good helper and teacher and how much trust you must develop to benefit from such a helping situation. In this exercise, limits should be set on where the children are allowed to guide their partners. They should be told to stay clear of stairways and other dangerous areas since they are not experienced guides!

Act Out a Sentence

This exercise is very similar to the popular game of Charades, except that it uses no signs or symbols. The children are simply asked to guess what one child is acting out without words. Examples of sentences or situations to be acted out are: "Close the door." "I like you." "You make me mad!" "I like to play baseball." "I get scared when people yell." After this experience, the children again discussed the frustrations of not being understood or able to understand. A further discussion centered around the relief and happiness the actor felt when someone finally understood what he or she was trying to say. These issues were related to the handicapped children, and examples were given as to how difficult it may sometimes be for special children to make themselves understood. This exercise also gave us an opportunity to discuss signing as a means of communication, especially in regards to autistic children.

Talk with Ball in Mouth

A further extension of the issues raised in the previous exercise may be gained through another exercise in communication problems. In this one, the child is asked to tell a story to the group while holding a ball in his or her mouth. The ball should be large enough that there will be no danger of a child swallowing or inhaling it.

Communicate a Drawing

In this exercise, two children are selected. One is given a design which is then shown to the group. The remaining child (who has not seen the drawing) is sent to the blackboard (or a large paper in full view of the group) and instructed to draw according to directions given by the child with the drawing. The child

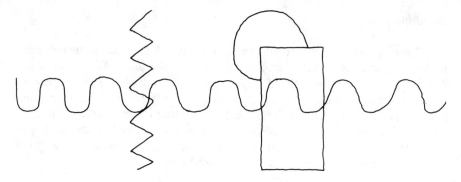

Figure 12.1 "Communicate a Drawing" example

with the drawing then describes the figure to be drawn to the other child, who attempts to follow the instructions exactly. Care should be taken in constructing the figure to be described so that unclear or ambiguous terms, such as *wavy* or *curved,* are likely to be used in describing it. This magnifies the communication problem presented in this exercise. (See Figure 12.1 for an example.) Following this exercise, the children discussed the frustrating experience of not being able to express themselves adequately and not being understood or able to understand. The children who had the experience of trying to draw the figure from their partner's description also talked of their impatience, a helpess feeling of dependence, and the embarrassment of not being able to perform adequately in front of the group. Once again these common problems relating to an inability to understand or be understood adequately were related to special brothers or sisters with various communication problems.

Where Is the Sound?

All the children are asked to sit in a circle approximately 15 feet in diameter. One child is blindfolded and instructed to sit directly in the center of the circle. It is important that there be a child directly in front and in back of the child in the circle. The children in the circle are instructed to clap their hands once when the facilitator points to them. The blindfolded child is to point in the direction from which he or she thinks the sound originated. Because of the physical mechanism of the hearing process, it is quite likely that the child in the center will mislocate sounds coming directly from in front or in back of him or her. If and when this occurs, the other children are likely to comment on the inadequacy of the subject on such a seemingly simple task. This lends itself to a discussion of relative task difficulty for persons of different abilities. The frustrations and embarrassment stemming from inadequately performing before a peer group may be used as a catalyst for a discussion of the feelings of handicapped persons in situations where it is difficult to function adequately.

Following Many Directions

In this exercise, one child is asked to leave the room. Together, the rest of the group makes up a list of four or five directions, and everyone copies them down before the child returns to the room. Upon returning, someone reads the directions out loud while the subject listens. Upon completion of the list, the child executes the directions. At the next child's turn, one more direction is added to the list. A new list should be devised each time so that the children cannot memorize the list before their turn. If you need to save time, several lists can be made up beforehand and one handed out for each turn. Depending on the age of the group, the children will start to make mistakes and forget directions when the list length is four to seven directions. The directions should be discrete, explicit, and observable so that the rest of the group can immediately tell the correctness or error of the child's attempt. An example of a list might be "open the window, pick up the chalk, jump, walk in a circle, touch the wall, close the door." This type of exercise lends itself to a discussion of differential mental abilities and frustration at not meeting your own expectations.

Task Analysis

A popular game with the group was asking one member to leave the room and having him or her describe to a child in the group how to complete a simple task. For example, a child might be asked to tell another how to put on a belt or tie a shoe. The child following the directions was instructed not to do anything he was not told. This often led to humorous situations in which the direction-giving child assumed essential steps (such as pulling the laces tight when tying shoes) and forgot to verbalize them. The importance of breaking down even simple tasks into sequential steps became obvious to the group during this game.

Following the exercise, the group discussed techniques for teaching autistic children and practiced teaching specific skills to each other. Special importance was given to gaining the child's attention, making directions simple, giving physical examples, and providing plenty of praise and rewards.

SNACK

After the group-oriented activity exercises, it was useful to have a short snack time in order to relax and settle the group in preparation for the more discussion-oriented second half of the session. Snack time became quite useful. It was often used by children to informally discuss their favorite exercises and how they related to their special siblings. Snack "duty" was assigned to a different group member each week and further served the purpose of allowing individual group recognition for the snacks the children brought. They often brought the group a snack which they had prepared themselves.

DISCUSSION/INFORMATION GIVING

With the particular group with which we were working, we felt a need to include an impetus for the discussion of major topics. In planning for each meeting, we made a great effort to match our discussion-prompting activities to the interests and age level of our group. We found several techniques to be especially useful in involving the children in major issues involved in dealing with their special siblings.

Interviews

Some of our most successful discussions evolved from questionnaires which the children filled out as if they were news reporters writing a story about their siblings. It was helpful to have the children work in pairs, with one child interviewing another about his sibling. It is more fun for the children if this can be done with a videotape recorder or, if none is available, with a tape recorder. The videotape is especially interesting to children, and it can be played back and discussed with the group. It is helpful to have the group themselves make up the questions for the interview. In this way, those topics of interest to the particular children are likely to be brought up. This is especially true if, when making up the interview questions, the children are directed to think about "What would you like to know about (another group member's) brother or sister?" or "What would you like other people to know about your brother or sister?" or "What do you think are some of the things people wonder about special kids?" Here is a sample of the questions and answers one group of children made up.

Special Brother Interview

What is your brother's name? Paul

How old is he? 7 years old

What does he look like? He has blue eyes and brown hair. He's shorter than me.

What are his favorite things to do? He likes to play with blocks. But he doesn't build with them. He sort of drops them. He likes to eat french fries, too. So do I.

What things are hard for him to do? He has trouble paying attention, and he gets mad a lot. Also he can only say a few words. But he can show you what he wants with his hands.

Do you help him? How? Yes. I help him stay calm and pay attention. Sometimes I just put my arm around him. Other times I hold his face so he looks at me and say, "Paul, now pay attention. Look at me."

Does he ever help you? Not very much.

What games does he like? He likes hide-and-seek. And me and my friends play with him but we sometimes hide in easy places so he can find us. He likes that a lot.

What things make him sad or happy? He gets sad if he can't have his way—like if we don't let him play in the water. He's happy to go to school.

Do you ever get mad at him? What do you do when you get mad? Yes. I don't spank him 'cause he really doesn't understand (even though I want to sometimes). Usually I hold his hands down and say "no" very loud.

How did he get to be special? I don't know. I think he came like that.

What are some good things about having a special brother? You can come to groups like this. Also you can help them and sometimes you're the only one in the whole world that can teach them something and that makes you real proud.

What are some bad things about having a special brother? Well, it's hard 'cause you have to babysit a lot. You know that takes a lot of time and sometimes you have to hide your things so he won't break them.

Is there anything else you would like to say? Yes. I would like to say they should teach regular kids about special kids in school so they would see they aren't so bad. Then they could learn about them and how to help them and stuff, and it would be easier for the special person.

Thank you very much!

With this particular type of activity, it is relatively easy for all the children to join in the discussion because they have all previously considered answers to these questions in their own interviews. Discussions may center on any of the topics raised, and should be moderated and directed by the facilitator to insure that topics of interest and importance to most of the children are covered. For example, with the interview given above, the discussion afterward centered mainly on two of the questions, "How did special brothers and sisters get that way?" and "What do you do when you get mad at a special brother or sister?" It seemed that several children had been quietly wondering about these sensitive issues and were only able to bring them up in the less personal context of "What would someone else want to know about a special child?"

Drawing

Another discussion-facilitating technique we found useful, especially with this age group, was drawing. During several sessions the children were invited to draw anything they wanted in relation to their special sibling. Some children used this open invitation to draw a scene reemphasizing the exercise of the first part of the session, but most children picked up on topics which were either specifically important to them or which had been covered, but not in enough depth or specifically enough for them. Some children chose to express their fears or anger in the drawings.

Such was the case with one 10-year-old girl. Her picture expressed one of her fears, that her disruptive, troublesome brother would interfere with her wedding. Her drawing depicts a girl in bed, thinking of a scene where her brother is hanging monster-like from the ceiling, biting off the groom's hat just as the preacher says: "Dearly beloved, we are gathered here...."This child's drawing spawned a conversation in which the group members shared their fears concerning their handicapped siblings. Common fears included:

- Their brother or sister embarrassing them in front of friends.
- Their sibling not being able to get a job or live independently in the future.
- Not being able to date or marry because of a responsibility to care for the handicapped child.
- Others taking advantage of their brother or sister or treating the sibling unfairly.

Discussions about fears centered not only on the expression of common fears, but also on information and a process helpful in dealing with fears. For example, alternative residences, group homes, and sheltered workshops were discussed as possible future plans for disabled adults, and the children encouraged each other to talk to someone, either friends or family members, about their fears. As one child put it, "It's so much easier to worry with someone than it is to worry alone." During this part of the discussion, the group members and facilitators decided to share phone numbers as "hot lines" to be used if one member had a problem he or she wished to share with another member.

Drawings were even used as a problem-solving technique by several children. One interesting sequence was drawn by an 11-year-old boy. He depicts a child running around (supposedly out of control) along the top half of the picture. The bottom half is divided into two sections, labeled "right" and "wrong." The "right" side shows two figures seated and talking. The "wrong" side shows one figure spanking the other.

Following the presentation of this drawing to the group, we had a lively discussion regarding major problem behaviors of autistic kids and some ways to deal with them. This included:

1. *Lack of play skills and need to adapt games.* Children shared experiences they had had and their ideas of how to adapt their favorite games (baseball, hide-and-seek, etc.) to include a handicapped child. Several of the children spontaneously demonstrated the games they had adapted, and the group had great fun making up alternate rules for baseball, kickball, tag, and other games.
2. *How to discipline.* Group members discussed the need to correct and limit their brother or sister at home. Consensus was that talking to the child, using a limited vocabulary ("No," "Hands down," etc.), was better understood and more effective than physical punishment (hitting, spanking).
3. *How to explain to friends.* Kids shared feelings of anger at others' misunderstanding of sibling's problems. "I get so mad I feel like dumping a

bowl of spaghetti on their heads...but I guess it's better to explain."
They also discussed different ways of explaining handicaps: "He doesn't
talk, but he likes people to say hello to him," "He has trouble listening
and learns things more slowly," and so on.

4. *How to get a child's attention.* The need to gain a child's attention before teaching a skill was discussed, and the siblings made a list of their
   own helpful behaviors, such as "hold his head so his eyes look at you,"
   "touch him," "call his name."

5. *How to calm a frightened child.* Here also the kids spoke of what works
   for them: "Just put your arm around them, say, 'It's okay,' " "Keep to
   a schedule," and so on.

A final major purpose of the drawing time was to express frustration. One
child used her drawing to relate her frustration and that of her whole family
when they are unable to quiet the handicapped child's crying. Other members
also discussed their own reactions to frustrating situations and admitted how
hard it is to be supportive and calm at times when the sibling is upset for no observable reasons. The group seemed relieved that other members had also had
these experiences and feelings.

Books—Reading/Writing

During our search for ideas and materials helpful to siblings of autistic kids,
we discovered a number of children's books dealing with handicaps and children's reactions to them. We used a variety of these books to stimulate discussion and increase the awareness of our group. Most often the children reacted
positively to the books and were pleased to read that others had run into the
same difficulties or questions regarding handicaps. However, in some instances
our youngsters strongly disagreed with ideas put forth in the books, and this led
to some of our most lively discussions. For example, "It says here that this kid
was embarrassed because people stared at her brother. Well, not me! I just go up
and tell 'em he's different, that's all. And they shouldn't be staring. And how
would they like it..." etc., etc., etc.

The books we used dealt with a variety of handicaps, and we used this to
help children generalize in discussions of individual differences and abilities and
again to emphasize the fact that they were not alone in their special family situations. Some of the most useful children's books are listed at the end of the
chapter.

Another technique which we found helpful in initiating discussions and
clarifying ideas was to suggest to the children that we write a children's book together. Again the children were asked, "What do you think children might like
to know about special kids?" This led to topics such as: What is autism? How
do you get it? What do you tell friends about an autistic brother or sister? What
things make brothers and sisters sad, mad, worry, afraid, happy? What do you

do to help a special brother or sister? How do you get help with the special problems of being in a special family? Answering these questions proved quite involving and, in fact, took several group meetings to complete satisfactorily. This was helpful, however, because it allowed children the opportunity to "take issues home with them" and discuss them not only with the group but also with family members, in preparation for the next group meeting.

During the group discussions, the children were reminded of the powerful effect they could have on their siblings. Together we explored and outlined training techniques to help children set limits and teach skills to their sibling. The kids put all these suggestions and some drawings together in a book "for the use of other brothers and sisters" and "so we could remember when we're alone what we talked about in the group."

The children were extremely proud of their book. In fact, we would suggest that groups might consider doing a few more product-oriented activities. Too late we thought how nice it would have been to display our group's drawings and book on the bulletin boards in school.

FOLLOW-UP

After our series of sessions, we arranged for each of the siblings to visit their brother or sister at school. This has been reported to be highly successful in terms of helping children see positive characteristics in the handicapped child outside of the family situation (Berg, 1973; Parfit, 1975). Several of our group members, who had formed friendships, found that they had brothers in the same class and arranged to come together. This encouraged discussion during the visit, and in fact we would encourage anyone arranging brother/sister visits to use pairs if at all possible. With the advantage of hindsight, we are now also able to see that it would have been better had we arranged visits *during,* and not *after,* the completion of our sibling group sessions. The experience of seeing teachers and children interacting and intervening with their siblings would have been a good base for our discussions of interventions and training of techniques for controlling or teaching behaviors. Even at the completion of our sessions, however, our sibling visits were a major success in allowing the children:

1. To see that other people (teachers and children) do indeed experience and deal with the same problems with handicapped children that they have at home.
2. To see a range of materials or games which can be used productively with their brother/sister.
3. To share with teacher any helpful ideas they had used successfully at home with their handicapped brother/sister.
4. To "demystify" what goes on in school programs designed for handicapped/autistic children and show that to some degree the children are able to partake in normal school experiences such as music, pre-academics, and gross motor activities.

5. To be exposed to the special services their siblings receive—language, perceptual training, learning to play.
6. To see that there are a range of children experiencing behavioral and communication problems.
6. To see their brother/sister in a *positive* light—going to school, responding to directions and interactions.

The other aspect of our follow-up program involved the continuing use of the hot line for individual members to contact each other and the facilitators. Over the 18 months since the group met, it seems this has developed more into a way of continuing friendships formed in the group than of asking for emergency service. We have also used the children's hot line and book to introduce new siblings to the school and put them in touch with former members of our group.

FEEDBACK/EVALUATION

Once again, with the wisdom of hindsight, we can see we could have benefitted from a more systematic method of obtaining feedback. As it was, we informally gathered information from children and parents as to changed behaviors at home, different ways of dealing with the handicapped child, and more or different questions to parents indicating a heightened awareness of the sibling's handicap and feelings. The results of our sessions seemed quite evident. More than half of the families reported a dramatic positive change in the "normal" sibling/handicapped sibling interactions. Most frequently, normal siblings were reported to be more patient and more confident and to spend more time in their dealings with the handicapped children. This is similar to the results Weinrott (1974) reports from his training sessions with siblings of handicapped children. All of the families reported the siblings to be trying new methods of teaching and including the handicapped sibling, with a high percentage of positive results.

Although our informal observations do indeed seem positive and encouraging, we would encourage those involved in future sibling support groups to gather information before and after the group regarding attitudes and information, much as Bookbinder (1977) has done. This would allow for more precise evaluation of the group's effectiveness with relation to its goals than we were able to accomplish. We would also encourage an evaluation over a long period of time (1 to 2 years) to ascertain how long the effects of the group last. Our informal measures over 1½ years indicate that those children who most earnestly incorporated new teaching behaviors in their interactions with the children have maintained them, and all of the children retained their heightened awareness and range of intervention possibilities. About half of the group requested and received a second follow-up visit to school a year after our group ended in order to "keep up with new developments in school." We have been quite pleased with the continued interest from these members.

In terms of our own (adult) evaluation, we should mention that at the outset, we decided to have two adults (parent worker and school psychologist) function as group facilitators. We made our own evaluations of the group effectiveness as it went along. In fact, we decided midway in our series of sessions that, because of the dynamics of our particular group, the sessions were more productive and lively with only one adult as facilitator. We then followed through in the rest of the group meetings with only one of us directly involved.

In this presentation of our experience, we do not mean to imply that sibling groups function best with one adult in charge, or with only six members, or in fact with any of the specifics we mentioned. We do mean to encourage those who embark on such an adventure to consciously make decisions based on their particular goals and group dynamics. Indeed, some groups may function better with two or even three adults, or with a less activity-based, more cognitive approach, or meeting weekly rather than monthly as we did. Group dynamics are bound to change with different age groups and different numbers of children. We do want to emphasize that in our experience it seems valid, no matter what the goals, ages, or number of the group, that the group facilitator(s) be very familiar with autistic children and group dynamics. The adult(s) involved must be comfortable with the informational (etiology, interventions, etc.) and attitudinal questions that arise with respect to this specific and complicated group of children. Furthermore, for a successful group, it is necessary to know how to put a group at ease, encourage discussion, adapt to specific group goals, and evaluate and change as needs become evident.

Tables 12.1, 12.2, and 12.3 present those ideas and activities we considered before, during, and after our group met. In effect, it is an outline of our group's life. We would encourage future groups to map out similar schemes in order to most effectively assess and meet their specific needs and evaluate their performance.

Table 12.1   Considerations for beginning a sibling support group

1. *Define the Need*
    Informal contact with parents and siblings
    Newsletter notice
    Phone call to sibling (child's decision to join)
    Identify target age group
    Lunchbox reminder to siblings

2. *Define the Goals*
    Raise children's awareness of handicaps
    Provide forum for sharing experience
    Encourage problem solving
    Impart information
    Provide skill training

3. *Scheduling*
    Arrange meeting time and day
    Arrange transportation
    Decide on structure of group which best fits needs and age of group

Table 12.2 Group structure, sibling support group

Activity	Purpose
1. Introduction	
Initial information sharing (including picture of sibling)	Group introduction and cohesiveness
Confidentiality discussion/ agreement	Encourage trust and comfort of group members
	Awareness that others have similar problems with siblings
2. Experience/Awareness Activities	
Write Name in Mirror	Experience frustration and relate it to handicaps
Dizzy Balance Beam Walk	Experience uncoordinated movements; relate to autistic child's perceptual problems
Taste/Smell Identification	Discuss various senses, inability of some kids to use them or take in appropriate information
Blindfold Walk	Experience how important trusting relationship is between helper-helpee
Act Out a Sentence	Experience frustrations at not being understood, able to understand
	Discuss alternative forms of communication
Talk with Ball in Mouth	Extension of discussion of communication difficulties
	Frustration of inability to communicate
Communicate a Drawing	Discuss complexity of language, communication problems
	Experience frustration, embarrassment of handicapped
Where Is the Sound?	Experience and discuss differential abilities of different people
	Discuss peer influence and embarrassment of inadequate performance
Following Many Directions	Experience limits of memory; discuss differential abilities of both handicapped and nonhandicapped persons
Task Analysis	Demonstrate the importance of breaking down tasks to sequential steps when teaching; need to be explicit and discrete in teaching steps
	Practice teaching skills
	Discuss importance of praise, rewards, consistency
3. Snack	Informal discussion of activity
	Peer relationships formed
	Group recognition of individuals for snack contribution
4. Discussion/Information Giving	
Interviews (Children interview each other about siblings—video or audio tape)	Children discuss what they or others would like to know about special kids: etiology, treatments, recognition of feelings, future consideration
	Alleviate feeling of isolation; awareness that others encounter similar problems
Drawing (Open or suggested topics)	Expression of feelings; fears, anger, frustration, joy, helplessness, usefulness, jealousy, love, etc.
	Problem solving of specific problems—how to discipline, how to explain to friends, how to get a child's attention, how to teach a child a skill, how to calm a frightened child
Reading/Writing Books	
Reading books	Explore others' ideas about handicaps, compare to own
	Gather information about etiology, treatment
	Awareness that others have similar problems
Writing books	Express feelings; share information
	Create useful product to be shared
	Stimulate discussion of variety of topics: expression of feelings, problems that arise, how to cope, etc.

Table 12.3 Follow-up, sibling support group

1. Follow-Up Activity for Group

		Purpose
A. Visit to Jowonio School	Demystify sib's schooling
	See sib in positive, normalizing situation (learning, responding)
	See that others encounter problems in dealing with handicapped child
	Observe/comment on methods of teaching, relating, dealing with conflict
	See variety of individual differences among handicapped/nonhandicapped children
B. Continued use of "hot line"	Available for contact with group members for friendship and/or support

2. Feedback/Evaluation

A. Continuous evaluation throughout sessions	Assess effectiveness in meeting group goals, group dynamics, and cohesiveness; make changes if necessary
B. Compile information from parents and siblings after sessions.	Evaluate long-term effectiveness
	Contemplate changes

In summation, we would only note that we have found involvement in such a group to be rather expensive—in terms of commitment, time, planning, and emotional investment. However, we also believe we got what we paid for—it seems obvious to us that in terms of developing a therapeutic environment for autistic children, involving those outside the school also dealing with this child has observable benefits to all concerned.

REFERENCES

Berg, K. Christina loves Katherine. *Exceptional Parent,* 1973, *3*(1), 35-36.

Bookbinder, S. What every child needs to know. *Exceptional Parent,* 1977, 31-35.

Coletti, G., & Harris, S. Behavior modification in the home: Siblings as behavior modifiers, parents as observers. *Journal of Abnormal Child Psychology,* 1977, *5*(1), 21-30.

Grossman, F.K. *Brothers and sisters of retarded children.* Syracuse, N.Y.: Syracuse University Press, 1972.

Kaplan, F. Siblings of retarded. In S.B. Sarason & D.J. Sarason (Eds.), *Psychological problems in mental deficiency* (4th ed.). New York: Harper & Row, 1969.

Klein, S. Brother to sister, sister to brother. *Exceptional Parent,* 1972, *2*(1), 10-15. (a)

Klein, S. Brother to sister, sister to brother. *Exceptional Parent,* 1972, *2*(2), 24-27. (b)

Klein, S. Brother to sister, sister to brother. *Exceptional Parent,* 1972, *2*(3), 24-28. (c)

Lavigeur, H. The use of siblings as an adjunct to the behavioral treatment of children in the home with parents as therapists. *Behavior Therapy,* 1976, *7*, 602-613.

Parfit, J. Siblings of handicapped children. *Special Education: Forward Trends,* 1975, *2*(1), 9-21.

Schreiber, M., & Feeley, M. Siblings of the retardate: A guided group experience. *Children,* 1965, *12*(6), 221-225.

Weinrott, M. A training program in behavior modification for siblings of the retarded. *American Journal of Orthopsychiatry,* 1974, *44*(3), 362-375.

BOOKS FOR CHILDREN

Barnes, E., Berrigan, C., & Biklen, D. *What's the difference?* Syracuse, N.Y.: Human Policy Press, 1978.

Brightman, A. *Like me.* Boston: Little, Brown, 1976.

Christopher, M. *Long shot for David.* Boston: Little, Brown, 1973.

Cleaver, V., & Cleaver, B. *Me too.* New York: J.P. Lippincott, 1973.

Fassler, J. *One little girl.* New York: Human Sciences Press, 1969.

Gold, P. *Please don't say hello.* New York: Human Sciences Press, 1975.

Kraus, R. *Leo the late bloomer.* New York: Windmill Books, E.P. Dutton, 1971.

Lasker, J. *He's my brother.* Toronto: George J. McLeod, 1974.

Peterson, J. *I have a sister, my sister is deaf.* New York: Harper & Row, 1977.

Sobol, H. *My brother Steven is retarded.* New York: Macmillan, 1977.

13
An Outreach Service Model: Beyond Techniques for Motivating Autistic Children

Sheila Merzer

INTRODUCTION

Keith is about to enter third grade in his rural elementary school. It is not predicted that he will need any special services. He reads, writes, and does math at age level. He also laughs, talks, and plays with his friends. It is difficult now to believe that at age 5 Keith was diagnosed as autistic and functioning in all areas at least 2 years below age level. He rarely spoke, scribbled all over his papers, made no attempt to play with children, and "tuned out" most of what was happening around him. Keith is unusual in that little now reminds us of his previously severe disability except for the shadows of blankness that now and then pass across his eyes. He is not unusual in that he is an autistic-like child who has made continuous growth attending an integrated program in a regular setting which was modified and intensified to meet his special needs. Keith is one of at least 200 children currently being served on an outreach basis by Minneapolis Children's Health Center's Program for Autistic and Other Exceptional Children.

The Program for Autistic and Other Exceptional Children was begun in 1972 at the University of Minnesota when Dr. Uwe Stuecher received a Bureau for Education of the Handicapped grant to educate master's level students to work with children who were then considered unreachable and unteachable. At that time there was little awareness of autism in our area and no public-school based services to meet the special social-emotional, behavioral, and learning needs of children with autistic characteristics. Our demonstration classroom opened with three severely handicapped autistic-type children and three practicum teachers. What began as an experimental pilot project has grown substantially in size and scope in response to an ever-increasing demand for services. In addition to the original demonstration classroom, which is now providing intensive direct service to six to eight preschool autistic-type children, and an integrated 6-week summer program providing similar services for children of different ages (2 to 12) and differing special needs as well as their nonhandicapped siblings, our program has developed a wide range of outreach services intended to enable seriously handicapped children to make meaningful growth while remaining at home and attending a local school.

Our outreach model began as a makeshift attempt to provide service to children whom we could not accommodate in our small demonstration classroom. What began as an informal, almost token effort to serve a child our program had no space to accept has grown into our most popular, perhaps most effective, intervention model. We began our outreach program hesitantly because we were skeptical about the possibility of effectively intervening with such difficult children outside of a specialized, self-contained setting. It therefore came as quite a surprise when many of our outreach children began developing meaningful communication and improving affectively, socially, behaviorally, and cognitively in ways we had, to that point, not seen in the similarly handicapped children then attending our special project classroom or other equally specialized programs. In fact, we have watched children who had been interacting, learning, and communicating in regular settings with special assistance lose their communicative language (i.e., become echolalic) and deteriorate behaviorally to varying degrees when placed in their district's newly opened program for autistic children. We therefore began to explore the variables that may have accounted for the progress in our outreach children and to accordingly modify both our understanding of the autistic disorder and our intervention procedures. We have by no means become advocates of an integrated program for every child. However, we have come to believe that, while most settings designed primarily for autistic children do teach skills, some aspects of their self-contained environment and frequently repetitive routinized teaching procedures may unwittingly maintain and ingrain the child's autistic functioning patterns.

A Perspective on Autism

It is a fact—if there are any facts in the field of autism—that autistic children do not respond with growth to the kinds of nurturance, teaching, and management that would allow a nonautistic child to develop. The study of autism has therefore given birth to a wide range of approaches and techniques to teach these children skills and modify their behaviors. The settings thus created may in a sense be said to provide abnormal environments (where no children play normally, where no children interact) with abnormal teaching (overly structured and repetitive) and forms of behavior control that you rarely see used with nonhandicapped children. Our rural settings, instead, have found ways to provide these children with intensive individualized assistance within a normal learning environment. We have come to believe that this is a key to the effectiveness of these programs. Finding that those children who received intensive integrated services at an early age were indeed in many cases able to learn how to learn, to develop creative play and spontaneous language, to make friends and become socially integrated, made us rethink our earlier ways of understanding autism and of intervening.

We used to describe autistic-type children as lacking an inner motivation to cooperate and to learn. We would describe the children as engaging in a wide variety of "avoidance behaviors" ranging from "tuning out" (actively not focusing on the task materials) to hyperactivity (or hyper-reactivity—the hyperactivity appeared in response to external stimulation or control) and distractibility to tantrum-like resistance. Since we saw the autistic disorder as being based at least partially in a motivation problem, we approached intervention by attempting to build an intense relationship between each child and his or her individual teacher. It was through this relationship that we attempted to motivate interaction and learning. We also devised a variety of techniques intended to motivate focused cooperation in a disinterested child.

Others would look at the avoiding child behaviorally. Their approach (summarized simplistically) would be to eliminate those behaviors that are interfering with learning, teach attending behaviors, and then train skills.

Both approaches are more or less effective with different children, and both continue to have validity and a place within our current intervention model. However, as we watched the development of a large number of children over time, we began to notice some alarming repetitive patterns.

- Skills seemingly gained in one setting were not voluntarily used in another; thus in many cases school programs "reteach" a child the same skills year after year.
- Self-stimulatory, destructive, or other inappropriate behaviors decreased or eliminated in one situation tended either to reappear or be replaced by other, sometimes less desirable behaviors when the children changed settings or when a specific behavior management technique was no longer used. As we checked the histories of children who had become self-destructive, we noticed that very frequently in their histories some less difficult interfering behaviors had been eliminated.
- The children would develop specific language patterns that they used appropriately but very often repetitively and monotonically without learning to converse spontaneously with other children and adults and without learning to generate the communicative language necessary to express feelings and personal thoughts.
- The children would learn to use specific toys in specific ways; however, they usually did not develop exploratory play. They learned to imitate but not to create.

- The children would become what we call "responders"; in other words, they would learn to comply without at the same time learning to initiate.

We used to believe that these functioning patterns were part of the nature of autism. We still do. We also believe that all too frequently they may be perpetuated and further ingrained because of the ways most autistic children are taught.

For the purpose of intervention, we no longer define *autism* as a behavioral syndrome or as a motivation-based syndrome, but rather as a coping syndrome. In most children we assume the disorder has its basis in physiological or metabolic or other organic differences (the etiology undoubtedly differs from child to child) which somehow make interacting or communicating or learning unusually difficult. We look at the child's autistic behaviors as a way of coping with these difficulties. The child's way of coping limits his or her growth since the function of most of the autistic behaviors is to isolate the child from other people and from many of the "normal" learning opportunities available in the environment. The goal of our intervention is thus to enable the child to develop more adaptive, constructive ways of coping which allow for growth.

Focus of the Program

Although there is little that is true of *all* children identified as having autistic characteristics, we have noticed that almost universally those children who initially appeared to actively avoid cooperating in the learning situation actually appear in many ways to be perfectionists when they do cooperate. In many instances we have found that changing some aspect of the way we present tasks results in an immediate increase in cooperation and focus. In other words, the avoidance behaviors may have initially been related to the fact that the child had genuine difficulty with some aspect of the task as originally presented.

We now perceive the avoiding child as having an exceptionally low frustration tolerance and difficulty modulating body tension and incoming stimuli. From a very young age, these children must have become quickly overstimulated, overanxious, or overfrustrated in response to any attempts at maintaining interaction or focused attention. For the purpose of intervention (our intent here is to give a rationale for an intervention approach—not an explanation of autism), we see the seemingly negative children as habitually (consciously or unconsciously) choosing not to try rather than to try and then experience the resulting internal frustration and tension.

In addition, many of our children seem to learn skills the way I learned physics; that is, master the skill, demonstrate it to criterion, then drop it—because (in our interpretation) the skill is often not functional or relevant or useful to their lives. This may be because it is in the autistic child's nature to learn skills without necessarily learning the purpose of the skills. For example, the fact that they learn to imitate motor or other behaviors in one task situation does not mean that they will begin to spontaneously imitate activities in the world around them (in a sense, they have missed the purpose of imitation). The children typically do not integrate the skills that are taught to them in isolation. Perhaps some of their avoidance behaviors are related to the fact that, to them, the tasks being repeatedly presented are meaningless or irrelevant.

To summarize, in our intervention as well as in our outreach consultation, our focus has moved away from techniques to improve motivation and approaches to decrease or increase specific behaviors toward reproducing a more natural developmental and learning process which in these children did not occur naturally. We now see the child's avoidance behaviors as a cue that we need to modify our teaching. In order to illustrate the ways some of the perspectives presented in this introduction can be translated into a school-based intervention, in the next section I will focus primarily on one child, describing both our outreach consultation process and our intervention program.

PAUL

Paul was referred to our program by his resource room teacher with his parents' permission. He had been attending this resource room (designed primarily for educably retarded children) for 2 years and had reportedly made only minimal growth. Paul's lack of progress was frustrating for his parents, and their relationship with the school staff had deteriorated because of it. The school staff members were frustrated with Paul because he did not seem to benefit from their extensive efforts to serve him. They were also frustrated with his parents for being frustrated with them, since they were trying their best.

It is not uncommon for a referral to our program to be triggered by frustration and for the parents and professionals to be blaming, rather than supporting, one another. Our referrals are perhaps even more frequently triggered by dissent among the professional staff. Quite often, by the time a referral reaches us, the most difficult problems to deal with are not so much with the child but with the communication difficulties among the various adults involved and committed to the child's life. One of our primary roles as consultants is thus to understand the different people's differing, but often all quite useful, perspectives and enable them to put them together in a valid way for the child's total program.

From the moment Paul was referred, we began listening to the perspectives of both the family and school staff to understand their perceptions of Paul and of each other, their frustrations, and their needs. We consistently clarified that our role was not to take sides, but rather to understand and support all concerned and assist them in designing a more effective program.

Evaluation

Our outreach service for Paul began, as it does for most children, with what we call an *educational evaluation*. Our purpose in this initial contact is not to pinpoint the child's skill levels (since our children are typically not "testable" in the traditional sense) or come up with a differential diagnosis (since our children generally receive a long string of different, often contradictory, diagnoses). Instead, we observe and explore the child's communication and interaction with staff and his or her response to materials, to external demands and control, to frustration, and to a variety of teaching and management procedures.

Paul's parents and the participating professionals observed the evaluation session through a one-way mirror. In this way they were able to give us immediate feedback as to whether Paul's functioning during the evaluation represented his typical behavior. We also video taped Paul's evaluation, both in order to keep a visual record of his functioning at the time of referral and to use for staff meetings and inservice training with his school personnel. The video tapes generally have the side effect of building positive communication at a placement conference since they focus the attention and interest of the group on the child. They also reduce arguing, since people very rarely argue when they can see and hear the reasons for all service requests.

At the conclusion of Paul's initial evaluation, we met with his parents and teachers to discuss our evaluation observations (included elsewhere), to discuss his functioning at school and at home, and to formulate a beginning intervention plan. In this evaluation conference we usually detail the child's needs as we see them, based on our initial observations and staff input. We also verbally explore the resources available in the community. Among the variables we may discuss are the kinds of classroom options available; the different teachers' strengths, weaknesses, and attitudes; the family's needs as well as available guidance and support; funding; and other administrative issues. From this information we come up with a beginning plan. In many cases this plan involves the district's hiring a paraprofessional who can be trained to provide intensive individualized teaching to the autistic child wherever needed and who can facilitate the child's participation within the group. In Paul's case we did not make this recommendation since he already was receiving sufficient individual time. We decided to leave Paul's basic placement intact (since the staff appeared to be competent and interested in learning new ways to work with him) and find ways to modify the service within this framework.

School Observation

The next step of our involvement with Paul was to schedule a day to observe him at school. The following is a brief description of Paul's functioning at the time of his referral.

> Our overall initial impression of Paul was of a generally cooperative but uninvolved "detached" child. He went through the motions of the school day, willingly performing familiar tasks, but showing little interest in or enjoyment of the activities. His affect could be described as "flat," with little observed variation in facial expression in response to interaction or activities.

Paul did become invested in maintaining control over some aspects of his life and would protest (sometimes adamantly—by screaming, tantruming, and actively refusing involvement)—the introduction of change into his life routine. He protested new experiences and new activities, including a strong resistance to attempting interaction with other children.

If told that he could go to a desired place, or if he decided himself that he wanted to do so, Paul was likely to perseverate, repeating the same words (e.g. "go swimming") over and over again. Paul would answer a variety of factual questions (often saying "yes," no matter what the question) in short monotonic phrases. Other than the repetition of desires and the expression of specific needs, he did little spontaneous conversing with adults and none with other children. Paul might generally have been described as a "responder." He would respond to questions and directions, but sorely lacked visible initiation or creativity. If not involved by an adult at school, Paul would sit on the radiator self-stimulating; left to himself at home, he might choose to eat, watch TV, and spend long periods of time pacing and waving his arms. He would also spend long periods of time on the trampoline, where he would willingly, successfully, and adeptly imitate and invent new bouncing patterns.

Most of Paul's self-care skills appeared age-appropriate, although his limited ability to verbally negotiate would make one hesitate to trust him to care for himself. However, he could toilet, feed, and dress himself, even managing a winter snowsuit. He acted responsible for his own belongings and carefully (perhaps compulsively) put each item in its place. In some ways Paul's self-sufficiency contributed to our impression of him as "detached," since at least at school he did not need others to satisfy many of his needs, and appeared most content when allowed to do "his own thing" his own way.

During our educational evaluation as well as during our school observation, Paul was generally focused and cooperative, demonstrating an adequate attention span (working 15 to 30 minutes without interruption) in an individual teaching situation when he understood the task and could successfully do as requested. When the task was in some way confusing, frustrating, or "different," anxiety triggered avoidance behaviors; i.e.,he might become nonfocused and unresponsive, he might self-stimulate by flapping his arms or making noises (thereby "tuning out" the request), or he might become echolalic (repeat what was said to him without necessarily processing the words) and perseverative (giving back the response that had been correct the time before without showing an understanding of the question or the response). At these times repetition or drilling of the specific activity did little to improve Paul's cooperation or grasp of the lessons because his avoidance behaviors (and accompanying low frustration tolerance) interfered with his ability to "tune in," process, and learn from teaching.

We observed Paul's school staff members giving him a candy reward for not self-stimulating during structured activities. Through this approach they demonstrated that Paul could control his hand stimulation if he were rewarded for not self-stimulating for specific periods of time in specific situations. However, at a meeting following our observation, both Paul's parents and the school staff agreed that this was not leading to less self-stimulation at other times or to more spontaneous involvement in the world around him. As we pointed out at the meeting, Paul's self-stimulation accelerated both during times when he was not involved in structured activities and when he was frustrated, anxious, or confused. Therefore, instead of rewarding Paul for not self-stimulating, it was decided to focus instead on finding ways to teach him so that the learning situation would become less frustrating and on teaching him to initiate more constructive activities during unstructured times.

Inservice Training

The next step in our consultation service for Paul consisted of inservice training. A small part of our inservice training involved Paul's entire school staff, including regular classroom teachers, administrators, the librarian, the janitors, cooks, and so on. Our purpose in involving all building staff members was to increase their understanding of Paul so they would know how to effectively interact with him in the halls, in the lunchroom, or anywhere else, as well as to facilitate the development of an interested support staff for the teachers directly involved in his program. The second part of the inservice training was more intensive and was designed to increase their understanding of Paul's learning differences. The following list summarizes some of the issues covered during this inservice training. Specifics of Paul's learning process are included here because we have found that autistic-type children of many different functioning levels learn in some similar ways.

- One of the tasks illustrated on videotape demonstrated some of the difficulties experienced by Paul and his teacher in the structured learning situation. The task material was simple, involving paper and pencil only. On the paper was written a single line of alphabet letters (e.g.,C D S L F), which Paul easily recognized. Paul was first asked to "touch the C." He easily did so. The next request was that he "draw a line under the D." His response was to circle the D. I next illustrated the desired response by saying "I'm going to draw a line under the L. Now you draw a line under the D." Paul easily drew the line under the D. Next he was asked to "circle the S," then to "draw a line under the F," both of which he easily did. But when asked to draw a line "on top of" another letter, he drew a line under it. In my interpretation, Paul's way of responding to this task was to related both to the nature of his handicap and to his prior experiences with structured teaching. Much of Paul's earlier teaching had been done in a repetitive kind of format, meaning that the response pattern (e.g., circle the letter) established in the first response remained the same throughout the entire task. This made it possible for Paul to correctly complete a task by focusing more on single words or phrases (related to the target variable being taught) than on whole sentences and by taking his cues more from the materials than from teacher explanation. On tasks involving comprehension rather than memory and following varied as opposed to repetitive directions, Paul's ingrained habit of repeating rather than processing interfered with his ability to understand the task. The problem did not appear so much to be that he could not learn to understand the language, but rather that he approached learning with a well-established set toward repetition rather than processing.

- Paul seemed to have learned many skills while sometimes missing the purpose or meaning of those skills. For example, his well-developed visual discrimination abilities and visual memory led to his becoming a good sight word reader. When we first met Paul, he read aloud at second grade level, but demonstrated minimal reading comprehension. Some of his difficulty with reading comprehension was obviously linked to the apparent gaps in his receptive language. However, to me his major difficulty in building comprehension appeared linked to the fact that he seemingly read to word call, not to gain information or follow a story; i.e., he had missed the main purpose of reading. Thus, it was understandable that he typically responded to tasks requiring reading comprehension by circling the first response or all the responses or by echoing the answer the teacher gave him. In my estimation, the basic problem in teaching him was not that he could not learn to understand, but rather that he seemed as yet unaware that there was something else to understand—i.e., that there was a purpose to the reading comprehension tasks other than the process of reading aloud and circling some words.

- Similarly, Paul would learn speech and language patterns and use them appropriately but repetitively (without variation in wording or intonation) in specific situations or in response to specific questions or material stimuli. However, the fact that he had learned new language patterns did not necessarily lead to much increased spontaneous use of language. In fact, while occasionally Paul would spontaneously come out with an appropriate self-initiated original communicative phrase, hinting that his inner language might be better developed than his general expressive language indicated, Paul did not typically initiate using speech other than to make requests. He did not voluntarily share experiences, verbally express feelings, or otherwise converse. In a broad sense, he had learned speech, but missed one of the important functions of language—communication.

- Paul's immediate avoidance response to situations that were difficult for him seemed linked to the fact that he was in some ways a perfectionist. He has his own idea of how things ought to function in his life routine, and he did not welcome any interruption in his order. On cognitive tasks, he wanted immediate assurance that he was putting down the correct response and would require (by looking at the teachers or repeating his answer) teacher approval before going on to the next question. Here again, his purpose did not appear to be to better understand the task (he would correct an incorrect response choice, paying no visible attention to the reason for the change). His purpose seemed to be, rather, to go through the process of completing his paper perfectly. His seeming need for immediate feedback after each response made it dificult for him to work independently on task assignments.

- Contributing to his use of avoidance behaviors was the fact that his language was not developed to the point where he could ask questions that would help pinpoint his difficulty or verbally express the reason for his resistance to attempt a given activity.
- Paul's language difficulties, coupled with his tendency to "tune out" when he did not understand, made it difficult for him to benefit from small- or large-group teaching. Since a teacher in front of a room tends to vary her language and mix task-related statements with unrelated comments regarding behavior, and so on, and since other children speak quickly with little repetitive pattern to what they say, Paul's general response to a group situation was to withdraw by tuning out or self-stimulating.
- Paul's resistance to interacting with other children was also probably closely linked to his difficulty with language (other children are more difficult to understand than adults), to his difficulty with free play (which is not repetitive and which does not have "rules" that can be systematically trained), and to his lack of desire to attempt that which he had not mastered.

Intensive Intervention

One of our recommendations at the conclusion of the inservice training was that Paul participate in our summer program for several weeks of intensive intervention and that a member of his school staff participate with him, both to observe his functioning and to receive training. The main purpose for Paul's participation in our summer project was to see how he would function in a new setting where he had no pre-established routines and no habitual functioning patterns. (We have a diagnostic classroom during the school year which offers a similar option for intensive intervention in a new setting along with staff training and participation. This insures that any gains made in this setting transfer to the child's community school.) Our major concern in Paul's case was to find ways to promote affective development as well as to increase his spontaneous language, group participation, and interaction with peers. The following are some of the observations made during the summer weeks.

- One of the program goals was to explore ways to develop in Paul the desire to initiate in a positive way. To this end, Paul and his tutor Marie tried a variety of program options (e.g., group activities, music, and arts and crafts). The second time specific options appeared, Paul was given a choice as to which he preferred. Marie observed that he always made a choice as to which he would like to do (as opposed to only saying "no" to ones he would not like) and that he was definite about his selections. (To avoid power struggles when an activity was required, it helped to clarify verbally before introducing the activity when he had a choice and when he needed to participate.)

- Paul appeared to especially enjoy our daily music sessions. He independently began to make many of the motions that accompany our songs and to sing some of the words. He also spontaneously began requesting that specific songs be sung. One of his apparent favorite songs was "Old MacDonald" and he would loudly announce the names of the animals that he wanted included. One of the factors that may have contributed to Paul's enjoyment of these music sessions was that he was at times among the more competent of the group members. This may have given him a boost in self-confidence which triggered his motivation to participate. Additionally, the verses and motions to the songs were repetitive, and the pace was slow enough to allow him to master the words and movements easily. We were pleased to see that in this activity, as well as in several others, Paul could generate enthusiasm while participating in a group.

- When involved in group activities, Paul observed other teacher-child pairs and made some verbal comments regarding what he heard and saw. Interestingly enough, Paul was observed relating nonverbally to some of the less advanced autistic-type children. He and another child with a similar pattern of self-stimulation were seen self-stimulating near each other, stopping and starting their hand movements together, and moving with parallel rhythms.

- Paul appeared to be a tireless hiker. On the field trips, he moved rapidly. Writing language experience stories regarding field trip experiences seemed to be a workable route toward expanding Paul's use of language and building connections between what he wrote, read, and actually did. Asking Paul to use more language to explain or describe was sometimes successful in increasing the length and complexity of his sentences. Phrasing the question in such a way that a yes-no response was not possible was also helpful in getting Paul to listen and respond rather than just say "yes" (a response he gave seemingly to satisfy the questioner without investing in the interaction). The quality and quantity of Paul's verbal output both improved when his arousal level (level of excitement, anticipation, and involvement) was high.

- One of the summer staff teachers and her son (who is approximately Paul's age) included Paul in some social outings. Paul was willling to go and referred to the teacher's son as his "friend" in a positive way— rather than making his earlier heard protests of "no friend" when it was suggested that he might like to do something with another child.

Program Planning

At the conclusion of the summer program, we again met with the staff of Paul's school to design his program for the following school year. Everyone concerned felt that Paul's program included certain basic necessary service components:

- A small group resource room to function as a home base;
- Daily speech and language services;
- Daily academic tutoring;
- The opportunity for integration into a mainstream program.

Perhaps most importantly, it was apparent that the staff members involved in Paul's program were flexible, open to input, and willing to try varied approaches to find the most effective ways to help Paul learn and grow. At the staffing, the rationale for Paul's educational intervention programing was summarized as follows.

- Since it was observed that Paul's language output was better when he was interested and involved, it is probable that Paul's difficulty with communication is in some ways linked to difficulty with interaction. In other words, designing Paul's program to increase the ways in which he interacts with others and his desire to be involved should lead to increased language as well.
- In our summer school enviornment, where activities were designed so that Paul could easily participate if he tried, Paul appeared willing and occasionally almost enthusiastic about successful involvement. Staff members in Paul's school are attempting to structure some of Paul's group activities similarly to allow for more success, while teaching Paul the skills he needs to function in less specialized situations. To multiply Paul's small group experiences, his academic and speech sessions were scheduled wherever possible with other children.
- In the academic task situation, it was suggested that the focus be as much on the learning process as on teaching specific skills. In other words, increasing Paul's ability to process the language of instruction; to respond in a more affective, routinized, repetitive manner; and to accept and enjoy new activities should lead to improved learning in all areas.
- With regard to speech and language, the focus would be on increasing the spontaneity, variety, complexity, and frequency of Paul's ability to process increasingly varied and complex verbal input.

- When working with Paul, consistent attention would need to be paid to avoid establishing rote response patterns. In other words, a balance needs to be found between structuring the interaction (language, task, schedule) enough that Paul understands and is able to respond, but not structuring so much that he locks into a pattern.

FOLLOW UP

For all of our outreach children, follow up observation and consultation services are scheduled either at periodic intervals ranging from every 4 to 6 weeks to every 3 months (depending on need and distance from Minneapolis) or on an "as needed" basis. We prefer regularly scheduled consultation because it allows us to better know the parents, school staff, and child. The purpose of the follow up is to allow us to observe the child's response to intervention over time and suggest any needed program modifications. The follow up is also a valuable means of providing support for the school staff and the child's family. It is often easier for us as outsiders to see growth in difficult children than it is for those dealing with them every day. In a rural school, we are often able to reassure families and professionals that they are doing as well for their unique child in their own community as would be done anywhere else.

Paul's school is not far from our hospital, and thus his follow up is scheduled every 4 to 6 weeks. At the staff meetings following our observations of Paul in school, we attempt to detail those areas where growth is apparent as well as make recommendations for programming changes. The following changes were noted in Paul's functioning after the first 3 months of his new school year.

- Since so many of Paul's difficulties appeared linked to his limited comprehension, the year began with a strong emphasis on building Paul's understanding of what he heard and read. It did not take long for Paul to begin to respond to comprehension activities related to his own experiences by very confidently saying "no!" to incorrect choices and circling the correct choice, saying "yes!" with a smile and expression in his voice. Paul's reading comprehension has shown gradual steady improvement since he visibly first began to understand. He is now showing increasing ability to gain meaning from a text and answer nonroutinized questions. Along with his understanding, he has begun to show some definite preferences for some stories over others. He has also begun to get meaning from the pictures accompanying the stories rather than merely labeling the items. With his understanding has also come a still inconsistent but sometimes apparent investment in participating in the learning activity. For example, during one of my observations, he grabbed the chalk from the teacher to show her his idea of how the picture ought to look. In other words, he cared.

- An early emphasis in the area of speech and language focused on building affective involvement by finding ways to physically involve Paul in activities and by getting him to smile frequently (i.e., enjoy the activity). It was found that using manipulative materials (such as small animals, clay, or puzzles) in semistructured format increased Paul's interest in the language sessions (and decreased his self-stimulation, since his hands were otherwise occupied). There is at this time more noticeable variability in Paul's facial expression during social interaction. Seemingly related is the fact that at times Paul's speech loses its monorhythmic quality and emotion (e.g., enthusiasm, anger, frustration, giggling enjoyment) enters his tone.
- Since most children develop language partly in order to be able to initiate contact and control adults, a parallel early communication goal was to get Paul to initiate choosing specific activities. Soon Paul began walking into the room with a ready idea for what he and the speech therapist should do. When the choosing itself seemed to have become a pattern, the teacher began varying the format, sometimes allowing Paul to choose any activity, sometimes giving him a choice of two or three activities. Role reversal was also used during language activities whenever possible, giving Paul a turn to tell the teacher what to do rather than always responding to her directives. Games like Simon Says also proved to be good ways to elicit spontaneous language and a high level of involvement on Paul's part.

INTEGRATION

One of the discussions at an earlier follow-up staff meeting concerned modifying the integration component of Paul's program. Because of Paul's high level word recognition skills, he had been placed in a regular second grade reading group. His participation in this mainstream class was promising at first (Paul seemingly wanted to be in the group), but soon deteriorated to the point where he would enter the group, isolate himself, and self-stimulate. Since this attempt made it clear that Paul began the school year without the prerequisite social and language skills to function in the group, a special reading group comprised of Paul and one other child (Billy) was begun. The primary objective of this group was to teach Paul to learn in other than a one-to-one teacher-child situation. It has been exciting to watch the growth Paul has made since this group was begun less than 2 months ago. Specifically, Paul has begun to:

- Share the teacher's attention with another child while staying tuned in to the activity.
- Read silently (i.e., follow along) while the teacher or other child reads aloud.

- Independently complete a worksheet without needing continuous approval or reminders to stay on task; along with an understanding of meaning, he has begun to show signs of confidence that he knows he is right. He now requests help during an independent task only when he is unsure of the response.
- Show some self-confidence by helping Billy when he needs assistance in word recognition (for this purpose, a child was chosen whose sight word skills were slightly lower than Paul's).
- Willingly play learning games with Billy.
- Accept rather than reject Billy's overtures.

Billy appears to enjoy working with Paul and sees him as a friend, seeking him out during lunch and recess.

In other words, because Paul could not function in the mainstream reading group, we decided to teach him how to function in a reading group through the process of "reverse integration"—where a mainstream or more typical child is brought into the special setting for a specific activity. We suggest the process of reverse integration in a situation like Paul's, where the child needs to be taught to function in a specific kind of group or in a situation where the mainsteam group is just too large. We also might suggest reverse integration where a child is too disruptive to function in a mainstream classroom, but would benefit from the opportunity to play and learn with children who function more appropriately.

Another suggestion we recently made to Paul's staff was to integrate him for part of the day into some regular kindergarten activities. Although Paul is 10 years old, socially and cognitively he is in many ways at the level of a kindergarten child. We have in many cases found that allowing a child to reexperience the kinds of play and learning experiences that he or she was not able to benefit from as a younger child can be more beneficial than more traditional remediation attempts. In one situation, a 14-year-old functionally retarded autistic-type girl was placed part-time in a preschool and told she was a "helper." In this environment, she began to use language to communicate and develop pre-academic skills she had missed the first time around.

For most young autistic-type children (preschool and kindergarten age), we suggest a primary placement in an early intervention program geared for mildly handicapped children or in a regular kindergarten (depending on age and functioning level) once the child has begun to interact, to initate, and to develop the beginnings of receptive and expressive language. We have found that no other force is as powerful in promoting social growth as a large group of children playing normally—if the special child is given the needed help to benefit from the experience. We usually intensify this mainstream placement by adding a paraprofessional to the classroom. We train the paraprofessional to facilitate the participation of the special child and provide additional services (such as tutoring or small-group teaching) where needed. As the autistic child learns to function in the group, the aide gradually becomes a classroom assistant, providing additional teaching time for all the children.

IN LIEU OF A SUMMARY

It would have been simpler for me to put together this text if we had one system for serving all children. The truth is that we design as many service systems as we see children. The one common thread is flexibility and a willingness to attempt to modify any program that is not promoting meaningful change. One of our priorities is to be kind to the families that come to us and communicate openly and honestly with parents and professionals. All of our interventions are positively oriented. We do not believe in treating children negatively in the hope that in the long run they will be better off. Since we cannot predict the future, all we have is the present; thus to us the means is as important as the end.

Many times I as an individual—and we as a program—have been asked what are objectives are and how we measure our effectiveness. We have our systems, and we help the schools adapt theirs. However, I wonder what kind of change is the most important. And what about the child who is neurologically damaged to the point where growth is not a real possibility? My personal goal is to look at every child and every family and in some way make their lives a little smoother or a little happier. It may be just as important to Susie's family that her school learn to accept, teach, and enjoy her despite her on-going deteriorating physical disability as it is to Keith's family that he is able to go to school and have friends like most other children. Teaching others not to always equate growth with value and not to judge...parents or children or professionals...may be the most important function of our outreach service.

One day a 12-year-old child visited our demonstration classroom with his open school class. He had been afraid to come because he worried that he would get depressed. Upon leaving our classroom, he said to his teacher, "I wonder what it would be like if all the world were autistic and people could show love to one another." I wonder too.

Part V

Fostering Positive Attitudes toward Handicapped Children and Teacher-Child Relationships

14
Living Together:
Teacher Behaviors That
Promote Integration

Ellen Barnes

The teacher's role in an integrated setting is crucial. Teachers can facilitate or inhibit the integration of typical and special children through their interventions. This chapter describes a range of teacher behaviors that promote social interaction as well as the problems and challenges of mainsteaming from the teachers' perspectives, in their own words. The data used in this chapter are taken from interviews with teachers as well as specimen recordings of interactions in the classroom.

Teachers talked about their definition of an integrated setting as much more than being in the same classroom together—"living together, working together, being aware of each other, socializing together." As another teacher put it, "I think it means kids being involved with each other, caring for each other, helping and hugging each other, wanting to do things with and for each other, and learning about each other is a big part of it." Individualization and diversity seem to be central concepts. Individualization, not just in terms of the process of teaching but in terms of how children are seen, allows all children, no matter what their ability level, to be treated as special. Diversity as a positive value was mentioned by several teachers. As Helen said,

I think that integration implies a very different opportunity for handicapped children from the very beginning of their lives in the actual culture that exists in our society. Integration...for me means making our schools look like our society;...it means having each class or each community, each school group, look more like the community that it's in. Our community, our society includes many people with very different kinds of disabilities. I think most people ignore that. When you actually look at the figures—the population figures—it breaks down percentages of people who are disabled by what you call *mental illness*. It's shocking really to think of it because we don't think of it as being that many people. And in the American sense of the word it's in actuality a pluralistic system which is what the culture is.

Integration, then, is providing "equal opportunities" for all children and at the same time serving individual needs. Those teachers who mentioned the value of diversity felt that their environment needed *more* diversity in types of disabilities and ethnic backgrounds.

The teachers here obviously saw integration as much more than just proximity of special and typical children. It was based on a philosophical commitment to equal access principles for the special children. It also involved a focus on the socioemotional development of children in terms of accepting and valuing differences. One teacher describes her perspective.

> I think basically what I've seen here is typical kids and special kids together and interacting as human beings would—not a situation where you try to force an interaction but you do try to help an interaction occur, where kids have questions answered about differences. They learn to appreciate the differences and those differences that they don't like they can say that they don't like and that's okay. They can feel better about themselves. Special kids get to be with kids that have not been so severely injured by life as they've been and they can grow from that and open up from that. That's what I see—not forcing something or staging relationships, but helping people.

None of the staff mentioned fulfilling a law. They all spoke of a commitment to quality interactions between children with differences and noted that the school setting tries to foster quality relationships between them. The teacher's role in doing this is very significant and often problematic. In the next few pages, some of the ways in which teachers affect interaction between typical and special children will be illustrated.

TEACHER PRESENCE AS AN ATTRACTION

When teachers focus on special children, typical children may be drawn toward them and become involved with the special child as a secondary effect. The attractiveness of teacher attention and perhaps the nature of the activity the teacher and special child are engaged in draws the typical child. Here's an example in which Jean approaches Kevin at lunch time, even though Kevin's behavior around food is often difficult. She approaches because she wants the contact with Dottie, the teacher.

> Jean comes over. Dottie is still holding Kevin. She says, "I don't know if there is much room here." Jean sits next to Dottie after struggling to move a

chair. Dottie, looking at Kevin, says, "Would you like some more Kool Aid, Kevin?" Kevin drinks without spilling. Dottie says to Kevin, "We have a dinner guest." "I'm always going to eat here," says Jean. "We have cake for you, Kevin," says Dottie. Kevin looks at Jean now and then and seems to be looking over to the other table where a teacher and other children sit conversing and joking. Kevin appears oblivious to the conversation Dottie and Jean are having. The only sign of his awareness is his occasional short stares at Dottie and Jean. "He's learning to pick up his drink now, " says Jean. "He is learning. He's getting a lot better, " Dottie says. "Good drinking, Kevin," Dottie says to him. He watches the other table, not watching where the food is going. Dottie says, "You are interested in what's over there, hey Kevin." He leans against Dottie's arm, which is resting on the top of the chair.

Dottie pulls out another sandwich. Jean says, "Kevin has a big lunch." Dottie says, "Yes, he does." Dottie opens the sandwich and gives small pieces one-by-one to Kevin, who stretches his mouth to chew them. His mouth seems to move like a machine, very rhythmically and stretching. He picks up his drink and does not spill it this time. Dottie says, "Good drinking, Kevin. Excellent. Excellent." He sucks the empty cup, hoping to get more juice from it. He looks in it.

Dottie picks up the food on the floor. Jean is, meanwhile, busy eating her lunch and making comments to Dottie about the kind of lunch she brought. "I have a big lunch. I'm almost full," she says. Kevin looks at Jean as she eats but seems more focused on the food she has on the table. Kevin looks again to the other table.

In the following situation, Dawn seems intrigued by the book that Danny and Helen, the teacher, are reading; and Danny's interfering behavior doesn't affect her.

Danny and Helen are reading the *Let's Eat* book at the small table behind the partition. Dawn goes over and leans beside them, watching and smiling. She's rocking back and forth, looking at the book. Danny is saying the words in the pictures. Helen says, "How about the next page, Danny?" Dawn turns the page for him. Danny gets up, reaching for the shelf, and pulls over its contents. Things fall down. He screeches. Helen says, "That surprised you, didn't it. Let's pick them up." Dawn stands watching. They come back to the book. Dawn is asking questions about the pictures in the book, "What's that?" Danny is identifying them by name. They get to the last page, and he closes the book. (Dawn appeared to genuinely not know the names of things; she wasn't asking for teaching purposes.) Danny gets up and screeches, pushing at Helen. They move toward the door. Dawn says, "Where are you going?" Helen turns to Dawn and says, "You know, Dawn, Danny's real mad this afternoon. He's been screaming and hitting me. Do you know why? Why do you think?" Dawn says, "I don't know. Who's that from?" pointing to a picture on the wall. Helen answers and then goes into the hall with Danny.

Teachers can also encourage children to interact with each other, especially using sensorimotor activities. Here Vera and Kathy, teachers, begin by tickling

Greg and Lottie, a special and a typical child. In the end Greg receives tickling from both Lottie and Janet, another typical child, and everyone has a good time.

> Greg and Lottie are playing with Vera and Kathy, tickling and laughing. Then Lottie is tickling Greg and they are both shouting and giggling. Lottie pushes Greg toward Kathy, laughing and saying, "Here's your tickler." Greg is touching Lottie. Vera and Kathy are laughing and tickling Greg and Lottie and Janet. They are on the floor and couch. Kathy says to Janet, "Tickle Greg." She does, and they both are laughing. Greg sits on Kathy's lap, smiling and saying, "Tickle! Tickle!" Lottie comes over and falls on both of them.

.   Teacher attention can be used as a very effective "carrot" to start interaction between typical and special children. Children are drawn to the adults and to the activities adults are involved in. Teachers must be able to use the opportunity for interaction. In the following example, the extent of teacher attention may have prevented children from interacting.

> Janet and her teacher, Kathy, are working with Cuisenaire rods. Carol comes over to their table. Kathy asks if she wants to play with the rods. Carol nods. Kathy says, "Yes or no?" Carol says, "Yes." Janet is a foot away, watching Carol and Kathy intently. Kathy and Carol take out more rods. James comes over and begins to work with Janet on the rods. The two pairs work side-by-side.

Teachers must learn to involve children with each other and to recognize that too many adults may limit occasions for two children to interact.

TEACHER SPONTANEOUSLY INCORPORATES CHILDREN INTO JOINT ACTIVITY

In these situations a teacher will make a suggestion to involve a special or typical child in an integrated interaction. This may take only one brief suggestion, or it may require more extended participation by the teacher to maintain the involvement of the special child. Here Helen's suggestion was sufficient to have the children help; they seemed interested in the activity itself as well.

> Danny is sawing to make clayboards. Gena is leaning on John, thumb in mouth, watching him. John, a teacher, says, "Danny is cutting us some clayboards. " Gena watches for another couple of seconds and then gets up and walks away. John gets up and follows her. Danny is still sawing. Kara walks over and stands next to him, watching him saw, her hand on the licorice in her mouth. Helen is holding the cardboard. Mark comes in and goes over to them. He's watching, then talking to Helen. Gena has come back over and is standing on a chair next to Danny, watching him. Danny begins sawing at

another place. Helen: "Danny, the line is over here. We need big clayboards." She points to the line and helps Danny move the cardboard. Gena and Mark are watching and Kara too. Helen: "We need to hold it for him." Mark and Gena hold it, leaning over it watching the saw go, with their hands on the board. Mark says something to Helen about putting the snack in the refrigerator. They get up to leave. Helen says, "Gena, will you be careful to hold the board. Oh, Kara, too." Gena and Kara have already leaned over, kneeling with their weight on the cardboard. Helen leaves the room to go with Mark.

Another teacher describes her approach one day in a free play sitiation.

At times when the typical kids are doing some kind of group activity like playing store or house, they won't try to incorporate the special kids. Yesterday when I was playing with them, I wanted Greg to come and be my "son." At first they were reluctant. Then they said O.K.

Sometimes typical children react negatively to attempts to include special children in the process. Teachers handle this rejection in different ways. Here Vera ignores it.

Vera and Lottie are playing a game, Trouble, at the table. Vera asks Greg to come play Trouble with her and Lottie. He gets up and moves toward them. Lottie says to Vera, "No. I want you to play." Greg sits next to her. Vera ignores Lottie and shows Greg how to push the bubble for his turn. He figures out how to do it and keeps on doing it over and over. Vera says, "Greg, wait! It's Lottie's turn. Wait. Wait." She says this three times. "Wait. Just keep it under control." He stops and waits for Lottie's turn. They keep playing, with Greg pushing the bubble for Vera and Lottie then taking her turn.

Helen also matter-of-factly denies Kara's desire to "do it myself." Helen says to Kara, "Kara, can you help Danny color the planboard today?" Helen gets the crayons and the planboard and props it against the blackboard. Kara and Danny both move over toward her. Kara says, "I want to do it myself." Helen: "Danny's going to do it, too. Danny, color in Monday, June 7th." She hands him the crayons. Danny squeals,"Stop bossing." Helen is beside him, touching him. Kara and Danny are sitting side-by-side, both taking paper off the crayons. They begin coloring. His hand runs into Kara's. She says impatiently, "Danny!" He gets up and walks away. He says over and over to himself: "Stop bossing. You stop bossing." He walks back over and continues to color. Kara gets up to leave; she appears finished.

Helen's persistence in trying to overcome Nell's resistance to working with Danny is demonstrated in another situation around coloring the planboard.

Danny is coloring in the large block letters on the planboard. Helen says to Nell, who is sitting next to Danny, "Nell, do you think you can help Danny fill in the A and the Y?" Nell: "No" (quietly). Helen: "Danny's been having a little trouble staying inside the line, and you've been practicing those letters." Nell doesn't answer and does not work with the letters. She goes back to drawing, and Helen starts to help Gena with the guinea pig cage. Helen focuses back on Danny as he becomes distracted. She says to him, "Can you draw the A and the Y and ask Nell for help if you need it?" Nell says, "No" (smiling). "Well, you can just be there for back-up, " says Helen.

These situations were ones in which teachers spontaneously tried to involve special and typical kids together. They had to be aware of circumstances when interaction was possible and how to involve two children so that they are both interested in the activity. Sometimes teachers did not take advantage of circumstances as in these next two situations.

Greg is sitting at a table in the Brown Room doing a puzzle. Lottie is also working on a puzzle across the table from him. Greg works on the puzzle, quietly fitting each piece in its place. Lottie works quietly, and so does Greg. No words are exchanged between the two. Greg continues to work on the puzzle, not looking up, swinging one leg under the table. Lottie leaves after she has finished her puzzle. Greg does not look up...Vera comes over to the table to help Greg. Lottie walks back across the room. She leans over the table, watching Vera and Greg doing the puzzle. Greg makes some noises and Lottie imitates them. Vera ignores her, and continues to help Greg fit the puzzle pieces into place. Lottie leaves.

Bobby sits down at the table, and Bradley goes over to him and touches the play dough Bobby is using. Bradley leans toward Bobby and says "Oui Oui." Bobby stands up and walks a few steps over to the easel to paint. Bradley goes and stands beside him. Jan says warningly to Bradley, "You need to say 'paint' first." Jan: "Bradley, want to play with the playdough?" He sits beside her, looking at Bobby. Jan: "You're watching Bobby paint. You're watching Bobby paint, huh, Bradley. You're tired. You should go to bed earlier." Bobby turns to them, "You know something? My mom lets me watch TV sometimes." Bobby turns back to his painting. Jan to Bradley: "I'm going to make a bowl." Bobby: "How do you make a bowl?" Bradley watches. Then he gets up and walks across the room. He climbs up on the bookcase. Jan says, "No, Bradley," and he gets down. He walks over to Fran and takes her hand; he says "Oui. Oui." Fran says it back to him. Then Fran says, "I'm listening to Linda's directions, Bradley." Bradley then walks and sits on the arm of the chair where Dottie is reading to Randy. He's sitting and smiling, touching Dottie. She's holding out fingers and she's telling him the number of fingers. Randy is looking around with his thumb in his mouth. Bradley goes over to Bobby, who's painting. He's watching him and moves close to him. "No! Wash your hands!" Bobby says loudly, but he's smiling. Jan: "Bradley, you know you can't paint unless you say 'paint.' You can take a piece of paper and draw at the table."

In the first situation, the teacher appeared to be so focused on her own goal with the special child (that is, puzzle completion) that she ignored the opportunity for socialization. Bradley, in the second incident, seemed to be very focused on other people. He approached Bobby several times but was turned back by Jan's intervention. He then went to two other teachers who were working with children (Fran with Linda, Dottie with Randy) and was either rebuffed or not included. Jan persisted in reading Bradley's approach to Bobby as an interest in painting rather than in Bobby, and she continued to resist his attempts to make contact. These examples are included to demonstrate that often children may not be naturally included but in fact may require strong activity on the part of the teacher. This may require a commitment to integrated socialization as a conscious goal.

PLANNING ACTIVITIES FOR ALL

The teaching staff members see the integrated nature of the program as imposing another need for planning; not only do they focus on developing activities to meet the individual academic and behavioral needs of the children, but they also must consciously create opportunites for integrated interaction. As Vera put it, "I feel there's a real pressure to find activities that everyone can participate in. I feel like that's always on my mind." Activities that seem to allow for more interaction are discussed more fully in the next chapter. They include sensorimotor and gross motor experiences, group games, and activities centered around food. Helen gives an example from her classroom.

The sort of environmental structure is important—setting up activities where kids can be together, like painting...things that don't isolate.... I'm not always hitting on the right combination.... It's not subconcious. I think it's just something that teachers do with all kids really. If your goals are to have kids learning independently a lot from each other, you try to pair kids of somewhat different abilities that will stimulate one another. It's always a very conscious thing in the planning: How are we going to include Danny? How are we going to do something that will make him more involved and make him more accessible to people as well as what kind of skill he will get out of it? Like today when we planned out the papier mache activity, I know there would obviously be something in there for him, for Danny, to do...like ripping the paper. And that there would be a lot of chances for him to be equally involved with kids, even in fact to be giving things to kids but that it wouldn't be something holding back the other children, that it would be a real experience for other kids too.... I mean I try to send David out for water for the guinea pig or something—filling up pails of water with another child...things like that—I will do a lot of that sort of from across the room—like help somebody to get over to the carpentry table when Danny is there and...from across the room at key moments throw out a suggestion to be involved with him...trying to make what Danny is doing be attractive like when he's doing something by himself so that other kids will come over.

Teachers plan activities in which they pair or arrange small groups with typical and special children. Often maintaining the momentum of both the activity and the interaction requires active adult participation. Here is an example.

> Dottie and Fran sit with Linda, Kynna, and Randy at a screen, pushing needles with yarn through burlap to make designs. Randy, with Dottie's help, pushes the needle through to Kynna, who is pushing it back to Randy. Dottie: "Can you pull this through, Randy?" He does. Then he turns away watching Rick, from Dottie's lap. Fran to Kynna: "Push that through to Randy, he's waiting over there. " She does. Dottie says, "Randy, can you put it through?" Kynna responds, "No, I want it this way." Dottie: "Well, Kynna, that's where Randy wants to put it."

Helen describes the first day in a math time using Cuisenaire rods in which she integrated Danny and a number of the typical children.

> That was the first day I worked with the group. We're starting a little period in the morning time on numbers and stuff. I don't know how successful it was, but I had the whole box of rods and each child had a can and I had them take out some of each color so that they could get a sense that there were 10 different ones and stuff like that. I had to help Danny an awful lot with that, and the other kids could really help each other more. It's more like aiming for his total involvement knowing that I have to support him a great deal. For Danny really it was more like following a command and putting things in the can. I scaled it down and then he was doing something else. They were building structures with the rods and I had him doing length discrimination kinds of stuff. It was very hairy and I wasn't too happy with it. My thinking was, of course, to start out with something where he could be involved with the group, even if it was just being at the table with the group and sharing the common lot and in incidental stuff that comes up—like whose hand is in the box, just hitting into kids, and then just breaking it down further.

All the classrooms had some sort of group meeting each day as well as group games and singing. In most cases the special children took part, even if they required help from adults or other children.

> From the beginning we have expected that they would participate. When we go around the circle, we as teachers always asked Bradley, asked Randy.... We have assumed they would be part of the plan. We were dividing up class jobs the other day and we did it including Randy and Bradley. I think the children assume they would participate, maybe at a different level, but participate.

These examples all involve teacher *planned* experiences in which adults were present and active. Another dimension to planning is to set up materials and pair children and then step back and let interaction proceed. This seemed to work when the children involved are active enough interpersonally. Either the special child must be able to engage more mutually and reinforce the social behaviors of the typical child, or the typical child must be willing to actively pursue and reinvolve the special child. In the following play situation, Fran begins by being involved verbally with Bobby, a typical child. She sees Randy being interested and encourages him to join them. Then she moves back and lets them play.

> Fran and Randy are sitting on the floor with toys. Bobby comes over and says, "This is the gas station." Fran: "And this is the barber shop where you get your hair cut. Like you got a hair cut." Randy looks at them. Bobby tells Fran about the sliver in his finger, showing it to her. Fran says, "It's a sliver." They continue to talk. Then Fran says to Bobby, "Did you come over to play with Randy?" Fran moves back and Bobby goes closer. Bobby: "This is a toy shop." They both begin moving the Fisher-Price objects. Bobby is hammering. Randy is making sounds, smiling. They are both moving the cars in the garage. Every now and then, Randy looks at Fran and smiles. They play side-by-side. Randy moves around behind Bobby. Randy looks at Fran, now reading to Bradley, and says, "Kynna! Kynna!" Fran: "You can go talk to Kynna; she's at the table." Randy smiles and turns back to the blocks. Linda comes over and becomes involved in the play. Randy says, "Ah! Ah!" loudly. Jean and Kynna imitate the sound from across the room, "Ah!" Randy says, "Ah!" Dottie says: "Shh!" They quiet down. Bobby says, "I have to go to the bathroom." When Fran says, "O.K.," Bobby leaves. Randy says, "Bye." He focuses back on the cars. Linda: "O.K., Randy." Randy touches Linda's hair, smiling. She's playing with the cars. He's looking at the door, then back to the cars. They are sitting side-by-side, playing, Randy with blocks now, not looking at each other. Linda drops a car. Randy looks at it and says, "That hurt." Linda is humming, talking softly to herself, as she works the toy garage. Randy continues moving the car around and props it up with a Lincoln log. Bobby has come back in—and is sitting at the table with the chalk painters. Randy to Linda: "A red car is pretty car, red," pointing to car. Linda looks but doesn't say anything. She continues with the cars. Linda seems very engrossed, talking to herself. She makes a car roll down the ramp into Randy's lap. He laughs and so does she. Randy says, "I like it, I like it." Randy gets up and walks to the bookshelf. Then he goes back to the shelf and the Fisher-Price toys, next to Linda. Jean, Linda, and Bobby leave the room to wash their hands. Randy turns to watch them. Then he goes back to the cars.

In all of these activities, teacher planning and intervention facilitated interaction between typical and special children, often through the choice of activity. The teachers' verbal mediating efforts also provided redirection for the children, encouraging them to focus on each other. More examples of this kind of adult intervention will be discussed in the following section.

DIRECTING CHILDREN TOWARD EACH OTHER

Typical children can ignore the presence of special children by not including them in a conversation or activity, or they can treat them as if they cannot understand or respond. The most frequent instance of this is when a typical child will ask a teacher to communicate with a special child rather than doing so directly himself or herself. This may be built on realistic expectations about the special child's inability to speak, or it may reflect an attitude of condescension toward the special child. The teacher intervention often used at this point is to suggest that the typical child speak directly to the special child.

> Danny goes across the room to the workbench where the paper and markers are. "Draw saber saw," Danny says. "O.K., draw it," says Helen. Dawn approaches and asks Helen, "What is Danny drawing?" "Ask Danny," says Helen. Dawn: "Danny, what are you drawing?" There is no response from Danny.

Teachers can also direct children's attention to the presence and desires of the special child. Here Helen directs attention to Carol.

> Jean comes over with a bag of potato chips. She offers Rick one. Helen: "Carol might like one." Jean: "No. I don't want to give her one. Only people." Rick: "Carol is a person." Jean: "Well, not a person like that. Not little kids." Bobby: "I'm not a little kid." Helen: "See, Jean, Carol's reaching out her hand like this. I think she wants one." Jean hands Carol one. Rick: "I'm giving mine to Bobby, because Jean wouldn't give him one."

Extending an interaction that has already begun is another function of teachers—to help it continue and to make the content a learning experience. Vera describes an interaction that occurred in the car on the way to a field trip.

> On the way to Green Lakes in the car Martin was making sounds. He said "light," which was one of his really big words and a lot of the kids said it after trying to say it exactly the same way that he had. Then he was making sounds like a sucking-in air noise, and the kids were making sounds like that. It seems to me that one of the kids—it may have been Jane again—did that back to him, like took another sound and said it to him and wanted him to repeat it. Sandy then said, "Well, you know, 'light' was an l-word. Maybe you could think of other l-words that Martin could also say." Lottie especially started trying to think of l-words that he could say. I felt like that was an acceptance kind of thing. We were all going to the same place and it was really neat.

The children here had made Martin a part of their group experience and had started an imitation activity appropriate to his skill level. The teacher expanded on it and helped their interaction with Martin continue. Again there are times that children may initiate contact and the teacher ignores or actually interferes with the peer interaction rather than facilitating it. The following anecdote illustrates this kind of situation.

> Jan and Bradley are sitting at the table with a pegboard, pegs, and a peg pattern. Bradley picks up the red pegs. Jan says, "Blue, Bradley, blue." Bradley

continues to place all colored pegs in no consistent order. Jan keeps repeating, "Blue, blue." Jan takes out all the colored pegs except the blue. She says, "You need to do blue right across this row. You need blue, Bradley, blue." Jack says, "You need to put blue on," looking up from his work with the inch cubes. "I'm talking to *Bradley,* Jack," says Jan. Jack returns to his work, mumbling about blue pegs, saying "Bradley doesn't know what to pick." Bradley puts in a blue peg. "Good for you, Bradley!" says Jack, clapping his hands. Jan says, "Jack, I'm working with Bradley." Bradley ignores this. He finishes with the blue pegs. Jan says, "Good, Bradley." Jan takes another card and says, "We're going to do orange." Bradley looks at the card, but picks up a yellow peg. "Not the yellow, the orange," says Jan. "Orange," Jack says, mimicking. Jan says, "I'm doing this with Bradley, Jack." She appears to be getting disturbed. "Get the orange," Jan says.

Rather than capitalizing on Jack's interest in Bradley, Jan, the teacher in this situation, continues to cut off interaction. She focuses so intensely on the task that she wants Bradley to accomplish that she cannot seem to tolerate Jack's intrusion. Rather than building on Jack's interest in Bradley and helping extend their contact, she does the opposite.

INTERVENING WITH PROBLEM BEHAVIOR

Teachers actively intervening in situations of aggression or interference can help the children learn to deal with each other and can prevent negative experiences between typical and special children. The intense focus on feelings and behavior mean that conversations often occur about problems between children. In the following encounter, John helps Gena talk with Jack, a special child, about why he doesn't like her.

Gena, who is sitting beside John, says to Jack, "Why don't you like me?" in a puzzled voice. Jack looks at Gena, then to his sandwich, still rocking, and says, "I don't like Gena." He goes on talking about Gena. "But why, Jack?" says Gena. No answer. "What makes you do that?" says Gena. Jack rocks back and forth and sadly says, "She is not nice to people. You have to be nice to people." John interrupts the conversation and says, "Do you think you should be nice to people, Jack?" "Yes," says Jack. Can you be nice to Gena?" says John. "No," says Jack. Gena listens. "He says no," says Billy, listening to the conversation. Jean interrupts: "He doesn't like me, either." She stands as she directs this statement to John. "Who is *he*?" says John, asking for specifics. "Him," says Jean, pointing to Jack. "Who's him?" says John. "Jack," Jean finally says. "Jack doesn't like you," says John, repeating the entire sentence. Jean says Jack bothers other people when other people would like to believe that they are bothering him. "Don't talk to me. I won't listen," says Jack angrily. "I'm not bothering you, Jack, so why don't you like me?" says Gena, still not understanding Jack's reasoning. "Gena is still wondering why you don't like her, Jack," says John. "I just don't," says Jack. He goes back to eating his sandwich. Gena and Jean resume eating. Billy leaves the table.

At snack time in the next anecdote, teachers intervene to prevent further aggression and to direct the actions of the special child as he interacts with typical children. They use verbal restraints and verbal directions to work on behavior that inhibits social interaction by its arousal of fear or its inappropriateness.

> Martin goes over to Janet. He stands with his hands around her under her arms. She puts her hands on his, not pushing him away. She's talking to Sandy about snack. James says, "Martin, come sit down," and he does. Martin gets up and goes over to Janet, grabbing her arm to get the cups. Sandy says, "Martin, don't hurt. You can pass out the cups, but don't hurt." He sits down and passes the cups out. Janet asks, "Can Martin get the cups to me so I can pour?" Sandy answers, "Martin, pass out the cups." He grabs Lottie and Sandy disengages them. Sandy: "Pass the cups to Janet so she can pour the juice." He gets up and brings over the cup. Martin stands behind Lottie and tightens the grip on her arm. "Martin!" She says emphatically. He moves back. Sandy gets him to sit down. Martin is giving out the Rice Crispie snack. Billy: "Can I have one?" "Can I have one, Martin?" He hands him one. Greg is making sounds and standing up. Kathy: "Give one to Greg, Martin. Here's Greg." Martin gives one to Greg. Lottie: "Can I have another one?" He hold out his to her. James: "Who are you asking?" Janet: "Martin." He holds out his own. James says, "No." Lottie says, "Take one out of here and give it to Janet." Janet: "Martin, yes, yes. Thank you," as he holds one out to her. Lottie says to Martin, holding out her hand: "Martin, may I have a cookie, please?" He gets it. Kathy: "Want to give one to Greg?" Lottie: "He's giving one to him now." Janet: "Martin, can I have another one?" He looks at her. "Me," she says. He stands up, walks over, and gives her one.

Teachers working to reduce those difficult behaviors (aggression especially) can affect integration by helping typical children be more comfortable in approaching special children. Teaching children how to handle aggressive or interfering behaviors is an important approach. It gives children a sense of control over their experiences; they will feel less fearful and victimized and probably be more willing to initiate and respond to special children. The following vignette shows a teacher (Lynn) instructing Jean on an approach to Kevin's behavior; Nell, a typical child from Kevin's classroom, also helps by telling Jean to talk to Kevin and by giving him another puppet.

> Jean is visiting from the Blue Room. She has picked up bristle blocks on the shelf and put them on the floor and is building with them. Nell walks over and says: "Those are Kevin's. Those are Kevin's." Jean doesn't respond verbally and continues to play. They then proceed to play together with the blocks. Kevin walks between them and knocks part of Nell's structure. She squeals. Lynn asks, "Nell, what happened?" Nell reports that Kevin knocked her building down. Lynn says, "Say 'Be careful, Kevin.'" Lynn hands Kevin a puppet. Kevin is standing right next to them, puppet in his hand, putting

things in the puppet. He suddenly reaches over for a piece of Jean's construction and knocks it apart. Jean is shouting, moaning, "Oh! Oh! Oh!" Nell sees this. She says, "Just talk to him." Jean: "I wanted to show everybody." She is moaning. Lynn comes over and leans over Jean. Lynn: "How did it get broken?" Jean points and says, "Kevin." Lynn asks, "Why didn't you talk to Kevin about it? Talk to him and tell him it's your work. If you don't talk to him, he won't understand. Next time say 'No, Kevin. No. That's my work.' Why don't you do that? Because he likes little pieces to put in his puppet." Lynn is touching Jean. Then Lynn helps her get the pieces together. Lynn gives Kevin some Fisher-Price people. She says, "See, you give Kevin some other things." Jean is rebuilding her structure, while Kevin sits right next to her putting little pieces in his puppet. She seems calm. Kevin is standing there, watching. He leans over and grabs at the blocks. Jeans says, "No, Kevin, no, Kevin, no." Kevin lets go. Nell leans over. "No, Kevin." Nell hands him the other puppet. Jean continues building carefully. She then picks up the structure and takes it over to the Blue Room.

The teacher's intervention here included a wide range of behaviors: instructing the typical child about verbal restraint of the special child, diverting the special child, suggesting a competing responses approach (that is, give Kevin some things). Rather than dealing directly with Kevin to stop his behavior, she diverts him (by giving him a puppet) and focuses her attention on the typical children, using the opportunity to teach an assertive approach to Kevin's interference. Direct instruction is important for both positive and negative behaviors. Children can be instructed about ways to interact by teaching (for instance, singing or using controlled vocabulary for language teaching) and how to involve special children in play; they also can learn how to deal with behaviors that are disconcerting for them like the ones above.

EXPLANATIONS

Many of the children express curiosity about the special children. An important role for teachers is answering questions and providing explanations of the idiosyncratic and problematic characteristics and behaviors of the special children. Having explanations should help typical children develop an understanding approach toward the special children; these occasions also allow for the transmittal of values and attitudes by the teacher to the typical children. In the example below, the teacher describes a conversation with two typical girls who were complaining about the messy eating habits of one of the special children.

Lottie was talking about how slobby Carol was. I said hadn't there been a time in her life when she was slobby? Like when she was a baby? And Kynna just beamed and said, "When I was a little baby, I used to eat spaghetti with my fingers." Janet said, "Yeah...and I sometimes dripped milk on my shirt."

I said, "Lottie, did you do any of those things?" and Lottie said, "Well...I guess." So we talked about how a lot of those things are learned and we could help...like her parents had helped her to learn we would help with some of the special kids or some of the kids who just do things less well. And so I feel in the long run that really does help.

It seemed common for the typical children to label some of the special children "babies" because of their delayed behavior. In the incident that follows, Bobby, who had just turned 4, was struggling with the issue of Kevin, age 6, not being toilet-trained. Dottie gives him an explanation for why Kevin wears Pampers.

Bobby is standing on the stairs waiting for the skill group to end so he can eat lunch in the Brown Room. He's looking at the powder and box of Pampers on the shelf. Bobby: "What's these?" Dottie looks. Bobby says, "Powder," and Dottie repeats, "Powder." Bobby says, "Kevin's a baby." Dottie: "No. Why do you say that?" Bobby: "Because these are only for babies." Dottie: "Not always." Bobby: "Yes." Dottie explains, "Those are to help Kevin— because sometimes he can't tell us when he wants to go to the bathroom." Bobby asks, "He can't say that?" Dottie: "No, so these keep him from getting his pants wet." Bobby says, "He has to pull them down." Dottie asks, "Does Sally wear Pampers?" Bobby replies, "No. Sometimes she pees in her pants. She used not to but now she does sometimes." Bradley runs by. Bobby looks up and says, "No, Bradley." As Dottie goes to get him, Bobby goes to the door to look.

Teachers' discussions with children, like this one, help children conceptualize some of the differences of the special children and make analogies to their own lives and feelings. All this promotes comfort and therefore more interaction between typical and special children.

MODELING

Modeling is perhaps the most important intervention by teachers in an integrated setting. The modeling includes demonstrations of what things to do with a child (e.g., particular kinds of play activities), how to communicate (e.g., controlled vocabulary, simple syntax, signing), how to intervene in problem situations (e.g., redirecting, verbal restraint), how to express affection and caring. By including special children in all activities, teachers model inclusion for children. Teachers model by asking special children questions or asking them to participate, even if they may not be able to function on the same level as the typical children. Helen describes her perspective on the importance of modeling.

I model all the time. I hope, I try, I tend to think that's probably the most effective thing...much better than direct instruction, like saying you should do this. It's much more subtle and really it's just so effective. I see children using the words I use. I've had to model children talking in simple sentences, say, to Danny, or talking in grammatical structures that he'll understand because he doesn't understand the whole range and variety of language. So if they want something from him they have to say to him, "Give me the _____." They've picked it up. That's the more overt things. I've tried to model the attitude a lot—just including David—that he's valuable and that he needs limits to be set, that you can tell him that you don't like things, that you can ask him to participate. And hopefully a lot of things I hope I modeled, like patience and respect. I think I see that those are value issues; but, if anything, this year has convinced me of the strength of modeling, because I see kids really doing that helping stuff. It's not direct imitation; it's really different.

The crucial nature of the teacher's role is evident when you see the power of modeling. Teachers will focus more on their own behavior when they realize what a powerful tool modeling is.

I'm very aware this year especially of what I say and what my behavior is... 'cause I really see the kids modeling...you know.... I try to make sure that the words I use are always as positive as they can be...and the language that I use I try to make as consistent as I possibly can.... Depending on who I'm talking to, I try to be as definitive as I can in what I say to a child. I try to use the same kind of language that other teachers use.... I feel that that really helps. I see that happening a lot where the things teachers do with the special kids when they're playing and interacting they all try to do. Play is really an easy thing to be able to do, so I try and play with all the kids an awful lot, tickle games or peek-a-boo games or whatever. I think the typical kids watch you. They are very much aware of how you deal with special kids, and I've seen them pick up on what I do and react to it. I've also heard myself and I think, Oh, my God, do I do that? You know that kind of thing.... That's helped me to take a step back.

Obviously seeing yourself through your behavior as modeled by children is strong and vivid feedback—something that will help most teachers be more conscious of their actions.

PROBLEMS OF INTEGRATION FOR TEACHERS

In their interviews, teachers discussed several aspects of an integrated setting that were problematic for them. The most frequent issue mentioned was the difficulty of responding to a wide range of children. At the same time, they describe this range as one of the greatest benefits.

It's more difficult to teach in an integrated setting. I have no idea because I haven't taught in anything but an integrated setting, but I think it's harder teaching in an open, integrated setting than it would be in a more rigid kind of situation, but it is also more rewarding. I mean it's more difficult because you need to know more and you need to be on top of things, have to react with and plan for and be aware of and tune in to so it obviously requires more awareness on your part. But the benefits are enormous. You have that wide range of people and abilities. It's much more of a little cosmos that you're involved with. It's more realistic. It's more like what life really is.

I think it's harder but it's what I believe in.... It's not easier. You have to have a million things at your fingertips and in your head at all times and you have to be able to respond in 10 different ways at once. But it's ultimately more like believing in people living together and learning together from each other and with each other. So I'm learning as much as everybody else learns.

One teacher focuses on the specific conflicts she feels when children are at different developmental levels.

I would say that what continues to trouble me—a hurdle I haven't been able to solve completely—is that if you have a child like Kevin who is at a low developmental level—the toddler kind of stage of whisking things off tables and emptying shelves—that makes it difficult to leave things out for kids who are really ready to have on-going projects. So I think that's really one of the things I haven't solved in my mind about an integrated setting. Again, I don't think that it's the integrated special, labeled/nonlabeled child in the same sense as it is the same range. If we are going to meet needs and needs are high for a lot of individual time and a lot of lap-sitting and a lot of supportive work, it's really hard to do that at a time that we are trying to press discovery learning and problem solving and decision making and choices for kids who are 6 and 7. So that means it's hard to teach effectively without losing somebody.

A solution to this problem suggested by several teachers was to reduce the age range of children in any particular class. Here's one teacher's comment.

I think it would also mean somewhat more selectiveness as to age. I could see having a group on a class basis of children who were closer in age developmentally; instead of having a 3 to 8 or a 3 to 12, it would be more like 3 to 6, and many of the younger handicapped children would fit much more easily into that. I find here that a lot of the activities that we plan for the youngest children are so appropriate for the labeled kids...for the typical kids too. The kinds of things we provide for 3-year-olds and 4-year-olds are very, very different from the experiences that a 7-year-old needs. I find I'm falling over my feet all the time trying to do both, but I think that the youngest groupings are really appropriate for the younger children and I think in that sense we've really done very well by them. I would really try to include a different—a wider range of children—like kids who were not labeled but not fitting in as well. And more typical kids—I think there should be more—a bigger ratio of typical children, like 5 to 1 actually. Even more diversity in types of handicaps would really be beneficial.

So while a narrower age and developmental range would ease the teacher's load, they suggest more diversity of labeled children and a higher ratio of typical to special children.

The crisis nature of responding to the needs of special children was frustrating to several teachers. They saw that the need to be on top of the problem behavior like interference and aggression drained them and kept them from meeting everyone's needs. "How do you give so much attention to everyone when you're spending a lot of the time with the needs of the special children, people running, people screaming? It takes it away from the typical kids." One staff member suggests a role of crisis teacher or having staff functions as a rover.

> The biggest difficulty has been to be in a situation where you know there has to be a lot of time set aside for staff members to be away with kids working on problems; to describe, to discuss, and to set limits, follow through on those kind of things, and not have to worry about deserting your partner in skill group or not worrying about who's going to cover for you while you're doing that. We should do that. We need to be able to do that and it's a hard thing to do, to go out in the hall with a kid or go into the corner with a kid and spend a lot of time when it has been planned for you to be doing something else. And therefore, it's a hardship for the other staff member to cover. So this whole ideas of having crisis people, I think, is nice. It's good. It's necessary. Or having enough staff members so that, you know, one person can be a rover and can take care of problems or can sit in on activities while another staff member is away. So much stuff has to be ignored. It's just too much. Too many of the problems have to be ignored down there because we can't get away and talk about them and follow through on them and come back to them later on.

Issues of independence-dependence were a concern of teachers, too—in terms of what teachers expect and what they foster in children. One teacher felt that the high degree of adult involvement with special children reduced the amount of integration; teachers always present to help meant that typical children didn't have to initiate as much with special children. Another teacher describes his feelings about high teacher involvement with special children.

> I guess my expectations were lower for special kids. I feel they need more support. I don't demand as much in terms of independent work. It's easier actually for me to be supportive, in some ways to be more patient—which can be a trap—I realize it now. It's not that I don't expect, it's that I don't expect the same, especially around independence. I'm a lot more careful in how I plan out things step-by-step for a disabled child. I'm much more careful. I'm less worried about upsets with normal kids than with special kids. A lot of upsets I just feel they have to work through. With the special kids I am very nervous about it. I think at times I tend to oversupport because of that—with special kids—because I've seen a lot of times with my own kids that I just couldn't—I knew I was going to be there and they had to realize that they had to struggle through some pain. But with a special kid, very

> often I am afraid to allow him to do that so that's a difference I feel. I am not
> sure what their strengths are so it's very difficult. And I think that leads to
> too much being there at times actually.

One staff member expressed her focus on developing typical chldren who
could be givers with special children.

> There is a lot of independence for the kids and in a lot of ways that's good,
> but if it's a detachment or self-centeredness, then I don't think it's good.
> That's what we're talking about, how to foster not less individuality but less
> self-centeredness. I think some of the self-centeredness grows out of the one-
> on-one times with such a strong focus on everybody being different. I think
> it's hard for kids to separate out that it's O.K. to be different, to be yourself,
> but it's not O.K. to be selfish.

What she seems to be saying is that the amount of adult attention the typical
children receive as well as the message they receive that they are all valued could
promote more egocentrism and less "giving" behavior.

The last issue mentioned as a concern in an integrated setting was the need
for clinical help to teachers faced with a wide range of children with very special
needs.

> We need to have more specialized kind of support help built in for the teach-
> ers, like people who are more versed in physical therapies and language ther-
> apy, and to be able to use those people well. I could see that in the life of the
> school it would be evolving where we'd have relationships with more specific
> people who felt good about those kinds of skills. I mean, it's hard for each of
> us to be an expert in all the areas that each kid needs. And if we want to keep
> taking in kids that are so different...the expectation for each of us to become
> a Spina Bifida expert or whatever could happen.

WHEN TO INTEGRATE

During the period in which the data were being collected for this study, teachers were actively considering and debating to what extent special children should
be integrated. That is, should they be involved with typical children 100% of the
day, or was it justifiable to "segregate" special children for some time in order
to meet particular needs. As one of the teachers says, "One of the big problems
of an integrated setting is deciding when to and when not to integrate and for
what specific reasons."

> I think the individual programming was really sort of necessary and I feel like
> a lot of the one-to-one time is really necessary for all the kids. I don't think
> that makes the school less of a stimulating or safe or exciting place to learn—
> but I think it tends to take away from a total kind of cohesion sometimes.

Helen gives the rationale for those periods of the day in which special children are removed from the family group and given intense programming, either alone or with other children with special needs.

> I don't think that the integration has to be 100% all through the day. I don't think it's being prejudicial to say that at this time what those kids need are a more specific close kind of contact and a more structured environment because it's like that at that time of the day. It's really like a practice period for those kids. They're getting a chance to have the full attention of an adult and to have a very, very structured learning experience and to have a structure without the other children that they don't have any other time. I don't see it as contradictory because I think it meets their needs and it works well and because we're not approaching it from the viewpoint that these kids are harmful to the other children.... I don't think they need it all day long.... I think doing it for a small part of the day is really very beneficial for them. Maybe because I've seen the kinds of results of that time because they can take the learning, they can take the strengthening that goes on, and I don't think it would work any other way. I don't think that just having them live on love all day would be of value. The proof is when they go back into the family group. I think it takes a lot of development. Some kids could benefit from a kind of transitional integrated group where it is a lot safer and there is closer adult attention. And I don't think it makes sense to say, well I advocate diversity and that means that everybody should be together all the time for all day.

SUMMARY

This chapter presents teacher perspectives and behaviors related to achieving social integration of typical and special children. A variety of interventions used by teachers is described, including teacher presence, spontaneous incorporation, planning activities for all children, directing children toward one another, intervening with problem behavior, giving explanations for special child behavior, and modeling. The data used as the basis of these categories were specimen recordings and teacher interviews. In addition to interventions, the chapter also includes a discussion of issues or teacher-identified problems raised by an integrated setting.

While the teachers were struggling with various issues about how to implement their ideal integrated setting, they all expressed their desire to continue to teach in such a situation. Here is the kind of learning environment they want to create.

> I think primarily what I'm trying to achieve is to have a place where children can feel really safe and positive about themselves and their activities, their achievements, whatever they are, as well as learning whatever they need to learn in the way of reading and writing and math and stuff. In a way, it means to start out with a good mental health background. They learn to be

people in a very positive way, learn about other people, are treated with more respect. And along with that, children learn to communicate their own ideas and thoughts. In most ways I see that helped by the presence of kids who are very different. I think that there's a sort of heightened sensitivity at the school for individual differences because they're pretty obvious. They're right out there and we have to deal with them all the time.

I want to have a setting which is a safe place for kids to learn, but it's also a stimulating place for kids to learn...an emphasis on affective and cognitive growth...for kids to make some choices and to initiate their own learning. I also feel that it's really important to establish a kind of environment where people feel that they are individuals, that they can be different, and where they value the differences.

It is clear that the teachers are as focused on the affective and social development of the children as they are on their academic growth. Conscious planning for the total environment may affect the successful integration of disabled and typical children.

15
The Classroom Social Behavior of Children Labeled Autistic

Carroll J. Grant

There is considerable disagreement concerning the behavioral symptoms that define the syndrome of autism. There is little dispute, however, that inability to relate normally is one of the major diagnostic features of this disorder. It is surprising, therefore, that "the social behavior of autistic children, its nature, causes, and effects have received little attention" (Richer, 1976b, p. 898), and that there are few research projects that focus on the social behaviors of children labeled *autistic*. This chapter will review some of the research done on this topic, describe research I carried out on the interactive behaviors of children labeled *autistic* and their assigned teachers, and draw some implications for classroom application from the results of these research endeavors and practical experiences.

RESEARCH ON THE INTERACTIVE BEHAVIORS OF CHILDREN LABELED AUTISTIC

Hutt and Ounsted (1966, 1970) were among the first to intensively study the social behavior of autistic children. They observed the social behavior of eight such children in a hospital playroom and garden, and they found these children nearly always engaged in solitary play. On occasion, however, they would run to a nurse and climb into her lap or raise their arms to be picked up. When physically hurt, they would always run to an adult. "These approach gestures were normal in form, that is indistinguishable from those of normal children, except for one feature—aversion from the face" (Hutt & Ounsted, 1966, p. 347). The adult would reach for the child and the child would stretch his arms out also, indicating a readiness to be picked up, but the face was held down so that the adult's face was not in full view. "Even when the child is in the adult's arms, it keeps its face averted from the adult's face and any attempt to make it fixate upon the adult provokes the child to shield its eyes with its hands" (Hutt & Ounsted, 1966, p. 347). The children similarly avoided looking at the adult's face when manipulating the adult's limbs to perform certain actions. These observations indicate that, apart from face aversion, all other components of the social encounters of the children labeled *autistic* were those shown by normal, nonautistic children.

These authors further explored the autistic child's facial aversions through an experimental study. They used five models depicting five different faces, a happy, a sad, and a blank human face, a monkey face, and a dog face. These faces had similar outlines in black and white and were mounted on stands 3 feet high. "The stands were placed around the periphery of an otherwise empty room at approximately equal distance from each other; the positions of the models were systematically varied for each child" (Hutt & Ounsted, 1966, p. 348). Eight autistic children and six nonautistic children, who were of the same age group and also in-patients, were brought individually into this room. An observer recorded their spontaneous behaviors.

The mean number of encounters per child with the different faces as well as with the other environmental fixtures revealed that the nonautistic group showed the least amount of time attending to the blank face, with all the other faces being encountered more or less equally often. On the other hand, the autistic group encountered the happy face less frequently, the blank and animal faces more frequently, and the environmental stimuli (light switches, taps, windows) most often. When the manners in which the two groups of children inspected the figures were compared, it was found that the nonautistic group's visual and manipulatory inspection of the faces were closely synchronized, while the autistic children's encounters with the faces were not always accompanied by visual inspection. This was less true, however, of their encounters with other environmental stimuli.

"The results of this preliminary experiment, while by no means conclusive, would suggest that the human facial configurations elicit more avoidance than nonhuman ones in autistic children; the smiling face evokes the strongest avoidance reaction" (Hutt & Ounsted, 1966, p. 346). These authors hypothesize that this is so "probably because this combination of features has been most closely associated with approach and hence social demands" (Hutt & Ounsted, 1966, p. 346).

Richer (1976a) has done a series of studies on the social behavior of autistic children that is built on and supports the findings of Hutt and Ounsted. One of his major endeavors was an observational study of eight autistic children and eight disturbed and retarded children, matched for age and sex, during free play time at an outdoor playground. To give some comparison with normal children, a group of nine children from a local nursery school were similarly observed.

The behavior of the subjects was unobtrusively observed and recorded. The behaviors recorded were a variety of interactional behaviors, stereotypes, non-stereotyped object manipulation, and approaches by other people.

The results of this research indicate that there are five characteristics which differentiate autistic from nonautistic children:

1. Autistic children rarely start or continue social interaction compared to nonautistic children.
2. They act to reduce the probability of social encounters by avoiding eye contact and by being on the edge of an area.
3. They move away from others more often.
4. They are less aggressive than nonautistic disturbed children and have a higher frequency of defensive behaviors than either group.
5. Their threshold for "defensive/flight" behaviors is much lower than nonautistic children's. (Richer, 1976b)

Richer has developed a perspective on the autistic child's social behavior based on his own studies (Richer, 1976a, 1976b; Richer & Coss, 1976; Richer & Richards, 1975) and the findings of others. He describes these children as predominantly avoiding social interactions which seem to be the "net result of conflicting social approach and avoidance motivations, where avoidance is much stronger than in nonautistic children. However, social approaches, often ambivalent, are observed" (Richer, 1976a, p. 1). He defines two immediate casual factors which influence whether or not an autistic child will approach or avoid.

> One is the difficulty of, or uncertainty in, the mutual activity. Autistic children are more likely to avoid the more uncertain the activity.... The second factor is the behavior of other people. An autistic child is more likely to avoid someone who looks at him compared with someone who does not; (Richer & Coss, 1976) to avoid someone who reacts intensely to his looks or other approaches compared with someone who reacts less intensely (Richer & Richards, 1975); and to avoid someone who threatens him compared with someone who does not. The child's responsiveness to these two factors fluctuates. In other words his threshold for avoidance changes and this is associated with many factors...[such as] when a child has just been avoiding, he is more likely to respond with avoidance to a subsequent approach than if he had not just been avoiding. (Richer, 1976a)

Often the immediate effect of avoidance is that it leads to approaches by adults, which in turn leads to more avoidance by the child. This avoidance suggests that the adult's approach is aversive. "Thus the social encounter is aversive, and the tendency to avoid social interactions is reinforced. This is called a *reflexive* mechanism—the avoidance maintains itself via the adult's reaction" (Richer, 1976a, p. 1). Autistic children seem to have been avoiding from a very young age, which leads Richer to believe that this reflexive mechanism is in operation from this early time. Social avoidance, by inhibiting normal communication interactions, affects the child's acquisition of language and other skills for communication and cooperation.

It is partly in these interactions that, from an early age, normal children acquire cultural competence. Autistic children's particular avoidance of these interactions retards this aquisition, it retards the acquiring the meaning of words, negotiating social relationships, etc. In addition, the reflexive mechanism is very likely to operate in these communication interactions. Catch 22. (Richer, 1976a, p. 1)

The last study to be reported is an ecological investigation done by Lichstein (1976). He explored the everyday behavior, including social interactions, of an autistic child in his own environment using naturalistic methodology. The observations of the child were recorded on a pre-established instrument in three settings: the school in the morning, the school in the afternoon, and the home in the afternoon.

Lichstein analyzed the behaviors to identify the child responses that occurred within certain behavioral settings and to see if there were correlations between the child's responses and the preceding stimuli. The results of the study may be summarized as follows.

1. The child showed a diversity of behavior over time in a given setting and across settings. There were significant changes in approximately 70% of the behaviors from setting to setting, and similar changes occurred within settings over time.
2. The child showed a marked absence of relatedness to other, nonautistic children and a far greater responsivity to adults.
3. A few self-stimulatory behaviors were inversely correlated with a number of behaviors which denote an awareness and responsiveness to environmental stimuli. That is, when the child was attending to his environment, he infrequently performed some self-stimulating behaviors.
4. Adult attention was inversely correlated with a number of self-stimulatory behaviors. This suggests that noncontingent adult attention interrupted the self-stimulatory sequences, causing their reduction and accompanying increase in attentiveness to the environment.
5. A number of self-stimulatory behaviors correlated inversely with each other. This implies that planned reduction in one self-stimulatory behavior could cause unplanned increases in other self-stimulatory behaviors.

The results of Lichstein's study are noteworthy and valuable because they include both the naturally occurring behavior of the child and the behavior of those with whom he interacts. The following study explores in even greater detail the social behavior of children labeled *autistic*.

INTERACTIONS OF CHILDREN LABELED AUTISTIC AND THEIR TEACHERS

Ecological Perspective on Autism

The ecological perspective in psychology assumes that all behavior is a function of a person interacting with his or her environment. This interrelationship between organism, behavior, and environment includes behavior that is perceived as deviant. When the ecological viewpoint is applied to children labeled *autistic,* the implication is that the manner in which another person interacts with the child will influence the child's behavior. As discussed above, research measuring the effects of social environmental influences on the child labeled *autistic* substantiates this belief (Lichstein, 1976).

Of particular interest and concern to educators is information on the spontaneous behavior of children labeled *autistic* in response to their teachers' behaviors. Like all teachers, teachers of children labeled *autistic* are in a position to tremendously influence the lives of their students through their interactions. However, one of the main diagnostic features of autism is the inability of these children to relate to people in ordinary ways (Hutt & Hutt, 1970). This characteristic of the autistic child makes the teacher's interactions with him or her unique and creates phenomena that need to be extensively explored. Presently, there is considerable literature written about various successful intervention programs with children labeled *autistic,* but most fail to fully describe what the adult did in an encounter with the child. Did the adult touch the child, make demands, ask questions, look at the child, yell, smile? (Grant, 1978). There is also considerable literature on the behavior of children labeled *autustic,* but rarely is it a complete compendium of the child's behavior repertoire. As discussed above, these children exhibit much normal behavior which goes unheeded or unappreciated (Lichstein, 1976). Furthermore, rarely do researchers look at the preceding social environmental forces in an attempt to understand the child's behavior. Hutt and Hutt write that, although relating socially is a major problem for these children, "little attempt seems to have been made to specify or to investigate systematically what particular aspects of social interaction are impaired" (1970, p. 147).

It is apparent that there is a gap in the research done on autistic children. Investigators have skipped the necessary steps of comprehensively observing and analyzing how adults, particularly teachers, interact with a child labeled *autistic* and how the child responds in uncontrived situations. Barker (1969), Hutt and Hutt (1970), Raush (1969), and Willems (1965), among many others, strongly emphasize the need to know the environmental effects on behavior under natural conditions. It is especially important to know the natural history of behavior if you are going to attempt to modify it (Hutt & Hutt, 1970).

> Before such interventions into the environment may occur, however, one must accurately observe, describe, and identify the environmental forces operating within the environment and the behavior resulting from this interaction between the child and his environment. (Gibbons, 1971, p. 4)

Presently we are attempting to modify the behavior of children labeled *autistic* before it has been comprehensively examined in situ. I (Grant, 1978) have carried out research to begin filling this void of information by making an extensive assessment of the naturally occurring interactions between teachers and children with autistic-like behaviors, studying their verbal and nonverbal behaviors in their classroom environment. These behaviors were then analyzed to find any relationships between the teachers' behaviors and the children's subsequent responses.

In order to examine the spontaneous social behaviors of children labeled *autistic* and their teachers, it was most profitable to use a naturalistic approach. The research methodology and procedures are further explained in the following section.

Methodology and Procedure

I attempted to gain a greater understanding of the natural behavior of children labeled *autistic* by studying their spontaneous social interactions with their teachers. Naturalistic methodology was chosen as the most efficient means to examine the relationship between the teachers' behaviors and the children's behaviors. The naturalistic or ecological approach advocates the intensive study of the "natural" existing interrelationships and interdependencies between the organism and his or her environment (Barker, 1969). The term *natural* refers to uncontrived conditions where nature has been the inducer of the events. The role of the investigator is that of a receiver or transducer of these events, rather than a manipulator of variables. He or she translates the stream of behavior into a written record as completely as possible (Barker, 1969).

In this study, both the teachers' behaviors and the children's behaviors were observed, recorded, and analyzed in a natural setting. Four teacher-child pairs were studied; a pair consisted of a teacher and his or her assigned child labeled *autistic*. The children were four 7-year-old boys labeled *autistic* by a certified professional. The teachers were each child's (subject's) teacher-advocate who had the responsibility for planning the child's educational program and implementing any individualized teacher-initiated work. All of these individuals attended or worked at Jowonio.

In order to study several characteristics of both the teachers' behaviors and the children's behavior, an instrument was devised specifically for this research. This instrument, the Flanders-Swan Interaction Analysis, delineates and categorizes teacher behaviors into four variables: I Action, II Physical Contact and Prompts, III Gaze, IV Intensity. It similarly delineates and categorizes child behaviors: V Action, VI Verbalization, VI Gaze, VII Intensity. The Flanders-Swan Interaction Analysis thus separates and defines eight variables of each teacher-child interaction (Grant, 1978).

Four separate 15-minute videotapes were made of each teacher-child pair while they were engaged in a one-to-one individualized teaching session. The pairs' interactions were then coded by the Flanders-Swan Interaction Analysis. All the data concerning the interactive behaviors of a particular child and his assigned teacher were analyzed separately in order to find patterns within that pair's behavior repertoire. The analysis process focused on the manner in which a teacher and an assigned child interacted with one another—that is, how did a teacher verbally (e.g., lecture, praise, questions) and nonverbally (e.g., touch, gesture, look at) interact with the child, and how did the child behave (e.g., respond appropriately, work, talk, look) in the interchange. The data on each pair were then compared with the other three pairs to find similarities and differences. The end product of the analysis was separate data in the interactive behaviors of four teacher-child pairs and on how these four pairs compared with one another.

Summary of Results

Teacher Behaviors

1. Each teacher employed indirect behaviors (accepting, encouraging, praising, questioning) and direct behaviors (lecturing, directing) in a ratio that suggests that they responded to the needs of the children and provided the necessary structure to the sessions. The ratio of occurrence of indirect to direct behaviors further indicates that their teaching styles had the flexibility needed to appropriately address various classroom situations. Furthermore, none of the teachers ever reacted intensely to the assigned child. Most all of their interactive behaviors were performed calmly and patiently, using simple short sentences without any tangible rewards.
2. Each teacher-child pair was sitting next to one another and were, therefore, physically close. Often the pair had physical contact, or the teacher gave prompts to the child. The teacher contact was never restraining or negative, and it was either accepted or initiated by the child, with a few rare exceptions.
3. Each teacher consistently looked at the child or the child's face, with only a few rare exceptions, while the child most frequently responded with looking at his task.

Child Behaviors

Each child responded to his teacher's behavior with a very high frequency of cooperative social behavior, the majority of which was task-oriented. In fact, the most frequent response to the vast majority of teacher behaviors was on-task behavior and eye gaze. The high occurrence of appropriate behavior and eye gaze, including the children looking at their teacher when being looked at, suggests that the children found these sessions nonthreatening.

One factor to note in evaluating these findings is that this research was done in the spring semester of the school year. The teachers had been working with their assigned children in sessions similar to the ones analyzed for about 8 months. We can speculate that these results are the product of an established teacher-child relationship, and they could have been different if the study had been done in the fall, before the relationship had developed. Accepting the context within which the research was done, the research findings have important implications for classroom teachers.

IMPLICATIONS OF RESEARCH FINDINGS FOR THE CLASSROOM TEACHER

The data gathered in this study provide a wealth of information concerning the naturally occurring social behaviors between teachers and children labeled *autistic*. This information is valuable because of the present void in our knowledge about the syndrome of autism in general and specifically about such children's spontaneous interactive behaviors. Furthermore, these findings are significant because they provide strong support for the appropriate placement of children labeled *autistic* in educational settings and guidelines for implementing interventions with these children.

Support for Educational Placement

Too often children labeled *autistic* are excluded from educational opportunities. As Sullivan writes, "It is probably safe to say that there are no handicapped citizens who have been subjected to more discrimination or received fewer community services than those labeled 'autistic.' They are the last to be included, last on the waiting list—the 'hardcore' handicapped" (1978, p. 13). This discrimination is based on the prevailing belief that autistic children are ineducable, more specifically, "that autistic children cannot function in normal classrooms, not only because of their disruptive behavior, but also because of their serious behavioral limitations. They do not use language, understand instructions, pay attention or interact with others" (Schreibman & Koegel, 1978, p. 7).

These research findings (Grant, 1978) strongly contradict this sterotypic belief that all children labeled *autistic* should be left out of educational settings because they are too disruptive or are too behaviorally limited. The findings on the children's behavior very clearly challenge this view.

1. Each child behaved appropriately 93% to 97% (the range of behaviors is the range of the four children's individual scores) of the observed time.
2. Each child most frequently responded with on-task behaviors (65% to 81%) and gaze (73% to 92%) to the teacher behaviors.
3. Each child frequently looked at the teacher (6% to 17%) and initiated physical contact (8% to 24%).

These are very appropriate behaviors for a classroom situation. They are not only appropriate, in the sense of not being disruptive, but they also strongly indicate that the children were "understanding instructions," "paying attention," and "interacting" with their teachers. These behaviors are all indications of learning. An understanding or an explanation of these behaviors can be best obtained by studying the context within which they occurred, that is, by studying the teacher behaviors to which the children were exposed. Analyzing the teacher behaviors not only provides valuable insight into the children's behaviors but also provides the necessary information to develop guidelines for teachers working with these children.

Guidelines for Intervention

The research findings are the first to describe in detail the natural interactive flow between the teacher and his or her child during a work-oriented session. In this research, as in most classrooms, the teacher is a major influence in the child's ecosystem. Knowledge of the quality of the teacher influence, therefore, is of utmost importance in understanding the nature of the child's behavior.

In addition to contributing information about the child labeled *autistic,* the findings concerning the teacher behaviors also provide guidelines for adults working with these children. Presently, there is a paucity of information regarding the specific intervention behaviors of adults, particularly teachers (McDonald & Shepherd, 1976). Several theroretical frameworks are advocated for educating children labeled *autistic* (Bettelheim, 1967; Des Lauriers & Carlson, 1969; Kozloff, 1973; Wood, 1975), but all fail to describe the interaction between the teacher and the child. My research findings begin to fill the gap in our knowledge about interventions with these children. The following guidelines for implementing interventions with autistic children are derived from my research (Grant, 1978) and experiences, as well as the research of others.

A general statement about an effective teaching process for working with autistic children is that it is similar to the style of any good teacher. That is, there is little in the teacher's repertoire of behavior that is unique to working with autistic children. An effective teacher with a particular age group probably has the basic necessary skills for working with most children labeled *autistic* of the same age group. After all, a child labeled *autistic* is essentially a child who has a mixture of "normal" characteristics interwined with characteristics that are atypical of most children of comparable age. It is these behaviors, characteristic of the syndrome of autism, that must be considered when working with an autistic child.

Be Flexible

Be flexible in order to appropriately meet the child's needs. This is a concept frequently used by Amidon and Flanders (1967) and aptly describes the teaching style of the adults in my research. Flexibility is the ability to shift teaching behavior to appropriately meet a student's needs at a particular time. A flexible teaching style characterizes one who is sensitive to the child's thoughts and feelings and is able to accurately discern when to follow the child's initiative (those verbal or nonverbal actions based on the child's feelings and thoughts) and when to impose his or her ideas on the child. Both responding to the child and directing the child are necessary and valid ways of relating; however, it is an art to know when it is most effective to shift from one to the other.

For example, suppose you have planned a lesson of sorting colors using different shaped blocks and the child becomes interested in sorting the blocks by shapes. You can either respond to the child's interests in the shapes by acknowledging the child's efforts or stop his or her activity in order to focus on the colors. A person with a rigid or inflexible teaching style would probably not acknowledge the child's interest and ability to sort by shape and redirect his or her attention to studying the colors. A person with a flexible teaching style would probably comment on the child's activity and then, depending on how important the teacher deemed the shape sorting, either allow the child to continue or redirect the child to sort by color. The major differences in these two styles are that the flexible style frequently acknowledges the child's self-initiated activities, either neutrally or positively, while the inflexible style acknowledges the child's behavior infrequently and stays with the predetermined task. A flexible teacher uses a balance of responsive and directive behavior; an inflexible teacher uses predominantly directive behavior.

The behaviors that are commonly defined as responsive are questions, praise, encouragement, and acceptance of feelings and behaviors (Flanders, 1970). These behaviors tell another person that you are interested or even value what he or she is thinking, feeling, or doing. The intent of listening, accepting, or praising another is conveyed verbally as well as nonverbally. A little nod of the head with a smile can tell someone that you hear and approve of his or her thoughts and behavior.

The behaviors that are commonly defined as directive are lectures, directions, and criticism (Flanders, 1970). These behaviors have the intent of controlling another's behavior. Lecturing conveys information, facts, and opinions to another person. Directing and criticizing are means to change the behavior of another. As is true for responsive behavior, directive behaviors can be verbal as well as nonverbal. A frown with a pensive look can be a criticism; a pointed finger can be a direction.

As I have mentioned, a good teaching style consists of responsive and directive behaviors; both forms of interacting are necessary. A teacher with a flexible teaching style has a balance of both of these types of behaviors in his or her repertoire. A teacher with an inflexible teaching style, however, uses few responsive behaviors. These teachers rarely acknowledge or encourage any child's thoughts or feelings.

Based on my research (Grant, 1978) and experience, I believe that a flexible teaching style is highly effective with children labeled *autistic*. An analysis of the teacher-child interactions in my study revealed that the teachers definitely provided structure to the work sessions by setting a framework of expectations; however, they also frequently acknowledged and encouraged a child's self-initiated behaviors. The children responded to these teachers with a very high percentage of work-oriented behavior. The teachers seemed to attend to their assigned child intensely and to base their behaviors on the messages the child gave. If a child was showing signs of frustration, a teacher might say, "You are getting tired; this is hard work," but then he might add, "Let's do a few more and then we'll try another game." The teacher acknowledges the child's feelings, but then sets an expectation that more work will be done. On some days and with some children, however, it was best to end the session. The degree to which you can push a child will vary, depending on a multitude of factors which this chapter cannot address. The point being made here is that teachers need to be sensitive to the needs of the child and vary their directive or responsive behavior accordingly.

One further comment concerning flexibility in the process of teaching children labeled *autistic* needs to be made. The adults in my research employed a flexible teaching style which did not include any strict behavior modification procedures. Neither rewards nor punishments were used systematically to encourage appropriate behavior in any of the situations observed. These findings, therefore, suggest that a variety of intervention techniques are appropriate at different times with different children. This information cautions us not to assume that a behavior modification procedure is the most efficient means of teaching all children labeled *autistic* at all times.

Be Nonthreatening to the Child

Richer's (1976a) work has contributed an interesting perspective on the behavior of children labeled *autistic*. This research suggests that autistic children have a predominant tendency to avoid social interactions. More specifically, these children are more likely to avoid interacting (by performing stereotyped movements, moving or turning away, or gaze averting) when the person confronting or reacting to them is threatening or when the activity is threatening or uncertain. Richer (1975) states that "the tendency to escape from or avoid social interactions is greatly enhanced if any uncertainty or difficulty arises in the interaction."

I believe that there is some validity to Richer's theory. The teachers in my research could be viewed as nonthreatening because of their high percentage of responsive behaviors performed very patiently and calmly. Because these adults were sensitive to and acknowledged their children's needs, the children might have perceived their teachers as nonthreatening, and therefore, responded appropriately in the situation. This is one possible interpretation of data. The concept of being nonthreatening is congruent with the concept of being flexible and further describes an effective teaching style.

Teachers should interact with their students in an intrusive but nonetheless nonthreatening fashion. That is, be sensitive to the child's feelings and thoughts so as to know when he or she is ready to follow a directive or needs some reassurance. Also, talk and interact with a child calmly and patiently, using a normal tone of voice and normal eye contact. These behaviors should encourage a sence of trust instead of fear. Projecting a nonthreatening image is particularly important when the child is already performing some avoidance behaviors. For example, if a child is actively performing stereotyped behaviors and whining, he is apt to respond better to someone firmly saying "no" in a normal tone of voice and using smooth body movements than to someone yelling "no" and moving quickly.

Finally, to be nonthreatening, it is important to challenge a child with tasks that are within his or her capacity to understand and perform. Tasks that are extremely novel or demanding, especially those which are prolonged, should be avoided. Teachers have to understand the stages of development, in all areas of growth, in order to discern what tasks are appropriate for a particular child at a particular time.

Be a Good Observer

The two sections above emphasize the importance of being sensitive to the child's needs in order to determine when it is most appropriate to be directive or responsive and when you are threatening the child. Most children, especially children labeled *autistic,* are incapable of expressing their needs; therefore, adults working with them must discern their needs by observing their behaviors. Furthermore, observations need to include not only an awareness of the child but also his or her social and physical surrounding. Children's behavior is a response to their interaction with their environment; therefore, the environment must be considered. Teachers must develop the art of observing.

Use Physical Contact and Prompts

Teachers communicate nonverbally as well as verbally. In fact, nonverbal messages frequently have more impact than verbal ones. The most obvious nonverbal messages are given through physical contacts and prompts. A warm hug from a teacher tells the child, "I care." A gentle but firm holding of the hands can say "no." A variety of gestures, including pointing, can cue the child as to what is expected.

The teacher's physical closeness to a child should also be considered. Some children might find this closeness comforting, while others might need some defined space between themselves and another person. If a child is receptive to sitting near the teacher, the teacher can utilize his or her body as a shield to prevent distractions, to appropriately direct the child to the task, and to give positive physical contact as suitable.

There is no conclusive evidence to support or negate the value of making physical contact with or providing prompts to children labeled *autistic*. My research findings indicate that the teachers gave a high percentage of physical contact and prompts to the children, and the children responded appropriately. Probably the types and frequencies of physical contacts and prompts beneficial to autistic children are determined by the preferences of the individuals involved. It is important, however, that teachers be aware of their nonverbal behaviors and the child's response to these behaviors in order to determine the most efficient teaching style for that child.

Modify Your Language

Modify your language to meet the child's ability to understand. Most children labeled *autistic* have a language deficit which is characteristic of the syndrome of autism. It is important, therefore, that a teacher adjust his or her communication to meet the receptive language ability of the child.

The children in this research were 7-years-old autistic boys with language delays. The teachers presented the children with a wide variety of questions, directives, and statements, all of which were phrased in short, concise sentences, such as: "Good work," "Show me the ball," "Do you want a cookie?" and "Sit down."

Not all children labeled *autistic* need to be talked to this way. The language abilities of autistic children vary, but most show some delay. All teachers, therefore, need to be aware of a child's receptive language ability and to appropriately adjust their language in order to be understood.

Consider the Use of the One-to-One Teacher-Child Relationship

Most children labeled *autistic* can benefit initially from a one-to-one teacher-child relationship. These children tend to have difficulties coping with complex stimuli; therefore, a group situation can be overwhelming. In a closely supervised work situation, the teacher can encourage the child to attend and provide needed help and reassurance. As the child succeeds at work-oriented activities, he or she should be challenged with more independent tasks and working with or next to the other children. Once a child can attend in a group situation, group activities should be encouraged so that he or she can benefit from the interaction with other children.

Be Positive

Be positive in your expectations of the child's abilities. Expect that the child is capable of succeeding at work activities. Your underlying conscious and unconscious perceptions of an individual will shape your expectations for that person, which will invariably influence the treatment you will offer. It is critically important that teachers working with children labeled *autistic* believe that these children can learn new skills and behave appropriately within an educational setting. Teachers need to study their students and then apply the most appropriate teaching techniques and style to encourage their skills. It is your responsibility to discover each child's learning ability—an ability that everyone has to some degree.

REFERENCES

Amidon, E.J., & Flanders, N.A. *The role of the teacher in the classroom.* Minneapolis: Association for Productive Teaching, 1967.

Barker, R.G. Wanted: Eco-behavioral science. In E.P. Willems & H.L. Raush (Eds.), *Naturalistic viewpoints in psychological research.* New York: Holt, Rinehart & Winston, 1969.

Bettelheim, B. *The empty fortress.* New York: Free Press, 1967.

Des Lauriers, A.M., & Carlson, C.F. *Your child is asleep: Early infantile autism etiology, treatment and parental influences.* Homewood, Ill.: Dorsey Press, 1969.

Flanders, N.A. *Analyzing teaching behavior.* Reading, Mass.: Addison-Wesley, 1970.

Gibbons, S. Environmental forces impinging upon normal and disturbed children in a regular classroom. (Doctoral dissertation, University of Michigan, 1971). *Dissertation Abstracts International,* 1972, 66617B. (Order No. 72-74, 873)

Grant, C.J. *An ecological study of the interactions of children labeled autistic and their assigned teachers.* Unpublished doctoral dissertation, Syracuse University, 1978.

Hutt, S.J., & Hutt, C. *Direct observation and measurement of behavior.* Springfield, Ill.: Charles C Thomas, 1970.

Hutt, C., & Ounsted, C. The biological significance of gaze aversion with particular reference to the syndrome of infantile autism. *Behavioral Science,* 1966, *11,* 346-356.

Hutt, C., & Ounsted, C. Gaze aversion and its significance in childhood autism. In S.J. Hutt & C. Hutt (Eds.), *Behavioral studies in psychiatry.* New York: Pergamon Press, 1970.

Kozloff, M.A. *Reaching the autistic child: A parent training program.* Champaign, Ill.: Research Press, 1973.

Lichstein, K. *The ecological assessment of an autistic child.* Unpublished doctoral dissertation, University of Tennessee, 1976.

McDonald, J.E., & Shepherd, G. The autistic child: A challenge for educators. *Psychology in the Schools,* 1976, *13,* 248-256.

Raush, H.L. Naturalistic method and the clinical approach. In E.P. Willems & H.L. Raush (Eds.), *Naturalistic viewpoints in psychological research.* New York: Holt, Rinehart & Winston, 1969.

Richer, J. Unwillingness to relate: The autistic child and his world. *New Behavior,* 1975, *17,* 98-101.

Richer, J. *The partial noncommunication of culture to autistic children—An application of human ethology.* Paper presented at the international Symposium on Autism, St. Gallen, Switzerland, 1976. (a)

Richer, J. The social-avoidance behavior of autistic children. *Animal Behavior,* 1976, *24,* 898-906. (b)

Richer, J.M., & Coss, R.G. Gaze aversion in autistic and normal children. *Acta Psychiatrica Scandinavica,* 1976, *53,* 193-210.

Richer, J., & Richards, B. Reacting to autistic children: The danger of trying too hard. *British Journal of Psychiatry,* 1975, *127,* 526-529.

Schreibman, L., & Koegel, R. Autism a defeatable horror. In *Readings in autism.* Guilford, Conn.: Special Learning Corporation, 1978.

Sullivan, R.C. Autism: Current trends in services. In *Readings in autism.* Guilford, Conn.: Special Learning Corporation, 1978.

Willems, E.P. An ecological orientation in psychology. *Merrill-Palmer Quarterly,* 1975, *11,* 317-343.

Wood, M.M. (Ed.). *Developmental therapy: A textbook for teachers as therapists for emotionally disturbed young children.* Baltimore: University Park Press, 1975.

Part VI
Evaluating Children and Programs

16
Evaluating Peer Interactions in an Integrated Setting

Ellen Barnes
Debra Isaacson

A major argument made for mainstreaming is the positive peer modeling opportunities offered to special children through their contact with nonhandicapped children. Opponents of mainstreaming raise concerns about the rejection and scapegoating of special children by typical children. Peer interactions in a mainstreamed setting are important because they represent a major socializing opportunity for both the typical and special children. For the special children to be accepted as part of the typical community and for the typical children to learn to interact constructively with the special children, there must be contact and positive peer interaction when they are young.

The naturally occurring interactions between the typical and special children in our integrated setting were recorded in a variety of ways over time. This chapter reviews the aspects of peer interaction studied, methodologies used, and some of the results. The major focuses of the research are the actual behaviors and the expressed attitudes of the children toward each other. The procedures and data will be presented in three parts: describing interactions using specimen recordings, describing interactions using SWAN (Systematic Who-to-Whom Analysis Notation), and sociometrics and children's attitudes analyzed qualitatively.

SPECIMEN RECORDINGS

Specimen recording is the "scheduled continuous observing and narrative recording of a behavior sequence under chosen conditions of time and life setting" (Wright, 1960, p. 83). This approach allows us to capture "the range, variety, wealth, and subtlety of the behavior" (Wright, 1967, p. 87) and to describe the behavior in its situational context. The raw data of interactions are captured without omitting material because of selective observing or because of limits set by a particular theory. A complete description of this approach can be found in Wright (1967).

A major value of specimen recordings is that the material can be coded and quantified and the data can also be qualitatively analyzed. In the following pages, we will describe the procedures we used in enough detail to be replicated, and we will report some of the results in evaluating peer interactions.

Procedures

Each child in the integrated setting was observed for 5-minute periods in each of three situations—work, play, and snack or lunch. (The 5 minutes was deemed sufficient time, but any consistent length is possible.) In this case, each child was observed four times in each of the three situations for a total of 60 minutes of specimen recording. The question was whether child-child interaction varied in the different situations where both stimulus activity and degree of adult intervention varied. The data were collected over time to minimize the effect of observer bias. Pretraining of observers, periodic critiquing of completed observations, and spotchecks in which two observers recorded the same child for the same 5 minutes also maximized reliability. Here is an example of a 5-minute sample on Amy, in a play situation.

> Amy is in the top of the loft alone and walks to the edge, watching Jude and the volunteer. Amy blows on her hands and watches Jamila and Nova arguing down below at the table. They stop. Amy blows loudly on her hands and continues to watch them. Amy sits down and pushes her truck. Amy looks out of the loft and calls in baby talk to Mieke, " ge, ge, sissy." Mieke, who is sitting at the table, asks, "What, honey?" Amy says, "ge, ge, come here." Mieke comes to the loft, says something to Amy, then walks away. Amy sits on the floor of the loft with a truck, watching Mieke and Jamila at the table. Amy looks at Andy, who is sitting at the table below drawing with a magic marker. Amy looks back again at Jamila and Mieke. Mieke gets crayons and paper and climbs to the loft with Amy. The girls talk and color.

After the data have been collected, they are coded so that comparisons can be made between samples. The specimen recordings were coded using an adaptation of the Social Reinforcement Scale by Charlesworth and Hartup (1967). This instrument was chosen because it identifies a variety of categories of social behavior between people in some detail. For a detailed description of the development of the adaption, see Barnes (1978). Every behavior which is exhibited by the target child toward another person or directed by another person toward the target child is scored. Here is the sample record from above, with the coding.

Amy is in the top of the loft alone and walks to the edge, watching (*1a*) Jude and the volunteer. Amy blows on her hands and watches (*1a*) Jamila and and the volunteer. Amy blows on her hands and watches (*1a*) Jamila and Nova arguing down below at the table. They stop. Amy blows loudly on her hands and continues to watch them. Amy sits down and pushes her truck. Amy looks out of the loft and calls (*1j*) in baby talk to Mieke, "ge, ge, sissy." Mieke, who is sitting at the table, asks (*1h*), "What, honey?" Amy says (*1g*), "ge, ge, come here." Mieke comes (*3g*) to the loft, says (*1j*) something to Amy, then walks away. Amy sits on the floor of the loft with a truck, watching (*1a*) Mieke and Jamila at the table. Amy looks at (*1a*) Andy, who is sitting at the table below drawing with a magic marker. Amy looks (*1a*) back again at Jamila and Mieke. Mieke gets crayons and paper and climbs (*1i*) to the loft with Amy. The girls talk (*1j*) and color (*3h*).

After the samples are coded, the frequencies of each category are tallied to determine totals of behaviors initiated and received by each target child in work, play, and snack/lunch. Figure 16.1 shows the form used for the tallies for each child. R are behaviors received by the subject and I are those initiated by him or her. In the end, the tally sheet will show not only the total number of times a particular behavior (e.g., 9a) occurred, but also in what situations and by whom toward whom.

Figure 16.1

Amy

Categories	Play						Work	Snack/Lunch
	John		Mieke		Nova			
	R	I	R	I	R	I		
1a								
1b								
1c								
•								
•								
•								
•								
9a								
9b								

The coding categories can be grouped for more manageable manipulation of the data into three kinds of interactions: positive (categories 1-4); neutral (category 5); and negative (categories 6-9). Each child's interactions with typical and special children can be expressed on a 5 "x 9" card, as shown on Figure 16.2.

These cards can then be sorted to perform a variety of manipulations on the data, as will be indicated by the results below. The most crucial procedure is the

Figure 16.2

Jude (Typical Child)

		Special Children			Typical Children			
		Play	Snack	Work	Play	Snack	Work	Totals
Positive	I	1	2	0	25	21	8	57
	R	3	0	0	21	9	5	38
Neutral	I	0	0	0	1	1	2	4
	R	0	0	0	0	0	0	0
Negative	I	1	0	0	1	4	0	6
	R	0	0	0	1	6	0	7
Totals		5	2	0	49	41	15	112

initial recording. Rich, full, and accurate recording takes an alert eye and a quick pen. The importance of skill in detailed description rather than interpretation cannot be underestimated. With good specimen recordings, many different means of organization and analysis can be used to make sense of the natural interactions between children.

Results

In this setting, there were three typical children for each special child; this ratio should be kept in mind when interpreting the data in the following tables and figures.

Frequencies and percentages of all interactions (typical; special; typical-typical; typical-special; special-typical; special-special) during all time periods

As shown in Table 16.1, typical children had three times more interactions than special children. Of those, 90% were with other typical children rather than with special children. Special children interact three times more often with typical children than with special children. These frequencies and percentages reflect the 3:1 typical:special child ratio in each class and are expected probabilities pointing to equal rates of interaction for each group.

Frequencies and percentages of all interactions (typical; special; typical-typical; special-special; special-typical; typical-special) in each of three situations—play, work, snack/lunch

Most interactions occur at play for all groups and combinations of groups (see Table 16.2.) For the majority, the lowest number occur in work. Special

Table 16.1 Number of interactions across all time periods

Initiator/Receiver	No.	%
Typical/All	1019	76
Special/All	317	24
Typical/Typical	928	91
Typical/Special	91	9
Special/Typical	243	77
Special/Special	74	23

Table 16.2 Frequencies and percentages of interactions in each situation

	Play		Work		Snack/Lunch	
	No.	%	No.	%	No.	%
Typical	507	50	178	17	334	33
Special	166	52	64	20	87	28
Typical/Typical	458	90	158	89	312	93
Typical/Special	49	10	20	11	22	7
Special/Typical	129	78	42	66	72	83
Special/Special	37	22	22	34	15	17

children interacted least with other special children at snack/lunch. Half (50%) of all interactions occur at play. For typical children, 90% are with other typical children. For special children, 78% of the interactions are also with typical children. Special children were more positive to typical children than to other special children.

Quality of interactions per group in each situation. Percentage positive, negative, and neutral in play, work, snack/lunch for special, typical, special/ special, special/typical, typical/typical, typical/special

Tables 16.3 and 16.4 show that typical children were positive 88% to 90% of the time with other typical children. With special children, typical children were positive 68% and 75% (work and snack/lunch) of the time. Special children were positive 79% to 86% of the time with typical children, but only 59% to 67% with other special children.

Figures 16.3 through 16.12 present these results graphically.
1. Frequencies of integrated and nonintegrated interactions—all time periods. Typical/typical interactions occur most frequently, while special/special occur least often (Figure 16.3). Typical children interact

Table 16.3   Positive, neutral and negative interactions of typical children in each situation

		Total		Play		Work		Snack/Lunch	
		No.	%	No.	%	No.	%	No.	%
Typical to Typical 928	Positive	822	89	404	88	143	90	275	88
	Neutral	14	1	9	2	4	3	1	1
	Negative	92	10	45	10	11	7	36	11
Typical to Special 91	Positive	75	82	45	92	15	75	15	68
	Neutral	2	2	2	4	0	0	0	0
	Negative	14	16	2	4	5	25	7	32
Typical to All 1019	Positive	897	88	449	89	158	89	290	87
	Neutral	16	2	11	2	4	2	1	0
	Negative	106	10	47	9	16	9	43	13

Table 16.4   Positive, neutral and negative interactions of special children in each situation

		Total		Play		Work		Snack/Lunch	
		No.	%	No.	%	No.	%	No.	%
Special to Typical 243	Positive	194	79	96	74	36	86	60	83
	Neutral	4	1	3	2	0	0	1	1
	Negative	47	20	30	24	6	14	11	16
Special to Special 74	Positive	47	64	24	65	13	59	10	67
	Neutral	1	1	0	0	0	0	1	7
	Negative	26	35	13	35	9	41	4	26
Special to All 317	Positive	239	75	120	72	49	77	70	80
	Neutral	5	2	3	2	0	0	2	2
	Negative	73	23	43	26	15	23	15	18

with each other almost three times more than they interact with special children. This is slightly less than we would expect with the typical:special child ratio of 3:1.

2. Percentages of integrated interactions in each of the three situations—work, play, snack/lunch. Of all the integrated interactions, 75% occur at play, less than 19% at work (Figure 16.4).

3. Percentages of interactions initiated by typical and special children during each of the three situations (play, work, snack/lunch). Figure 16.5 results are consistent within each grouping of children. All children interact most in play and least in work.

Figure 16.3 Frequencies of interactions between children

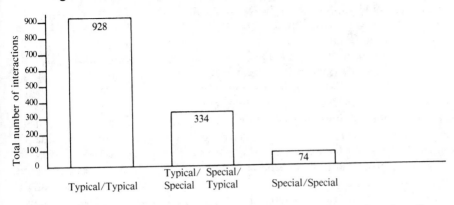

Figure 16.4 Percentages of all integrated interactions by situation

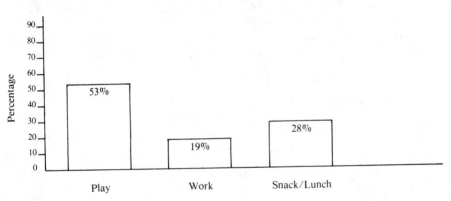

Figure 16.5 Percentages of interactions in three situations

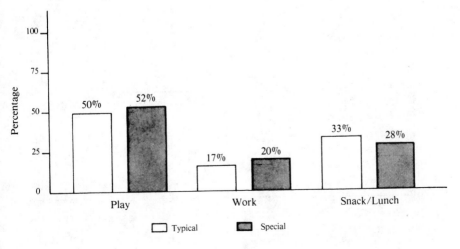

4. Percentages of interactions in each situation which are integrated. In *all* situations, about 25% of the interactions occur between typical and special children. This is expected with the 3:1 ratio of typical:special children (Figure 16.6).
5. Frequencies of integrated and nonintegrated interactions in play (Figure 16.7), work (Figure 16.8), and snack/lunch (Figure 16.9). In all situations, typical/typical interactions occurred with the greatest frequency while special/special occurred least often.
6. Quality of initiating behaviors in each situation (play, work, snack/lunch) (Figure 16.10). The quality (positive, negative, neutral) of the initiating behavior is consistently positive, ranging from 72% to 77%, in all three situations. In general, 89% of typical children's interactions are positive. In general, 77% of special children's interactions are positive.
7. Quality of each group's initiating behavior—percentages positive, negative, and neutral (Figure 16.11). In all situations, typical children have 13% more positive initial behaviors and 13% fewer negative initial behaviors than special children.
8. Quality of all integrated interactions. Figure 16.12 shows that 80% of all special/typical or typical/special initiations are positive.

Figure 16.6   Percentages of interactions by situation which are integrated

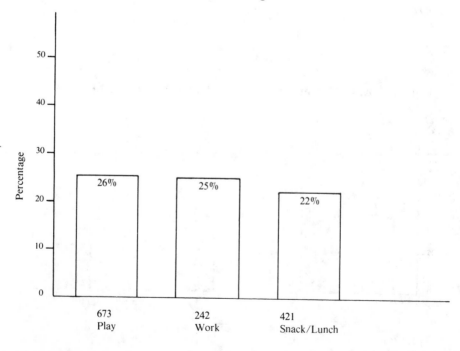

Figure 16.7   Play interactions

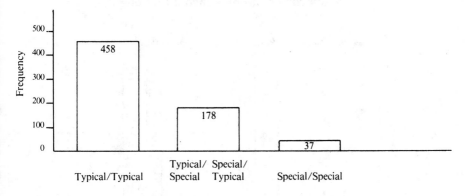

Figure 16.8   Snack/lunch interactions

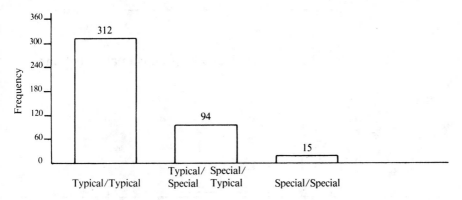

Figure 16.9   Work interactions

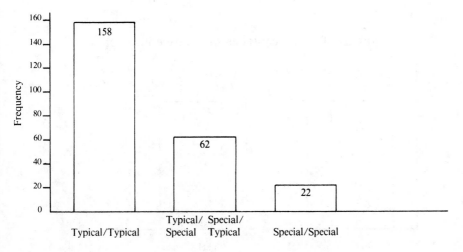

Figure 16.10   Quality of interactions initiated by typical and special children in each situation

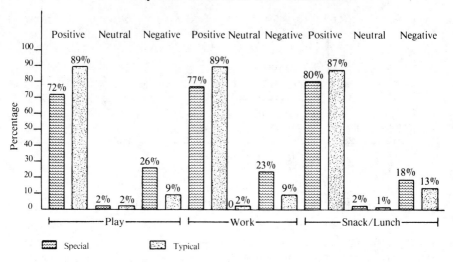

Figure 16.11   Quality of interactions by groups in all situations

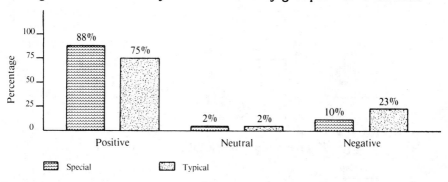

Figure 16.12   Percentages of positive interactions

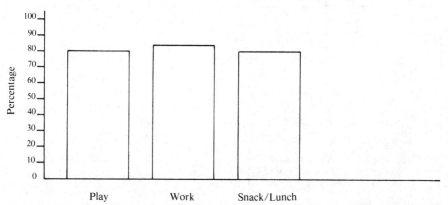

THE SWAN (SYSTEMATIC WHO-TO-WHOM ANALYSIS NOTATION)

The Systematic Who-to-Whom Analysis Notation (SWAN) is a coding system to use for on-the-spot observation and is based on Flanders' Teacher Interaction Analysis. Created by William Swan (1973) at the University of Georgia, it uses 1-minute observation periods with notations at 3-second intervals. There are nine general categories involved in the notation technique: observes, physical contact, follows directions, works, verbalizes, physical activity, waiting in turn, nondirected activity, and removal from view. Subcategories number 18, making 27 total categories which can be used to describe the behaviors (see Appendix).

Procedures

A color coded SWAN observation form was created for each room. Included on the form are the names of the teachers and the children in each room as well as some empty spaces to use for visitors or group situations. After the 1-minute observation, the 20 notations are then tallied into appropriate, inappropriate, and neutral behaviors and recorded on the form.

SWAN completed a total of 4 minutes of observations per child and drew inferences from those data. In our situation, it seemed that more observations would lead to more objective and complete data. Therefore, each typical and special child in this integrated setting was observed once each month in three different activities: work, play, and snack/lunch. *Work* was defined as any activity that was teacher directed. *Play* was defined as any activity that was not teacher directed, and transitional activities were not observed. Each special child was observed at least twice per month in each of the activities.

At the end of 4 months, enough data had been gathered to make some general statements about each child's behavior. The target of the analysis was the percentages of appropriate, inappropriate, and neutral behaviors and the integration of typical and special children in a variety of situations. Two forms were designed to accommodate the information gathered on the individual SWANs.

First, the percentages of appropriate, inappropriate, and neutral behaviors were tallied and an average percentage obtained for each situation. The integration of special and typical children was described by recording the number of times each typical child had some interaction with a special child and the names of those children in each of the three situations. For each special child, interactions were recorded with teacher, typical children, and other special children in each of the three situations. The names of those people were noted, as were the number of observations in each situation.

At this point the information could be used by the teachers of the various children to see what activities seemed to promote interaction, which children seemed to have high percentages of inappropriate behaviors and in which situations, and which children seemed to interact most readily. At the end of the school year (5 more months), the summaries were again completed and compared in graph form to the previous 4-month summaries. Again, general statements can be constructed, utlizing the data from the two summary sheets.

Results

From Table 16.5, reporting the percentage of daily interactions occurring at the various activities, we can see both consistencies across classes and differences between and within each class in the fall and spring.

These data may be analyzed room by room, activity by activity, or group by group. For example, the Orange Room had more teacher interactions in work and play as compared to snack, and these percentages were higher in the fall. Typical children in this room interacted most often during snack; special children, during play. However, when the direction of these interactions in considered, a very complex picture emerges. Not only can we see room differences, activity differences, semester differences, and group differences, but combination differences as well. There are 270 specific situations within these five classes.

Another table, not shown here, depicts the number of each individual child's interaction with other children, both initiated and received. Here we can see which children interact with many children, which are isolated, which do not reciprocate to others, and which are not reciprocated to. Another way of recording and interpreting sociograms is shown in Table 16.6.

Table 16.6 is a room-by-room tally of children who interact with all other children. It is evident that the Spring Room had the highest mean number of interactions, but the lowest number of children receiving attention from all others. So it may be that one or two children are interacting a great deal—leaving many alone.

The Rose Room had the second highest mean number of interactions, but the lowest number of children interacting with others. All special children in this room initiated interactions to all other students. In contrast, none of the Blue Room's special children received interactions from all children and only one special child initiated interactions to all other children.

Figures 16.13, 16.14, and 16.15 depict individual child patterns of inappropriate, appropriate, and neutral behaviors and their changes over the years. Special child A's appropriate behavior increased, inappropriate behavior decreased, and neutral behavior decreased over the year. Typical child 1 showed no change. Special child B and typical child 2 displayed an identical pattern, showing the increase of appropriate behavior and decrease in negative or neutral behavior of special children. This pattern is true for snack and play. While at work, special child A did not change, but special child B increased appropriate and inappropriate behaviors and decreased neutral ones. The least amount of change seems to have occurred during work.

Table 16.5   Percentages of interaction by room during three activities in the fall and spring

ACTIVITY	ROOM	TOTAL TEACHER F	TOTAL TEACHER S	TOTAL TYPICAL F	TOTAL TYPICAL S	TOTAL SPECIAL F	TOTAL SPECIAL S	TYPICAL TEACHER F	TYPICAL TEACHER S	TYPICAL TYPICAL F	TYPICAL TYPICAL S	TYPICAL SPECIAL F	TYPICAL SPECIAL S	SPECIAL TEACHER F	SPECIAL TEACHER S	SPECIAL TYPICAL F	SPECIAL TYPICAL S	SPECIAL SPECIAL F	SPECIAL SPECIAL S
Snack	Orange	19.13	14.25	11.38	9.38	2.0	4.88	17.8	10.4	15.8	13.4	1.38	7.6	19.67	20.67	4.0	2.67	1.67	.33
	Blue	26.44	16.1	25.89	17.9	1.56	1.6	14.8	14.17	34.5	24.8	2.3	2.33	49.67	19.0	4.3	7.5	0	.5
	Butterscotch	14.22	8.44	15.11	13.11	2.89	.44	15.17	8.67	20.0	16.0	4.33	.5	12.33	8.0	5.33	7.3	0	.33
	Rose	16.89	18.11	9.89	10.89	3.0	4.72	17.5	18.83	10.17	10.67	2.67	5.5	15.67	16.67	9.33	11.33	3.17	3.17
	Spring	16.4	14.78	6.7	7.11	1.0	3.44	16.43	12.83	7.29	7.17	1.14	4.5	16.3	18.67	5.33	7.0	.67	2.67
Work	Orange	21.25	24.5	10.75	8.83	3.0	.75	18.8	16.8	16.6	13.0	4.8	1.0	25.33	37.33	1.0	.67	0	.33
	Blue	35.0	23.8	16.11	4.7	1.11	2.6	29.0	22.67	20.33	5.33	1.0	2.5	47.0	25.5	7.67	3.75	1.33	2.75
	Butterscotch	21.11	14.78	14.4	8.44	1.33	3.0	20.5	16.67	16.0	11.5	1.33	3.83	22.33	17.67	11.33	2.33	1.33	1.33
	Rose	26.67	27.22	8.89	5.61	.78	1.39	26.0	27.17	12.33	7.33	.67	1.83	28.0	27.33	2.0	2.1	1.0	.5
	Spring	14.4	21.33	7.2	8.11	1.45	1.78	12.0	19.0	8.71	9.5	1.86	2.5	20.0	26.0	3.67	5.33	.5	.33
Play	Orange	21.25	17.88	9.88	13.25	4.5	7.0	22.8	12.6	14.2	20.8	5.8	10.6	18.67	26.67	2.67	.67	2.33	1.0
	Blue	22.38	23.0	21.88	15.5	2.38	.6	24.17	21.33	25.83	19.5	3.17	.67	17.0	25.5	10.0	12.0	0	.5
	Butterscotch	8.78	15.56	16.22	13.56	1.56	.89	8.67	14.0	21.83	16.33	1.0	.5	9.0	18.67	5.0	8.0	2.67	.83
	Rose	19.0	23.78	9.61	7.39	.67	2.44	18.5	22.33	13.83	9.67	.5	3.5	20.0	26.67	1.17	2.83	1.0	.33
	Spring	13.3	13.11	16.9	7.89	2.3	3.33	9.14	14.0	20.29	9.83	2.86	1.67	26.33	11.33	3.0	4.0	1.0	6.67

Table 16.6   Compiled interaction data

Room	Children Inter-acted With	Children Receiving Interaction From All In Room		Children Initiat-ing Interac-tion To All In Room	
		Total	Special	Total	Special
Orange	9.875	6	2	3	0
Blue	10.2	5	0	1	1
Butterscotch	9.89	4	1	3	1
Rose	11.44	7	1	6	3
Spring	12.1	3	0	3	1

Figure 16.13   Behavior patterns of selected children during snack in the fall and the spring

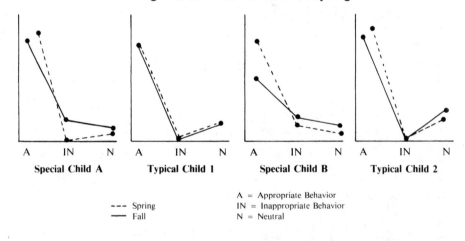

Special Child A   Typical Child 1   Special Child B   Typical Child 2

--- Spring
— Fall

A = Appropriate Behavior
IN = Inappropriate Behavior
N = Neutral

Figure 16.14   Behavior patterns of selected children during work in the fall and the spring

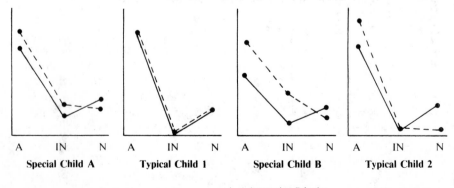

Special Child A   Typical Child 1   Special Child B   Typical Child 2

--- Spring
— Fall

A = Appropriate Behavior
IN = Inappropriate Behavior
N = Neutral

**Figure 16.15   Behavior patterns of selected children
during play in the fall and the spring**

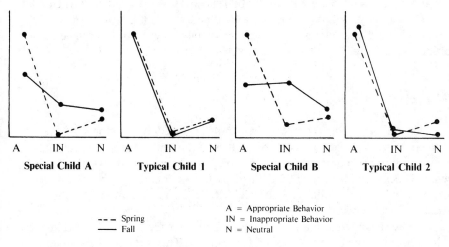

A IN N	A IN N	A IN N	A IN N
Special Child A	Typical Child 1	Special Child B	Typical Child 2

- - - Spring
——— Fall

A = Appropriate Behavior
IN = Inappropriate Behavior
N = Neutral

INTERVIEWS AND SOCIOMETRICS

In addition to the observational techniques described above, interviews and sociometrics were used to assess the relationships between typical and special children in this integrated setting. Structured interviews with verbal children give their perception of others, a perception which may or may not seem consistent with how they behaved during the observations. Even children as young as 3 and 4 years old are able to respond to questions. Our interviews were structured by using pictures and a standard and limited set of questions. The data from the interview process were analyzed with sociometric techniques; a qualitative content analysis was also performed.

Procedure

Laminated pictures of the children's faces were used as stimuli for the taped interview. The subject child was given the pictures of the children in his or her class and asked to sort them into two piles according to the following three criteria: Like/Not Like; Afraid of/Not Afraid of; and Would Ask for Help/Would Not Ask for Help. After the child sorted the cards into Like/Not Like, the interviewer took the Like pile and spread the cards out on the table, asking the child to rank them (i.e., "Who do you like best? Next best?"). Then the interviewer asked "Why?" each of these children was liked. The same procedure followed for Not Like and for the other polarities. After the sorting process, each child was asked to talk about the school ("What do you think about it? What do you like? Not like?") and about each of the three special children in his or her classroom. The questions about the special children were open-ended, geared toward eliciting perceptions of the child. Questions might include the following: "Tell me about John. What do you think about him? How do you know when John wants something? What do you think he'll be like when he grows up?"

Each child's responses were noted by the interviewer on a data sheet; in addition, direct statements were transcribed from the tapes.

Analysis

The material from the interviews can be analyzed in a number of ways. Sociometric analysis gives a picture of each child's popularity, peer structure, and reciprocity in each class. Quantitative analysis of rankings shows the degree to which special children were integrated as far as friendships were concerned. Content analysis of children's interviews offer an understanding of their perspective on the special children.

In the sociometric analysis, the first place votes received by each child were tallied for both the Like and Not Like categories. This total number of choices a child received was diagrammed for each class (see Figure 16.16). After each child is located, it is easy to see the most "popular" children (highest number of choices) fall in the center, while the least-favored children are on the periphery. Lines can be drawn between each child and his or her peers who either chose or were chosen; reciprocal choices have arrows at both ends. In Figure 16.16, the three starred children were labeled *special*.

The special children are clearly integrated here. One of them is designated most popular. The child with the fewest like votes is a typical child. In general, this target shows very evenly distributed peer choices with no isolated children (e.g., receiving one or no choices). The special children received as many choices as the typical children.

Other ways of looking at the interview data give a larger picture of how the special children are seen by typical children. Table 16.7 depicts the class-by-class distribution of Like and Dislike votes received by the special children.

The percentages of Like and Dislike votes are then compared to the percentages expected in proportion to the special children in each class. Thus, in the Spring Room in 1976, 30% of the class was comprised of special children. Yet special children received 33% of the Like votes, 3% more than their share. Likewise, they only received 26% of the Dislike vote, although they comprised 30% of the class. Other class sociograms provided different data. The general trend shown may be interpreted as quantitatively insignificant. No one class had special children drastically excluded or pampered, and the overall differences between special and typical kids in Like and Dislike votes is negligible. This seems to show that in class, the children do not necessarily differentiate special children from typical ones in terms of friendship choices.

Figure 16.16 Sociogram of "Like" choices, Rose Room

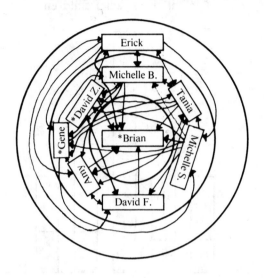

Table 16.7 Class by class

1976-77	% of Like votes received by special children	% of special children in class	% of Not like votes received by special children
Butterscotch Room	25	33	58
Rose Room	37	33	40
Spring Room	33	30	26
Orange Room	36	37	46
Blue Room	24	25	44

1977-78	% of Like votes received by special children	% of special children in class	% of Not Like votes received by special children
Butterscotch Room	25	30	45
Rose Room	29	30	15
Spring Room	19	23	15
Sun Room	21	30	36
Blue Room	18	30	39

Figures 16.17 and 16.18 (Like votes) show that, for the entire school, both years, the special children generally received about the expected number of Like votes, based on their percentage in the classroom. An interesting pattern emerges between 1976 and 1978. In 1976 (Figure 16.17) the Like votes are

**Figure 16.17   Like votes received by whole school:
Typical and special children**

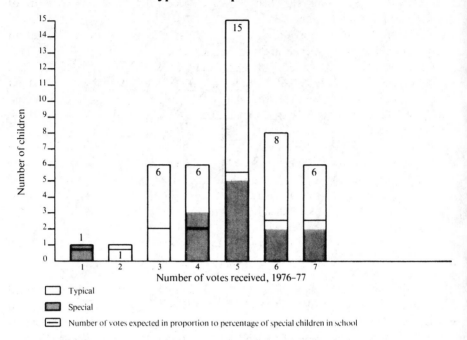

Typical

Special

Number of votes expected in proportion to percentage of special children in school

**Figure 16.18   Like votes received by whole school:
Typical and special children**

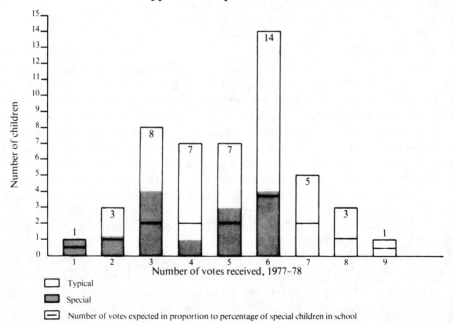

Typical

Special

Number of votes expected in proportion to percentage of special children in school

relatively evenly spread at the middle and upper levels, while the special children did not individually receive as few Like votes as the typical children. In 1978 (Figure 16.18), however, the special children received proportionately more of the lower and middle range Like votes, but were excluded from the upper levels.

On the Not Like vote figures, 1977 to 1978 (Figure 16.20), there is an almost even spread between special and typical children at all levels. In 1976 to 1977 (Figure 16.19), another interesting pattern arose. At the lower end of the scale, receiving only 1 to 2 Not Like votes, the special children received more than their share, but no special child received 3 or 4 Not Like votes, while the typical children got 3. At the other end of the scale (i.e., the most Not Like votes) (5), both children were special.

When sorting the reasons given for disliking and liking special children, the Not Like reasons are mainly limited to specific actions, while reasons for liking special children are almost evenly divided between general characteristics and special actions (Table 16.8). This indicates, on the one hand, that it is not the children themselves who are disliked but some of their specific behaviors. On the other hand, it is the children who are liked, as well as some of their positive behaviors. Furthermore, the specific acts of special children which bother typical children are not indigenous to the special children. They are also given as reasons for disliking typical kids.

Aggression is a major concern for typical children; specific acts mentioned include "hits me," "scratches," "pinches," "bites," "pulls hair." They seem to have developed explanations for this aggression. Examples of these explanations include: "He hits me 'cause he has to do his work." "He pinches to get your attention." "He's mad 'cause he has to do his work." "He pulls hair because he's angry.... I don't know that he's angry but he always looks sort of angry." The typical children also try to understand the communication problems and the idiosyncratic behaviors of the autistic-like children in our setting. "He eats paint. He thinks the color looks good and it might taste good. Some of it looks really appetizing, but you're not supposed to eat it." "He yelled; I think he wanted to teach me about up and down." "He's saying that because he's trying to talk and he doesn't know what words to say."

The children seem to have a psychodynamic point of view. They describe feelings as motivators of behavior, and they assume the special children are like themselves in motivations (upset, angry, etc.). They have learned to adapt to nonverbal and unusual communication patterns; for instance, they test out whether a special child wants something in a variety of ways. "He doesn't use words. When I give him something, he takes it." "He just comes up and sees me and pinches me to eat or play." "The way I find out is to put it on the floor and see if he wants to be with it or not." When the children talk about how they spend time with the special children, they describe both "equal" interactions and interactions in which the typical child acts as a helper or teacher. Activities of peers include both parallel roles and cooperation. "I play house with him and doctor with him. I be the doctor and he be the patient." "He and I like to jump off boxes." "Mostly G. and I were the leaders 'cause we were the first ones sitting on the steps." "I slide down the slide and bump into him."

**Figure 16.19   Not Like votes received by whole school:
Typical and special children**

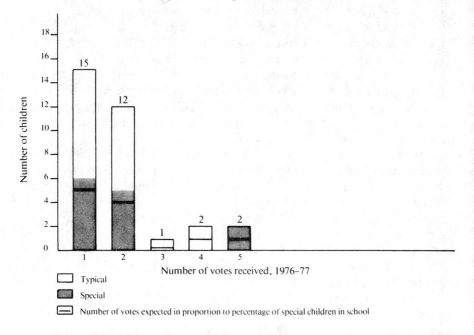

Typical

Special

Number of votes expected in proportion to percentage of special children in school

**Figure 16.20   Not Like votes received by whole school:
Typical and special children**

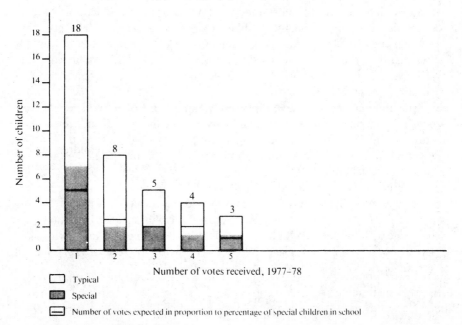

Typical

Special

Number of votes expected in proportion to percentage of special children in school

Table 16.8 Expressed reason for Like/Not Like choices

Reasons for dislike of special children

Specific actions	Frequency	General characteristics	Frequency
Aggressive acts	36	Unattractive appearance	11
Noisy; screams	9	Hurts feelings	5
Disrupts play	4	Is different	1
Disrupts lunch/snack	5	Can't learn	1
Wiggles things	1	Doesn't do nice things	1
Sucks fingers	1		19
Wets pants	1		
Says "get outta here"	1		
Won't play with me	1		
Doesn't do nice things	1		
	60		

Reasons for like of special children

Plays with me	6	Is my friend	1
Says "hi"	1	Is funny	2
Helps clean up	1	Is cute	2
Colors in books	1	Has a tooth out	1
Shares with me	1	Shares with me	1
	10		7

In terms of functioning as teachers, the typical children describe helping with the achievement of school tasks and with behavior problems. "I help him do his work. I do it a couple of times and then just leave him alone and let him do it by himself." "I get paper for him and help him draw pictures. He scribbles too much." "I work with him. I help him and I read stuff to him. I show him what to do by putting pegs in the board. I show him how to make stuff with the clay." " I help him color and be quiet." "When he's crying I tickle him. He laughs." "I keep him away from certain things he shouldn't be at." "I help him by being with him so he won't get scared. 'Cause when he's alone, he's afraid and starts to pinch."

Interviews with children allow adults to see peer interactions from the child's perspective. The matter-of-fact way in which the typical children view their special classmates supports the data from the observations. There seems to be a lot of positive feeling and comfortable interactions.

SUMMARY

This chapter describes procedures used to assess the naturally occurring interactions between typical and special children in an integrated setting. Two kinds of observation methods (specimen recording and the SWAN Systematic Who-to-Whom Notation) used with the typical and special children yielded similar results of primarily positive interactions in the three different situations of play, work, and snack/lunch. There is some variation in these situations, and the majority of integrated interactions occur at play. Analyzing the SWAN data by classroom allowed an analysis of interactional patterns in a group, including the spread of contacts and the degree to which any child is isolated. Interviews with verbal children and the use of sociometrics gave an opportunity to gain the children's perception of others. The sociometric data corroborate the results of the observations—that special children are well-integrated into the classroom group, being chosen by their peers in proportion to their numbers. The children were able to express their reasons for liking and disliking particular children, as well as how they see themselves interacting with special children.

This decription was an attempt to communicate in fairly specific detail several methods used to evaluate interactions in an integrated setting in hopes that the procedures could be replicated. In addition, the results of the data not only demonstrate the process of analysis and reporting, but describe what was actually happening in this setting between children.

REFERENCES

Barnes, E. *Peer interaction between typical and special children in an integrated setting: An observational study.* Unpublished doctoral dissertation, Syracuse University, 1978.
Charlesworth, R., & Hartup, W. Positive social reinforcement in the nursery school peer group. *Child Development,* 1967, *38,* 993-1002.
Swan, W.W. *An observational instument based on the objectives of a special educational curriculum.* Paper presented at the meeting of the American Educational Research Association, New Orleans, February 1973.
Wright, H.F. *Recording and analyzing child behavior.* New York: Harper & Row, 1967.
Wright, H.F. Observational child study. In P. Mussen (Ed.), *Handbook of research methods in child development.* New York: John Wiley, 1960.

APPENDIX: SYSTEMATIC WHO-TO-WHOM ANALYSIS NOTATION

1. *OBSERVES:*   When a child looks at someone (who is not talking) or something in the classroom, category "O" is recorded.
   In response to child's name being called: When the child observes someone who has just spoken his name, category "ON" is recorded.
   While talking: When a child is looking at another person while that person is talking, category "OT" is recorded.
2. *PHYSICAL CONTACT:*   When a child initiates physical contact such as tapping another on the shoulder, patting another on the back, placing an arm around the shoulder of another, holding hands with another, sitting in another's lap, or any similar physical contact, category "C" is recorded.
   Inappropriate: When a child hits, slaps, kicks, knocks, grabs, pushes, or pinches another or makes some similar physical contact, category "C − " is recorded.
   Restraint: When a child must be physically restrained or physically moved by the teacher, category "—" is recorded in the teacher's who-to-whom column.
   Receives: When a child receives appropriate physical contact, category "CR" is recorded.

Receives inappropriate: When a child receives inappropriate contact, the category "CR – " is recorded.

3. *FOLLOWS DIRECTIONS*: When a child conforms (motor behavior) to instructions given by the teacher and when such conforming is not the result of being physically moved (above, "Restraint"), category "F" is recorded.

Does not follow directions: When a child does not follow directions to conform, category "F – " is recorded.

4. *WORKS*: When a child works on something during any structured, individual activity time such as "work time," "art time," "organized game time," looks at the story book during "story time," or eats and drinks during "snack time," category "W" is recorded.

Works, but not appropriately sitting: When a child is doing work, but is not appropriately sitting, category "W – " is recorded.

5. *VERBALIZES*: When a child initiates talk with a peer, teacher, or group, or is engaged in conversation with a peer, teacher, or group, and the language is understandable, category "V" is recorded.

Inappropriate: When a child screams, yells, uses obscene language, or is generally boisterous, or any similar behavior, or when any verbalization is indicated to be inappropriate by the teacher, category "V – " is recorded.

Nonunderstandable verbalization: When a child verbalizes and the verbalization cannot be understood by the recorder and there are no teacher cues to indicate that the talk was understandable (including humming when not inappropriate), category "VN" is recorded.

I-statements: When a child uses a first person singular pronoun, i.e., *I, my, mine,* or *me*, category "VI" is recorded.

Group-Rules: When a child verbalizes concerning group rules, category "VG" is recorded.

In response: When a child verbalizes in response to a stimulus, such as when the teacher asks the child a question, and the stimulus is noted by the observer, category "VR" is recorded.

6. *PHYSICAL ACTIVITY*: When a child walks from one part of the room to another, moves a chair, or performs any similar physical (motor) behavior, category "A" is recorded.

Inappropriate: When a child knocks over a chair, lies on the floor when he is supposed to be sitting at the table, throws an object in a classroom, or some similar behavior, category "A – " is recorded.

Parallel play: When a child plays in the same, or a parallel, activity as a peer simultaneously, and does not interact in any way with this peer, category "P + " is recorded.

Play: When a child is participating in an activity or with materials with another child or children or by himself, and this play is not classified as parallel play, category "P" is recorded.

Responding Activity: When a child nods his head or "hunches" his shoulders or some similar physical activity while another is talking to him or in response to a question from another, category "RA" is recorded.

7. *WAITING IN TURN*: When a child is appropriately waiting in turn (appropriately sitting or standing) during play, special, or other times, and he appears to be observing those engaged in the activity, category "T" is recorded.

8. *NONDIRECTED ACTIVITY*: When a child exhibits unusual, bizarre, or otherwise indescribable physical behavior such as types of rocking, clapping, or withdrawn

behavior, such as sitting in a corner by one's self during free time, nose-picking, or some similar behavior, category "N" is recorded.

9. *REMOVAL FROM VIEW*:

By self: When a child, of his own volition, is not in view because he has gone to a corner of the room which cannot be seen from the observation window, category "/" is recorded.

By teacher: When a child is not in view because the teacher has taken him outside of the classroom (generally but not always for inappropriate behavior), category "//" is recorded.

17
Informal Diagnostic Assessment of Autistic Children

Cindy Bodenheimer

This chapter describes an informal assessment battery designed to evaluate autistic children. The battery is based on a developmental approach, congruent with the often uneven rate of learning autistic children display in various cognitive and motor areas. The framework of the assessment is such that psychologists and teachers can clinically determine and plan for individual educational needs of children in the areas of Behavior, Socialization, Communications, and Pre-Academics.

BACKGROUND MATERIAL

For the past several years, Jowonio: The Learning Place has provided a unique learning environment for both typical and autistic or autistic-like children. Typical children were, for the most part, referred by their parents who had heard about the setting by word of mouth. These parents were interested in having their children in an environment where they would be exposed to and learn to accept and interact with handicapped youngsters. Most of the parents were interested in the individual attention given to academic and affective development which could be offered in a setting with a high teacher/child ratio. In selecting typical children for our class, we had little difficulty. Our major concerns were in maintaining an appropriate peer group and varied racial and economic groupings of children.

Selecting autistic children, however, proved to be quite a difficult and delicate task. Children were referred fron a variety of sources: pediatricians, Association for Retarded Citizens, public and private schools, psychologists, and speech and hearing centers. The referrals included a functionally wide range of children. There were severely involved, totally withdrawn children, and those who had age-appropriate motor and accademic skills, but were socially unaware and nonrelating. Which children could we best serve? Which group would benefit most from integration with typical peers? Which ones were most severely autistic and had no other program options? There were many complicated factors involved in our selection of handicapped children.

One of our primary concerns was to serve the needs of a functionally wide range of autistic-like youngsters. In an environment which has as one of its primary goals to teach typical children to interact with and respond to handicapped children, it is important that there be a variety of special children. This aids greatly in teaching children to accept and look at individual differences rather than to generalize or categorize handicaps. We were also aware that in our locale there was a dearth of services for those severely involved children with autistic characteristics.

It was clear to us that we needed a framework within which to evaluate the children referred to us. As anyone familiar with standardized psychological testing is aware, these instruments are often inappropriate for the assessment of autistic children. In fact, many of the children referred to us were accompanied by reports which began: "Johnny is untestable by traditional psychological measures at the present time." We found that even those tests which were able to be used successfully with some children, such as the *Peabody Picture Vocabulary Test* (Dunn, 1965), *Illinois Test of Psycholinguistic Abilities* (Kirk, McCarthy, & Kirk, 1968), *Stanford-Binet Intelligence Scale* (Terman & Merrill, 1973), *Columbia Mental Maturity Scale* (Burgemeister, Blum, & Lorge, 1972), or the *Leiter International Performance Scale* (Arthur, 1950), gave us relatively little usable information relevant to our decision-making process. A number of these tests are too dependent on language to give an accurate picture of the autistic child's skills, and others are too specific to assess the child who functions on various developmental levels in different areas. It was from this need to have a usable, flexible, developmentally oriented framework that we set about the task of developing an informal assessment battery which would enable us to diagnostically evaluate the wide variety of autistic and autistic-like children who were being referred for services at our setting.

JOWONIO INFORMAL DIAGNOSTIC ASSESSMENT BATTERY

In planning our assessment battery, we were constantly reminded that, in order to be most useful, it would need to be:

1. Developmentally oriented around a number of skill areas;

2. Able to give information which was directly translated to program planning. For these reasons, we decided it would be most advantageous to assemble a number of tasks which would allow us to assess and describe a given child's functioning in the areas of Language, Behavior, Pre-Academics, and Socializa-

tion. These are the major groupings of curriculum goals for children in our set-ting (derived from *Developmental Therapy,* Wood, 1975).

Within these areas, we first had to decide which behaviors we would be in-terested in eliciting and evaluating. What were the primary "autistic" behaviors which differentiated these children from those evidencing generalized retarda-tion, language delay, and learning disabilities?

Controversy has surrounded the definition of *autism* since Kanner first de-scribed his group of children with "autistic disturbance of affective contact" in 1943. Even today there is no single, accepted description of this elusive disorder. Over the years, several major authors have varied the terminology and redefined the salient characteristics. Interested readers are directed to Mahler, Ross, and DeFries' (1949) discussion of the "more benign psychosis," Mahler's (1952, 1959) description of the pseudodefective schizophrenic child, Goldfarb's (1961) discussion of childhood psychosis, Creak's (1961) nine criteria for the schizo-phrenic syndrome in childhood, Rimland's (1964) and Bettelheim's (1956, 1967) discussion of infantile autism, and Wing's (1966) and Rutter's (1978) descrip-tions of the autistic child. For our purposes, the general behavioral characteris-tics which appear to differentiate this group include:

1. Uneven and inappropriate language development;
2. Uneven development in cognitive and perceptual skills;
3. Inability to relate appropriately to people and the environment;
4. Insistence on sameness and rigidity of behavioral patterns.

With these characteristics in mind, we assembled a series of play and pre-academic tasks around which we could evaluate these general behaviors and get an estimate of a particular child's developmental levels in our four major cur-riculum areas. We based some of these tasks on those described by Schopler and Reichler (1976) in their *Psychoeducational Profile* and the *Language Acquisition Program* developed by Kent (1974). However, instead of looking at a child's per-formance on a scale including pass, emerging, and fail as did Schopler and Reichler, we chose to describe a child's functioning in each of the areas, keeping in mind as we did the four characteristics of autism mentioned previously and es-timating developmental levels in our curriculum areas. We were interested in tai-loring our assessment tool very closely to our program planning in order to ob-tain the most directly usable psychoeducational information.

It is our contention that you gain the most valuable information about autistic and other traditionally untestable children through a clinical observation of the child's functioning in a play-oriented situation. It is in such a situation that the child is likely to feel least threatened and to perform most adequately. Also, in such a situation, the subtleties of the child's ability to relate to others are likely to be evident. Thus, our assessment battery is designed to include a series of developmentally oriented tasks and activities presented informally to the child in a play session with an adult who interacts with, observes, and records the behavior of the child. Table 17.1 presents an outline of the various tasks in our assessment, as well as our organizational scheme for them. In the following sec-tions of this chapter, each of these tasks will be fully explained, as will the di-agnostic information to be gained in presenting each task.

Table 17.1
Jowonio informal assessment tasks

I. *BEHAVIOR*
  A. *Affect*
      Sensory stimulation/awareness of environment
      React to reflection in mirror
      React to playful physical intrusion, tickling
      Appropriate tolerance for frustration, interruptions
  B. *Perception*
      Bubble play
      Find treat under cup/peek-a-boo
      Show interest in simple picture book
      Completion of puzzle—2-5 years or 4-6 years
      Match 5 objects according to color (toy cups and saucers)
      Identify 3 objects in pouch

II. *SOCIALIZATION*
  A. *Play and Interest in Materials*
      Imaginative play with trucks, cars, blocks
      Symbolic play with tea cups
      Symbolic play with puppets
  B. *Relating, Cooperating, Human Interest*
      Observe interactions throughout all tasks presented
      (Specifically focus on maintaining eye contact; initiating
      interactions; seeking help from examiner; awareness of ex-
      aminer's presence; cooperation; ability to take turns; reac-
      tion to physical contact)

III. *PRE-ACADEMICS*
  A. *Fine Motor*
      Play-dough: modeling-imitation
      Color simple picture/scribble on paper
      Stack blocks
      Copy shapes
      Cut paper with scissors
      Copy letters; numbers
      Draw self
  B. *Cognitive Performance*
      Find missing object game
      Sort cards by color, function
      String beads by pattern
  C. *Gross Motor*
      Walk, run, climb, descend stairs
      Catch, throw, kick ball
      Clap hands, stand on 1 foot
      Jump up and down on 2 feet

IV. *COMMUNICATION*
Preverbal Section
A. *Attending*
Sitting still
Look at objects
B. *Motor Imitation*
Specific motor imitation
Vowel, consonant imitation
Word imitation and approximation as contingency

Verbal Section
A. *Basic Receptive Phase*
Demonstrate understanding of familiar labels
Demonstrate understanding of simple body part labels
(basic self-awareness)
Demonstrate understanding of simple directions, requests
B. *Basic Expressive Phase*
Name objects
Name body parts
Counting; ABC's
Picture book—who, what, where, why questions

TASKS AND ORGANIZATIONAL SCHEME

General Testing Consideration: Informal Assessment

The basis of informal assessment is clinical observation of a child through a series of planned activities. In such a situation, the observational skills of the evaluator are far more important than the specific tasks presented. The evaluator must be able to remain flexible and react individually to each child's particular style and needs. It is not my intention to give the impression that the tasks per se are unimportant. However, their major value, in an informal assessment, lies in the fact that they serve as a vehicle for the evaluator's observations.

Within the framework of the tasks available for presentation, the evaluator must judge which would be most appropriate or revealing for each individual child. In each of the four general areas (Behavior, Socialization, Communication, and Pre-Academics), the evaluator should attempt to give only as many items as are required to gain a descriptive developmental level of functioning in that area and obtain information relevant to the four specific autism criteria.

The series of tasks in each area of the Informal Assessment are arranged in ascending developmental difficulty. The evaluator must make an initial judgment as to the child's overall functioning level in presenting the first task. Initially, it is often valuable to give the child a choice of tasks to choose from and thus begin with a high interest task for each child. It is within the nature of this assessment that the evaluator is free to vary the number and order of the tasks. Evaluators should be sensitive to the child's activity level, attention span, and tolerance for highly structured activity when presenting the table tasks (coloring, puzzles, etc.). It has been found helpful, especially with developmentally young children, to vary activity-focused and sedentary activities in order to maintain interest and avoid frustration.

Time and Place

Length of an informal assessment varies from 30 minutes to 1 hour, with most evaluations taking approximately 35 to 40 minutes. Most of the assessment should be conducted in a relatively quiet, brightly lit room. However, the evaluator may want to walk with the child throughout the (school) building in order to see how the child reacts to new places, people, children, stairs, and so on.

Developmental Age Range

The range of tasks included in the assessment allows the evaluator to assess children functioning *developmentally* between the ages of 2 and 7 years. However, it is relatively easy to add items at either end of this developmental range to include children functioning slightly lower or more advanced than the given developmental range. This is because it is primarily the clinical observation skills of the evaluator, not the specific tasks presented, which are crucial to the successful evaluation of the child.

Materials

Specific items have been chosen for their appeal to various developmental levels, potential for creativity and interaction, ability to elicit cognitive and behavior styles, and capacity to draw out language. The following is a list of the items found most useful in assessing children of varying developmental levels. With these items, all of the tasks listed in Table 17.1 may be presented.

1. Sturdy woman's make-up mirror, 4″ square.
2. Soap bubbles with wand in screw-top plastic container.
3. Plastic toy cups and saucers, e.g., "Tipsy Teacups" by Gabriel.
4. Sturdy, simple colorful picture book, with words, e.g., *Let's Eat* (Gyo Fujikowa, © 1975 Zokeisha Publications, Ltd.; Canada).
5. Candy, raisins, etc.
6. Colorful wooden puzzles, 2 to 5 year, 3 to 6 year level by Playschool, Fisher-Price.
7. Large 8″-10″ ball.

8. Clay, play-dough.
9. Toy car (Matchbox).
10. Small 2″-3″ ball.
11. Paper.
12. Large crayons.
13. Blunt scissors.
14. Cloth sack or paper bag.
15. Simple coloring book, e.g., *Animals to Color* (Lois Ehlert, a Whitman Book; 1967; Western Pub. Co., Inc.; Racine, Wis.).
16. Small (1″) wooden blocks to stack.
17. Two or more animal puppets.
18. Colored (1″) wooden beads to string.
19. Cards to sort by color, function (from magazine pictures or purchased from firms such as Developmental Learning Materials).

Parent Interview

It is important to keep in mind that, no matter how much clinical and diagnostic information you can gain from an initial evaluation of a child, this sample of the child's behavior may or may not be representative of his or her functioning in other settings. In order to put initial evaluation information on a child into perspective, it is helpful to solicit certain information from the child's parent. Parents, after all, almost always know more about their children than we do, and they are usually quite willing to share this information. It is unfortunate that some settings which still rely on a "blame the parent" approach often cut off this most helpful source of information.

In interviewing a parent before an initial evaluation, it is often helpful to remove the child to the care of a supportive staff member. This allows the parent and evaluator to speek freely, out of the child's presence, about the child's development and problems. You may think this is overly cautious in the case of some severely delayed youngsters, but in terms of concern for the child, it is better to err on the side of overcaution than to allow a child to overhear information which could be damaging to his or her self-concept. At a later date, of course, with some children, it is possible to sensitively discuss their problems and plans and enlist their support in their own development. Another advantage of removing the child is that parents are often more relaxed in an interview if they do not have to be concerned with also caring for or comforting their child.

Within the parent interview, the following points should be covered.
1. Birth history—any unusual problems?
2. Developmental history—unusually uneven or slow in certain aspects?
3. Health history—any reason to suspect organic causes for delays? Vision and hearing screening performed?

4. Present behaviors—positive aspects of child's behavior and specific concerns?

The parent interview may also give the evaluator a general look at the child's specific abilities—what can and cannot be expected from the child during the assessment. This is often very helpful in deciding when to demand language or set limits with a child during an initial evaluation.

TASK ANALYSIS AND INFORMATION GAINED

The following is a specific description of each task and the clinical and diagnostic information to be gained from it. Note that many tasks yield information applicable to several categories. For example, the task of Bubble Play, listed under the Perception subheading of Behavior, encompasses diagnostic questions of fine motor skills, attention span (cognitive development), visual tracking (perception), and social interaction. In these cases, tasks are listed under the heading or subheading dealing with the *major* source of information for that specific task.

Note also that no tasks are listed under part B of Socialization, Relating, Cooperating, and Human Interest. Information for this category is to be gathered from the child's overall social functioning on all the tasks presented.

I.   *BEHAVIOR*

   A. *Affect*

      Task: SENSORY STIMULATION/AWARENESS

      Materials: Water; sand; uncooked rice; large container, such as commercially manufactured water or sand table.

      Description: Examiner shows child material and physically tries to interest child by assisting in scooping, pouring, covering hands, etc.

      Information to be gained: Is child aware of materials? Does child enjoy sensory stimulation? Is child creative or rigid in play? Does child even minimally react to or explore material?

      Task: REACT TO REFLECTION IN MIRROR

      Material: Woman's cosmetic mirror with protective cover, approximately 4 " square or diameter.

      Description: Examiner shows child mirror closed in case. Examiner opens and looks at mirror (which is facing away from child) and models mirror play (making faces, smiling, etc.), hoping to arouse curiosity for mirror in child. If child fails to react, examiner structures activity and tries to engage child in mirror play.

      Information to be gained: Does child watch examiner's mirror play? Is child *interested* enough *in material* to spontaneously explore it? Does child use mirror *appropriately* (as opposed to mouthing or banging)? Does child react to his or her image in mirror?

Task: REACT TO PLAYFUL INTRUSION, TICKLING

Materials: None.

Description: Examiner tickles and plays with child in a physical, rough-housing manner. Examiner may roll child on floor, swing child in air, etc.

Information to be gained: Is child aware of examiner's presence (does he or she look at examiner, react to examiner's touch, words, sounds)? Is child *more* reactive/aware in active play sessions than in quiet tasks (books, table tasks)? Does child react appropriately to tickling, touching of body, or does he or she seem indifferent or afraid? When child is swung in air, does he or she grab for adult's body for security? Is he or she unusually afraid of/resistant to being picked up?

Task: REACT APPROPRIATELY TO FRUSTRATION, INTER-RUPTIONS

Materials: None; incorporated at opportune time into session.

Description: Examiner induces mild frustration and interruptions and notes child's reaction. This may include requiring child to sit longer than desired, holding child on lap when he or she wants to get down, interrupting play by ending a task early, removing material.

Information to be gained: Can child engage himself or be engaged in activity intensely enough to be frustrated by an interruption? What is child's reaction to frustration? Is it aggressive? If so, self- or other-directed? Is child easily frustrated or upset by examiner's varying routine or intervening in child's (stereotypic or repetitive) play?

B. *Perception*

Task: BUBBLE PLAY

Materials: Plastic jar of soap bubbles and wand.

Description: Examiner gives child bubble container. If necessary, direct child to open jar, blow bubbles. Add further direction and modeling if necessary. Examiner tries to engage child in interactional play, take turns, break each other's bubbles, etc.

Information to be gained: Does child accept and use material appropriately? Does child have fine motor ability (eye-hand coordination) to unscrew top, bring wand to mouth, catch bubbles? (Gross motor abilities may also be evident from child's movement about room after bubbles.) Can child blow or learn to blow through imitation, trial-and-error? Is child willing to take turns with examiner, play interactionally? Does child exhibit any unusual body tremors, self-stimulation, when excited by bubbles or running about room? Can child visually track bubbles?

Task: FIND TREAT UNDER CUP/PEEK-A-BOO

Materials: Small treat for child—predetermined earlier according to child's reported preferences (candy, chips, string, small toy, etc.).

Description: Examiner places treat under cup in full view of child. This may be coupled with a peek-a-boo type activity.

Information to be gained: Is child motivated and focused enough to look for treat (person in peek-a-boo)? Does child realize that treat (person) still exists even when out of view (object permanence)? Is child pleased with own performance when he or she finds treat/person?

Task: SHOW INTEREST IN SIMPLE PICTURE BOOK

Material: Simple colorful picture book with a few simple words on each page. There should be familiar objects clearly pictured, suitable for labeling, describing.

Description: Have child sit on examiner's lap and look through picture book. Describe and ask questions about book; see if child will look, label, describe, point appropriately.

Information to be gained: Will child willingly sit in examiner's lap, or is he or she opposed to physical contact? Can child's attention be sustained through visual material? Does child look appropriately or try to bang, tear, or mouth it? Is child interested in pictures or unusually drawn to patterns, letters, words? Does child insist on controlling materials (holding book, turning pages), or is he or she willing to be directed or take turns? What is the quality and quantity of language? Is it spontaneous or must it be elicited by examiner? Can child label, describe, point to pictures?

Task: COMPLETION OF SIMPLE PUZZLE

Materials: Commercially manufactured colorful wooden puzzle. Examiner may want to obtain several on different levels of difficulty (2-3 years, 4-6 years. etc.), so task can be matched with child's estimated ability.

Description: Examiner presents puzzle to child who is seated at table or on floor. If child does not engage himself productively, examiner models and verbally directs child to complete puzzle. If necessary, examiner may do several puzzle pieces with child's hand and praise for correct performance.

Information to be gained: Can child use material productively? Does child look to examiner for direction, praise, approval? Can child follow directions? How developed are child's problem-solving skills? (Does he or she approach task in trial-and-error fashion? Is activity ordered? Task focused? Does child match pieces and shapes?) Is child's fine motor skills developed enough to place and pick up pieces without difficulty?

Task: MATCH 5 OBJECTS ACCORDING TO SHAPE/COLOR

Material: Toy set of 5 plastic colored cups and saucers, color coded: red cup and saucer, yellow, etc.

Description: Examiner presents child with material. If child fails to explore or use appropriately, examiner directs activity so that child is required to match cups and saucers by color. If necessary, examiner may model and teach matching. Child can also be directed and taught to sort by function cup/saucers. Cups and saucers can be stacked and knocked down.

Information to be gained: Does child spontaneously explore materials? Does child initiate appropriate activity? Is child able to understand matching/sorting? Are child's fine motor skills adequate for task?

Task: IDENTIFY 3 OBJECTS IN POUCH

Materials: Toy car, ball, block.

Description: Examiner makes sure child is able to receptively identify all three objects. ("Give me car, ball, block.") In full view of child, examiner places all three items in bag or pouch, and then directs child to retrieve each item individually. ("Give me ball, " "Can you find the ball?" etc.).

Information to be gained: Can child receptively identify objects? Is child willing to search for item out of view? Can child tactilely discriminate objects? Is child fearful of putting hand in pouch?

II. *SOCIALIZATION*

A. *Play and Interest in Materials*

Within this area, it is desirable to note the child's exploration of the environment and presented material.

Task: IMAGINATIVE PLAY WITH TRUCK, CARS, BLOCKS

Materials: Variety of large, small toy vehicles, blocks.

Description: Examiner engages child in play with toys. Symbolic play is encouraged. (Examiner might help child build "road" with blocks and have truck "drive" down road with accompanying noises, etc.) Examiner should fade his or her interaction to see if child can continue playing alone.

Information to be gained: Does child use materials spontaneously, appropriately? Does child engage in symbolic play, or is play strictly concrete and manipulative? Is child unduly fascinated with the objects or with manipulating them (e.g., spinning wheels on trucks, dropping the toys)? Can child engage in solitary play, or is adult direction needed for appropriate action? Is child able to play interactionally with examiner? Is child's play organized, logical? Does child use words (noises) to explain, enhance play?

Task: SYMBOLIC PLAY WITH TEA CUPS

Materials: Toy plastic cups and saucers.

Description: Examiner attempts through verbal and visual means to engage child in a "tea party." If child is obviously unable to respond at this level, examiner may explore play at a lower level (having child imitate drink from a cup, eat from a plate, etc.)

Information to be gained: Can child interact on symbolic level? Can child imitate play behavior? Does child initiate play? Is child creative with materials? How much verbal interchange does the child spontaneously offer?

Task: SYMBOLIC PLAY WITH PUPPETS

Materials: 2 or 3 interesting animal puppets with clearly delineated features (eyes, ears, mouth, etc.).

Description: Examiner initiates puppet play with child and offers a puppet to child. If child accepts and uses puppet, interactive symbolic play is encouraged. If child is unwilling or unable to play with puppet, examiner continues to try to engage child with puppet, possibly through conversation about body parts. ("Can you find my eyes? Oh, yes, I have big eyes! Where are your eyes?" etc.)

Information to be gained: Can child play symbolically, creatively with materials? Can child play interactionally with examiner, examiner's puppet? Does he or she enjoy this interaction? Can child engage in conversation with puppet, examiner? Is content and manner of play logical, abstract, organized? Does child know body parts, enjoy finding them?

B. *Relating Cooperating, Human Interest*

No tasks. Throughout session note eye contact, initiation, awareness of other's presence, reaction to physical contact, cooperation, resistance, control needs, need for direction and praise.

III. *Pre-Academics*

A. *Fine Motor*

Task: PLAY-DOUGH: MODELING-IMITATION

Material: Nontoxic soft clay or play-dough.

Description: Examiner presents child with play-dough in can. If child makes no attempt to explore material, examiner partially opens container, or if necessary gives material to child. Examiner may then ask to share some of child's clay. If child does not cooperate, examiner takes some, explaining that each needs some to play with. Child is then left to play with material, while examiner does the same. After examiner has had time to note child's spontaneous play style, examiner encourages child to make a product and/or imitate the product the examiner makes (ball, snake, bowl, etc.). Children who are not on an imitative level may be helped by examiner to explore the play-dough, squeeze, bang, roll it.

Information to be gained: Does child use material productively? Can child be induced to explore material and become aware of or enjoy it? Can child imitate? Does child take pride in his product? Seek examiner's approval? Can child share materials? Can child play spontaneously and creatively, or is play rigid or concrete? Does child use hands cooperatively, transfer material from hand to hand?

Task: COLOR SIMPLE PICTURE/SCRIBBLE ON PAPER

Materials: Large crayons, magic markers, simple coloring book with well-delineated pictures, plain white paper.

Description: Present child with crayons or magic markers and books. Allow him or her to choose the picture and color. If necessary, verbally and physically direct child. If child is not yet to the level where he or she could be expected to color a picture, present paper and direct coloring and scribbling. Examiner should try to interest child in the product.

Information to be gained: Does child have enough motor control to stay within lines of picture? How does child hold crayon/marker? (Immature first grasp, fine finger control?) Can child comfortably make a choice of color, picture? Does child know names of colors, pictured objects in book? Can child take directions? Does child take pride in product? If child needed adult structure to begin task, does he or she eventually understand task and become self-directed? Hand dominance?

Task: STACK BLOCKS

Materials: Small (1½") square wooden blocks, preferably with letters and numbers on them. (These are distributed by several manufacturers of early child toys.)

Description: Present blocks to child. Allow child to examine and play with them. Eventually examiner directs child to stack them (up to 28), knock them down, and imitate a pattern of blocks examiner has constructed. Examiner may also ask child about letters and numbers on blocks, spell child's name, etc.

Information to be gained: Does child approach material productively? Is child resistant to adult direction? Is child inordinately occupied with stacking or ordering blocks in a certain arrangement? Can child stack blocks (fine motor control)? Will child knock blocks down? Does he or she become frightened or overexcited when blocks fall? Can child imitate examiner's play with blocks? Does child know letters/numbers on blocks? Can child count blocks? Can child follow verbal direction to put blocks back in box? Will child take turns or share blocks with examiner? Hand dominance?

Task: COPY SHAPES

Materials: Crayons, markers, paper.

Description: This activity should be entirely adult-directed. Examiner asks child to "Make one like this," as he or she proceeds to draw a horizontal line, circle, cross, square, triangle, and on to more intricate shapes (diamond, etc.) if appropriate. If necessary, examiner may have to take marker in child's hand and imitate his or her own actions before child understands task.

Information to be gained: How much fine motor control does child display? Does he or she know names of shapes? Can he or she imitate examiner? How well does child take direction, limits? Hand dominance?

Task: CUT PAPER WITH SCISSORS

Material: Blunt-ended scissors, marker, paper.

Description: Examiner directs child verbally, gesturally, or by demonstration to cut along a line drawn on a paper. Higher functioning children may be directed to cut out the picture they colored in the coloring book.

Information to be gained: How much fine motor control does child exhibit? Can child focus on task? Task completion? Does child take pride in accomplishment? Hand dominance?

Task: COPY LETTERS, NUMBERS

Material: Marker, paper.

Description: Examiner prints several upper-case letters (preferably several in child's name), and asks child if he or she can name them. If not, examiner may ask child to point to specific letters. Child is then directed to copy letters and/or write his or her name. Repeat with numbers.

Information to be gained: Does child have any particular interest or overexcitement about letters, lines, or numbers? Does child insist on patterns with letters or become upset if numbers or letters are presented out of sequence? Does child recognize numbers or letters? Know certain words?

Task: DRAW SELF

Material: Paper, markers/crayons.

Description: Child is instructed to draw a boy or a girl (or draw Johnny, etc.).

Information to be gained: Is drawing reality-based? How sophisticated is drawing in terms of body parts, fine motor skills? Can child describe picture? Hand dominance?

B. *Cognitive Performance*
(Estimates of cognitive performance also include imitation, problem-solving skills, academic readiness, and symbolic play found in other sections.)

Task: FIND MISSING OBJECT GAME

Material: Several small toys: car, ball, top, block (preferably familiar to child), cardboard square.

Description: Examiner presents toys to child one at a time and asks child to label toys. Toys are presented two or more at a time; then out of child's view, one is removed (behind cardboard shield). Child is then asked what is missing.

Information to be gained: Can child label toys? Is visual memory adequate for task? Is attention span adequate for task?

Task: SORT CARDS BY COLOR, FUNCTION

Material: Commercially manufactured (by Developmental Learning Material) set of cards able to be sorted by function; set of various one-color cards.

Description: Demonstrate sorting by sorting four cards into appropriate places (colors with lower functioning children; function with higher functioning).

Information to be gained: Does child have basic classification skills? Can child follow directions? Can child attend to task until completion? Does child seek adult approval, praise, direction?

Task: STRING BEADS BY PATTERN

Material: Set of colored wooden beads; two strings.

Description: Present child with material and verbal instruction to string beads. After initial play with beads, ask child to imitate and *continue* simple color pattern (such as yellow, red, yellow, red...or yellow, blue, blue, yellow, yellow...) examiner demonstrates on his or her string.

Information to be gained: Can child follow directions? Can child recognize and continue pattern without adult assistance? Is fine motor coordination adequate for task?

C. *Gross Motor*

Task: WALK, RUN, CLIMB, DESCEND STAIRS

Materials: None.

Description: Child's ability to walk, run, manage self on stairs should be noted at appropriate opportunities.

Information to be gained: How developed are child's motor skills? Taking into account chronological age, is the child balanced, confident in his or her movements? Can child walk up/down stairs, one foot per step, or does he or she appear unsure of depths, hesitant to move, grab for assistance, overstep or understep? Does child watch where he or she is going? Does child exhibit unusual or perseverate movement patterns or spastic jerky movements?

Task: CATCH, THROW, KICK BALL

Materials: Colored 12″ child's ball.

Description: Examiner gives ball to child. If child plays unproductively with ball or not at all, examiner directs child to throw ball to him or her. If child is still uncooperative or confused, examiner takes ball and throws (or rolls) it to child. (It often helps distractible, unfocused children to sit and roll ball rather than to stand and throw ball.) Examiner then attempts to engage child in game of catch. Examiner may find it necessary to make noises, clap, or tickle child to get child's attention before ball is thrown. Child may also be asked or taught to kick the ball.

Information to be gained: Could child attend to task? Was play interactional? How developed are child's gross motor skills? Is child agile, clumsy, swift, coordinated? Was child able to visually focus on and track ball? Was child interested by ball or interactional play or did he or she prefer to occupy self through self-stimulation?

Task: CLAP HANDS, STAND ON 1 FOOT

Materials: None.

Description: Examiner asks child to "clap hands." If child fails to respond, examiner demonstrates and indicates to child to imitate. If child still fails to respond, examiner claps child's hands and encourages him or her to repeat action. Repeat with standing on one foot.

Information to be gained: Does child have motor coordination (balance) to accomplish tasks? What type of directions does child respond to best (verbal, gestural, modeled, combination)? Does child understand task and refuse to comply?

Task: JUMP UP AND DOWN ON 2 FEET

Materials: None.

Description: Examiner encourages child to stand, hold hands, and jump with examiner.

Information to be gained: Does child seem to enjoy interactions with adult? Does child prefer to jump alone? Can child jump with 2 feet? Does physical activity tend to overexcite the child, cause him or her to self-stimulate or have difficulty concentrating on directions or the task?

IV. *COMMUNICATION*

   Preverbal Section

   A. *Attending*

      Task: SITTING STILL

      Materials: None

      Description: Throughout the session, examiner should note the child's capacity for sitting still and attending.

      Information to be gained: How long is the child able to focus on another person or materials? Is there anything which appears to help the child attend—"John look," "John sit and listen," sitting child in chair, on lap, touching child, gently directing child's head in direction of activity, coupled with "look" or "look at me," etc.? Is there any self-stimulation which interferes with child's ability to focus? If so, what kind (arm flapping, rocking, repeating words, screaming, etc.)? What happens if child is restricted from engaging in self-stimulation?

Task: LOOK AT OBJECTS

Materials: 4 or 5 small objects: toy car, ball, block, crayon, cookie, etc.

Description: Examiner presents materials one at a time with the verbal direction, "Look at this."

Information to be gained: Can child's attention be directed to specific objects? How long can child sustain that attention? What are major interfering behaviors if child cannot attend?

B. *Motor Imitation*

Task: SPECIFIC MOTOR IMITATION

Materials: Several small objects—toy car, ball, block, crayon, cookie, etc.

Description: Examiner involves child in a Simon Says game in which the following tasks are performed at the direction "Do this" or "Johnny do."

- Point with one finger to object on table.
- Extend both arms in front of body.
- Point to nose.
- Point to eyes, one with each forefinger.
- Cover eyes with hands (peek-a-boo).
- Stand up.
- Sit down.

If child does not immediately imitate, examiner may have to physically guide child through actions at first to see if child will then repeat the action.

Information to be gained: Can child spontaneously imitate motor tasks? What directions are most helpful for child? If child does not imitate, is it because he cannot perform the act, does not understand the direction (or imitate in general), is not focused enough on the examiner or the task, or because of resistance or a need to control the situation and not cooperate? How long is the child's attention span for responsive, focused tasks such as this? Does child understand games and look to examiner for direction?

Task: VOWEL, CONSONANT IMITATION

Materials: None.

Description: Examiner makes vowel and consonant sounds and directs child to imitate. During convenient time throughout session, examiner may imitate child's sound and see if child will enter into sound imitation game.

Information to be gained: Does child have ability to make various sounds? Will child cooperate in verbal imitation? Does child like to be imitated, and continue with new, different sounds, or stop making sounds at all? Does child babble with inflection and appear pleased with adult response? Are child's vocalizations repetitive, perseverative, self-stimulating, used to avoid situations and people?

Task: WORD IMITATION AND APPROXIMATION AS CONTINGENCY

Materials: None.

Description: During opportune times throughout session, examiner asks child for word approximation before performing obviously desired action. For example, if child likes to be picked up, adult may ask child to say "up," before being picked up. If child will or can not cooperate, adult may require child to raise arms before being picked up. (Action may have to be demonstrated for or with child.) Other opportunities may be requiring "out" or pointing before leaving room, or water ("wa") or giving cup to adult for water.

Information to be gained: Does child have ability to link sounds deliberately? Can child understand verbal contingencies? Will child cooperate and communicate if required for desired action? Does child quickly learn gestural communication? Will child only communicate under situations of desire, or is communication generalized and spontaneous?

Verbal Section

A. *Basic Receptive Phase*

Task: DEMONSTRATE UNDERSTANDING OF FAMILIAR LABELS

Materials: 4 to 5 familiar objects—ball, block, book, etc.

Description: Examiner and child are seated at table. Three or more objects are set out in front of child. Examiner encourages child to point to or indicate in some way each particular object. Commands "Show me (ball)," "Give me (ball)," or "Where's (ball)?" may be used.

Information to be gained: Can child demonstrate understanding of several familiar words? If child does not respond correctly, does he or she at least try to respond (by giving incorrect response), or is child completely resistant or confused by the task? Is the child interested in the concrete uses of the objects to a degree which does not allow him or her to respond to examiner's commands?

Task: DEMONSTRATE UNDERSTANDING OF SIMPLE BODY PART LABELS (BASIC SELF-AWARENESS)

Materials: None.

Description: Examiner asks child to respond to simple requests, "Show me your (or Johnny's) *nose*," or "Where's your *nose*?" etc.

Information to be gained: Does child have basic understanding of body part labels? Does child have minimal self-awareness demonstrated by differentiating different body parts? Does child enjoy interaction centering around his or her body and discussion thereof?

Task: DEMONSTRATE UNDERSTANDING OF SIMPLE DIRECTIONS, REQUESTS

Materials: Varied; any set of items from play sessions would be appropriate.

Description: During opportune times throughout evaluation session, examiner gives child simple directions and requests and notes response. Examples: "No," "Give me," "Put the block in the box," "Open (close) the door," "Put the ball down and stand up" (2-part direction).

Information to be gained: Can the child comprehend and comply with simple or complex directions? Does child seemingly understand and resist by ignoring or acting contrary to that which is requested? If child is resistant, how strong is the resistance? What happens if examiner is insistent and persistent with requests? Can child remember verbal directions for short periods of time?

B. *Basic Expressive Phase*

Task: NAME OBJECTS

Materials: 4 to 5 familiar items such as ball, book, toy truck, block.

Description: Examiner presents items throughout session, asking child "What's this?" or "What do you want?" and notes child's response. Examiner should consciously vary gestural directions with these requests.

Information to be gained: How extensive is child's expressive vocabulary? How much does child understand? Does gestural addition to direction aid in child's understanding? How cooperative is child? Does child look to adult for direction?

Task: NAME BODY PARTS

Materials: None.

Description: At opportune time during session (perhaps during physical interaction with child—tickling etc.), examiner asks child to name various body parts. "What's this?" Examiner may also see if child can name examiner's body parts.

Information to be gained: Can child name basic body parts? Does child have basic self-concept allowing him to differentiate body parts? Can child generalize knowledge to name examiner's body parts? Does child enjoy interaction centering around his or her body? Does child enjoy being touched? Can child quickly learn new body part label (e.g., elbow)?

Task: COUNTING, ABC's

Materials: None required, blocks may be used.

Description: Examiner asks child to count. May demonstrate by starting "one, two, three," Children who appear to have understanding of numbers may be asked to count items such as blocks.

Child is asked to recite ABC's. Again, examiner may prompt child by beginning ABC or having child repeat letters.

Information to be gained: What is the range of child's ability to make various sounds? Can child learn sequence of sounds by rote memory and reproduce them? Does child have understanding of one-to-one correspondence? Does child have particular interest in numbers or letters, or in ordering or sequencing them? Will child repeat sound, words, after an adult?

Task: PICTURE BOOK: WHO, WHAT, WHERE, WHY QUESTIONS

Materials: Simple picture book.

Description: Sit with child and encourage conversation around pictures in book through who, what, where, and why questions.

Information to be gained: What is extent of child's expressive vocabulary? Is child's conversation reality-based and logical or perseverative or out of context? How is child's understanding of questions? What is child's ability to answer such questions?

Throughout the session the quality and quantity of the child's spontaneous verbalizations should be noted so you can answer the following questions.

- Is the child verbal?
- Does the child have some consistent system (verbal or nonverbal) of communicating wants? If nonverbal, describe the system—gestures, pulling adult's hand, screaming, etc.
- Does child have basic desire to communicate? Or is communication only used to meet specific needs ("out", "cookie")?
- Are child's verbalizations communicative, perseverative, self-stimulating, echolalic, or a combination?
- What is the range of child's expressive and receptive vocabulary (length of word sequences emitted and understood)?
- Does child use personal pronoun "I," "me," "mine," or refer to self not at all or in the third person ("Johnny wants")?

RECORD FORM

While conducting an informal assessment, the evaluator should use a record form such as the one presented here. This format allows the evaluator to take notes on each task and to get an overall view of the items presented.

RECORD FORM—INFORMAL DIAGNOSTIC ASSESSMENT

Child:_____   Date of Birth: _____   CA: _____
Parent: _____   Address: _____   Phone: _____
Date: _____   Examiner: _____
Child's Current Placement: _____

I.   Parental Concerns and Pertinent Background:

II.   Tasks Administered:

I. *Behavior*
☐ Sensory stimulation
☐ Mirror play
☐ Playful physical intrusion, tickling
☐ Appropriate tolerance for frustration, interruptions
☐ Bubble play
☐ Peek-a-boo
☐ Picture book
☐ Puzzle completion
☐ Matching objects
☐ Identifying 3 objects in pouch
☐ Other _____

III. *Pre-Academics*

☐ Play-Dough; Modeling-Imitation
☐ Color simple picture/scribbling
☐ Stack blocks
☐ Copy shapes
☐ Cut paper with scissors
☐ Copy letters; numbers
☐ Draw self
☐ Find missing object game
☐ Sort cards by color
☐ String beads by pattern
☐ Walk, run, climb, descend stairs
☐ Catch, throw, kick ball
☐ Clap hands, stand on 1 foot
☐ Jump up and down on 2 feet
☐ Other _____
☐ Other _____

II. *Socialization*
☐ Imaginative play with trucks, cars, blocks
☐ Symbolic play with tea cups
☐ Symbolic play with puppets
☐ Other _____
☐ Other _____

IV. *Communication*
Preverbal Section
☐ Sitting still
☐ Look at objects
☐ Specific motor imitation
☐ Vowel, consonant imitation
☐ Word imitation
Verbal Section
☐ Understanding of familiar labels
☐ Understanding of body part labels
☐ Understanding of simple directions
☐ Name objects
☐ Name body parts
☐ Counting, ABC's
☐ Picture book questions
☐ Other _____
☐ Other _____

III. *Notes and Comments*
    I. *Behavior*

        A. *Affect*
        Task: Sensory stimulation/awareness
        Note: Response to material; awareness of environment; creativity/rigidity of play.
        Task: React to playful intrusion
        Note: Aware of E's presence; reaction to touching; reaction to being held, picked up.
        Task: Mirror Play
        Note: Interest in material; reaction to image.
        Task: React to frustration, interruptions
        Note: Aggressive? Self- or other-directed? Interruption in routine bring undue frustration?

        B. *Perception*
        Task: Bubble play
        Note: Fine motor coordination; visual tracking; appropriate use of materials; self-stimulation; interactional play.
        Task: Find candy/peek-a-boo
        Note: Object permanence; visual tracking; motivation.
        Task: Picture book
        Note: Reaction to physical contact; attention span; interest in material (pictures, words); control issues; quality and quantity of language.
        Task: Puzzle
        Note: Follow directions; look to E for assistance, praise; problem-solving skills; fine motor coordination.
        Task: Match objects
        Note: Use of materials; initiate activity; cognitive understanding; fine motor skills.
        Task: Identify objects in pouch
        Note: Receptive language; tactile discrimination; fear.
        Behavior: Other notes and comments

    II. *Socialization*
        A. *Play and Interest in Materials*
        Task: Play with cars, trucks, blocks
        Note: Initiation of activity; interest in materials; symbolic play; interactional play; organized, logical activity.
        Task: Play with tea cups
        Note: Symbolic play and interaction; imitation; creativity; language.
        Task: Puppets
        Note: Symbolic interactional play; language, body part identification.
        B. *Relating Cooperating, Human Interest*
        Note: Eye contact; initiation, awareness of other's presence; reactions to physical contact, cooperation.
        Socialization: Other notes and comments

III. *Pre-Academics*

    A. *Fine Motor*

    Task: Play-Dough
    Note: Interest in material; imitation skills; pride in product; share materials; creative play; use hands cooperatively, adeptly.

    Task: Color picture/scribble
    Note: Fine motor, grasp of crayon, choice making, color names; follow direction; hand dominance.

    Task: Stack blocks
    Note: Fine motor; hand dominance; appropriate use of material; rigidity; counting, sharing; taking turns.

    Task: Copy shapes
    Note: Fine motor; name of shapes, imitation; hand dominance.

    Task: Cut with scissors
    Note: Fine motor; attention span; follow directions; hand dominance.

    Task: Copy letters, numbers
    Note: Interest in letters, lines, numbers, patterns; letter, number recognition; fine motor; hand dominance.

    Task: Draw self
    Note: Fine motor skills; body image; language; hand dominance.

    B. *Cognitive Performance*

    Task: Find missing object
    Note: Visual memory; attention span; language.

    C. *Gross Motor*

    Task: Catch, throw, kick ball
    Note: Attention span; gross motor skills; coordination; visual tracking; interactional play; follow directions.

    Task: Sort cards by function; color _
    Note: Cognitive understanding of classification; cooperation; ability to follow directions; attention span. _

    Task: String beads by pattern
    Note: Ability to recognize and continue pattern; fine motor.

    Task: Walk, run, climb, descend stairs
    Note: Gross motor skills; confidence; balance; unusual movement patterns; activity level.

    Task: Clap hands; stand on 1 foot
    Note: Motor coordination, imitation; cooperation.

    Task: Jump up and down
    Note: Balance; coordination; self-stimulation.

    Pre-Academics: Other notes and comments

IV. *Communication*

    Preverbal Section

    A. *Attending*
    Task: Sitting still ✓
    Note: Attention span; self-stimulation.

Task: Look at objects
Note: Attention span; self-stimulation.

B. *Motor Imitation*

Task: Specific motor imitation
Note: Imitation skills; ability to focus on E; control issues; cognitive understanding.

Task: Vowel, consonant imitation
Note: Range of sounds; resistance; perseveration.

Task: Word imitation and approximation as contingency
Note: Ability to link sounds; cooperation; resistancy, gestural communication.

Verbal Section

A. *Basic Receptive Phase*

Task: Understanding of labels
Note: Receptive vocabulary; distractibility; cooperation; resistance.

Task: Body parts; self-awareness
Note: Receptive vocabulary; self-awareness.

Task: Simple directions
Note: Receptive vocabulary; cooperation; resistance; control issues.

B. *Basic Expressive Phase*

Task: Name objects
Note: Range of expressive vocabulary; cooperation.

Task: Name body parts
Note: Expressive vocabulary; ability to learn new words; body awareness.

Task: Counting; ABC's
Note: Range of sounds; verbal imitation; rote memory; interest in letters; numbers; readiness skills.

Task: Picture book; *Wh-* questions
Note: Expressive vocabulary; cognitive ability to respond to *Wh-* questions; general quality of language.

Communication: Other notes and comments

INTERPRETATION AND REPORT

As with any psychological or educational report, that written for the Informal Assessment should basically answer the presenting questions. As stated earlier, the initial evaluation is designed to address the following concerns: (*a*) Does the child exhibit those autistic characteristics which make him or her appropriate for a particular educational/therapeutic setting? (*b*) If so, what initial programming suggestions can be offered?

Format

The following format for summarizing the information of the initial evaluation and suggesting program goals and approaches is suggested.

1. *Referral Information*
   Name   Date of Birth   Chronological Age
   Parent   Address   Phone
   Date   Evaluator   Current Placement
2. *Reason and Source of Referral*
3. *Parental Concerns and Pertinent Background*
4. *Summary of Observations*
   Social/Affective Responses
   Cognitive/Perceptual Functioning
   Language
5. *Summary and Recommendations*
6. *Initial Programming Objections and Suggestions*
   Behavior
   Communication
   Socialization/Affective Development
   Pre-Academics

Example of Complete Report

The following is an example of the report containing information gained through an informal assessment of an "untestable" autistic-like child who was referred for placement in a special educational preschool setting. Note that the programming recommendations contained in the report are a logical outgrowth of the child's functioning on tasks presented throughout the informal evaluation. These goals are adapted from the *Developmental Therapy* curriculum (Wood, 1975).

PSYCHOEDUCATIONAL EVALUATION

Name: Tommy Parks   Parent: Mrs. Joan Parks   DOB: 2-18-74
Address: 41 Smith Street, Phone: 432-1234   CA: 5 yrs. 2 mos.
         Syracuse, N.Y.
Examiner: Cindy Bodenheimer

Present Placement: Currently involved in no organized clinical or educational program.

Reason for Referral: Tommy was referred by Joan Smith, a social worker at Community Services, for an evaluation to determine if Jowonio: The Learning Place would be the most appropriate placement for him in the fall of 1979.

Pertinent Background/Parental Concerns

Tommy's mother, Mrs. Parks, accompanied him to the evaluation session. Tommy lives at home with his mother and 2-year-old sibling, David. His father has recently separated from Mrs. Parks and visits occasionally.

Mrs. Parks reports Tommy's prenatal and birth history as normal and unremarkable. His development, however, was slow and uneven. He walked at 2 years and ate and slept poorly as an infant. Mrs. Parks' major concerns include Tommy's (1) lack of language, (2) poor self-help skills (especially feeding and dressing), and (3) disinterest in the people and things around him. If left alone, Mrs. Parks reports, he will walk around the room mouthing and banging toys.

Mrs. Parks would like to enroll Tommy in a school designed to meet his special needs. Until recently, she was unaware that he was eligible for educational assistance. She is now very concerned about and aware of his uneven development as she compares him to his normally developing 2-year-old brother. In general, Mrs. Parks impresses one as a concerned and capable parent.

Summary of Observation

Upon his arrival at Jowonio: The Learning Place, Tommy was willingly led to a room where this examiner presented him with a series of informal play tasks and observed his behavior for approximately 35 minutes. Tommy's interactions were also observed briefly in a preschool classroom at Jowonio.

Social/Affective Responses

Tommy showed little interest in people. He appeared to use them in a physically manipulative way, as a means to some desired goal. Several times he sought out adults to lead by the hand when he wanted to go out. Tommy consistently avoided eye contact in a variety of situations, from quiet coloring to being lifted high in the air and swung from side to side. He ignored even the most intrusive of the children during his brief visit to the preschool class. During the evaluation, Tommy was not seen to imitate the examiner, even when encouraged to do so by bouncing a ball or clapping hands.

There were several activities in which Tommy was able to participate and display minimal skills. He smiled, clapped his hands, and looked directly at the examiner when he, at the examiner's request, placed a block on top of the two the examiner had stacked. Tommy also had a favorable reaction to squeezing (and licking) play-dough. Upon seeing this, the examiner decided to further explore his reaction to other highly stimulating sensory activities. Tommy was directed to a "water table" filled with uncooked rice. He thoroughly enjoyed squeezing and pouring this substance, to the point where he eventually climbed into the table, assisted by the examiner. It might be also noted that Tommy was attracted to running water and smiled as he splashed in it. He displayed some problem-solving abilities by climbing on a box so that he could reach the flowing water with his mouth. However, when he was given a cup, he tried to drink from the empty cup, and made no attempt to fill it with the running water.

Tommy's gross motor skills appear approximately 3 years underdeveloped for his chronological age. He had difficulty maneuvering his way down a flight of stairs, and evidenced some perceptual difficulty by lifting his leg as though expecting another step when he had reached the floor. Possibility of depth perception problems should be more fully investigated.

Cognitive/Perceptual Function

Initially Tommy moved about the confined evaluation area in a nondirected way, briefly examining objects. He frequently shook objects, holding them close to his right ear. He was seen to smile at the noise a rattle-like object made.

When presented with various toys, Tommy consistently grasped the toy, shook it vigorously, and either dropped the item or handed it to the examiner. He did allow the examiner to physically guide him through scribbling with a crayon. Immediately afterward he drew a short, curved line unassisted. By avoiding eye contact, squirming, and pushing toys away, Tommy managed to resist participation in most examiner-initiated activities, such as playing with a ball, a kaleidoscope, or car. Left to his own devices, he occasionally engaged himself in a self-directed activity, such as looking at a book. However, as soon as the examiner tried to participate in or structure the activity, Tommy lost all interest and moved away. It should be noted that Tommy's preference was to use objects in a perseverative fashion, such as randomly flipping the pages of a book or spinning a block.

Language

At this point, Tommy has few communication skills. He was occasionally heard to whine or grunt when either bored or frustrated. He shook his head from side to side on two occasions, and it was unclear as to whether he intended this to mean "no," although this remains a possibility. He responded to very few verbal commands, but was seen to respond immediately to his name, by turning toward and coming to the speaker. He stood up when a hand was extended to him along with the command "stand up." It was noted that, during the evaluation, Tommy responded selectively to sounds, at times ignoring loud noises produced quite close to him, yet noticing inconsequential sounds, such as a door squeaking behind him.

Summary and Recommendations

Tommy impressed this examiner as a severely delayed, nonverbal child with many autistic characteristics, notably a disinterest in and manipulative use of people, perseverative use of objects, minimal eye contact, and the display of much nondirected activity. He remains highly resistant to both peer and adult overtures and is not amenable to physical or verbal imitation at this point. Tommy is unskilled in many basic self-help and readiness areas, such as putting on his coat, puzzle work, coloring, or playing appropriately with toys. His gross motor abilities are somewhat delayed, and he prefers help in coming down stairs, although he is able to balance himself by holding on to a railing. There is evidence of some visual perceptual impairment, which should be further investigated by an ophthalmologist.

Tommy was very interested in highly stimulating sensory activities, such as playing in water, play-dough, and uncooked rice. He was able to search out adult assistance or approval the few times he needed help or was able to cooperate in a task. However, it seemed clear he wanted adult intervention only on his own terms, through his initiation.

It is this examiner's opinion that Tommy would benefit most from a program designed to help him focus his attention, specifically using highly stimulating sensory awareness activities (water, play-dough, tickling, etc.).

This type of sensorimotor emphasis would best be presented through much individual adult attention, and in a highly intrusive, yet playful context, including much physical contact. It would be beneficial if this adult attention was offered frequently enough to give Tommy a solid feeling of security and trust, yet withheld at specific times during high interest tasks in order to encourage Tommy to seek out and respond to people.

It could be anticipated that, through this type of programming, Tommy would progress in terms of sensory awareness, attention span, and body image. It would also be expected that he could develop a healthy relationship with an adult, and some awareness of his peers, through full-time participation in a program with such a sensorimotor focus.

In light of this, it is recommended that Jowonio: The Learning Place would be a most appropriate placement for Tommy in the fall of 1979.

Initial Programming Objectives and Suggestions

Behavior

Goal 1. Develop the ability to respond to stimulus by sustained attending to the source of the stimulus.
Suggestions: Present Tommy with highly stimulating materials such as bright colored objects, musical or noisy objects, and strong-smelling foods or other substances. Use strong inflections in your voice as you present the material to Tommy, waving the object before his eyes, rattling the object, or moving strong-smelling substance below his nose. As Tommy makes a move toward the object, praise him in a vibrant voice. At first it may be necessary to move Tommy through the manipulation of the object, but gradually phase this out. Tommy should maintain attention to an object for 1 to 3 minutes without physical intervention.
Goal 2. Develop the ability to respond with motor responses to sensory stimulating materials and simple verbal directions.

Suggestions: With activities such as sand, water, and small Styrofoam pieces in a tub, place Tommy's hands in the medium, saying "Tommy play!" At first, it may be necessary to move Tommy through some actions, such as stirring and pouring, in order to maintain interest in the activity and continue verbal support. Make parallel movements in the medium.

Start to direct Tommy in play with balls. Sit opposite Tommy with your legs enclosing him at first. Throw or roll the ball to him, then say, "Roll it!" and move Tommy through the action, slowly withdrawing with time your physical support.

Goal 3. To actively assist in learning self-help.

Suggestions: Tommy will take his coat most of the way off himself. He needs verbal and sometimes physical direction to start. He needs the adult to guide his right hand over to pull the left sleeve free from his hand. After he has taken his coat off, move him through hanging it up. His visual deficits may give him difficulty with finding the hook.

To put on coat, place the coat on the floor in front of Tommy with the collar toward him. Have him place his hands in the sleeves and then lift the coat over his head. He does not have the fine motor capability to help with his zipper.

Feeding—Tommy cannot manage to eat half of a sandwich bite by bite at this point. Cut his sandwich into bite-size pieces, and put them all in his bowl. Require Tommy to pick up the pieces using a pincer grasp. When Tommy has mastered this, increase the sandwich piece size so that he must eat it in two bites. Do not let him put the entire piece in his mouth. As each stage is mastered, increase the size of the piece until the sandwich is eaten in halves.

Goal 4. To respond independently to several play materials.

Suggestions: Place materials such as music toys, colored blocks, etc., in his vicinity. Manipulate them within his sight, then lay them down within his reach, and physically assist him in playing with toys. Gradually fade physical support.

Communication

Goal 1. To produce a variety of sounds.

Suggestions: Tommy is just beginning to experiment with sounds. Encourage this by imitating the sound after him and responding physically and enthusiastically to sound he makes. Maintain eye contact if possible.

Goal 2. To attend to person speaking.

Suggestions: Encourage Tommy's attention by turning his body and face toward you when you address him. He will usually stop when his

name is called. If he does not, turn and go over to him so that he is facing you when you speak to him. Say, "Tommy, look at me."
Goal 3. To respond to verbal command, with motor behavior.
Suggestions: Encourage Tommy to respond to the simple commands of "Tommy, come here," "Tommy, do this," while doing a simple motor task such as clapping, patting knees, touching nose, etc., and "stand up."

Tommy should be given every opportunity to wave when adult says "bye-bye" when leaving the room or the school for the day. Move him through it at first, gradually withdrawing pressure of your hand.

Socialization/Affective Development

Goal 1. To attend to others' behavior.
Suggestions: Work with Tommy on activities such as dump and fill (with spoons, shovels, etc.), opening various jars and boxes, form-boards, stacking cones, and making two-block towers out of large and small blocks. Make sure he understands what you are requiring of him. Model activity and use verbal and physical direction.
Goal 2. To imitate simple familiar acts of adult.
Suggestions: Encourage imitation of "bye-bye" at opportune times. After adult modeling, have Tommy transfer objects such as blocks or small animals from table to inside box. Give direction "put it in," and praise him enthusiastically for the accomplishment.

CONCLUSION

The clinical observation of children with special needs, especially those severely impaired to the extent that they are labeled *autistic*, is a complicated and most valuable skill. It is hoped that this detailed account of one approach toward this end is helpful to those practitioners evaluating and planning for this difficult and challenging population.

Furthermore, we hope and intend that teachers working with and planning for these children every day will be able to extrapolate from the particular informal assessment presented those skills which they can use in their teaching situations in order to more fully understand and plan for individual needs of children.

REFERENCES

Arthur, G. *Arthur Adaptation of the Leiter International Performance Scale.* Chicago: Stoelting, 1950.
Bettelheim, B. Schizophrenia as a reaction to extreme situations. *American Journal of Orthopsychiatry,* 1956, *26*, 507-518.

Bettelheim, B. *The empty fortress.* New York: Free Press, 1967.

Burgemeister, B.B., Blum, L.H., & Lorge, I. *Columbia Mental Maturity Scale* (3rd Ed.). New York: Psychological Corporation, 1972.

Creak, M. Schizophrenic syndrome in childhood: Progress report of a working party. *Cerebral Palsy Bulletin,* 1961, *3,* 501-4.

Dunn, L.M. *Peabody Picture Vocabulary Test.* Circle Pines, Minn.: American Guidance Service, 1965.

Goldfarb, W. *Childhood schizophrenia.* Cambridge, Mass.: Harvard University Press, 1961.

Kanner, L. Autistic disturbances of affective contact. *Nervous Child* 1943, *2,* 217.

Kent, L.R. *Language acquisition program for the retarded or multiply impaired.* Champaign, Ill.: Research Press, 1974.

Kirk, S., McCarthy, J., & Kirk, W. *Illinois Test of Psycholinguistic Abilities* (Rev. ed.). Urbana: University of Illinois Press, 1968.

Mahler, M.S.. On childhood psychosis and schizophrenia: Autistic and symbiotic infantile psychosis. *Psychoanalytic Study of the Child.* New York: International University Press, 1952, *7,* 287-305.

Mahler, M.S., Furer, M., & Settlage, C.F., Severe emotional disturbance in childhood: Psychosis. In S. Arieti (Ed.), *American handbook of psychiatry,* New York: Basic Books, 1959.

Mahler, M.S., Ross, J.R., & DeFries, Z., Clinical studies in begign and malignant cases of childhood psychosis (schizophrenic-like). *American Journal of Orthopsychiatry* 1949, *19,* 295.

Rimland, B. *Infantile autism.* New York: Appleton-Century-Crofts, 1964.

Rutter, M. Developmental issues and prognosis. In M. Rutter & E. Schopler (Eds.), *Autism, A reappraisal of concepts and treatment.* New York: Plenum Press, 1978.

Schopler, E., & Reichler, R. *Psychoeducational profile.* Chapel Hill, N.C.: Child Development Products, 1976.

Terman, L.M., & Merrill, M.A. *Stanford-Binet Intelligence Scale* (1972 norms ed.; Form L-M). Boston: Houghton-Mifflin, 1973.

Wing, J.K. Diagnosis, epidemiology, aetiology. In J.K. Wing (Ed.), *Childhood autism: Clinical, educational and social aspects.* London: Pergamon Press, 1966.

Wood, M.M. *Developmental therapy: A textbook for teachers as therapists for emotionally disturbed young children.* Baltimore: University Park Press, 1975.

Author Index

Adler,J., 47
Albers, R., 155, 174
Almond, P., 46,48
Alpert, C., 181, 189
Amidon, E., 129, 134, 283, 288
Apter, S.J., 30
Arick, J., 46, 48
Arieti, S., 345
Arthur, G., 316, 344
Atwood, T., 8, 13
Auerbach, A.B., 200, 208, 210, 211, 213, 215
Ayres, A.J., 7, 13

Bachrach, A., 45, 48, 49, 57, 67
Baker, A.M., 8, 13
Balow, B., 6, 13
Baltaxe, C., 155, 156, 174
Barker, R.G., 279, 280, 288
Barnes, E.B., 13, 16, 20, 30, 235, 255, 274, 291, 292, 312
Barnes, K., 104, 107, 118
Barsch, R.H., 199, 200, 215
Bartolucci, G., 155, 174
Bates, E., 159, 164, 174
Benaroya, S., 179, 189
Benigni, L., 159, 174
Berg, K., 218, 230, 234
Berko-Gleason, J., 173, 174
Bettelheim, B., 6, 13, 200, 215, 283, 288, 317, 345
Berrigan, C., 235
Betts, C., 38
Biber, B., 67
Biklen, D., 235
Binder, A., 14
Binder, V., 14
Bissell, H., 120, 135
Black, M., 107, 118
Bliss, C., 177, 189
Bloom, L., 156-157, 159-160, 167, 168, 171, 172, 174

Blum, L.H., 316, 345
Bodenheimer, C., 12, 13, 217, 315
Bonvillian, J.D., 177, 189
Bookbinder, S., 221, 231, 234
Brady, D.O., 179, 189
Branston, M., 161, 175
Bretherton, T., 159, 174
Brightman, A., 235
Bruner, J., 95, 118, 164, 174
Bryson, C.Q., 177, 189
Burgemeister, B.B., 316, 345

Camaioni, L., 159, 164, 174
Carkhuff, R.R., 129, 135
Carlson, C.F., 7, 13, 283, 288
Carpenter, R., 158, 174
Carr, E.G., 177, 179, 185, 189
Carrier, J.K., 177, 189, 190, 191
Cartwright, D., 207, 215
Casey, L.O., 177, 179, 189
Cazden, C., 174
Chapman, R., 161, 175
Charlesworth, R., 292, 312
Chastain, L.D., 11, 138, 139
Cherry, C., 115, 118
Chiarandini, I., 155, 175
Christopher, M., 235
Churchill, P., 155, 174
Clarke, E., 179, 189
Cleaver, B., 235
Cleaver, V., 235
Cohen, M., 179, 189
Coleman, J., 197, 215
Coletti, G., 217, 234
Corrigan, R., 159, 174
Coss, R.G., 277, 288
Creak, E.M., 3, 4, 13, 317, 345
Creedon, M.P., 179, 185, 189
Cunningham, M., 155, 174

Davis, O., Jr., 129, 135
DeFries, Z., 317, 345

347

DesLauriers, A.M., 7, 13, 283, 288
Dewey, J., 107
Doherty, L., 155, 174
Dunn, L.M., 345

Ehlert, L., 321
Everard, M., 3, 13, 38
Eyde, D.R., 7, 14

Fassler, J., 235
Fay, W.H., 176, 189, 191
Feeley, M., 218, 234
Feingold, B., 7, 14
Fish, B., 155, 175
Flanders, N.A., 129, 134, 283, 284, 288, 301
Folstein, S., 7, 14
Foster, R.E., 179, 189
Fouts, R.S., 177, 179, 189
Franklin, A.W., 175
Fredericks, M., 164, 175
Freed, A., 131, 135
Freedman, P., 158, 174
Freeman, B.J., 4, 14, 107, 118
Fristoe, M., 190
Froebel, 107
Fujikowa, G., 320
Fulwiler, R.L., 177, 179, 189
Furer, M., 345
Furfey, P.H., 65-66, 68

Gallagher, J.J., 8, 14
Garvey, C., 95, 96, 118
Gesell, A., 95, 104, 118
Gibbons, S., 279, 288
Gleason, J. Berko-
    See Berko-Gleason, J.
Glucksberg, S., 173, 175
Gold, P., 235
Goldfarb, W., 155, 174, 317, 345
Gordon, E.G., 179, 189
Gram, R.K., 135
Grant, C.J., 12, 275, 279, 280, 282, 283, 284, 288
Graziano, A.M., 16, 30
Greenfeld, J., 200, 215
Grossman, F.K., 218, 220, 234
Guest, P.M., 135
Guralnick, M.J., 107, 118

Harris, S., 217, 234
Hartup, W., 292, 312
Hegrenes, J., 190
Hehner, B., 190
Heiko, R.L., 11, 120
Hereford, C.F., 208, 215
Hermelin, B., 177, 189
Heskett, W.M., 7, 13
Hodges, W., 67
Hollis, J.H., 177, 189, 190, 191

Howe, L.W., 120, 135
Hunt, J. McV., 67, 159-161, 175
Hunter, C.P., 120, 135
Hutt, C., 275-276, 279, 288
Hutt, S.J., 279, 288

Ingram, D., 158, 159, 175
Isaacson, D., 13, 291

James, S.L., 11, 155
James, W., 107
Jencks, C., 215
Jernberg, A., 7, 14
Jolly, A., 95, 118

Kahn, J., 159, 175
Kanner, L., 3, 4, 6, 14, 317, 345
Kaplan, F., 218, 234
Kates, B., 190
Kaufman, B.N., 200, 215
Kent, L.R., 87, 93, 317, 345
Kipilka, M., 129, 135
Kirk, S., 316, 345
Kirk, W., 316, 345
Kirshenbaum, H., 120, 135
Kirshner, K., 164, 175
Klein, L.S., 179, 189
Klein, S., 218, 234
Klips, B., 164, 175
Knapczck, D.R., 104, 118
Knoblock, P., 3, 15, 16, 20, 30, 31
Koegel, R., 282, 288
Kollinzas, G., 179, 189
Konstantenareas, M.M., 179, 189
Kozloff, M.A., 45, 48, 283, 288
Kraus, R., 235
Krauss, J., 164, 173, 175
Krug, D., 46, 48
Kugelmass, J., 12, 195

Lahey, M., 156-157, 159-160, 167, 168, 171, 172, 174
Lansing, M., 46, 48
Lasker, J., 235
Lavigeur, H., 217, 220, 234
LaVigna, G.W., 179, 189, 190
Leibovitz, S.F., 179, 189
Lempers, J., 164, 175
Leonard, L., 158, 175
Lewis, M., 174
Lichstein, K., 278, 279, 288
Lloyd, L.L., 174, 190
Lock, A., 175
Lorge, I., 316, 345
Love, H.D., 200, 201, 215
Lovejoy, K.M., 179, 189
Luria, A.R., 179, 189

Mahler, M.S., 345
Marshal, N., 190
McAfee, O.D., 197, 198, 208, 216
McCandless, B., 67
McCarthy, J., 316, 345
McDonald, J.E., 283, 288
McDowell, P., 179, 189
McLean, J.E., 93, 177, 179, 189, 190
McLean, L.P., 177, 179, 189, 190
McNaughton, S., 190
Meany, M., 179, 189
Medinus, G.R., 216
Meisels, S., 30
Menolascino, F.J., 7, 14
Merrill, M.A., 316, 345
Merzer, S., 12, 150, 236
Michelman, S.S., 95, 110-112, 115, 118
Miller, J., 161, 175
Minifie, F., 174
Mlinarcik, S., 9, 49
Montgomery, J., 107, 118
Morehead, D., 158, 175
Morse, K., 129, 135
Mosley, A., 45, 48, 49, 57, 67
Musil, A., 179, 189
Mussen, P., 312

Nedler, S.E., 197, 198, 208, 215
Nelson, K.E., 177, 189
Ninno, M., 10, 71
Nitzburg, A., 67

O'Connor, N., 177, 189
Ogilvie, H., 179, 189
Ornitz, E.M., 7, 14
Ounsted, C., 275-276, 288

Palomares, U., 120, 135
Paluszny, M.J., 38
Parfit, J., 217, 230, 234
Park, C.C., 38, 200, 216
Parten, M., 95, 104, 118
Peterson, D.R., 201, 216
Peterson, J., 235
Piaget, J., 95, 97, 104, 118, 159, 167, 175
Premack, A.J., 177, 189, 191
Premack, D., 177, 189, 191
Pronovost, W., 179, 189

Raaz, N., 6, 14
Raush, H.L., 279, 288
Rees, N., 158, 175
Reichle, J., 161, 175
Reichler, R.J., 46, 48, 208, 216, 317, 345
Reilly, M., 95, 100, 104, 118, 119
Richards, B., 275, 288
Richer, J., 275, 276-278, 285, 288
Ricks, D., 155, 175
Rimland, B., 7, 8, 14, 200, 216, 317, 345
Ritvo, E.R., 4, 7, 14, 38, 200, 216

Roberts, A., 155, 175
Rosenblum, L., 174
Ross, J.R., 317, 345
Routh, D.K., 179, 189
Ruttenberg, B.A., 72, 93, 179, 189
Rutter, M., 7, 14, 38, 155, 175, 189, 200, 216, 317, 345

Salvin, A., 179, 189
Sanders, K., 164, 175
Sarason, D.J., 234
Sarason, S.B., 234
Satir, V., 135
Says, S., 67
Schachter, F., 164, 175
Schaeffer, B., 179, 189
Schiefelbusch, R.L., 93, 175, 189, 190
Schopler, E., 38, 46, 48, 208, 216, 317, 345
Schreiber, M., 218, 234
Schreibman, L., 282, 288
Schubert, A., 11, 176
Schuler, A.L., 176, 189, 191
Settlage, C.F., 345
Shapiro, E., 67
Shapiro, T., 155, 175
Shearer, D.E., 89, 93
Shepherd, G., 283, 288
Shervanian, C., 155, 175
Silverman, H., 179, 189, 190
Silvern, S.B., 99, 119
Simmons, J., 155, 156, 174
Simon, N., 177, 190
Simon, S.B., 120, 135
Smart, M.S., 54, 67
Smart, R.C., 54, 67
Smilansky, S., 95, 97, 104-105, 118
Smouse, A.D., 179, 189
Sobol, H., 235
Spicker, H., 67
Sullivan, R.C., 282, 288
Swan, W.W., 291-292, 301, 311, 312
Swindle, F., 45, 48, 49, 57, 67
Swisher, L., 155, 174
Sylva, K., 95, 118

Takata, N., 119
Teece, C., 95, 103, 104, 119
Terman, L.M., 316, 345
Tubbs, V.K., 177, 190

Uline, C., 10, 94
Uzgiris, T., 159-161, 175

Valett, R.E., 61, 68
Vermeulen, S., 10, 71
Volterra, V., 159, 164, 174

Wakstein, D.J., 179, 189
Wakstein, M.P., 179, 189
Watrin, R., 65-66, 68

Weinrott, M., 217, 231, 234
Wellman, H., 164, 175
Wesley, S., 179, 189
Wiegerink, R., 8, 14
Wilbur, R., 190
Willems, E.P., 279, 288
Wing, J.K., 317, 345
Wing, L., 38, 155, 159, 175, 189
Wolf, E.G., 72, 93
Wood, M.M., 17, 21, 30, 38, 45, 47, 48, 54,
    58-62, 64, 65, 67, 68, 72-77, 86-89, 92,
    93, 101, 104, 108, 110, 113, 119, 121,
    283, 288, 317, 339, 345
Wright, H.F., 291, 312

Yawkey, T.D., 96-97, 99, 119
Yoder, D.E., 93
Yoppi, J.O., 104, 118

Zander, A., 207, 215

Subject Index

Academics, teaching of, in mainstreamed environment, 44-46
Affective development
  Alternative communication systems and, 188
  Assessment methods, 123, 134, 136-137, 318, 322-326, 336
  "Awareness program" at Jowonio School, 24-25, 120-137
  Families and, 197, 217
  In outreach service model, 245-248
  Mainstreaming and, 11, 20, 24-29, 126-127, 130, 255-256, 273-274
  Music activities in, 246
  Play and, 20, 104, 106-108
  Teachers as facilitators of, 128-129, 131, 125-136
  Values clarification exercise, 25
  (*See also* Self-concept, development of; Social development of autistic children)
Affective skill levels, assessment of, 123, 136-137, 318, 322-326, 336
Aloofness in autistic children, 3, 12-13
  (*See also* Detachment in autistic children)
Alternative communication systems, 11-12, 176-192
  Comparison of, 178-184, 186-188
  Definition, 191
  Effects on behavior and development, 183-184, 186-188
  Implementing, 182-188
  In case study, 72-73, 85-86, 89
  Integration and, 183-184, 186-187
  Language development and, 176, 184-186
  Parents' involvement in, 89, 183-184, 186-188, 204-205
  Siblings' involvement in, 183, 223, 233
American Sign Language (Ameslan or ASL), 186, 191
Anxiety in autism, 4, 239
  Avoidance behaviors and, 239

Assessment methods, for use with autistic children
  Autism Screening Instrument for Educational Planning, 46, 48
  Behavior Rating Instrument for Autistic Children (BRIAC), 72
  Behavioral Characteristics Progression, 61, 67
  Developmental Therapy Objectives Rating Form (DTORF), 72, 113
  "Educational evaluation" (outreach service model), 240-243
  Flanders-Swan Interaction Analysis, 280
  Group Behavior Survey, 123, 134, 136-157
  Infant Psychological Development Scales (IPDS), 159-162
  Informal Diagnostic Assessment (Battery), 13, 21, 315-345
  Language Acquisition Program, 317
  Social Reinforcement Scale, 292
  Sociograms and sociometrics, 123, 136-137, 280-282, 291-314
  Sociometric interviews, 305-312
  Specimen recording, 291-294, 311-312
  SWAN (Systematic Who-to-Whom Analysis Notation), 291, 301-314
Association for Retarded Citizens, 315-316
Autism
  Definitions, 3-8, 317
  Diagnosis and assessment, 4, 315-345
    (*See also* Assessment methods, for use with autistic children)
  Etiological and therapeutic theories
    Affective development approach, 11, 317
    Behavioral approach, 7, 238, 242-243
    Biophysical theories, 7, 239
    Brain dysfunction theory, 4-5, 7-8
    Coping syndrome, 239
    Developmental learning disability approach, 4, 8-10, 238-240
    Ecological approach, 217, 278-280

Autism (Continued)
  Genetic influences, 7
  Motivational theory, 238
  Neurophysiological disorder in arousal
    systems of brain, 7
  Nutritional therapy, 7
  Psychoanalytic theory, 6, 200-201, 208
  Sensorimotor theories, 7, 11
  Sensory integration theory, 7, 200-201
  Sensory stimuli, abnormal responses to,
    4-5, 7-8, 238-239
  Incidence, 4-5
  Symptomatic behaviors (*See* Autistic
    children, characteristics of)
*Autism Screening Instrument for Educational
  Planning*, 46, 48
Autistic children, characteristics of, 3-13, 155,
  158-165, 238-240, 244-245, 275-283, 317
  (*See also* specific characteristics)
Aversion from the face, 275-278
Avoidance behaviors in autistic children, 3, 7,
  12-13, 72, 237-244, 275-278
  Anxiety as a cause, 239, 242
  Difficulty or meaninglessness of tasks, and,
    239-240, 242
  Effect on acquisition of language and social
    skills, 277
  Reinforced by some teacher behaviors, 237-
    240, 243-244, 275-278

Backwards integration, 106, 149-150, 250
Behavior modification, 10
  In case study, 74, 90-93
  Limitations of approach with autistic chil-
    dren, 238, 242-243, 278, 285
  Parents trained in, 71
  Siblings trained in, 217
Behavior Rating Instrument for Autistic Chil-
  dren (BRIAC), 72
Behavioral approach to autism, 7, 238, 242-243
Behavioral Characteristics Progression, 61, 67
Biophysical theories of autism, 7, 239
Blissymbols, 177-178, 180-182
  Definition, 191
Brain damage in autism, 7
Brain dysfunction in autism, 4-5, 7-8
Bureau of Education for the Handicapped, 16,
  236

Catatonia in autism, 4
Cause and effect (concept of)
  And language development, 159-162
  (*See also* Sensorimotor concept development)
Causes of autism (*See* Autism: Etiological and
  therapeutic theories)
Change, resistance to, in autism, 3-4, 239, 317
Chemical food additives, and hyperkinesis, 7
Classroom location, for mainstreaming, 37
Classroom scheduling, for integration, 10, 17-
  18, 20-27, 39, 56-57

Classroom social behavior of autistic children,
  275-288
Clinging (behavior), 4
Clinical teaching instruments, 45-46
Cluster model (mainstreaming), 30
Columbia Mental Maturity Scale, 316
Communication board, 176-179,
  Definition, 191
Communication book, 180, 183-185, 187-188
  Definition, 191
Communication disorders in autism, 3-5, 11,
  155, 158-165, 238-239, 317
  (*See also* Language development; Language
    content; Language use)
Communication skills, assessment of, 159-162,
  317, 319, 330-335, 337-338
Communication systems, alternative (*See* Alter-
  native communication systems)
Communicative functions, failure to under-
  stand, 163, 169-172, 244
  (*See also* Language development; Language
    use)
Content (language) (*See* Language content)
Coping behaviors, in autistic children, 239-240
Cross-modal association
  And alternative communication systems, 177-
    179
  Definition, 191
Curriculum, and integration, 22-27
  (*See also* Jowonio School: Curriculum)

Detachment in autistic children, 241-243
  (*See also* Aloofness; Avoidance behaviors in
    autistic children)
Developmental delay in autistic children
  In definitions of autism, 3, 5
  In Jowonio School teaching approach, 9-10,
    317
  Related to coping behaviors, 239-240
Developmental learning problems in autism, 4,
  8-10, 238-140, 317
Developmental Therapy, 17, 21, 30, 38, 45, 47-
  48, 54, 57, 58-62, 64-65, 68, 72-77, 86-89,
  92-93, 101, 104, 108, 110, 113, 119, 121,
  283, 288, 317, 339, 345
*Developmental Therapy for Young Children
  with Autistic Characteristics*, 45, 48-49, 57,
  67
Developmental Therapy Objectives Rating
  Form (DTORF), 72, 113
Diagnostic assessment (*See* Informal Diagnostic
  Assessment (Battery))
Diagnostic teaching, 21, 67
Discrimination against autistic children, 282

Early infantile autism, 3, 317
Echolalia in autism, 4, 179, 237
  Definition, 191

Echopraxia, 185, 188
 Definition, 191
Ecological view of autism, 217, 278-280
"Educational evaluation" (outreach service
 model), 240-243
 (*See also* Assessment methods)
Enjoyment (*See* Pleasure)
Epilepsy, 4-5, 71
Equal opportunity, and integration, 256
Expectations, effects of, on autistic children
 Of parents, 197
 Of teachers, 33, 271, 287-288
 Of typical children, in integrated program,
  150
Experience/awareness activities, for siblings,
 221-225, 233
 (*See also* Siblings of special children)

Facial aversion, 275-278
Families of autistic children
 Need for support, 5, 200-201, 205-208
 Structure, effect of, on children, 197
"Family groups," 17-18
Family histories, 130, 321-322
Family structure, 197
Fathers, in parent support groups, 213-214
Feingold Diet, and hyperkinesis, 7
Flanders' Teacher Interaction Analysis, 301
Flanders-Swan Interaction Analysis, 280
Form (language), definition, 157
 (*See also* Language content; Language use)

Generalization (of skills), 10
 Failure to learn, and tasks meaningless to
  children, 239-240
 Goal, in case study, 74, 84-85, 93
Genetic influences in autism, 7
Group Behavior Survey, 123, 134, 136-137

Hot line for siblings of special children, 231
 (*See also* Siblings of special children)
Hyperkinesis, diet therapy for, 7
Hyperkinesis in autism, 4, 7, 238

Idiosyncratic language in autism, 4, 155, 205
 (*See also* Language use)
Illinois Test of Psycholinguistic Abilities, 316
Incident of autism, 4-5
Individualized Educational Plan (IEP), 39, 61,
 89, 205
Infant Psychological Development Scales
 (IPDS), 159-162
Informal Diagnostic Assessment (Battery), 13,
 21, 315-345
Inservice training and orientation, 35, 47, 243-
 245
 Use of videotapes in, 241
Integration, 13, 17-27, 35, 46-47
 Affective education and, 11, 20, 24-29, 126-
  127, 130, 255-256, 273-274

Integration (*Continued*)
 Alternative communication systems and,
  183-184, 186-188
 "Backwards" or "reverse," 106, 149-150,
  250
 Child interactions in various activities, 292-
  304
 Classroom scheduling and, 10, 17-18, 20-27,
  39, 56-57
 Classroom social behavior of autistic chil-
  dren, 275-288
 Curriculum and, 22-27
 Difficulties for teachers, 269-272
 Evaluating peer interactions, 291-314
 Importance of, in development of handi-
  capped children, 49-50, 107, 150, 238,
  240, 247-250
 In outreach service model, 247-251
 Interactive behavior, assessment of chil-
  dren's, in various activities, 292-304
 Lesson plans for integrated activity, 62-63
 Materials for, 18, 23, 35, 46-47
 Meals and, 43, 293-299
 Music activities and, 149-151
 Play and, 10, 17, 20, 95, 100, 105-109, 112,
  250, 292-300
 Play, assessing peer interactions in, 293-299
 Sociograms and sociometric analysis, 123,
  136-137, 280-282, 291-314
 Teacher behaviors to promote, 12-13, 19, 24-
  25, 255-274
 Transportation and, 22, 42
 Typical children and (*See* Mainstreamed
  environment: Typical children in)
 (*See also* Mainstreamed environment)
Intermodal transfer (*See* Cross-modal associa-
 tion)
Interviews, sociometric, 305-312
IQ scores of autistic children, 5
 (*See also* Assessment methods; Standardized
  psychological testing)

Jowonio Informal Assessment Tasks, 318-319,
 322-334
 (*See also* Informal Diagnostic Assessment
  (Battery))
"Jowonio" (meaning of name), 15
Jowonio model (mainstreaming), 15-27
 Case studies, 49-62, 71-93
 (*See also* Integration; Jowonio School; Main-
  streamed environment)
Jowonio School
 Classes
  Class groupings ("family groups"), 17-18
  Classroom organization and furnishings,
   54-55
  Classroom programming (scheduling), 10,
   21-22, 39, 54, 56-57
  Stage One classroom: case study, 49-68
 Curriculum, 10-12, 20, 22-24, 62-67

Jowonio School (Continued)
History of, 15-16
Inservice training and orientation, 47, 51-52
Parent participation, 12, 15-16, 27, 195-216
As Board members, 198
In case study of autistic child, 89-90
In parent support groups, 12, 206-210,
212-215
In school social events, 196, 198-200
Parent-school communication, 201, 203
School's openness to parents, 198, 201
Sibling support groups, 12, 207, 217-235
Staffing, 20-21, 51-53, 203-206

Kanner syndrome, 3, 317

Language Acquisition Program, 317
Language content
Deficit in, in autistic children, 158-162
Definition, 156-157
Sensorimotor concept development and, 159-
162, 166-169, 170
(*See also* Language development; Language
use)
Language development
And alternative communication systems, 176,
180-188
And cognition of communicative functions,
163, 169-172, 244
And play, 20, 103-104, 168, 245, 249
And sensorimotor concept development, 159-
162, 166-169, 170
Assessment of, 159-162, 317, 319, 330-335,
337-338
Bloom and Lahey model of, 155-165
Effect of avoidance behaviors on, 277
Facilitation of, 11-12, 138, 147, 165-175,
247-249
Impact of, on general development, 176
In case studies, 51-52, 71-78, 85-86, 242-249
Music activities and, 138, 147
Language disorders in autism, 3-5, 11, 155,
158-165, 238-239, 317
(*See also* Language content; Language devel-
opment; Language use)
Language form, definition, 157
(*See also* Language content; Language use)
Language, idiosyncratic, in autism, 4, 155, 205
Language use
Definition, 157-158
Disorders of, in autistic children, 3-5, 155,
158-159, 163-165, 176, 186, 238-239,
244-246, 316-317
In alternative communication systems, 186
Understanding of communicative functions
and, 163, 169-174, 244
(*See also* Language content; Language devel-
opment; Language form)
Leiter International Performance Scale, 316

Let's Eat, 320
"Looking For Me" (film), 47
Low stimulus environment, 10
In case study, 74, 81, 83-84

"Magic circle," 18-19
Mainstreamed environments
Alternative communication systems and, 183-
184, 186-187
Beliefs, values in development of, 9, 31-34,
255-256, 273-274
Case studies, 9-10, 49-68, 71-93, 240-250
Classroom, location of, 37
Classroom scheduling for, 10, 21-22, 39, 54,
56-57
Difficulties of, for teachers, 269-272
Goals and objectives of, 11, 273-274
Importance of, in development of handi-
capped children, 49-50, 107, 150, 238,
240, 247-250
Inservice training and orientation for, 35, 37-
38, 47, 241, 243-245
Materials for, 18, 23, 25, 46-47
Meals in, 43
Parents of special children, advantages for,
199-200
Personnel, classroom, 42, 51-53
Personnel, resources, 39, 41
Play in, 10, 20, 107, 250, 292-304
(*See also* Integration: Play and)
Selection of children for, 37, 270-271, 315-
345
Social development in, 11, 247-251, 256
Social interactive behavior of autistic chil-
dren, not a barrier to, 282-283
Teachers as models in, 19, 24-25, 198, 268-
269
Teaching of academics in, 44-46
Transportation and, 22, 42
Typical children in
Affective education for, 11-20, 24-29, 120-
137
As models and teachers in play, 19-20,
107, 250
Attitudes of, towards special children, 19-
20, 26, 259, 263-267, 305-312
"Awareness program" for, 120-137
Benefits of, for, 49-50, 273-274, 315
Effects of their expectations on special
children, 150
Fostering positive attitudes in, 19-20, 26,
43-44, 255-274
(*See also* Integration; Jowonio School)
Mainstreaming models, 27-28
Cluster model, 30
Jowonio model, 15-27
Outreach service model, 12, 236-251
Regular class with supplemental services, 30
Tandem class model, 30

Mainstreaming models (Continued)
Teacher plus aide model, 29
Teaming model, 28
Transitional program model, 29
(*See also* Backwards integration; Public
schools, autistic children in)
Materials
For developmental play, 54-55
For integration, 18, 23, 35, 46-47
Meals, and integration, 43, 292-304
Medication, 5, 71
Megavitamin therapy, 7
Memory in autism, 3, 8
Short-term memory and use of nontransient
alternative communication systems, 177-
178, 191, 192
Mental retardation and autism, 4-5, 10
In case study, 71-93
(*See also* Developmental delay in autistic
children; Developmental learning prob-
lems in autism)
Metabolic disorders and autism, 4-5, 7
Minneapolis Children's Health Center,
Program for Autistic and Other Excep-
tional Children, 236-237
Models of mainstreaming (*See* Mainstreaming
models)
Morphology (language), definition, 157
Motivational theory of autism, 238
Multisensory input
And alternative communication systems, 179
Definition, 191
Music, 11, 138-151, 246
Affective education, use in, 246
As developmental teaching medium, 138,
141-147, 246
Integration, use in facilitating, 149-151
Language development facilitation and, 138,
147
Parent and sibling involvement through, 150
Sensorimotor development through, 11
Social development through, 138, 140, 144-
147
Songs, 140-149
Use with siblings of special children, 150

National Society for Autistic Children, 4-5, 8,
38
Definition of autism, 4-5, 8
Neurophysiological disorder in arousal system
of brain, in autism, 7
Non-SLIP (NonSpeech Language Intervention
Program), 177-178
Definition, 191
Nontransient systems (of communication), 177-
178
Definition, 191
Nutritional therapy, 7

Object permanence (concept of)
And language development, 159-162
In Jowonio Informal Diagnostic Assessment
(Battery), 324
(*See also* Sensorimotor concept development)
Oral communication
Definition, 191
Skills needed for, 176
Orientation and inservice training, 35, 37-38,
47, 241, 243-345
Use of videotapes in, 241
Outreach service model (mainstreaming), 12,
236-257
Approach to autism, 236-240
Case study, 240-250
"Educational evaluation" (assessment), 240-
243
Inservice training and orientation, 241, 243-
245
Integration in, 247-251
Summer project (affective development),
245-247

Parent behaviors and attitudes
Influence on child's school performance, 197
Modeled in Jowonio School classrooms, 198
Not a cause of autism, 200-201, 208
Reaction to child's handicap, 201, 208
Parent interview
In "educational evaluation" (outreach service
model), 241
In informal diagnostic assessment, 21, 321-
322
Parent involvement, 12, 27, 195-216
In alternative communication program, 183-
184, 186-188, 204-205
In "educational evaluation" (outreach service
model), 241
In Jowonio informal assessment, 321-322
In music program, 150
In social events, 196, 198-200
Parent-school communication, 201-213
Parent support groups, 12, 200-201, 206-216
Training in behavior modification, 71
(*See also* Jowonio School: Parent partici-
pation)
Parent-school communication, 201-203
Parent support groups, 12, 200-201, 206-216
Fathers in, 213-214
Models of, 210-212
Parent worker's role, 206-210
Parent worker (Jowonio School), 196, 203-206
In case study, 52-53
In parent support groups, 206-210
Parental behavior (psychoanalytic) theory of
autism, 6
Effects of theory on parents, 200, 321
Refutation of, 200-201, 208
Parents, single (*See* Single parents)

Peabody Picture Vocabulary Test, 316
Perfectionism in autistic children
  And avoidance behaviors, 239, 244
  And lack of meaning of tasks, 239-240
Phonology, definition, 157
Picture boards, 176-178
Pidgin Signed English, 186-191
Planning time, 35-36, 41
Play
  As a child's work, 49, 63-64, 107
  As a setting for clinical observation, 317
  As a symbolic activity, 10
  As an intervention, 100-105, 113-118, 250
  Autistic child's inability to play, 10, 107
  Definitions, 95-97, 100
  Developmental learning and, 95-100
  Developmental Therapy model and, 100-105
  Hierarchy of behaviors, 95, 100, 108
  In mainstreamed environment, 10, 20, 107,
    250
  In Stage One classroom, 97-99
  Integrated behavior in, 292-304
  Language development and, 20, 103-104,
    168, 245, 250
  Materials for (*See* Materials)
  Physical classroom environment, role of, 54-
    55, 110
  Planning for, 110-118
  Self-concept development through, 100
  Social development through, 11, 104, 250
  Social interaction patterns in, 292-300
  Typical children as models in, 107, 250
  With typical siblings, 228
  With younger typical children, 250
Pleasure, responding to environment with
  Importance in development, 10, 54
  Therapy goal, in case studies, 71-79, 245-247,
    249
Portage Guide to Early Education, 89, 93
Pragmatics (language use), and alternative
    communications systems, 186
Program for Autistic and Other Exceptional
    Children, University of Minnesota, 236-
    251
Project TEACCH, 28-29
Psychoanalytic theory of autism, 6, 200-201
Psychoeducational Profile, 317
Psychological testing, standardized
  Not useful in assessing autistic children, 241,
    316
Public schools, autistic children in
  Music program, 150-151
  Outreach service model (Minnesota), 12, 236-
    251
  Syracuse (New York) City School District, 9,
    28-29
  (*See also* Integration; Mainstreaming models)

Reading, and use of alternative communication
    systems, 186-187

Regular class with supplemental services (main-
    streaming model), 30
Reinforcement of autistic behaviors, by teacher
    behaviors
  Avoidance behaviors, 237-240, 277
  Repetitive behaviors, 243-244
Repetitive behavior in autistic children, 5, 317
  And failure to learn generalization of skills,
    238-240
  Reinforced by teaching methods, 243-244
Resistance to change, in autism, 3-4, 317
Reverse integration, 106, 149-150, 250
Rutland Center (Athens, Georgia), 21

Seguin form board, 3
Selection of children for mainstreaming, 37,
    270-271, 315-345
Self-awareness, lack of, in autism, 4
Self-concept, development of
  As goal of emotional development, 22, 24,
    59, 130
  Facilitated by classroom equipment, 54
  In play, 100
Self-stimulation behaviors in autistic children
  Limitations of behavior modification, 238,
    242-243, 278
  Reduced with increased involvement in envi-
    ronment, 243, 278
Sensorimotor concept development, in language
    development, 159-162, 166-169, 170
Sensorimotor theories of autism, 7, 11
Sensory integration theory of autism, 7, 200-201
Sensory stimuli, abnormal responses to
  As cause of autism, 7-8, 200, 238-239
  In definitions of autism, 4-5
Sibling support groups, 12, 217-235
Siblings of special children
  Adjustment and emotional support activities
    for, 218-219, 226-234
  And alternative communication systems, 183,
    223, 233
  Books for, 235
  Experience/awareness activities for, 221-225,
    233
  Hot line for, 231
  In music activities with special children, 150
  In outreach model summer program, 150, 237
  Special needs of, 217-219, 228-229
  Support groups, 12, 217-235
  Trained as behavior modifiers, 217-218
  Visit to special child's class, 230, 234
Sign language, 176-179, 180-181, 185-188
  Definition, 191
  In case study, 72-73, 85-86, 89
  Long-term considerations, 186-188
  (*See also* Alternative communication systems)
Single parents, 196, 206-210
Social development of autistic children
  In a mainstreamed setting, 11, 20, 25-26,
    247-251

Social development of autistic children (Continued)
Physical environmental factors, 54
Role of alternative communication systems, 183-184, 186-188
Through music, 138, 140, 144-147
Through play, 104, 250
(*See also* Affective development)
Social interactive behavior of autistic children
Assessment of, in classroom setting, 123, 134, 136-137, 275-283, 291-314
Not a barrier to mainstreaming, 282-283
Research in, 275-279
Teacher behaviors and, 277, 282-288
Social Reinforcement scale, 292
Sociograms and sociometrics, 123, 136-137, 280-282, 291-314
Sociometric interviews, 305-312
Songs, 140-149
Group activity songs, 140, 144
Individual songs, 140-144
Passing songs, 140, 146-147
Pre-academic songs, 140, 145
Quiet songs, 141, 147-148
Social interaction songs, 140, 145
(*See also* Music)
Specimen recording, 291-294, 311-312
Stanford-Binet Intelligence Scale, 316
SWAN (Systmatic Who-to-Whom Analysis Notation), 291, 301-304, 311-314
Symbol system (of communication), 177, 178
Definition, 191
Symptomatic behaviors of autism (*See* Autistic children, characteristics of)
Syntax
Definition, 157
In alternative communication systems, 186
Syracuse (New York) City School District, 9, 28-29

T.A. for Tots, 131, 135
Tandem class model (mainstreaming), 30
Teacher behaviors
And classroom integration, 12-13, 19, 24-25, 255-274
And progress of labeled children, 10, 279, 283-288
And social interactive behavior of autistic children, 279-288
And expectations, 33, 271, 287-288
As models, 19, 24-25, 198, 268-269
To facilitate working with autistic children, 285-288
Which reinforce autistic behaviors, 237-240, 243-244
Teacher expectations, effect of, on children, 33, 271, 287-288

Teacher plus aide model (mainstreaming), 29
Teachers as models
For integrated interactions, 19, 24-25, 268-269
For nonsexist values, 24
For parent behaviors, 198
Teaming model (mainstreaming), 28
Temporal sequencing
And alternative communication systems, 177
And autism, 8
Definition, 192
Theraplay, 7, 14
Therapy approaches to autism (*See* Autism: Etiological and therapeutic theories)
Toilet training, achievement of, in case study, 73, 77, 82, 93
Total communication (system)
Definition, 176, 192
Success of use with autistic children, 179, 186
Transactional analysis
In "awareness program" at Jowonio School, 130-131
Transient systems of communication, definition, 192
Transitional program model (mainstreaming), 29
Transportation, and integration, 22, 42
Typical children (*See* Mainstreamed environment: Typical children in)

University of Minnesota, 236

Values clarrification exercise, 25
Verbalizations
Definition, 192
Increase with signing, 179
Vestibular dysfunction in autism, 7
Videotapes, use in inservice training and orientation, 241
Viral infections, and autism, 4-5
Visibility of labeled child (in mainstreaming), 18, 24
Vocalizations
Definition, 192
In total communication system, 176
May increase with signing, 179
Voice synthesizer
Definition, 192
Used to supplement signing, 187

Withdrawal (from contact with people), 3, 7, 16
In case study, 72
Reinforced by teacher behavior, 276-278
(*See also* Avoidance behaviors in autistic children)
Written word alternative communication systems, 177-178, 187

Contributors

Ellen Barnes, PhD
Director, Jowonio: The Learning Place
Syracuse, NY

Cindy Bodenheimer, PhD
School Psychologist, Jowonio: The Learning Place
Syracuse, NY
Currently School Psychologist
New Interdisciplinary School for Handicapped Children
Medford, Long Island, NY

Lyle Chastain, MS
Program for Autistic Children
Minneapolis Children's Health Center
Minneapolis Medical Center
Minneapolis, MN

Carroll J. Grant, PhD
Director, Parent/Infant Program and Adjunct Assistant Professor
Syracuse University
Syracuse, NY

Rosalind Heiko, PhD
School Psychologist, Jowonio: The Learning Place
Syracuse, NY
Currently Assisstant Professor of School Psychology
University of North Carolina
Chapel Hill, NC

Debra Isaacson, PhD
School Psychologist, Jowonio: The Learning Place
Syracuse, NY
Currently Coordinator of Standards
New York State Division of Youth
Albany, NY

Sharon L. James, PhD
Associate Professor of Communicative Disorders
Division of Special Education and Rehabilitation
Syracuse University
Syracuse, NY

Peter Knoblock, PhD
Professor of Special Education and Rehabilitation
Syracuse University
Director, Jowonio: The Learning Place, 1970-1979
Syracuse, NY

Judy Kugelmass
School Psychologist
Special Children's Center
Ithaca, NY

Sheila Merzer, MS
Program for Autistic Children
Minneapolis Children's Health Center
Minneapolis Medical Center
Minneapolis, MS

Sandra Mlinarcik, MS
Principal, Jowonio: The Learning Place
Syracuse, NY

Margaret Ninno, MS
Head Teacher, Jowonio: The Learning Place
Currently Teacher, Preschool Special Education Program
North Syracuse Public Schools
North Syracuse, NY

Annegret Schubert, MS
Language Therapist, Jowonio: The Learning Place
Syracuse, NY

Cynthia Uline, MS
Head Teacher, Jowonio: The Learning Place
Syracuse, NY

Susan Vermeulen
Teacher, Jowonio: The Learning Place and Syracuse City School District
Syracuse, NY